SUNDAY in SAN FRANCISCO

By

Daniel Mangin

Catherine McEver

Kathryn Olney

Conceived by

Andrew A. Anspach

Fodor's Travel Publications, Inc.
New York • Toronto • London • Sydney • Auckland
http://www.fodors.com/

Second Edition

ISBN 0-679-03288-6

Fodor's Sunday in San Francisco

Editor: Amy McConnell
Contributors: Steven Amsterdam, Robert Blake, Judy Blumenberg, Catherine McEver, Danny Mangin, Katherine Olney
Art Director: Fabrizio La Rocca
Cartographer: David Lindroth
Cover Illustration: Lloyd Dangle

Special Sales

Fodor's Travel Publications are available at special discounts for bulk purchases for sales promotions or premiums. Special editions, including personalized covers, excerpts of existing guides, and corporate imprints, can be created in large quantities for special needs. For more information, contact your local bookseller or write to Special Markets, Fodor's Travel Publications, 201 East 50th Street, New York, NY 10022. Inquiries from Canada should be directed to your local Canadian bookseller or sent to Random House of Canada, Ltd., Marketing Department, 1265 Aerowood Drive, Mississauga, Ontario L4W 1B9. Inquiries from the United Kingdom should be sent to Fodor's Travel Publications, 20 Vauxhall Bridge Road, London SW1V 2SA.

PRINTED IN THE UNITED STATES OF AMERICA
10 9 8 7 6 5 4 3 2 1

Contents

Maps

Foreword

Sunday is the day to see the Bay Area at its best—not just because there are so many wonderful things to do, but because Sunday is the perfect day to do them. On Sunday tensions lift and moods lighten. Gone is the weekday frenzy, the emotional gridlock of a place hard at work.

On Sunday streets are busy but not crowded. Traffic moves along at a pleasant pace, and free curbside parking or reasonable garage rates are available almost everywhere. Getting around is no longer a major undertaking, and everything seems within easy reach. Sightseeing, dining, shopping, sports, the arts—whatever your pleasure—Sunday is the day to enjoy it.

Though this guide is tailored for Sunday activities, it's equally valuable for planning Saturdays, too. Whether you're a visitor from Vitebsk, a neighbor from Napa, or a hard-core San Franciscan who calls the city home, *Sunday in San Francisco* provides a detailed and eye-opening survey of all there is to do and see on weekends.

You'll find the popular attractions—"musts" for first-time visitors—as well as surprises even seasoned San Franciscans don't know about. There's backgammon, baseball, and bicycling—even boccie and ballooning. There are walks through gardens and groves of wildflowers. There are guided architecture tours and trips to great museums, as well as to many smaller ones showcasing specialized collections and art from all over the world. It's all here, along with where to get a manicure, rent a computer, buy a pair of suede boots—even best bets for children. With this book you'll see Sunday as an excellent time for getting things done and for enjoying the region's bountiful pleasures—enough to fill a lifetime of Sundays.

Fodor's wants to hear about your weekend experiences, both pleasant and unpleasant. When a restaurant, shop, or attraction fails to live up to its billing, let us know, and we'll investigate the complaint and revise our entries when the facts warrant it. And please feel free to let us know your own suggestions for what to see and do in San Francisco.

Send your letters to the editors of Fodor's Travel Publications, 201 East 50th Street, New York, NY 10022.

Andrew A. Anspach

About the Contributors

Andrew A. Anspach has produced arts programs for New York public radio and for the Canadian Broadcasting Company. From 1956 to 1986 he served as the managing director of New York's Algonquin Hotel, and on Sunday—his only day off—he developed the passion for exploring the city that sparked Fodor's *Sunday in . . .* series.

Daniel Mangin lived in San Francisco for 20 years before moving to New York, where he edits Fodor's guides. He has written about travel and the arts for the *San Francisco Chronicle*, *SF Weekly*, *Bay Area Reporter*, and other local Bay Area publications.

Catherine McEver is a freelance writer who has lived in the Bay Area for more than 20 years. She has covered the local food scene for *SF Magazine* and the *East Bay Express*.

Kathryn Olney is a San Francisco writer and editor. She was on the staff of *Mother Jones* magazine for 12 years, and she has published articles there and in *Parenting*, *Savvy*, and the *San Francisco Examiner*.

Amy McConnell, editor of *Sunday in San Francisco*, can't imagine a better city in which to spend a Sunday.

1 Essential Information

Visitor Information

By Kathryn Olney

Updated by Daniel Mangin

For general information and free booklets and maps, contact the **San Francisco Convention and Visitors Bureau** (SFCVB, Box 429097, San Francisco 94142, tel. 415/391–2000). The bureau publishes a quarterly guide, *The San Francisco Book* with up-to-date information on theater offerings, art exhibits, sporting events, and other special happenings. For a copy send $2 for postage and handling to the above address.

To pick up a guide, stop by the bureau's **Visitors Information Center** (tel. 415/391–2000; open Sun. 10–2) in Hallidie Plaza's lower level, at Powell and Market streets near the cable-car turnaround. The bureau runs a **24-hour events hot line** that lists city happenings week by week; to reach it, press 2 on your touch-tone telephone after dialing the above number.

The **Redwood Empire Association Visitor Information Center** (The Cannery, 2801 Leavenworth St. 2nd Floor, 94133, tel. 415/543–8334) will provide you with a wealth of free information on San Francisco and surrounding areas, including the Wine Country, the redwood groves, and the rest of northern California. Send $3 for the 48-page *Redwood Empire Visitor's Guide*, with useful maps, events listings, and recreation highlights for the region; also ask for a free quarterly calendar of events.

The San Francisco Bay Area encompasses dozens of towns, many of which have a chamber of commerce happy to provide travelers with information. A few of the largest are:

Berkeley Convention and Visitors Bureau (1834 University Ave., Berkeley 94703, tel. 510/549–7040).

Oakland Convention and Visitors Authority (550 10th St., Suite 214, Oakland 94607, tel. 510/839–9000 or 800/262–5526).

San Jose Convention and Visitors Bureau (333 W. San Carlos St., Suite 1000, San Jose 95110, tel. 408/295–9600).

A statewide calendar of events and 12 Northern California driving tours are available through the **California Division of Tourism** (tel. 800/862–2543). Its staff can also answer many questions about travel in the state.

Useful Phone Numbers

Transportation

Amtrak (tel. 800/872–7245).
Greyhound (tel. 800/231–2222).

Local

Bay Area Rapid Transit (BART, tel. 415/992–2278).
CalTrain and SamTrans (tel. 415/508–6200 or 800/660–4287).
San Francisco Municipal Railway System (Muni, tel. 415/673–6864).

Events and Entertainment

BASS (tel. 510/762–2277), for sports, concerts, and other events.
BASS Charge Performing Arts Line (tel. 415/776–1999), for cultural events—theater, opera, ballet, etc.
Events Hotline (tel. 415/391–2001).
Moscone Center (tel. 415/974–4000) for event information.
MovieFone (tel. 415/777–3465).
TIX Bay Area (tel. 415/433–7827).

Getting to San Francisco

By Car

From the south (San Jose), take U.S. 101 north to San Francisco. For a more scenic route follow I–280 on its winding path just east of the coastal foothills. In the late afternoon you can often view the approaching fog as it spills over the hills.

From the East Bay or the Central Valley, take I–80 across the Bay Bridge; if you are arriving from the southeast, take I–580 to I–80. From the bridge you get a dramatic view of the downtown skyline.

From the north, take U.S. 101 south across the Golden Gate Bridge.

It's best to avoid driving over the bridges late Sunday afternoon. That's when residents return to the city from weekend trips, and bridge traffic can get snarled.

By Train **Amtrak** (tel. 800/872–7245) serves the Bay Area. Two trains—the *Zephyr,* from Chicago via Denver, and the *Coast Starlight,* traveling between Los Angeles and Seattle—stop at Jack London Square (245 2nd St. at Harrison) and Emeryville (5885 Landregan St. off Powell). Buses from Emeryville shuttle passengers across the Bay Bridge to the Ferry Building (foot of Market Street at the Embarcadero) or the CalTrain terminal (*see below*) in San Francisco.

CalTrain (tel. 415/508–6200 or 800/660–4287) offers passenger service from San Jose to San Francisco, stopping at most of the towns in between; there is also an express service that stops only in key towns, such as San Mateo and Palo Alto. The San Francisco terminal is at the intersection of 4th and Townsend (tel. 415/495–4546).

By Bus **Greyhound Lines** (tel. 800/231–2222) serves San Francisco from the Transbay Terminal (1st and Mission, tel. 415/495–1575) and the Oakland terminal (2103 San Pablo at 20th St., tel. 510/834–3213).

Getting Around

Because San Francisco is relatively compact and because it's so difficult to find parking, we recommend that you do as much exploring on foot or by bus as you can. San Francisco is a wonderful city to walk about, provided you don't mind the hills. Walking is the best way to discover the nooks, crannies, alleys, and hidden staircases that are sure to charm your socks off.

As with any city these days, it's important to know which neighborhoods are not safe at night, especially if you're alone. Be wary in the Tenderloin, parts of the Mission (around 14th Street, for example), the lower Haight, and SoMa (south of Market) if you aren't near the clubs and nightlife.

"How to Get There from Union Square" is a handy free booklet that explains how to reach approximately 50 points of interest by public transportation. You can pick it up weekdays 9–5 at the Redwood Empire Association's Visitor Information Center (The Cannery, 2801 Leavenworth, 2nd Floor, tel. 415/543–8334); call or write for a copy.

By BART **Bay Area Rapid Transit,** or **BART** (tel. 415/992–2278), sends air-conditioned aluminum trains at speeds of up to 80 miles per hour across the bay to Oakland, Berkeley, Concord, Richmond, and Fremont. Trains also travel south from San Francisco as far as Daly City. Wall maps in the station list destinations and fares (90¢–$3.40). Sunday trains run from 8 AM to midnight.

By Bus The **San Francisco Municipal Railway System,** or **Muni,** includes buses, trolleys, surface streetcars, new subsurface streetcars, and cable cars. Service is round-the-clock, and the fare is $1. Transfers are good for two changes in any direction within 90 minutes. For bus information, call 415/673–6864 (Sun. 9–5).

If you're a tourist, your best bet may be a $6 All Day Cable Car Pass, good for unlimited travel on all bus and cable-car routes all day; it can be purchased at the police kiosk at Powell and Market streets (Sun. 9–9) and at the Visitor's Information Center in Hallidie Plaza (Sun. 10–2), just below the kiosk. A three-day pass, good for buses and cable cars, sells for $10 at the same locations.

The following companies—all three headquartered at the Transbay Terminal at 1st Street and Mission—will get you to the East Bay, Marin County, and the peninsula by bus. Their staffs can also advise you about the best route to take if you know your destination.

East Bay: AC Transit (tel. 510/839–2882 or 510/817–1717).
Marin County: Golden Gate Transit (tel. 415/923–2000).
Peninsula and San Francisco Airport: SamTrans (tel. 800/660–4287).

By Cable Car and Trolley "They turn corners almost at right angles, cross other lines, and for all we know, may run up the sides of houses," wrote Rudyard Kipling in 1889. In June 1984 the 109-year-old system returned to service after a $58.2 million overhaul. Because it had been declared a National Historic Landmark in 1964, renovation methods and materials had to preserve the character of Andrew Hallidie's system. The rehabilitated moving landmark has been designed to withstand another century of use.

The Powell–Mason line (No. 59) and the Powell–Hyde line (No. 60, the best route if you're riding just for fun) begin at Powell and Market streets near Union Square and terminate at Fisherman's Wharf. The California Street line (No. 61) runs west from Market Street near the Embarcadero to Van Ness Avenue. The fare is $2.

Cable cars are popular, crowded, and an experience to ride: Move toward one quickly as it pauses, wedge yourself into any available space, and hold on. The views are spectacular, and the sensation of moving up and down some of San Francisco's steepest hills in a small, clanging, open-air conveyance is not to be missed.

In 1995, Muni unveiled its new "F" line of antique open-air trolleys from the United States and around the world—Baltimore, Philadelphia, Hiroshima, Melbourne, Hamburg, Milan, and elsewhere. The trolleys presently run from Castro and Market to the Ferry Building—but by the end of the century, cars will run along the Embarcadero from 4th Street past the Ferry Building to Fisherman's Wharf.

By Taxi Cab rates are high, although most rides are relatively short. It's almost impossible to hail a passing cab, especially on Sunday. Either phone or use the nearest hotel taxi stand. Fares are $1.70 for the first mile and $1.80 for each additional mile, plus tip. A cab to the San Francisco Airport is about $30 with tip. Check the Yellow Pages under taxis for a number of choices. One reliable company is **Veterans** (tel. 415/552–1300).

By Car Driving on Sunday in San Francisco can be a challenge, what with the hills, the one-way streets, and the traffic. Take it easy, remember to curb your wheels when parking on hills, and use public transportation whenever possible.

The major east–west streets north of Market are **Geary Boulevard** (it's called Geary Street until Van Ness Avenue), which runs to the Pacific Ocean; **Fulton Street,** which begins at the back of the Opera House and continues along the north side of Golden Gate Park to Ocean Beach; and **Fell Street,** the left two lanes of which cut through Golden Gate Park and empty into **Lincoln Boulevard,** which continues on the park's south side to the ocean.

The longest street in San Francisco, **Mission Street,** heads southwest from the Embarcadero to Van Ness Avenue, then turns due south to Cesar Chavez Street (formerly Army Street), after which it resumes a southwest course into Daly City.

Among the major north–south streets are **Divisadero,** which becomes Castro Street at Duboce Avenue and continues past Cesar Chavez Street; **Van Ness Avenue** (it becomes South Van Ness Avenue a few blocks south of City Hall); and **Park Presidio Boulevard,** which empties into **19th Avenue.**

By Ferry During the week ferry boats are used by commuters; on the weekend they become not only a pleasant diversion but a good way to beat the Sunday traffic home to the city after an excursion to Tiburon or Sausalito. Prices for both are $5.50 each way; round trips average around an hour.

The Blue and Gold Fleet (Pier 39, Fisherman's Wharf on the Embarcadero, tel. 415/705–5444) conducts 1¼-hour tours under both the Bay and Golden Gate bridges, as well as excursions to Marine World Africa USA and other attractions.

Golden Gate Ferry (Ferry Building, foot of Market St., tel. 415/923–2000) takes passengers to Sausalito and Larkspur.

Red and White Fleet (Pier 41 and 43 1/2, tel. 415/546–2628) serves Sausalito, Tiburon, Muir Woods, Angel Island, and Alcatraz. In 1996, the Blue and Gold Fleet purchased the Red and White Fleet. At press time the purchase was subject to government and union approval.

Orientation

Most neighborhoods are laid out on a grid, so it helps to ask for the nearest cross street when getting directions to an address. West of Arguello Boulevard, you enter a section of the city known as the **avenues.** The avenues run north–south, starting with 2nd and ending near the ocean with 48th. Out in the avenues, south of Geary Boulevard, is a series of alphabetically named east–west streets, beginning with Anza and continuing south to Wawona and Yorba (there's no X or Z Street) just north of Sloat Boulevard (Rte. 35). Starting downtown on the south side of Market Street (SoMa) is a series of numbered **streets,** beginning with 1st and continuing south to 30th. The streets run east–west (southeast–northwest downtown). Be careful when reading addresses not to confuse streets and avenues.

Parking

Street parking in the city is better on Sunday in some spots, worse in others. Chinatown, the Marina, and North Beach tend to be just as bad as usual. But drive a few blocks from a neighborhood's main artery and your pickings become better on the weekend. Street parking around Golden Gate Park on Sunday is difficult unless you arrive before noon because street traffic is blocked off inside most of the park and the entire perimeter becomes lined with cars. Your best bets are on the avenues off the main arteries of Lincoln Boulevard (Sunset District side) and Fulton Street (Richmond District side). In North Beach, park near the bay (start looking around Broadway east of Battery Street) and walk up the hills, instead of trying to find a spot on the hilly streets. Downtown, stay away from Union Square. You can usually find spots in the Financial District or (better yet) south of Market, then walk back toward the main shopping areas. On Sunday in the Marina head away from Marina Green and the bay, and park on the neighborhood side streets.

Many parking garage rates go down on Sunday and after business hours. But the three best downtown garages—a bargain for shoppers, since they average only $1 per hour—are the Fifth and Mission Garage, the Ellis-O'Farrell Garage (across from Macy's), and the Sutter-Stockton Garage. All those listed below are near shopping and tourist attractions.

Downtown **Fifth and Mission Garage** (833 Mission, tel. 415/982–8522).
Ellis-O'Farrell Garage (123 O'Farrell at Stockton St., tel. 415/986–4800).
Ampco Embarcadero Center Garages (Embarcadero 1, 2, and 3, Sacramento between Battery and Davis Sts., tel. 415/398–1878).

Fisherman's Wharf **Pier 39 Garage** (Pier 39, Powell at Beach St., tel. 415/705–5417).
Wharf Garage (350 Beach St. at Taylor, tel. 415/921–0226).

Chinatown **Sutter-Stockton Garage** (330 Sutter, tel. 415/982–7275).
Portsmouth Square Garage (753 Kearny at Clay St., tel. 415/982–6353)

Civic Center/ Opera Plaza **Opera Plaza Garage** (Van Ness and Golden Gate Aves., tel. 415/771–4776).

Ghirardelli Square **Ghirardelli Square Parking Garage** (900 North Point St. at Polk St., tel. 415/929–1665).

Weekend Hotel Packages

Many hotels offer special packages that turn a weekend in the city into a wonderful minivacation. Packages may include free parking, Continental breakfast, wine and chocolates, use of health-club facilities and children's playgrounds, museum and/or shopping discounts, and—best of all—bargain room rates. San Francisco's smaller hotels, inns, and bed-and-breakfasts are less likely than the larger, business-oriented hotels to offer specials. However, select smaller properties in all price ranges offer seasonal promotions, such as a winter holiday "Shop 'Til You Drop"; for information, call 800/738–7477. The following hotels frequently offer weekend packages:

Fisherman's Wharf **Holiday Inn–Fisherman's Wharf** (1300 Columbus Ave. at North Point St., 94133, tel. 415/771–9000 or 800/465–4329, fax 415/771–7006).
Hyatt at Fisherman's Wharf (555 North Point St. at Taylor, 94133, tel. 415/563–1234 or 800/233–1234, fax 415/749–6122).
Ramada Hotel–Fisherman's Wharf (590 Bay St. at Jones, 94133, tel. 415/885–4700 or 800/228–8408, fax 415/771–8945).
San Francisco Marriott–Fisherman's Wharf (1250 Columbus Ave. at Bay St., 94133, tel. 415/775–7555 or 800/228–9290, fax 415/474–2099).
Sheraton at Fisherman's Wharf (2500 Mason at North Point St., 94133, tel. 415/362–5500 or 800/325–3535, fax 415/956–5275).

Nob Hill **Fairmont Hotel and Tower** (950 Mason at California, tel. 772–5000 or 800/527–4727, fax 415/772–5013).
Mark Hopkins Inter-Continental (999 California at Mason, 94108, tel. 415/392–3434 or 800/327–0200, fax 415/421–3302).
Ritz-Carlton San Francisco (600 Stockton at California, 94108, tel. 415/296–7465 or 800/241–3333, fax 415/291–0288).

Union Square **Chancellor Hotel** (433 Powell at Post St., 94102, tel. 415/362–2004 or 800/428–4748, fax 415/362–1403).
The Raphael (386 Geary at Mason, 94102, tel. 415/986–2000 or 800/821–5343, fax 415/397–2447).
San Francisco Hilton and Towers (333 O'Farrell at Mason, 94102, tel. 415/771–1400 or 800/445–8667, fax 415/771–6807).
San Francisco Marriott (55 4th St. at Mission, 94103, tel. 415/896–1600 or 800/228–9290, fax 415/777–2799).
Westin St. Francis (335 Powell at Post St., 94102, tel. 415/397–7000 or 800/228–3000, fax 415/774–0124).

Activities for Children

The Friday edition of the *San Francisco Examiner* has an excellent listing of upcoming events for children in its "Weekend" section. Also check the children's pages of the "Datebook" section (known as the Pink Section) of the Sunday edition of the *San Francisco Chronicle*. ***Parents Press*** (1454 6th St., Berkeley 94710, tel. 510/524–1602 or 800/994–4543) and ***San Francisco/Peninsula Parent*** (Box 1280,

Millbrae 94030, tel. 415/342–9203) are free monthlies with excellent services and events listings. *Parents Press* covers San Francisco, the East Bay, and Marin County; *Peninsula Parent* has listings for San Francisco and the Peninsula. Both are available at libraries, Safeway and Lucky grocery stores, hospitals, and children's and maternity shops. **Parent's Place** (3272 California at Presidio Ave., 94118, tel. 415/563–1041), a resource center (closed Sundays, though some programs are offered Saturdays) near Laurel Village, lists baby-sitting services as well as events; it's an excellent starting point for parents.

Places of Worship

Even in hip and secular San Francisco, churchgoing is part of Sunday. Meridian strips become sanctioned parking zones as churchgoers' vehicles crowd the few available parking places. Call ahead for information on child care and special hours for summer and holidays.

Assemblies of God **Glad Tidings Church** (1280 Webster at Ellis St., tel. 415/346–1111). Service: 10:45 AM. The first and third Sunday of every month there is also a service at 12:30 PM, followed by lunch ($2; first-time visitors free); the fourth Sunday there's a 6 PM service.

Baptist **19th Avenue Baptist Church** (1370 19th Ave. at Irving St., tel. 415/564–7721). This church offers services in Cantonese (9 AM), English (11:10 AM), Vietnamese (1:30 PM), and Arabic (7 PM). Call for Bible-study times in each language.

Buddhist **Buddha's Universal Church** (720 Washington at Kearny St., tel. 415/982–6116). The hand-built, five-story temple is decorated with murals and tile mosaics. It opens at 11:30 AM on the second and fourth Sundays of the month.

Zen Center (300 Page St. at Laguna, tel. 415/863–3136). The center conducts meditation classes (Saturday but not Sunday) and operates a hospice. It has four B&B-style guest rooms and runs Green Gulch (1601 Shoreline Highway, Sausalito, 94964, tel. 415/383–3134), which holds weekend retreats and Sunday meditation classes.

Christian Scientist **First Church of Christ Scientist** (1700 Franklin at California, tel. 415/673–3544). This century-old congregation is the oldest Christian Science church in northern California. Service: 11 AM.

Church of Christ **Civic Center Church of Christ** (250 Van Ness Ave. at Grove, tel. 415/861–5292) This racially diverse congregation includes Caucasian, African American, Indochinese, Filipino, and Japanese worshipers. Services: 10:30 AM, 6:30 PM. Bible class: 9:30 AM.

Eastern Orthodox **Holy Trinity Orthodox Cathedral** (1520 Green St. at Van Ness, tel. 415/673–8565). The oldest Eastern Orthodox church in the country was founded in 1857. Tours are available by appointment. Service: 10 AM.

Episcopal **Episcopal Church of St. Mary the Virgin** (2325 Union St. at Steiner, tel. 415/921–3665). The fountain in the courtyard of this 1891 church is fed by the same spring that used to water the neighborhood's dairies. Services: 8 AM, 9 AM, 11 AM.

Grace Cathedral (1051 Taylor at California St., tel. 415/776–6611). This historic building (*see* Architecture *in* Chapter 3) is the seat of the Episcopal Church in San Francisco. Services: 7:30 AM, 8:30 AM, 11 AM, 3:30 PM.

St. Aidan's Episcopal Church (101 Gold Mine Dr. at Diamond Heights Blvd., tel. 415/285–9540). This Southwest Mission-style church has a mural by Mark Adams and a hidden clerestory. Services: 8 AM, 10:10 AM.

Trinity Episcopal Church (1668 Bush St. at Gough, tel. 415/775–1117). The one-of-a-kind E. M. Skinner organ resonates amid near-perfect acoustics. Project Open Hand got its start in the church's kitchens, as did the nation's first Meals on Wheels program. Services: 8 AM, 11 AM; coffee and refreshments after the later service.

Independent Charismatic **Bethel Christian Church** (1325 Valencia at 24th St., tel. 415/285-1433). This evangelical fellowship holds services at 8:25 AM, 11 AM, and 6 PM.

Interfaith **Metropolitan Community Church** (150 Eureka at 18th St., tel. 415/863-4434). This gay congregation has been active in the Castro area since the 1970s. Services: 9 AM, 11 AM, 7 PM.

Religious Society of Friends (65 9th St. at Mission St., tel. 415/431-7440). The service is unprogrammed and anyone is welcome. Service 11 AM; adult religious discussion 9:30 AM except second Sunday of the month.

Jewish **Congregation Sherith Israel** (2266 California at Webster St., tel. 415/346-1720). This Moorish temple served as the seat of local government in the years after the 1906 quake, while the new civic center was being erected. In 1945, when the United Nations was founded in San Francisco, Jewish peace delegates met here for a commemorative service led by Rabbi Stephen S. Wise. Saturday service (Reform): 10:30 AM.

Temple Emanu-el (2 Lake St. at Arguello Blvd., tel. 415/751-2535). Temple Emanu-el's congregation dates to 1850. The current edifice, whose striking Levantine design combines Byzantine, Roman, and Mediterranean influences, was dedicated in 1926. Saturday service (Reform): 10:30 AM.

Lutheran **St. Mark's Lutheran Church** (1111 O'Farrell near Franklin St., tel. 415/928-7770). Henry Geilfuss, architect of this 1895 high-Victorian Romanesque-Gothic church, is well known for his lavishly detailed Victorian houses in the Bay Area. Services: 8:45 AM, 11 AM.

Methodist **Glide Memorial Church** (330 Ellis at Taylor St., tel. 415/771-6300). The dynamic Reverend Cecil Williams has made Glide in the Tenderloin the city's most famous church, popular for its gospel/rock-and-roll services and widely respected for its social programs (job training, aid to the homeless). Services: 9 AM, 11 AM.

Park Presidio United Methodist Church (4301 Geary Blvd. at 7th Ave., tel. 415/751-4438). This church is active in community affairs, supporting Emergency Family Services and the Food Bank, among other worthy causes; it's also the site of a youth guidance center, English-as-a-second-language classes, and a host of 12-step groups. Services: 9:30 AM (Chinese); 11 AM (English); 1:30 PM (Korean). Bible class (English) is held at 9:30 AM.

Mormon **Church of Jesus Christ of Latter-Day Saints (Golden Gate Ward)** (1900 Pacific Ave. at Gough St., tel. 415/771-3655). This Russian Hill district ward is the oldest in the city, but there are Mormon churches throughout the Bay Area. The church has served as a community base for many of the Samoan, Hawaiian, and Tongan immigrants to the Bay Area. Services run continuously from 9 AM to 12:15 PM: The first hour is devoted to the sacrament meeting, the second to Sunday school, and the third to the priesthood meeting.

Presbyterian **Calvary Presbyterian Church** (2515 Fillmore at Jackson St., tel. 415/346-3832). Calvary was rebuilt in the early 1900s using some of the materials from the original 1854 structure that once stood at Union Square. Services: 8:45 AM, 11 AM.

Noe Valley Ministry (1021 Sanchez. at 23rd St., tel. 415/282-2317). The ministry hosts music and dance events on the weekend (*see* Music *in* Chapter 7). The informal services are Presbyterian, but the congregation includes Jewish families from the church's Or Shalom Jewish Community (a group for mixed-marriage families, especially) as well as Catholics and members of other faiths. Service: 10:30 AM; religious study and discussion at 9:30 AM.

Roman Catholic **Mission Dolores Basilica** (3321 16th St. at Dolores St., tel. 415/621–8203). Constructed between 1782 and 1791, this is the sixth of the 21 missions founded by Father Junípero Serra in California—and one of the most intact. The cemetery in back includes the grave of Don Luis Antonio Arguello, the first governor (*see* Cemeteries *in* Chapter 6). The Mission Basilica, next door to the old Mission Dolores, holds Sunday mass at 8 AM and 10 AM in English and at noon in Spanish. There is only one service in the old Mission Dolores: Saturday at 5 PM.

Old St. Mary's Cathedral (660 California at Grant Ave., tel. 415/986–4388). Across the street from tranquil St. Mary's Park, this 1854 structure, built with granite quarried in China, was the city's first and only Catholic cathedral until 1891. Services: 8:30 AM and 11 AM.

St. Mary's Cathedral (1111 Gough St. at Geary Blvd., tel. 415/567–2020). There are 2,500 seats under the modern roof (formed by four paraboloids) of this 1970s cathedral, which also houses a high school, a convent, and a rectory. Services: 7:30 AM, 9 AM, 11 AM (in English); 1 PM (in Spanish).

Sts. Peter and Paul/Italian National Cathedral (666 Filbert St. at Stockton, facing Washington Square Park, tel. 415/421–0809). On the first Sunday in October, Sts. Peter and Paul holds its annual blessing of the fleet, which is followed by a parade to Fisherman's Wharf. Another popular autumn event is the Columbus Day pageant. Services: 7:30 AM, 9 AM, 10:15 AM (Chinese), 11:30 AM (Italian), 12:45 PM, 5:30 PM.

St. Vincent de Paul (2320 Green St. at Steiner, tel. 415/922–1010). This huge, gabled church, with its imposing tower, was built in 1916 by architect Frank Shea. Services: 8 AM, 10 AM, noon, 5:15 PM.

Swedenborgian **Swedenborgian Church** (2107 Lyon St. at Washington, tel. 415/346–6466). Nature feeds the Swedenborgian religious imagination, which explains the church's rough-hewn architecture (*see* Architecture *in* Chapter 3). Service: 11 AM.

Unitarian **First Unitarian Church** (1187 Franklin at Geary Blvd., tel. 415/776–4580). The original Romanesque-revival structure was built in 1888 next to the grave of Thomas Starr King, the Boston minister who founded the San Francisco congregation. (Among his other accomplishments, King helped keep California in the Union during the Civil War and founded the precursor to the Red Cross.) The newer portion, built in 1968 of redwood and concrete, blends in well. Service: 11 AM; Sunday forum 10 AM, breakfast 9:30 AM.

Vineyard **Vineyard Christian Fellowship** (1098 Harrison at 7th St., tel. 415/558–9900). According to its pastor, this church, a member of the Association of Vineyard Churches, "attempts to present Christianity within the context of contemporary culture. The emphasis is on worship and the ministry of the Holy Spirit." Services: 9 AM, 11 AM, and on the last Sunday of the month at 6 PM.

Seasonal Pleasures

There's something going on all year long in San Francisco. Fall and winter are the busiest times, but in the realm of culture, entertainment, and sporting events there's never a dry season. For extensive listings check the various guides in the "Weekend" section of Friday afternoon's *Examiner*, or the Sunday "Datebook" (the Pink Section) in the *Chronicle*. *Focus* magazine, available at newsstands, also offers hints, as does *Sunset* magazine's "Travel This Month" section. The *San Francisco Book*, published quarterly by the Convention and Visitors Bureau, lists sports, art, outdoor, and other special events over a four-month period; the bureau also offers an events hot line (*see* Visitor Information, *above*). The following is a selection of seasonal pleasures worth checking out. (For more information *see* Neighborhood Fairs *in* Chapter 3, Sightseeing, and Antiques Shows *in* Chapter 5.)

Winter Winter is an indoor time, and the city's performing-arts calendar is at its fullest. But some of the nicest days of the year can be spent outdoors in wintertime San Francisco—especially in February, when the fog doesn't roll in the way it does in the summer. Wetsuited surfers catch big winter waves at Ocean Beach; a few blocks away, rollerbladers ply the roads of Golden Gate Park. If you're yearning for summer, you can always get a taste in the park's splendid Victorian Conservatory (*see* Gardens *in* Chapter 6.)

January: San Francisco Sports and Boat Show will delight anyone who dreams of taking to the water. Cow Palace; tel. 415/931–2500 or 415/469–6065 for information.
MacWorld Exposition draws the computer-curious from the Bay Area and beyond. Moscone Center; tel. 415/974–4000.
February: Chinese New Year is celebrated with special banquets at nearly every Chinese restaurant in the city, and Chinatown's narrow streets become filled with red firecracker paper. The dragon-dance parade through Chinatown and beyond ends the festivities. Contact the Chinese Chamber of Commerce (730 Sacramento St., 94108, tel. 415/982–3000) for details.
First weekend in February: Golden Gate Kennel Club Dog Show, the largest west of the Mississippi, is held at the Cow Palace (Geneva Ave. and Santos St., Daly City, tel. 415/469–6065).
First weekend in March: Great Outdoors Adventure Fair, a three-day exposition that includes every nonmotorized sport, from rollerblading to kayaking to rock climbing—with demo and tryout areas, outfitters, and environmentalists—is held at the Concourse (8th and Brannan Sts., tel. 415/777–8498; contact the *San Francisco Chronicle* for details).

Spring In April the rhododendron dell in Golden Gate Park explodes with blooms. Cherry blossoms burst open all over the city (especially in Strybing Arboretum in Golden Gate Park), and Asian magnolias bloom everywhere. Tulips in the Queen Wilhelmina Tulip Garden gild the Dutch Windmill close to Ocean Beach.

April: Mountaintop Easter Services are held at the cross at Dalewood Avenue and Myra Way on Mt. Davidson (call the city's Recreation and Park Department weekdays at 415/666–7035 or, at Easter time, the New Life Church of the Nazarene at 415/564–7535 for information.) *See* Other Views *in* Chapter 6.
Mid-April: The **Cherry Blossom Festival** celebrates both the flowering trees and Japanese culture, culminating with a parade in Japantown (tel. 415/563–2313).
Late April–early May: San Francisco International Film Festival, the country's oldest film festival, is held at the AMC Kabuki 8 Theatres complex, the Castro Theatre, and other venues (tel. 415/931–3456).
May: The **Bay to Breakers Race,** sponsored by the *San Francisco Examiner* (tel. 415/808–5000, ext. 2222), is a 7½-mile course that draws crowds of runners—many dressed in hilarious costumes—and hordes of spectators, too (*see* Spectator Sports *in* Chapter 6).
May: Mural Awareness Week includes tours, performances, lectures, and open houses (tel. 415/285–2287).
Memorial Weekend: Carnaval (tel. 415/826–1401) sees the Mission District shedding the last of its inhibitions for a multicultural celebration with a parade, food booths, and live entertainment.

Summer Even though summer is the foggiest season in San Francisco, 'tis the season to be outdoors. So, as the days expand, city folk hit the beaches in Marin County or the East Bay. Sports fans pray for homers at Candlestick Park, and music lovers savor the Stern Grove concerts.

Weekend after Memorial Day: Union Street Spring Festival, on the swank shopping strip between Steiner and Gough streets, features award-winning arts and crafts and a tea dance in the street (tel. 415/346–4561).

Early June: Art Deco Weekend-By-the-Bay celebrates the city's Deco monuments (such as the Shell Building at 100 Bush Street) with walking tours, fashion shows, lectures, movies, antique sales, and a ball, all sponsored by the Art Deco Society (tel. 415/982–3326).

Mid-June: Juneteenth Festival, in commemoration of the Emancipation Proclamation of 1863, is a children's fair in San Francisco (tel. 415/776–0363) and a citywide festival at Lakeside Park in Oakland (tel. 510/238–3091).

Third or fourth Sunday in June: The **Lesbian-Gay Freedom Day Parade and Celebration** usually begins at the Civic Center and winds up at the Embarcadero (tel. 415/864–3733). The **San Francisco International Lesbian and Gay Film Festival** is held the week before the parade (tel. 415/703–8650), usually running along Market Street.

Last Sunday in July: Comedy Celebration Day, held on the Polo Fields in Golden Gate Park, has Bay Area comedians providing free belly laughs (tel. 415/777–8498).

July–August: Stern Grove Midsummer Music Festival offers performances by the symphony, opera, ballet, and other groups in an outdoor setting (tel. 415/252–6252; *see* Orchestral Music *in* Chapter 7).

August–October: Shakespeare in the Park presents one play by the Bard each year in San Francisco, San Jose, and Oakland (tel. 415/666–2221; *see* Summer Shakespeare Events *in* Chapter 7).

Autumn

Weatherwise, fall is San Francisco's summer. Temperatures soar in September and October, allowing you to sample nature in all its glory. By late October, when the air begins to chill, the city is too excited to mourn: Halloween is a big-league holiday here, with pumpkin festivals, fancy and down-and-dirty balls, and planned and impromptu street celebrations.

First weekend in September: San Francisco Fair includes such weird contests as the Impossible Parking Space Race and Fog Calling, as well as more predictable entertainment, exhibits, and food and wine tastings (Civic Center Plaza, Polk and McAllister Sts., tel. 415/703–2729).

Labor Day Weekend: A La Carte, A La Park (Golden Gate Park, Sharon Meadow, tel. 415/383–9378). Gourmet food (by some of the city's best), cooking demonstrations, a Shakespeare Day Camp for kids, and a music festival (past performers have included Bobby Caldwell and Queen Ida) are part of this annual festival.

September: Hayes Valley Autumn Block Party highlights this hip neighborhood's galleries (Hayes St. between Franklin and Laguna, tel. 415/255–9307).

September: Pacific Heights Home Tours, a fund-raiser for the San Francisco Historical Society, is your chance to peek inside some of the city's most lavish homes (tel. 415/775–1111).

Weekends, early September–early October: The **Renaissance Pleasure Faire** brings Elizabethan England alive with jousting, dancing, and theater performed by nearly 1,500 costumed players. There's also plenty of food, drink, and crafts (tel. 800/523–2473 for admission fees and directions).

Late September: Folsom Street Fair, one of the state's biggest one-day fairs, features music, comics, dancing, a beer garden, and lots of leather and flesh (Folsom St. between 7th and 11th Sts.; tel. 415/863–3247).

Last weekend in September: San Francisco Blues Festival, the nation's oldest, brings an array of regional talent from Louisiana and Texas, Chicago, the West Coast, and elsewhere (Fort Mason, tel. 415/826–6837).

First Sunday in October: Castro Street Fair (Castro and Market Sts.,

tel. 415/467–3354). San Francisco's gayest neighborhood becomes even gayer with an afternoon of food, entertainment, arts and crafts booths, and zany-costumed participants.
October: Open Studios is a month-long opportunity for the art-loving public to make weekend visits to the ateliers of hundreds of local artists (tel. 415/861–9838 for a $1 map).
October: Columbus Day Celebration and Parade is North Beach's festive homage to the famous explorer. (tel. 415/434–1492).
Mid-October: Pumpkin festivals are held in cities throughout the Bay Area. The **Half Moon Bay Art and Pumpkin Festival** has pony and train rides, crafts, and food booths (tel. 415/726–9652). On Polk and Vallejo streets in San Francisco, there's a costume parade and a biggest-pumpkin contest, along with food and crafts booths (tel. 415/346–4561).
November 1 and 2: The **Day of the Dead Festival** is a traditional Mexican feast in honor of the dead. Mission District merchants display colorful altars in their windows, and exhibitions at Galeria de la Raza/Studio 24 (2857 24th St. at Bryant St., tel. 415/826–8009) include both traditional and contemporary altars.
First weekend in November: The **San Francisco Bay Area Book Festival** brings together hundreds of national and local authors and publishers for readings, panel discussions, and other events (Concourse Exhibition Center, 8th and Brannan Sts., tel. 415/861–2665).

The Holidays During the holidays, many stores have extended hours on Sunday. Embarcadero Center buildings are illuminated just before Thanksgiving; Ghirardelli Square, Union Square, and the Stonestown Galleria usually light their trees and buildings a day or two after Thanksgiving. Lightings are often accompanied by choirs and other entertainment.

December: ***The Nutcracker,*** a San Francisco Ballet staple, features vivid sets and costumes and spectacular choreography. For 1996 only, while the the War Memorial Opera House undergoes repairs, the ballet will perform a truncated version at the Palace of Fine Arts, Nov. 29–Dec. 8 (tel. 415/865–2000).
December: San Francisco Girls Chorus Christmas Carol Sing-along is a yuletide Davies Hall event (tel. 415/673–1511).
December: Sing-It-Yourself Messiah, at Louise M. Davies Hall, offers you the chance to raise your voice in a chorus of hallelujahs (tel. 415/415/864–6000 for tickets or 415/759–3477 for information).
First two weekends in December: Celebration of Craftswomen, sponsored by the Women's Building, is held in the Herbst Pavilion at Fort Mason. In addition to crafts demonstrations and sales, child care, entertainment, and refreshments are provided (tel. 415/361–0700).
Last three weeks in December: The New Pickle Circus performs its acrobatic clowning at Cowell Theater at Fort Mason (tel. 415/544–9344).

Personal and Business Services

The following establishments are open on Sundays most of the year. Always call ahead, however, since some may close for vacations or holidays or in summer.

Automotive Services *Gas* Gas stations that are open on Sundays, from east to west, include
Fisherman's Wharf Union 76 (490 Bay St. at Taylor, tel. 415/771–7730).
Downtown Union 76 (390 1st St. at Harrison, tel. 415/957–1754).
APSI Chevron (Harrison at 6th St., tel. 415/863–3001).
Marina Chevron (2301 Lombard at Pierce St., tel. 415/929–9775).
BP (2831 Cesar Chavez St. at Bryant St. near U.S. 101, tel. 415/826–8855).
Market Street BP (2175 Market St. at 15th St., tel. 415/863–1250).

19th Avenue BP (1401 19th Avenue at Judah St., tel. 415/681–3860).
Carl and Dan's Chevron (6000 Geary Blvd. at 24th Ave., tel. 415/750–0111).
Roy's Super Shell (1070 Oak St. near Divisadero, next door to Divisadero Touchless Car Wash, tel. 415/864–3231).
Tom Higa Chevron (798 Stanyan St. at Beulah St., tel. 415/386–9802).

Car Rentals Most car-rental outlets at the airport and downtown are open Sunday. Reserve well in advance for summer weekends. The major companies are **Alamo** (tel. 800/327–9633), **Avis** (tel. 800/831–2847), **Budget** (tel. 800/527–0700), **Dollar** (tel. 800/800–4000), **Hertz** (tel. 800/654–3131), **National** (tel. 800/227–7368), and **Thrifty** (tel. 800/367–2277). Low-cost companies include **Continental** (tel. 415/441–1771) and **Enterprise** (tel. 800/325–8007).

Towing and Repairs The **California State Automobile Association** (CSAA, tel. 800/400–4222) provides help to members. The Yellow Pages list dozens of other services under Towing and Auto Repair.

Mechanics are on duty for minor or major repairs, subject to parts availability, at

Discount Brake and Clutch. *740 Valencia St. at 18th St., tel. 415/431–3500. Open Sundays 8:30–2.*
San Francisco Auto Repair Center. *611 Florida St. near 18th St., tel. 415/285–8588. Open Sundays 8:30–4.*

Car Wash For many, it wouldn't be Sunday without a vehicular scrub. There are self- and full-service car washes throughout the city:

Divisadero Touchless Car Wash. *444 Divisadero at Oak St., tel. 415/621–8676. Open Sun. 8–7.*
Seal Car Wash No. 1. *2 Bay St. at Embarcadero, tel. 415/391–4138. Open Sun. 9–5*

Baby-Sitters **Bristol-Haran Agency** (tel. 415/775–9100) offers daily 24-hour baby-sitting referrals in San Francisco, Marin County, and the East Bay from its office in San Rafael (tel. 415/459–0145). Two other options are **Bay Area 2nd Mom** (tel. 415/858-2469) and **Starr Belly Child Care Services** (tel. 415/541–8592), whose nannies are bonded and insured and trained in CPR and first aid.

Beauty Care and Haircuts The following San Francisco salons offer haircuts for men, women, and children.

Architects and Heroes. *2239 Fillmore near Sacramento St., tel. 415/921–8383. Open Sun. 10–5.*
Cinta Hair Studio. *San Francisco Shopping Centre, 865 Market St. at 5th St., tel. 415/777–3313. Open Sun. 11–6.*
Macy's Beauty Works. *Stockton and O'Farrell Sts., Union Sq., tel. 415/954–6363. Open Sun. 11–7.*

Delivery **Express-It Courier Services** (1855 Norman Ave., Santa Clara, 95054, tel. 408/988–1999 or 800/882–1000) delivers anything from an envelope to a truckload, anywhere in the Bay Area or the country.

Dentistry **Dental Society Referral** (tel. 415/421–1435) provides round-the-clock referrals on Sunday and holidays.

Dry Cleaning **Fulton Fabricare Cleaners** offers same-day service if you drop your items off early. *2900 Fulton St. at 5th Ave., tel. 415/387–6500. Open Sun. 8–8.*

Electronic Mail Every American home may not yet have access to the Internet, but patrons of many Bay Area cafés can log on to **SFNET.** For 50¢ you can debate the merits of the latest movie or flavored cappuccino with someone in another coffeehouse—electronically. Here's a list of cafés, each in a different neighborhood, with the 'NET. For a complete list, call 415/695–9824.

Brain/Wash (1122 Folsom between 7th and 8th Sts., tel. 415/861–3663) is a laundromat, too.

Cafe Milano (2522 Bancroft Way at Telegraph Ave., tel. 510/644–3100).

Coffee Zone (1409 Haight St. at Masonic Ave., tel. 415/863–2443).

Jammin Java (1395 9th Ave. at Judah St., tel. 415/566–5282).

Muddy Waters (521 Valencia at 16th St., tel. 415/863–8006).

Royal Grounds (1140 4th St. at B St., San Rafael, tel. 415/455–0107).

Yakety Yak (679 Sutter at Taylor St., tel. 415/885–6908).

Eyeglasses

City Optix offers some of the most stylish specs in town. If you're looking for designer frames, this is the place. *2154 Chestnut at Pierce St., tel. 415/921–1188. Open Sun. noon–5.*

Lenscrafters has many branches in the San Francisco area. Next to each is an **Eye Exam 2000** store (most of which close an hour earlier) that provides optometrist services on Sunday. *Stonestown Galleria, 19th Ave. at Winston Dr., tel. 415/566–9199; open Sun. 11–6. 685 Market St. at 3rd St., tel. 415/896–0680; open Sun. 11–5. 700 El Camino Real at Roble Ave., Menlo Park, tel. 415/329–8181; open Sun. 11–5. 325 Town Center Mall, Corte Madera, tel. 415/927–2616; open Sun. noon–6. 5707 Christie Ave. at Powell St., Emeryville tel. 510/547–8301; open Sun. noon–5.*

Site for Sore Eyes. *Serramonte Shopping Center, Daly City, tel. 415/992–8404. Open Sun. 11–7.*

Florists

There are sidewalk floral markets in just about every neighborhood on Sunday. In addition, a few shops are open for worldwide delivery:

Murata Floral Design specializes, as you might expect, in Japanese designs. *1737 Post St. at Buchanan St., Japantown, tel. 415/567–9133. Open Sun. 8 AM–9 PM.*

San Francisco Floral Exchange has balloons and gifts in addition to flowers. *200 Columbus Ave. at Kearny St., tel. 415/398–9888 or 800/398–9888. Open Sun. 10:30–4:30.*

Fiori offers European garden bouquets. *2314 Chestnut St. near Scott St., tel. 415/346–2432. Open Sun. 9–5.*

Pinelli's is a large shop that features seasonal garden bouquets. *714 Clement St. at 8th Ave., tel. 415/751–4142. Open Sun. 10–6.*

Health and Fitness Centers

24-hour Nautilus (1335 Sutter St. at Van Ness Ave., tel. 415/776–2200) has aerobics classes, fitness equipment, sauna, Jacuzzi, and steam room. Drop-in fee: $15. *Open Sun. 9–8.*

Embarcadero YMCA (169 Steuart St. at Mission St., tel. 415/957–9622), offers racquetball, an indoor track, a swimming pool, and aerobics classes. The $12 drop-in fee includes use of the sauna and whirlpool. *Open Sunday 9–5:45.*

Women's Training Center (2164 Market St. at 15th St., tel. 415/864–6835) is a complete workout center. The $10 day fee includes use of the sauna. *Open Sun. 10–5.*

Housekeepers

A Maid to Shine (tel. 415/379–9400 or 800/935–6243) provides bonded cleaners for home or office from 7 AM to 6 PM (later in emergency situations). A supervisor inspects the work before the cleaner leaves.

Limousine Services

Elegant Limousines (18 Robinson Dr., tel. 415/334–7179) is on call 24 hours a day, 7 days a week.

Locksmiths

Crown Lock (3615 Balboa St. at 37th Ave., tel. 415/221–9086 or 800/680–5625) can replace or open automobile or household locks.

Twin Peaks Locksmith (200 6th Ave. at California St., tel. 800/900–5397) offers a toll-free number in case you're locked out on a Sunday with no change.

Medical Services

Minor medical emergencies: San Francisco doesn't have the walk-in, immediate-care facilities that many suburbs do, although there is one at Mariner Medical Center in San Mateo (*see below*). Instead, use the emergency rooms listed below, or call the **San Francisco**

Medical Society (tel. 415/561–0850 or 415/561–0853) for names of doctors who work on weekends. (The regular referral hours are on weekdays, but in an emergency the answering service will contact the director on weekends.)

Mariner Medical Center (1261 E. Hillsdale Blvd. at Foster City Blvd., Foster City, tel. 415/570–2299) is an immediate-care center 25 minutes south of San Francisco. X-ray equipment, a lab, and a pharmacy are all on site. *Open Sun. 9–5.*

St. Francis Memorial Hospital (900 Hyde St. at Bush St., tel. 415/353–6000) offers a 24-hour emergency care and physician-referral service (tel. 415/353–6566), as well as rehabilitation and acute-burn care services (tel. 415/353–6255).

Howard A. Thornton, M.D. (395 5th Ave. at Geary Blvd., tel. 415/751–8616) makes house and hotel calls on short notice, 24 hours daily, for adults and children over 13.

UCSF Medical Center (505 Parnassus Ave. near 3rd Ave., tel. 415/476–1000) has a 24-hour emergency room (tel. 415/476–1037).

Office Services

Clerical Help

Most temp agencies (listed under "Employment, Temporary" in the Yellow Pages) can provide Sunday office help if you arrange for it by Friday. One reliable agency is **Total Support Services** (605 Market St. Suite 1250, tel. 415/543–4545).

Computer Stations

Kinko's Copies, Buckingham Way and Fillmore Street branches (*see* Copy and Fax Services *below*), have PC and Mac workstations for rent by the hour and a range of fancy printers.

Copy and Fax Services

Colorcrane Arts (3957 24th St. at Noe St., tel. 415/285–1387) offers photocopying and fax services and adult and children's art supplies. *Open Sun. 11–5.*

Kinko's Copies (555 Buckingham Way, near Stonestown Galleria, tel. 415/566–0572; 25 Stanyan St. at Geary Blvd., tel. 415/750–1193; 1967 Market St. at Duboce Ave., tel. 415/252–0864; and 3225 Fillmore St. at Greenwich St., tel. 415/441–2995). All four locations are open 24 hours daily.

Pharmacies

Ace Pharmacy delivers all over San Francisco. *2505 Noriega St. at 32nd Ave., tel. 415/731–3535. Open Sun. 10–3.*

Safeway Grocery Stores has five locations with pharmacies that are open on Sunday. *1335 Webster St. at Geary Blvd., tel. 415/921–5502 (10–6); 2300 16th St. at Potrero Ave., tel. 415/861–1334 (10–5); 850 La Playa at Fulton St., tel. 415/387–0481 (10–3); 2350 Noriega St. at 30th Ave., tel. 415/665–8456 (10–3); and 730 Taraval St. at 19th Ave., tel. 415/665–0119 (10–4).*

Walgreens has two San Francisco locations and one in Daly City with 24-hour prescription services. *498 Castro St. at 18th St., tel. 415/861–3136; 3201 Divisadero at Lombard St., tel. 415/931–6417; 395 S. Mayfair Ave., Daly City, tel. 415/756–4535.*

Photographic Services

Darkroom Rental

Rayko Photography Center (2423 Polk St. at Union St., tel. 415/567–9067) rents black-and-white darkrooms. *Open Sun. noon–8.*

Colorarts (449 Bryant St. at 2nd St., tel. 415/543–6717) has color darkrooms, but if you want to rent on Sunday, you must arrange it ahead of time.

Photo Processing and Passport Photos

Sapphire Photo (2761 Mission St. at 24th St., tel. 415/285–8678) offers one-hour photo processing and passport-photo services. *Open Sun. 11–5.*

Photo Motion (1835 Haight St. at Stanyan St., tel. 415/668–4687, open Sun. 10–7; 350 Bay St. at Mason St., tel. 415/398–6088, open Sun. 10–5; 1850 Fillmore St. at Bush St., tel. 415/346–1850, open Sun. 10–5:30) offers similar services.

Picture Framing

Cheap Pete's is a factory outlet store. *4720 Geary Blvd. at 11th Ave., tel. 415/221–4720; 1666 Locust St. at Civic Dr., Walnut Creek, tel. 510/945–1666; Montecito Shopping Center, 221 3rd St. near U.S. 101, San Rafael, tel. 415/455–8055. All open Sun. noon–5.*

Frame O Rama lets you do it yourself or have the staff do it. *1940 Polk St. at Pacific St., tel. 415/441–3636; 305 California Dr. at Burlingame Ave., Burlingame, tel. 415/343–8331; 210 Hamilton Ave. at Emerson Ave., Palo Alto, tel. 415/321–3939. Open Sun. noon–5.*
Frame of Mind custom frames photos and fine art. *1262 9th Ave. at Lincoln Blvd., tel. 415/759–2000. Open Sun. noon–5.*
The Great Frame Up provides custom service or, if you prefer, lets you do it yourself. *2358 Market St. at Castro St., tel. 415/863–7144. Open Sun. noon–5.*

Post Office The **main post office** (1300 Evans St., two blocks east of 3rd St., tel. 415/284–0755 for information) offers stamp-vending machines, a zip-code directory, postal scales and rates, and a bill changer in its lobby 24 hours a day, seven days a week. Two other full-service postal stations are open on Sunday: **Macy's Union Square Station** (121 Stockton St. at O'Farrell St., tel. 415/956–3570; open Sun. 11–5) and the **Stonestown Station** (565 Buckingham Way near 19th Ave., across from Emporium, tel. 415/284–0755; open Sun. 10:30–4:30). The **Airport Mail Center** (660 Road No. 6 at McDonnell Rd., tel. 415/742–1431) provides full postal services from 6 AM until 12 midnight. The **Postal Answer Line** (tel. 415/695–8760) has 24-hour recorded information.

Spas **Nordstrom Spa** provides facials, manicures, waxing, hydrotherapy, body wraps, and massages. *San Francisco Shopping Centre, 865 Market St. at 5th St., tel. 415/978–5102. Open Sun. 10–6.*
Kabuki Hot Springs offers hot and cold pools, sauna, massage, and steam rooms. *1750 Geary Blvd. at Fillmore St., Japantown, tel. 415/922–6002. Open Sun. 9 AM–10 PM.*

Veterinary Services **Pets Unlimited** (2343 Fillmore St. near Washington St., tel. 415/563–6700) is a nonprofit, 24-hour, full-service veterinary hospital.

Emergencies, Complaints, and Problems

Complaints and Emergencies
Better Business Bureau (tel. 415/243–9999).
Police (tel. 911 for emergencies or 415/553–8090).
Potholes and street repairs (tel. 415/695–2020).
Taxi complaints (tel. 415/553–1447).
Towed cars (tel. 415/553–1235).
24-hour rape hot line (tel. 415/821–3222).

Lost and Found Of the numbers that follow, only Amtrak answers on Sunday:
Amtrak (Jack London Square Station, tel. 510/238–4320; Emeryville Station, tel. 510/450–1087).
BART (tel. 510/464–7090).
CalTrain and SamTrans (tel. 415/546–4439).
Muni (tel. 415/923–6168).

2 Where to Eat

By Catherine McEver

Updated by Sharon Silva

When Sunday rolls around and everyone's favorite city gets even more mellow, the range of culinary possibilities becomes even broader. Kick back for a couple of hours with a cappuccino and a newspaper at a neighborhood café. Escort a budding Eloise to an elegant afternoon tea in one of the city's fine old hotels. Join in the tradition of family outings for dim sum in Chinatown, sampling the array of delectable dumplings that wheel by on tiered carts. Follow in the footsteps of the Beat Generation with a concoction of chocolate, steamed milk, and brandy at a vintage North Beach hangout where the jukebox plays sobbing arias. Comfort yourself with a plate of linguine and clam sauce in a family-run restaurant with red-checked tablecloths. Treat yourself to a cocktail or after-dinner drink and a twinkling view at a bar high above the city.

Alternatively, you can dine alfresco at Fisherman's Wharf, in Tiburon, or in Sausalito, taking in the spectacular bay views as you linger over brunch and a Ramos gin fizz. Explore the Marin Headlands and Pacific coastline and dine on gourmet fare at a mountain retreat. Cozy up to a fire at a seaside joint frequented by a steady neighborhood crowd. Plan an expedition to the Wine Country, where local produce and game, prepared by world-class chefs, serve as a perfect foil for a sampling of fine local wines.

The restaurants listed here can easily feed you for years of Sundays. They range from classics and neighborhood favorites to cutting-edge culinary happenings. The city's ethnic diversity is reflected in fare from every corner of the globe, and you'll encounter enough variety to fit every mood and budget.

Because many restaurants change their menus frequently to take advantage of seasonal offerings and because chefs play musical chairs, shifting to new restaurants or opening their own, specifics are mentioned mainly to suggest the house style. Unless otherwise noted, dress is casual and almost anything goes. Restaurants are listed by neighborhoods, which correspond to the maps in the back of the book.

Reservations Reservations are usually advised at all but the most casual restaurants. Here we have noted only when reservations are either not accepted or essential. Many restaurants that don't accept reservations for small parties will accept them for groups of six or more, sometimes even fewer; call ahead to see if your group qualifies. Always phone well in advance for holiday bookings, and keep in mind that at particularly popular restaurants it may be necessary to book a month or more in advance.

Smoking Many communities in the larger Bay Area (including San Francisco, Berkeley and Oakland) have already instituted nonsmoking ordinances for restaurants. An increasing number of restaurants in other areas maintain smoke-free environments, so smokers should always be prepared to step outside. Even in many alfresco dining situations, smoking is now considered politically (or socially) incorrect. If you're concerned, inquire about policies when making your reservations.

Sunday Hours Breakfast, when available, usually begins around 7:30. Brunch customarily runs from 11 to 3 or 4 and dinner from 5 or 6 to 9 or 10; kitchens often close in the interval between the two. Our listings note hours and meals for Sunday only; hours will be different on other days. Restaurants change hours from time to time based on the flow of business. Always call ahead to avoid disappointment.

Prices The price categories outlined below are based on dinner:

Category	Dinner Entrée	Dinner Cost*
$$$$$	over $20	over $45
$$$$	$15–$20	$30–$45
$$$	$12–$15	$20–$30
$$	$8–$12	$15–$20
$	under $8	under $15

**per person, including one drink and tip*

Saving Money Breakfast, lunch, and brunch prices are often a third to a half of those for dinner. Prix fixe meals can also offer excellent value and they are usually noted in the listings. Although the extravagant, prix fixe brunch buffets offered by a number of hotels and restaurants can be expensive, many charge greatly reduced rates for children, thus making it possible for parents to offer youngsters a grand-hotel brunch as a special but affordable treat. Brunch prix fixe menus usually include at least one drink and coffee. Prix fixe dinner menus also offer excellent value. If you're on a budget and crave bay views or an elegant and pricey setting, consider a visit for cocktails or dessert (*see* Sweets and Treats, *below*). And never let a waiter rattle off a list of specials without asking for prices!

Vegetarian Dining Because of talented chefs, new culinary trends, environmental awareness, health consciousness, and a rich abundance of farm-fresh produce, vegetarians in the Bay Area dine exceedingly well. We have included five popular vegetarian-only restaurants: **Greens** in the Marina, **Millennium** in the Civic Center, **Real Good Karma** in the Mission, **Vegi Food** in the Richmond, and **Long Life Vegi House** in the East Bay.

It's possible to dine well at both budget and all-star eateries by picking and choosing among appetizers, salads, and entrées. However, we've noted restaurants that highlight vegetarian specialties or that offer a good selection of vegetarian fare as part of their regular menu. Look for the symbol "VG" (vegetarian selections featured) at the beginning of each listing.

Dining with Children The restaurants included in this guide have been specifically queried about their attitude toward young customers. Establishments with a "CH" (good for children) symbol do more than simply tolerate kids—they welcome them with open arms. The nature of the welcome may include crayons, costumed waiters, special menus, reduced prices, unusual dinnerware, entertaining theme dishes, fish tanks, or fun drinks. Or it may simply mean reasonable prices and a friendly atmosphere for families.

Credit Cards The following credit card abbreviations are used: AE, American Express; D, Discover; DC, Diners Club; MC, MasterCard; and V, Visa.

Other Abbreviations Symbols at the beginning of an entry signify: CH: Good for children, L: Serves after 11 PM, MU: Live music, O: Outdoor dining, VG: Vegetarian selections featured, VU: Great view.

Restaurants

The Castro

Tourists drop by the Castro to catch the goings-on in the gay capital of the Western world, particularly on Lesbian and Gay Freedom Day in June. People-watching is a favorite pastime for everyone, including the inhabitants. You might want to grab a bite to eat before or after a film at the venerable Castro Theatre, the institutional anchor of the neighborhood.

American Casual *$$$$$* *O* **Patio Cafe.** This entire establishment is an enclosed, heated patio full of foliage, and there's always a line out the door for eggs Benedict and strawberry-banana daiquiris during Sunday brunch. *531 Castro St. at 18th near Market, tel. 415/621–4640. AE, MC, V. Sun. brunch 8:30–4:30, dinner 5–10.*

$ *CH, O* **Café Flore.** This crowded coffeehouse is a meeting place for neighborhood residents and their friends. Try the poached eggs with shiitake mushrooms and hollandaise sauce. Plan on sharing a table. *2298 Market St. near Noe, tel. 415/621–8579. Reservations not accepted. No credit cards. Sun. 7:30 AM–11 PM.*

$ *CH, L* **Sparky's Diner.** Black-and-white decor and glass brick walls create the right atmosphere for great scrambled eggs and other breakfast items, as well as pizza and beer. Best of all, it's open 24 hours a day. *242 Church St. between Market and 15th, tel. 415/621–6001. AE, MC, V. Sun. 24 hours.*

American Contemporary *$$$* **Market Street Restaurant.** Though the name is only temporary—a contest has been launched to come up with a permanent moniker—this sleek new Market Street eatery, brainchild of well-known restaurateur John Cunin, looks like it's here to stay. Here you'll find warm spinach and fingerling potato salad with apple-smoked bacon or chestnut-brown roast chicken crowned with crisp onion rings at night, and such appealing morning fare as Parma ham and Fontina on warm brioche or banana soufflé pancakes with chicken-apple sausage on the side. *2223 Market St. near Noe, tel. 415/431–0692. MC, V. Sun. brunch 10–2, dinner 5:30–10.*

Mexican *$–$$* *VG* **Pozole.** This colorful eatery was started by Jesse Acevedo, who also created Campo Santo. The fresh ingredients and light, innovative takes on traditional Mexican fare continue to draw a steady stream of customers. Crab quesadillas and Oaxacan tamales with mango salsa are among the best sellers. *2337 Market St., between Noe and Castro, tel. 415/626–2666. No credit cards. Sun. noon–11.*

Chinatown

Entertainment along these crowded streets includes culinary window shopping: plump golden hens, pressed ducks, roast pork, and Chinese sausage suspended from hooks; trays of chow mein, chow fun, and chicken feet; urns of preserved eggs; crates of exotic produce. A dim sum brunch of stuffed dumplings, egg rolls, and appetizer-size treats brought to your table on rolling carts and charged by the plate is a San Francisco must.

Chinese *$$$* *CH* **Gold Mountain.** This upscale eatery has the ambience of a ritzy Hong Kong restaurant, an entertaining array of dim sum by day, and such specialties as roast suckling pig and spicy fried crab for dinner. *644 Broadway near Stockton, tel. 415/296–7733. AE, MC, V. Sun. 8–9:30.*

$$–$$$ *CH* **Golden Phoenix.** The place is packed with families on Sundays, and since high chairs, boosters, and theme-name children's drinks are provided, it's a great place to bring the kids. Peking duck, shredded chicken salad, and seafood are specialties. *728 Washington St. between Grant and Kearny, tel. 415/989–4400. AE, DC, MC, V. Sun. 2:30–10:30.*

$$–$$$ *CH* **Oriental Pearl.** South China's Cantonese and Chiu Chow (Chao Zhou in Mandarin) cuisines, the latter being the seafood-based diet of a people some 200 miles north of Canton, are the specialties of this attractively decorated, professionally staffed Chinatown restaurant. Lunchtime brings a selection of dim sum—prawn dumplings, tiny spareribs in black bean sauce, pork and vegetables wrapped in bean-curd sheets—while dinner delivers a host of memorable dishes, from a delicate chicken meatball tucked into a crêpelike "bag" that's sealed shut with a Chinese chive to braised duck with a heady vine-

gar dipping sauce. *760 Clay St. near Kearny, tel. 415/433–1817. AE, DC, MC, V. Sun. dim sum 11-3, dinner 5–9:30.*

$$–$$$ *CH* **R & G Lounge.** On Sunday evenings Chinese families crowd into this highly regarded neighborhood restaurant for fresh pearly pink shrimp, steamed and served with a simple dipping sauce of soy and fresh chilies, Dungeness crab with scallions and ginger, tender stir-fried pea shoots, and other dishes that are pictured on a four-color menu that makes ordering easy. Choose either the simpler, less expensive, lively downstairs dining room or the pricier, rice-paper-outfitted, quieter room upstairs. *631 B Kearny St. near Commercial St., tel. 415/982–7877. AE, DC, MC, V. Portsmouth Square garage. Sun. 11–9:30.*

$$ *CH* **New Asia.** This monumental space is often full on Sundays, when hundreds of hungry diners flag down carts bearing dumplings, rice-noodle rolls, custard tarts, and dozens of other dim sum treats. It's less hectic at night, when a classic Cantonese dinner menu is offered. At either time you will find Chinese extended families occupying the many large round tables that furnish the room. *772 Pacific Ave. near Grant, tel. 415/391–6666. MC, V. Sun. dim sum 8:30–3, dinner 5:30–9.*

$–$$ *CH, L* **Hing Lung.** Whenever southern Chinese need a morning pick-me-up or a light but nourishing late-night snack, they sit down to a bowl of *juk* (also known as congee), a thick rice soup laced with nearly whatever they fancy, from pork meatballs to jellyfish. The kitchen here is famous for this homespun staple, and it also turns out a host of soup noodles, chow mein, rice plates, and barbecued items. In the evening, a dinner menu of well-prepared, modestly priced Cantonese dishes keeps patrons happy. *674 Broadway near Stockton, tel. 415/398–8838. MC, V. Sun. 8 AM–1 AM.*

$ *VG* **House of Nanking.** The Shanghai cuisine is terrific and the prices are a bargain, but you'll need to be cunning: They don't take reservations, and many of the best items—including the shrimp and green-onion pancakes in peanut sauce—aren't on the menu. Point to intriguing edibles on tables near you or plead with your waiter for advice. Arrive as early as possible to avoid the long lines. *919 Kearny St. between Jackson and Columbus, tel. 415/421–1429. Reservations not accepted. No credit cards. Sun. 4–10.*

Japanese *$$$* **Yamato Restaurant & Sushi Bar.** This cultural oasis has won an award from the emperor of Japan and kudos from locals. The lobby is a bamboo-and-reed reproduction of a rustic village, with a squeaking bridge, fountains, and fresh-flower ikebana arrangements. Try a sake martini with your teriyaki. *717 California St. near Grant Ave., tel. 415/397–3456. AE, D, DC, MC, V. Sun. 5–10.*

Civic Center

This cultural and civic stomping ground has more than 50 restaurants offering everything from pastrami sandwiches to world-class American cuisine. Most places are jam-packed before symphony and opera performances; many cater to postperformance crowds with romantic late-night suppers, exotic snacks, or seductive dessert menus. The enclave known as Hayes Valley (centered in Hayes Street), which has become an increasingly upscale gallery and shopping area, houses a handful of all-star eateries.

American Casual *$* *CH* **Bull's Texas Cafe.** Get ready for chicken-fried steak, Texas-style chili, ribs, links, and Cajun chicken wings in a noisy, down-home saloon with neon signs, Western art on the walls, chairs hanging from the rafters, and seating at big tables and benches. *25 Van Ness Ave. between Fell and Oak, tel. 415/864–4288. AE, DC, MC, V. Sun. 4–9.*

American Contemporary *$$$$$* *L, MU* **Stars.** You deserve a star if you can get in the door of the most popular bistro in town, owned by celebrity-chef Jeremiah Tower. The crowds are noisy, the lines are long, and everyone loves to critique the food. The truly hip drop in for a hot dog at the bar or late-night desserts. *150 Redwood Alley between Van Ness and Polk, tel. 415/861–7827. Reservations essential. AE, DC, MC, V. Sun. 5:30–midnight.*

$$$ **Ivy's Restaurant.** Innovative pastas, house-smoked trout, and lime pound cake are among the Sunday brunch and lunch options in this airy room with misty hues, changing art, and fresh flowers on every table. *398 Hayes St. at Gough, tel. 415/626–3930. AE, DC, MC, V. Sun. 11 AM–2:30 PM.*

$$$ **Stars Cafe.** Less raucous than the restaurant and popular with the symphony crowd, the café has a European ambience with colorful posters and bouquets. The mixed seafood—lightly fried and served with chips—is a favorite. Desserts (lemon cheesecake, devil's food cake) are stellar. *500 Van Ness Ave. at McAllister, tel. 415/861–4344. AE, DC, MC, V. Sun. brunch 11:30–2, late lunch and bar menu 2–5, dinner 5:30–9, late supper 9–10.*

Caribbean *$$$* *O* **Geva's.** The family photos in the entryway, banana-leaf light fixtures, intimate coral dining room, and inviting side patio and garden make you feel as if you're visiting friends in Jamaica. This friendly family makes its own breads and creates wonderful dishes with coconut and a pantryful of exotic spices. Try the jerk pork chops or chicken or the heavenly seafood stew. *482A Hayes St. between Octavia and Gough, tel. 415/863–1220. AE, MC, V. Sun. 5–8:30.*

$$$ *CH, MU, O* **Miss Pearl's Jam House.** Favorite fare at this colorfully wacko establishment includes black-eyed-pea fritters, catfish fingers, and jerk chicken. A swimming pool in the outdoor courtyard reminds diners that this tropical dining room is actually part of a motel. *601 Eddy St. between Larkin and Polk, tel. 415/775–5267. D, DC, MC, V. Sun. 5:30–9:30.*

Deli *$–$$* *CH, MU, VG* **Max's Opera Cafe.** Pig out on huge deli sandwiches and hefty slices of cake (and steer clear of overly ambitious dinner entrées) while the waiters take turns singing Puccini at the microphone. *Opera Plaza, 601 Van Ness Ave. between Turk and Golden Gate, tel. 415/771–7301. Reservations not accepted. AE, MC, V. Sun. 11:30–11.*

German *$$$* **Suppenküche.** If you hunger for bratwurst, red cabbage, and good German beer, this is the place to find all three. The atmosphere is decidedly young and hip, and communal seating makes new friendships an easy part of the dining package. Sunday brunch features Bavarian omelets, good-for-you muesli, and cold cuts and cheeses, among other German specialties. *525 Laguna at Hayes, tel. 415/252–9289. AE, MC, V. Sun. 10–10.*

Italian *$$$$* *O* **Vivande Ristorante.** Carlo Middione, San Francisco's best-known expert on the rustic food of southern Italy, showcases his culinary specialties in this handsome 200-seat restaurant just a little more than a block from the Opera House. The eye-catching entrance is a door shaped like an open mouth; the Venetian glass chandeliers, marble and slate floors, and large exhibition kitchen further add to the cosmopolitan atmosphere. There are plenty of delectable antipasti, inspired pastas, fragrant risottos, and tasty grilled meats and fish to tempt the diner and vintages from an all-Italian wine list to toast the meal. *Opera Plaza, 670 Golden Gate Ave. between Turk and Golden Gate, tel. 415/673–9245. AE, DC, MC, V. Sun. 11:30–10:30.*

$–$$ *CH, VG* **Spuntino.** This upscale, modernistic interpretation of a Milano café serves good pizzas, pastas, salads, and pastries and provides some prime people-watching. Lithe ballet dancers hit the cappuccino bar following afternoon performances. *524 Van Ness Ave. opposite Opera Plaza, tel. 415/861–7772. Reservations not accepted. AE, DC, MC, V. Sun. 10–7.*

Mediterranean *\$\$\$\$–\$\$\$\$\$* **Act IV.** This is a wonderful romantic hideaway of a place to eat, with a green marble fireplace, plush banquettes, Belgian tapestries, and lush flowers. Sample dishes—Mediterranean in spirit with a strong California influence—include roasted loin of rabbit stuffed with feta, spinach, and bell peppers and a selection of richly indulgent desserts. *Inn at the Opera, 333 Fulton St. near Franklin, tel. 415/863–8400. DC, MC, V. Sun. 7–10.*

\$\$\$–\$\$\$\$\$ *O* **Zuni Cafe.** Everyone-who-is-anyone's favorite hangout is the epitome of a European sidewalk café, with freshly shucked oysters, brick oven-roasted chicken, a perfect Caesar salad, and homemade ice cream—all prepared by chef Judy Rodgers. *1658 Market St. near Franklin, tel. 415/552–2522. AE, MC, V. Sun. 7:30 AM–11 PM.*

\$ *CH, VG* **Opera Plaza Grocery & Delicatessen.** Freshly made moussaka, Assyrian meatballs, layered spinach salad, tabbouleh, spanokopita, yogurt summer salad, and other exotic fast-food treats can be purchased for take-out or eaten here while you eye the well-stocked shelves of gourmet goods. *Opera Plaza, 601 Van Ness Ave. at Turk, tel. 415/441–2727. Reservations not accepted. AE, MC, V. Sun. 10–7.*

Pizza *\$* *CH, VG* **Vicolo.** This casually chic little joint, tucked away in an alley behind Davies Hall, serves Italian salads and great cornmeal-crusted pizza by the pie and slice. Among the popular toppings are andouille and smoked mozzarella and roast eggplant and blue cheese. Order at the counter and take a seat; a server will deliver your meal. *201 Ivy St. off Franklin, tel. 415/863–2382. Reservations not accepted. MC, V. Sun. noon–10.*

Seafood *\$\$\$\$* **Hayes Street Grill.** This comfortable grill with a vintage aura sports white tablecloths, bentwood chairs, an open kitchen, and a reputation for some of the best charcoal-grilled fresh fish in town. The place is partly owned by *Examiner* restaurant critic Patricia Unterman. *320 Hayes St. near Franklin, tel. 415/863–5545. AE, DC, MC, V. Sun. 5–8:30.*

Thai *\$\$* **Thepin.** In this small eatery, wines are carefully chosen to complement the exotic flavors in such dishes as calamari stuffed with ground pork or roast duck in red curry paste. *298 Gough St. at Fell, tel. 415/863–9335. AE, D, MC, V. Sun. 5–10.*

Vegetarian *\$\$\$* *VG* **Millennium.** Billing itself as "an optimal health cuisine restaurant," Millennium serves up a winning Mediterranean-influenced vegetarian menu built on dairy-free organic ingredients that are both low in fat and high in nutrition. Grilled portobello mushrooms, polenta torte layered with spinach and pesto, and saffron risotto topped with squash ragout can be paired with organic wines and beers at dinner, while brunch features such house-made creations as smoked veggie sausages, robust granola, and freshly baked bread with date spread. *246 McAllister near Hyde, tel. 415/487–9800. MC, V. Sun. brunch 10–2:30, dinner 5:30–10.*

Embarcadero

The sprawling, triple-tiered, eight-building Embarcadero Center complex at the foot of Market Street could be the mall to end all malls: It has linked bridges, walkways, and spiraling ramps leading to some 100 shops and more than 40 places to eat. The recent construction of a multiscreen movie theater specializing in foreign and domestic art films has brought even more people to the area. The surrounding neighborhood has a number of noteworthy restaurants, some with tranquil views of pocket-size parks or elaborate industrial landscapes. Near the waterfront are eateries with stunning views of the Bay Bridge and beyond.

\$\$\$ *CH, L, VU* **Gordon Biersch Brewery Restaurant.** Award-winning German-style beers brewed on the premises are matched by casual fare that goes

far beyond pub food: pan-roasted chicken breast with Tuscan bread salad, fresh grilled fish specials, and pizzas from the wood-burning oven. In the historic Hills Brothers Coffee building, it has mahogany, rose granite, and wrought-iron decor; great views of the bay; and lively crowds. *2 Harrison St. off the Embarcadero (1 block north of the Bay Bridge), tel. 415/243–8246. AE, D, DC, MC, V. Sun. 11–midnight.*

American Casual
$$–$$$

Fog City Diner. This trendy place—a ritzy chrome-and-neon railway car—remains impossibly popular. Reserve well in advance for a comfy booth. Order a number of small plates to sample the innovative regional cuisine—or opt for a chili dog. *1300 Battery St. between Greenwich and Lombard, tel. 415/982–2000. D, DC, MC, V. Sun. 11:30–11.*

American Contemporary
$$$$

Boulevard. When chef Nancy Oakes moved from a small storefront in the Richmond District to this showy waterfront palace, loyal fans were afraid her wonderful food might suffer. Despite those fears, Boulevard was busy from the moment the doors opened, with tables booked weeks in advance. Part of the reason for the continuing flood of diners is the elaborate interior, the work of restaurant designer Pat Kuleto. The rest, of course, is the food. The French-Californian menu changes often, and Oakes keeps coming up with new combinations to intrigue devotees and newcomers alike. The simple roast chicken with mashed potatoes is always first-rate, as is the unusual vanilla-cured pork loin. *1 Mission St. at Steuart, tel. 415/543–6084. Reservations essential. AE, D, DC, MC, V. Sun. 5:30–10:30.*

$$$$

One Market Restaurant. Superchef Bradley Ogden, famed for his rustic American cuisine and owner of the Lark Creek Inn (*see* Marin County, *below*), was one of the first big-name restaurateurs to move to this end of the Embarcadero in the early '90s, and many other savvy chefs have since followed. Book far in advance for a seat in the spacious, stark dining room, with its views of the Ferry Building. Singles can share a large round table near the open kitchen; another option is to squeeze into the bar lounge for a gourmet snack. Here Ogden's take on American fare has a melting-pot Italian accent, with generally good results: fried-onion salad with smoked salmon, pan-roasted halibut with lemon-saffron risotto, and grilled sweetbreads with pancetta are among the standouts. *1 Market St. at Steuart across from Ferry Bldg., tel. 415/777–5577. AE, DC, MC, V. Sun. brunch 10–2, dinner 5–9.*

$$$
CH, L, O

Park Grill. The club-room atmosphere is enhanced by rich Australian lace wood, while the patio (connected by a catwalk to Embarcadero One) provides a vacation from urban stress. Champagne flows during the prix fixe brunch, and the dessert buffet is satisfyingly sinful. Other options include early breakfast, afternoon tea, an any-old-time rolling dessert cart, dinner (with a superb seafood mixed grill), or an all-day bar menu with such picks as firecracker prawns. *Park Hyatt Hotel, 333 Battery St. at Clay, tel. 415/296–2933. AE, D, DC, MC, V. Sun. 6:30 AM–1 AM.*

Chinese
$$$$
CH, VG, VU

Harbor Village Restaurant. Sophisticated, classical Chinese decor and views of Justin Herman Plaza and the bay make this a favored site for daytime dim sum and noteworthy seafood dishes at night (try the seafood stew). Large, convivial family groups dominate on Sundays. *Four Embarcadero Center, lobby level, tel. 415/781–8833. AE, DC, MC, V. Sun. dim sum 10–2:30, dinner 5:30–9:30.*

$$
CH

Yank Sing. Though the specialty is dim sum, everything from shrimp, chive and mushroom, or lobster dumplings to deep-fried taro balls is top-notch. Prices are a bit cheaper than those at Harbor Village. *427 Battery St. at Clay, tel. 415/362–1640. AE, DC, MC, V. Sun. dim sum 10–4.*

Indian
$$$
VG, VU

Gaylord Indian Restaurant. North Indian specialties (tandoori, lamb kebabs, curries, vegetarian dishes), exotic drinks, and homemade ice creams are served in a setting fit for a raja, complete with candlelight, polished brass, potted palms, fine Indian art, and a sparkling view of the city. *1 Embarcadero Center, podium level, tel. 415/397–7775. AE, D, DC, MC, V. Sun. 5–10.*

Italian
$$$
CH, O, VG

Il Fornaio. Be seduced by the robust cuisine of Tuscany: grilled eggplant with sun-dried tomatoes; delicately fried baby squid; and wonderful pizzas, pastas, and breads. The trattoria has colorful murals, a marble and mahogany bar, an open kitchen, and alfresco dining. Or pick up picnic fixings at the bakery or take-out window and take advantage of the fountains and landscaped lawns of Levi Plaza. *Levi Plaza, 1265 Battery St. at Greenwich, tel. 415/986–0100. AE, DC, MC, V. Sun. brunch 9–2, dinner until 11.*

Mediterranean
$$$$
CH, O, VU

Splendido. The Kuleto-designed decor (marble tables, rough-hewn beams, huge skylight, exposed stone, black slate floors, pewter bar, dramatic lighting) looks like something out of a rustic French fairy tale, and the food (pan-roasted rabbit, exotic pizzas, shellfish soup) changes seasonally to offer a tour of the Mediterranean coast. Throw in outdoor patio seating, views of the bay, and a bar menu for the budget-minded, and you've got a winner. *4 Embarcadero Center, podium level, tel. 415/986–3222. AE, D, DC, MC, V. Sun. 5:30–9.*

Mexican
$–$$
CH

Chevys. Though it's part of a chain, this is still a steady winner in popularity polls, thanks to a festive atmosphere, fresh homemade tortillas, and tasty fajitas. *Two Embarcadero Center, tel. 415/391–2323. AE, MC, V. Sun. 11:30–9.*

Seafood
$$$–$$$$
O, VU

Scott's Seafood Grill & Bar. This is where locals go for fried calamari, oysters, crab, and fresh fish. Now that the Embarcadero Freeway is gone, there's a view of the Ferry Building from the dining room or outdoor patio. *Three Embarcadero Center, upper level, tel. 415/981–0622. AE, D, DC, MC, V. Sun. 4:30–9.*

$$$–$$$$
VU

The Waterfront Restaurant. This upscale eatery has soaring ceilings and seating on three tiers, affording terrific views of the bay. In addition to the seafood specialties (fresh abalone, lobster, oysters), there is a fine steak for the carnivores in your party. *Pier 7, Embarcadero (foot of Broadway), tel. 415/391–2696. AE, D, DC, MC, V. Sun. 10 AM–10:30 PM.*

Financial District/Jackson Square

A Sunday foray to the Financial District can make you feel like the sole survivor at the end of the world. It's actually possible to find a parking spot! Although many restaurants are closed, some choice eateries cater to Sunday crowds.

American Casual
$
CH, L, O

Clown Alley. An eclectic crowd gathers at this quintessential burger joint with an outdoor patio; a great oldies jukebox; and charcoal-grilled burgers, shakes, fries, beer, and espresso drinks. *42 Columbus St. at Jackson, tel. 415/421–2540. Reservations not accepted. No credit cards. Sun. 11–11.*

$$$
CH

MacArthur Park. A choice destination for meat eaters, this longtime favorite offers oakwood-smoked barbecued baby-back ribs and chicken, dry-aged steaks, chili, and burgers (as well as seafood, but why bother?) in a handsome, brick-walled, renovated pre-earthquake warehouse. Crayons and butcher paper keep kids busy. *607 Front St. at Jackson, tel. 415/398-5700. AE, DC, MC, V. Sun. 4:30–10.*

$$–$$$ **Perry's Downtown.** Perry's (*see* Union Street *below*) has been a Union Street institution for more than a quarter of a century; its success spawned this downtown branch. Here you will find creator Perry Butler's signature Chinese chicken salad, hearty chili with red onions and Cheddar, and juicy burgers in a comfortable clubby setting lined with yards of mahogany. More substantial fare is available as well. *185 Sutter St. at Kearny, tel. 415/433–4409. AE, MC, V. Sun. 11:30–10.*

American Contemporary

$$$$ *MU* **Bix.** Fashioned after a '40s supper club—complete with jazz piano, chic patrons, and classic American fare (chicken hash, potato-leek pancakes)—Bix is located off a back alley in a landmark building that was an assay office in Gold Rush days. This is a place to sip martinis at the bar and then grab a dining table on the mezzanine, where you can watch the action. *56 Gold St. off Montgomery, ½ block from TransAmerica Pyramid, tel. 415/433–6300. AE, D, MC, V. Sun. 6–10.*

$$$$$ *VU* **The Carnelian Room.** Walnut paneling and 18th-century art complete the haute ambience here on the 52nd floor of the Bank of America building, where a panoramic view of the city, the bridges, and the bay dazzles diners. Indulge in a prix fixe prime rib Sunday brunch or a seasonal, prix fixe three-course dinner and pretend you are king (or queen) for the day. *Bank of America building, 555 California St. at Kearny, tel 415/433–7500. Jacket required. AE, D, DC, MC, V. Sun. 10 AM–11:30 PM.*

$$$$ *CH, MU* **Cypress Club.** A cross between Toontown and an opulent Freudian fantasy, this is a place to show visitors or anyone who likes to be shocked. The fast-forward American fare (curry- and sesame-dusted veal; tandoor–roasted loin of lamb) arrives in presentations that demand double takes. The sculptural desserts are downright psychedelic, and live piano music adds to the cacophony. *500 Jackson St. near Montgomery, tel. 415/296–8555. AE, DC, MC, V. Sun. 4:30–11.*

$$$$ *CH* **Garden Court.** In the early 1990s, millions of dollars and many years were poured into restorative work that resulted in the resurrection of this stunning landmark, with its stained-glass dome, shimmering chandeliers, and willowy palms. It is a truly extravagant setting for a Sunday brunch buffet that is an old San Francisco tradition. You will find just about any breakfast item you can imagine here, from mountains of scrambled eggs to a sea of smoked salmon. *Sheraton Palace Hotel, 2 New Montgomery St. at Market, tel. 415/392–8600. AE, D, DC, MC, V. Sun. brunch times vary monthly; call ahead.*

Chinese

$$$$ **Tommy Toy's Haute Cuisine Chinoise.** Extravagance is the keyword here, from the celadon and muted rose decor (a re-creation of the 19th-century Dowager Empress's reading room) to the tuxedo-clad waiters to the rarefied Chinese cuisine with French preparation and presentation. The food doesn't always live up to expectations or inflated prices, but the ambience does. *655 Montgomery St. near Clay, tel. 415/397–4888. AE, D, DC, MC, V. Sun. 6–10.*

$–$$ **Hunan Restaurant.** The fiery Hunan cuisine and delectable smoked specialties served in this noisy converted warehouse in the farthest reaches of the Financial District have drawn compliments from food critics for years. *924 Sansome St. near Broadway, tel. 415/956–7727. AE, D, DC, MC, V. Sun. 11:30–9:30.*

Italian

$$$ *VG* **Ciao.** Garlands of red peppers, garlic, and sausage set the stage for fresh homemade pasta, grilled meats, fish, fowl, and regional Italian specialties at this upscale Milanese trattoria. *230 Jackson St. near Front, tel. 415/982–9500. AE, DC, MC, V. Sun. 4–10.*

Pacific Rim

$$$$–$$$$$ **Silks.** Like its sister restaurants at the world-class Oriental in Bangkok and the Mandarin Oriental in Hong Kong, this San Francisco hotel restaurant more than lives up to its reputation. The dining room

is decorated with wonderfully comfortable furniture in soothing colors of cream, gold, and earth tones. Thai coconut-lemongrass soup, grilled foie gras steak, roasted salmon, and sautéed banana-rum trifle appear on a regularly changing menu. Two-course, three-course, and four-course prix fixe dinner menus are offered. *Mandarin Oriental Hotel, 222 Sansome St. near Pine, tel. 415/986–2020. Jacket required. AE, D, DC, MC, V. Sun. 6–9:30.*

The Haight

Where did all the hippies go? The retro scene continues to thrive in the Haight-Ashbury, but the younger, hipper part of the Haight has now settled in at the opposite end of the neighborhood—the down-at-the-heels, heads-up section called the Lower Haight.

American Casual
$$
Kate's Kitchen. On Sunday mornings, breakfast aficionados crowd into this funky café for all their favorites: thick slabs of French toast, cornmeal-flecked buttermilk pancakes, zesty red flannel hash, flaky biscuits, and more. Kate offers a few lunch dishes, too, but most crave her breakfast plates, which she serves until closing. Checkered tablecloths, a linoleum tile floor, and a friendly staff complete the homespun picture. *471 Haight St. near Fillmore, tel. 415/626–3984. No credit cards. Reservations not accepted. Sun. 9–4.*

$–$$
CH
Pork Store Cafe. Expect a line out the door of this unpretentious little spot, where the bread is home-baked and the corned beef hash can't be beat. Breakfasts (omelets, pork chops with eggs, walnut pancakes) are the hot ticket here. *1451 Haight St. near Ashbury, tel. 415/864–6981. Reservations not accepted. MC, V. Sun. 8–4.*

$
VG, O
The Studio Cafe. This closet-size bistro has a bohemian atmosphere, offbeat art, background music—classical, jazz, and blues—and a relaxed crowd of neighborhood regulars. The fare (quiche, lasagna, veggie sandwiches, bread pudding) is homemade, the portions are hefty, and the price is right. *248 Fillmore near Haight St., tel. 415/863–8982. Reservations not accepted. No credit cards. Sun. 9–6.*

Caribbean
$$
CH
Cha Cha Cha. Tapas and exotic fare, such as Cajun shrimp and snapper wrapped in banana leaves, tempt a diverse—and occasionally downright weird—clientele to this lively place that's usually crammed to the rafters. The colorful Caribbean decor includes Santeria altars for those who like to cast spells after supper. *1801 Haight St. near Shrader, tel. 415/386–5758. Reservations not accepted. No credit cards. Sun. 11:30–11.*

English
$
MU, O
Mad Dog in the Fog. Bangers and mash and a dish called Greedy Bastard (bacon, sausages, eggs) are served with a selection of English brews in this roomy, relaxed, classic working stiff's pub with sports on the tube, a garden view from the patio, and live rock and roll after dinner. *530 Haight St. near Fillmore, tel. 415/626–7279. Reservations not accepted. No credit cards. Sun. 11:30 AM–2 AM.*

Indian
$$
CH, VG
Indian Oven. Locals consider these tandoori dishes and *thali* dinners (complete meals served on metal trays) some of the best in the Bay Area. The half-dozen vegetarian specialties and wide variety of breads more than satisfy nonmeat eaters. The corner location offers a view of the busy streets of the Lower Haight. *237 Fillmore near Haight St, tel. 415/626–1628. AE, D, DC, MC, V. Sun. 5:30–10.*

Mexican
$$
CH
Todos Santos. Images of the Virgin Mary and angels hovering at ceiling height are the major design themes in this busy and colorful Mexican outpost in the Lower Haight. Order huevos rancheros or stick with the house specialty—burritos. Carnitas or chorizo and black beans are good combinations for stuffing the big flour tortillas. *525 Haight St. near Fillmore, tel. 415/864–3721. No credit cards. Sun. 11–11.*

Middle Eastern
$
VG
Ya, Halla. The name means "welcome" in Arabic, and the owner-chefs, one a Palestinian Muslim and the other a Palestinian Christian, regularly greet customers as they enter this charming Middle Eastern café in the heart of the Lower Haight. An order of lemony dolmas washed down with Lebanese beer is a good beginning here. For the *shawerma* plate, the grilled lamb is cut from a rotating spit and served with pilaf, hummus, and salad. Chicken and lamb kebabs and a number of vegetarian main dishes satisfy both the meat eaters and vegetarians who cross the threshold. *494 Haight St. near Fillmore, tel. 415/522–1509. MC, V. Sun. 11–11.*

Thai
$$
VG
Thep Phanom. Rumor has it that superstar chefs from around the bay vie for seats here to sample such superbly prepared, out-of-the-ordinary Thai fare as minced duck salad, calamari salad, or seafood curry on banana leaves. *400 Waller St. at Fillmore, tel. 415/431–2526. AE, D, MC, V. Sun. 5:30–10:30.*

Japantown

The shoji screens, rock gardens, and reflecting pools of the three-block cluster of towers, plazas, and walkways that make up the Japan Center offer visitors the opportunity to explore the cultural and culinary wonders of the Land of the Rising Sun in the heart of San Francisco. With the Western Addition and its street gangs nearby, it's wise to be alert at night.

Japanese
$$$$
Fuku-Sushi. The intimate twilight lighting and attentive service make you feel pampered. The sushi is superb, but keep in mind that prices add up rapidly. *1581 Webster St., in Japan Center West near Post, tel. 415/346–3030. AE, MC, V. Sun. lunch noon–3, dinner 5:30–10.*

$$–$$$
CH
Iroha. The small courtyard entryway sports picture windows with plastic replicas of food. Diners sit at cozy booths bathed in light from paper lanterns, sampling top-notch tempura, sashimi, teriyaki, and noodle dishes, as well as fun theme plates for kids. *1728 Buchanan St., across from Japan Center, tel. 415/922–0321. AE, D, DC, MC, V. Sun. 11:30–10.*

$$–$$$
Isobune. The chef launches little wooden boatloads of sushi on a river of water that circles the counter; customers snag whatever catches their fancy as the vessels float by. *Kintetsu Mall, 1737 Post St. near Webster, tel. 415/563–1030. Reservations not accepted. MC, V. Sun. 11:30–10.*

$$
CH
Sanppo Restaurant. This popular, unpretentious place is a good pick for families. The wide selection of Japanese favorites (particularly the lightly battered vegetable and seafood tempura) is seductively low-priced. *1702 Post St. at Buchanan, tel. 415/346–3486. Reservations not accepted. MC, V. Sun. 3–9:50.*

$
CH
Mifune. Homemade noodles are the specialty at this comfortable café. Children get a charge out of special plates, such as a replica of Japan's famous bullet train loaded with noodles. *Kintetsu Mall, 1737 Post St. near Buchanan, tel. 415/922–0337. Reservations not accepted. AE, D, DC, MC, V. Sun. 11–9:30.*

Korean
$$
L
Korea House. The surroundings are stark, but the fiery traditional fare and the do-it-yourself tabletop grilling of marinated meats provide ample entertainment. *1640 Post St. (upstairs) at Laguna, tel. 415/563–1388. MC, V. Sun. 11 AM–1 AM.*

Pacific Rim
$$$$
YoYo Tsumami Bistro. The menu at this Pacific Rim bistro is wonderfully versatile, offering a score of small plates—*tsumami*—as well as larger appetizers and main courses. At the bar on the restaurant's upper level, enjoy a selection of tsumami, accompanied by beer or wine, as a good appetite tamer before a movie in the neighborhood. Main courses are served on the lower level, which resembles a traditional dinner house. The kitchen, which describes its efforts as French interpretations of Japanese dishes, produces such unique

fare as ginger-pickled salmon with wasabi crème fraîche and braised lamb shanks with azuki bean ragout. *Miyako Hotel, 1611 Post St. at Laguna, tel. 415/922–7788. AE, DC, MC, V. Sun. breakfast 6:30–11, lunch 11:30–2, dinner 5:30–10, tsumami bar 11:30–10.*

Marina

With bay views; kite-flying on Marina Green; and museums, galleries, and theaters at Fort Mason, the Marina is a vacation destination in its own right. Eateries range from neighborhood hangouts to restaurants renowned for their views.

American Casual
$$$ **Paragon.** A postcollege crowd gathers in this neighborhood bar and grill for the varied music lineup—jazz, blues, rock—and the trendy American food—pan-roasted salmon, barbecued pork tenderloin salad, braised lamb shank. Sunday evenings there are usually soothing dinner jazz in the early hours and a more serious program after nine. A reasonably priced prix fixe dinner, including champagne, an appetizer, main course, dessert, and coffee, helps to keep folks streaming into this hot destination. *3251 Scott St. between Lombard and Chestnut, tel. 415/922–2456. AE, MC, V. Sun. 4–2 AM.*

$ *CH* **Home Plate.** Homemade breads, apple-wood smoked meats, creative egg dishes (incorporating smoked salmon, fresh oysters, pine nuts, and more), and great pancakes (potato, fresh corn and bell pepper) have made this sunny, simple eatery one of the best breakfast spots in town. *2274 Lombard St. near Pierce, tel. 415/922–4663. Reservations not accepted. MC, V. Sun. 7–4.*

$ *VG* **World Wrapps.** This decidedly original spot should really fall under a category called American Multicultural; the food here couldn't be a more eclectic ethnic mix. The idea is simple: burritos stuffed with an international array of fillings, from Mandarin stir-fry and Thai chicken to the garden "wrapp," a mix of couscous and vegetables. The mostly Gen X crowd chases these hearty bundles with one of the distinctively different smoothies the staff whips up at breakneck speed. *2257 Chestnut St. near Scott, tel. 415/563–9727. No credit cards. Reservations not accepted. Sun. 8 AM–10 PM.*

Indian
$$ *CH, VG* **North India Restaurant.** This family-run operation is a perennial award winner in every local poll. Fare includes liberally spiced curries, tandoori specialties roasted over mesquite, and a tempting selection of vegetarian dishes. Everything is cooked to order with freshly ground spices in an exhibition kitchen. *3131 Webster St. near Lombard, tel. 415/931–1556. AE, D, DC, MC, V. Sun. 4:30–10.*

Italian
$$$–$$$$ *CH* **La Pergola.** The atmosphere is romantic, the waiters are friendly, the tables are intimately spaced, and the Northern Italian cuisine—especially the homemade pasta—is something to write home about. *2060 Chestnut St. near Steiner, tel. 415/563–4500. AE, MC, V. Sun. 5:30–11.*

$$$ **Cafe Adriano.** Here, in a sunny yellow-and-blue-green dining room, is where you'll find some of the city's most satisfying Italian fare. The menu changes daily, with delectable *antipasto misto*, any of the house-made fresh pastas, properly al dente risotto, and fresh seafood entrées among the best choices. An early-bird menu from 5 to 6 PM delivers two courses and glass of vino at a modest price. *3347 Fillmore St. near Chestnut, tel. 415/474–4180. D, MC, V. Sun. 5–10:30.*

$$$ **Cucina Paradiso.** You'll often hear Italian being spoken by both the staff and loyal clientele at this small and friendly neighborhood trattoria. The menu lists a pleasing antipasto of sautéed mushrooms with smoked mozzarella, excellent pumpkin-filled ravioli, a light and refreshing arugula salad with white grapes and Parmesan, and a good rendition of saltimbocca, among other choices. *2372 Chestnut St. near Scott, tel. 415/563-0217. AE, D, MC, V. Sun. 5:30–10:30.*

$$$ **Marina Cafe.** The excellent milk-fed white veal served in a top-notch rendition of veal piccata is rivaled by superbly fresh seafood and fla-

vorful pasta. Mahogany, marble, and a bar that's a work of art contribute to the inviting Old World decor. *2417 Lombard St. near Scott, tel. 415/929–7241. AE, MC, V. Sun. 5–10.*

$$–$$$ **Original Joe's No. 2.** This is a traditional Joe's-style joint, serving
CH Italian food at reasonable prices, with a modern twist. A few years ago this 1938 oldie was given a major facelift and a modern Italian menu that includes everything from fresh seafood items to the classic Joe's Special (a spinach, eggs, ground chuck, and onion scramble). *2001 Chestnut St. at Fillmore, tel. 415/346–4000. AE, D, DC, MC, V. Sun. 11–10.*

Mexican *$$–$$$* **Café Marimba.** Bold colors and charming Mexican folk art give this highly popular dining spot a cheerful demeanor. The mostly young crowd fills up on chunky guacamole served in lava-rock mortars, quesadillas stuffed with squash blossoms and *queso fresco,* sublime Oaxacan mole dishes, and red snapper–stuffed tacos. All the salsas are house-made, and each is a work of art. This fine food is the inspiration of Reed Hearon, the man behind SoMa's wildly successful LuLu (*see below*). *2317 Chestnut St. between Scott and Divisadero, tel. 415/776–1506. AE, MC, V. Sun. 10–11.*

Seafood *$$$* **Scott's Seafood Grill & Bar.** This is the original Scott's, a traditional seafood house with lots of wood paneling, windows, brass, and glass. Expect a great Sunday brunch (including fizzy drinks and every Benedict variation under the sun) and a vast selection of fresh seafood. *2400 Lombard St. at Scott, tel. 415/563–8988. AE, D, DC, MC, V. Sun. 11:30–10.*

Steak *$$$* **Izzy's Steaks & Chops.** The atmosphere is a perfect re-creation of a vintage SF saloon, and while the aged beef and steaks are prime features, it's the scalloped potatoes and creamed spinach that keep reeling the customers back in. *3345 Steiner St. between Lombard and Chestnut, tel. 415/563–0487. AE, D, DC, MC, V. Sun. 5–10.*

Thai *$–$$* *VG* **Gatip Classic Thai Cuisine.** Fans of sticky rice will love the northeastern Thai cuisine (curries, seafood, vegetarian dishes, and such specialties as beef with eggplant salad and papaya salad) at this colorful eatery decorated with Thai fabrics and crafts. *2205 Lombard St. at Steiner, tel. 415/292–7474. MC, V. Sun. 5–10.*

Vegetarian *$$$* *CH, VG, VU* **Greens.** The gourmet fare (and breads and pastries) are so good that the fact that the food is vegetarian is a side issue. The large, airy dining room, with eye-catching artwork and a wall of windows framing views of the Golden Gate Bridge, delivers a quintessential San Francisco experience. *Building A, Fort Mason Center, Marina Blvd. and Buchanan St., tel. 415/771–6222. D, MC, V. Sun. brunch 10–2.*

Mission District

The sunny Mission District enjoys a rich cultural mix and an eclectic range of ethnic food that reflects the city's history. There are Chinese and Italian restaurants, taquerias that rival the best that Guadalajara has to offer, small family cantinas serving Salvadoran or Nicaraguan cuisine, and offbeat cafés and counterculture eateries. Exercise routine caution when visiting the Mission after dark.

American Casual *$* *L, MU* **Radio Valencia Cafe.** Have brunch among bohemians, mingle with moody artists, and listen to the latest cutting-edge records. Later, you can chow down on sandwiches, house-made soups, salads, and small pizzas topped with pesto and sun-dried tomatoes. At night come for live bluegrass (cover varies). *1199 Valencia St. at 23rd St., tel. 415/826–1199. Reservations not accepted. MC, V. Sun. noon–midnight.*

Chinese *$$* **Yuet Lee Seafood Restaurant.** The Hong Kong–style crab or clams in black bean sauce are superior, but almost any of the fresh, delicately prepared seafood dishes here are a good pick, and the Hong Kong noodles are a delight. *3601 26th St. at Valencia, tel. 415/550–8998. MC, V. Sun. 4–10.*

Cuban/Puerto Rican *$$* **El Nuevo Frutilandia.** Here, authentic Cuban and Puerto Rican specialties are served in a festive Caribbean atmosphere. Try one of the hearty Cuban sandwiches at lunch and roast pork with plantains, yucca, and rice for supper. *3077 24th St. near Folsom, tel. 415/648–2958. MC, V. Sun. noon–9.*

French *$* *VG* **Ti Couz.** This little French oasis has a long counter where you can watch Brittany-style buckwheat crêpes being made with such fillings as smoked salmon, cheese and almond, mushroom, or ratatouille. Come up with your own herb-vegetable-seafood-meat combo or sample a lighter dessert crêpe made with white flour and stuffed with white chocolate or chestnut purée. Wash it all down with French cider on tap. This very popular place doubled in size not long ago, in response to the culinary gridlock experienced here every night. *3108 16th St. between Valencia and Guerrero, tel. 415/252–7373. Reservations not accepted. MC, V. Sun. 10–10.*

German *$$* **Speckmann's Restaurant.** The ambience at this neighborhood eatery resembles a friendly Bavarian Oktoberfest. The place has been serving traditional German dishes, such as sauerbraten and Wiener schnitzel, since 1963. *1550 Church St. at Duncan, tel. 415/282–6850. AE, MC, V. Sun. noon–9.*

Japanese *$* *CH* **We Be Sushi.** Some of SF's more interesting people patronize this bargain sushi-only pit stop decorated with offbeat artwork and beer signs. It's located between the only palm trees on Valencia. *1071 Valencia near 22nd St., tel. 415/826–0607. Reservations not accepted. No credit cards. Sun. 5–10.*

Mexican *$* *CH, L* **La Rondalla.** Christmas ornaments, balloons, stuffed birds, and a strolling mariachi band make for a festive atmosphere. The open kitchen has been turning out good Mexican standards since 1951, and first-rate margaritas soothe jangled nerves. *901 Valencia at 20th St., tel. 415/647–7474. No credit cards. Sun. 11:30 AM–3:30 AM.*

$ *CH, O* **La Taqueria.** This is fast food at its south-of-the-border best: fresh banana, strawberry, pineapple, and cantaloupe drinks; tacos and burritos made with whole (not refried) beans; a jukebox stocked with Mexican medleys; and sidewalk or patio seating. *2889 Mission near 25th St., tel. 415/285–7117. Reservations not accepted. No credit cards. Sun. 11–8.*

$ *CH, L* **Pancho Villa Taqueria.** The line moves quickly, so don't be discouraged when you first see it snaking out the door. A steady crew keeps the food—big burritos and soft tacos of *carne asada* (grilled steak), chicken, grilled shrimp—moving like clockwork into the hands of the hungry standees. There are dinner plates, too, but the tortilla-wrapped items are far and away the most popular. *3071 16th St. between Valencia and Mission Sts., tel. 415/864–8840. Reservations not accepted. No credit cards. Sun. 11 AM–midnight.*

$ *CH* **Taqueria La Cumbre.** When this stucco restaurant is packed—as it often is—sidewalk seating literally means sitting outside on the sidewalk. The carne asada and hefty burritos consistently win local popularity polls. *515 Valencia near 16th St., tel. 415/863–8205. Reservations not accepted. No credit cards. Sun. noon–9.*

$ *CH, L* **Taqueria San Jose.** This colorful cantina has terrific tostadas, quesadillas, charcoal-grilled steak, and a range of nontraditional taco fillings from tongue to brains, as well as an assortment of interesting salsas. *2830 Mission near 24th St., tel. 415/282–0203. Reservations not accepted. No credit cards. Sun. 8 AM–4 AM.*

Nicaraguan *$* **Nicaragua Restaurant.** Home-cooked regional specialties (tamales, fried bananas with sour cream, spiced beef with rice) have made this relaxed, friendly, family-run cantina a favorite for more than two decades. *3015 Mission between Army and 26th Sts., tel. 415/826–3672. No credit cards. Sun. 11–9:45.*

Peruvian *$$* *CH* **Fina Estampa.** Japanese-Peruvian chef-owner Julio Shinzato recreates regional specialties from his hometown of Lima to absolute perfection. Sample ceviche, deep-fried calamari, and a great rendition of *anticuchos* (marinated, skewered beef hearts grilled and served with a spicy cilantro sauce) in a cozy, narrow dining room. *2374 Mission near 20th St., tel. 415/824–4437. MC, V. Sun. 11:30–9.*

Salvadoran *$* *CH, L, VG* **El Zócalo.** This place serves the best *pupusas* (hand-patted, grilled corn flour rounds filled with meat or cheese) in town, accompanied by chopped cabbage salad doused with vinegar. About 1,400 are made every Sunday for avid fans who like to wash them down with cold beer. Other picks include fish soup, fried plantains, grilled shrimp, and tamales. *3230 Mission near 29th St., tel. 415/282–2572. Reservations not accepted. AE, DC, MC, V. Sun. 9 AM–3 AM.*

Spanish *$$* **Esperpento.** You'll feel like you're in Spain when you visit this wonderfully offbeat tapas bar in the heart of the Mission, particularly once you take a bite of the superb *tortilla de patatas*, eggs laced with onions and thinly sliced potatoes. Other choices are little plates of shrimp in a heady garlic and chili mix, grilled chicken croquettes, fried fish, serrano ham, Manchego cheese, and more. Paella, chockful of seafood and sausage, is also served. *3295 22nd St. between and Valencia Sts., tel. 415/282–8867. No credit cards. Sun. lunch 11–3, dinner 5–10.*

Thai *$$* *VG* **Manora's.** Passarin Prass named the original cozy restaurant after his daughter, who now runs an eponymous eatery (with full bar) of her own on Folsom near the Performing Arts Center. Both dish up great pad thai noodles, charbroiled jumbo prawns, and a range of seafood and vegetarian specials. *3226 Mission between Army and 29th Sts., tel. 415/550–0856; 1600 Folsom at 12th St., tel. 415/861–6224. MC, V. Sun. 5–10.*

Vegetarian *$* *CH, VG* **Real Good Karma.** This casual eatery (since 1967) dishes up tasty food to satisfy the strictest vegetarian or vegan (no dairy, no eggs). *501 Dolores at 18th St., tel. 415/621–4112. AE, MC, V. Sun. 11:30–9:30.*

Nob Hill

The home of Grace Cathedral, some of the city's finest hotels, and the very, very rich has indulgent dining options that range from extravagant brunches to suppers with sensational views. Though costs can soar as high as you'd expect when you're dining halfway to the stars, the budget-minded can sample the more opulent dining rooms by dropping in for afternoon tea or dessert or a drink at the bar.

American Contemporary *$$$$$* *CH, VG* **Fournou's Ovens.** Rich tapestries, antiques, and a massive European roasting oven embellished with hand-painted Portuguese tiles lend a Mediterranean mood for innovative American cuisine featuring roasted meats, fowl, and seafood. Breakfast specials include bluecorn waffles and southwestern omelets, while dinner offers a range of prix fixe options at various prices. *Stanford Court Hotel, 905 California St. at Powell, tel. 415/989–1910. AE, D, DC, MC, V. Sun. breakfast 6:30–11, brunch 11–2:30, dinner 5:30–10.*

$$$$ *CH, L, MU, VG* **The Big Four Restaurant.** Dark wood, green leather, Gold Rush memorabilia, a fireplace, and live piano music create an old boys' club atmosphere befitting a restaurant named after four robber barons. House favorites include double-thick pork chops, grilled Atlantic salmon, and angel hair pasta with Monterey prawns. *Huntington Hotel, 1075 California St. across from Grace Cathedral, tel. 415/771–1140. AE, D, DC, MC, V. Sun. breakfast 7–11; dinner 5:30–10:30.*

$$$$ *CH, VU* **Crown Room.** From the 24th floor of the Fairmont Hotel, the panoramic view of the city and bay is phenomenal—but prices can be just as breathtaking. Both the champagne brunch and the buffet dinner here are prix fixe and lavish, so bring an appetite and a couple of kids while you're at it. (Those under 12 dine free at brunch and half-price at dinner.) *Fairmont Hotel, 950 Mason St. at California, tel. 415/772–5131. AE, D, DC, MC, V. Sun. brunch seatings at 10, noon, 2; dinner 6–9:30.*

$$$$ *CH, MU, VU* **Top of the Mark.** The view from this celebrated 19th-floor aerie, which dates back to 1939, encompasses the entire city and bay. A classy lounge during the week, on Sundays it's the site of an equally classy brunch, with a pianist adding to the harmonious background. *Mark Hopkins Hotel, 1 Nob Hill at California and Mason, tel. 415/392–3434. AE, D, DC, MC, V. Sun. brunch 10–2.*

Italian *$$$–$$$$* **Venticello Ristorante.** The rustic charm of a Tuscan farmhouse, a friendly neighborhood ambience, and a glimpse of bay views create a perfect comfort zone. The fare includes good fresh pasta, salads, and pizza from a wood-burning oven. *1257 Taylor St. at Washington, tel. 415/922–2545. AE, DC, MC, V. Sun. 5:30–10.*

$$$ *CH, MU* **Bella Voce Ristorante & Bar.** Their voices may not be beautiful, but that doesn't keep the waiters here from breaking into operatic arias and Broadway show tunes now and then. The northern and central Italian dishes are moderately pleasing and moderately priced—but the singing's the reason to come. *Fairmont Hotel, 950 Mason St. at California, tel. 415/772–5199. AE, DC, MC, V. Sun. 5:30–10:30.*

$$$ *CH* **Vanessi's Nob Hill.** Some of the loyal crowd who followed this SF classic from its time-worn Broadway incarnation to the plush new Nob Hill rendition (warm woods, open kitchen, oversize booths) complain that the ambience is now too formal—but everyone agrees that the food (homemade pastas, fish, grilled meats) is fabulous. *1177 California near Jones St., tel. 415/771–2422. AE, DC, MC, V. Sun. 4:30–10.*

Mediterranean *$$$$* *CH, MU, O, VG* **The Terrace.** Though the Mediterranean-inspired menu is geared toward those of sophisticated palette, crayons and coloring-book menus keep children happy as well. Sunday offerings include a jazz brunch and a delightful afternoon tea. There's outdoor seating in the gorgeous garden courtyard, weather permitting. *Ritz-Carlton Hotel, 600 Stockton between Pine and California Sts., tel. 415/296–7465. AE, D, DC, MC, V. Sun. 6:30 AM–10:30 PM.*

Thai *$$* *VG* **Thai Spice.** An extensive selection of exotically spiced Thai dishes, including a range of vegetarian specialties, served in a light, airy dining room offers a nice break from lifestyles of the rich and famous. *1730 Polk St. between Clay and Washington, tel. 415/775–4777. AE, D, DC, MC, V. Sun. 11–10.*

North Beach

The concentration of restaurants, cafés, bakeries, delicatessens, and pizzerias makes this the most appetite-inducing section of town. Once known as Little Italy, this neighborhood now includes a rich selection of food from far-flung corners of the globe should you, God forbid, get your fill of Italian cuisine.

Afghani *$$* *CH, V* **Helmand.** Foodies and food critics alike adore the mix of exotic Kabul and Afghani vegetarian, lamb, and chicken dishes, graciously presented and affordably priced. *430 Broadway between Kearny and Montgomery, tel. 415/362–0641. AE, MC, V. Sun. 6–10.*

American Casual *$* *CH* **San Francisco Brewing Company.** The city's original brew pub serves burgers and fish-and-chips, as well as crab salad, salmon, and gumbo. The vintage saloon interior, with solid mahogany bar and brass trim, dates back to 1907. *155 Columbus Ave. near Pacific, tel. 415/434–3344. AE, D, MC, V. Sun. noon–1:45 AM.*

Basque *$$* *CH* — **Des Alpes.** Here you'll find Basque family-style dining at budget prices in an unpretentious paneled dining room with checked tablecloths. Some prefer the funky Basque Hotel, but both have staunch fans. *732 Broadway near Powell St., tel. 415/391–4249. MC, V. Sun. 5:30–9:30.*

$ *CH* — **Basque Hotel & Restaurant.** Tucked away in an alley, this restaurant offers one of the best deals in town: In a dimly lit room with picnic-table seating, mismatched china, and an inimitable atmosphere, a five-course dinner features such Basque comfort food as oxtail stew, sweetbreads, roast lamb, duck leg, and the like, all served family-style. *15 Romolo Pl., off Broadway between Columbus and Kearny, tel. 415/788–9404. MC, V. Sun. 5–10.*

American Contemporary *$$$–$$$$* *MU, VU* — **Moose's.** When Ed Moose sold San Francisco's most famous saloon, the Washington Square Bar & Grill, back in 1990, locals mourned the end of an era. Two years later, he and his wife, Etta, launched their new venture right across the square; now loyal fans and celebrities in search of a hangout vie for seating amid rich mahogany, mirrors, and crystal chandeliers. The regularly changing menu offers an outstanding Caesar salad, contemporary pizzas, and dishes imaginatively created from what's fresh in the market. There's a great view of Washington Square, plus live music in the evenings. *1652 Stockton St. between Union and Filbert, tel. 415/989–7800. AE, DC, MC, V. Sun. 10:30 AM–11 PM.*

French *$$$–$$$$* *VG* — **Café Jacqueline.** All they serve at this intimate café are soufflés of several glorious variations: Try the shiitake mushroom and fresh asparagus or the Gruyère, garlic, and prosciutto. Late-night reservations are available for the equally divine (and expensive) dessert soufflés, including the white chocolate and fresh blueberry or the Grand Marnier and fresh raspberry. *1454 Grant Ave. near Union St., tel. 415/981–5565. AE, D, DC, MC, V. Sun. 5:30–11.*

Italian *$$$$$* *VU* — **Julius' Castle.** This is a clear winner in the category of most romantic: a turreted castle perched high on Telegraph Hill, complete with crystal chandeliers, candlelight, and spectacular views of the bay. Attentive waiters deliver impeccable service, contemporary Italian cuisine (pastas, risottos, roasted fish and meats), and a fantastic chocolate tart with chocolate sauce and chocolate ice cream. *1541 Montgomery off Union St., tel. 415/392-2222. AE, DC, MC, V. Sun. 5–10.*

$$$–$$$$ *CH, O* — **Fior d'Italia.** Founded in 1886, this is one of the oldest Italian restaurants in America. The traditional northern Italian fare—veal, pasta, calamari, and a more contemporary Caesar salad—is served in an Old World atmosphere complete with a trickling fountain and a view of Washington Square. *601 Union St. at Stockton, tel. 415/986–1886. AE, D, DC, MC, V. Sun. 11:30–10.*

$$$ *CH, L* — **North Beach Restaurant.** A vintage North Beach ambience and an award-winning wine list accompany seductive northern Italian cuisine: homemade pasta and prosciutto, exquisitely fresh fish, and veal prepared nine deliciously different ways—from scaloppini to piccata. *1512 Stockton St. off Columbus, tel. 415/392–1700. AE, MC, V. Sun. 11:30 AM–11:45 PM.*

$$$ *MU* — **Washington Square Bar & Grill.** The old "Washbag" still draws a crowd, and great piano players can still be heard in the evenings. The fare ranges from Italian seafood and pasta to burgers. *1707 Powell St. at Union St., tel. 415/982–8123. AE, DC, MC, V. Sun. brunch 11–3, dinner 5–10:30, bar until 1 AM.*

$$–$$$ *CH* — **Gira Polli.** This popular spot has hand-rubbed peach-color walls, a view of Washington Square, and some of the best chicken in town—it's roasted on a unique rotisserie over a wood fire. *659 Union St. near Columbus, tel. 415/434–4472. AE, MC, V. Sun. 4–9.*

$$–$$$ *CH* — **Little Joe's on Broadway.** The food is cheap, portions are huge, the open kitchen and colorful mural of the city are entertaining, and everything from pasta with clams to veal parmigiana is great . . .

but their motto is "Rain or shine there's always a line." Folks with kids should try midafternoon to avoid an uncomfortable wait. *523 Broadway near Columbus, tel. 415/433–4343. Reservations not accepted. AE, DC, D, MC, V. Sun. noon–10:30.*

$$ *CH* **Cafferata Restaurant.** The Cafferata Ravioli factory started turning out fresh pasta back in 1886. The restaurant has a friendly family atmosphere and a tempting selection of ravioli, tortellini, and fresh pasta noodles. *700 Columbus Ave. at Filbert, tel. 415/392–7544. AE, MC, V. Sun. 11–11.*

$$ *CH, VG* **The Stinking Rose.** Not the place for a first date, this garlic mecca has everything from 40-clove chicken to garlic ice cream. It's not Italian per se, but the pasta selections aren't bad. Vegetarian specials are featured, and a few nongarlic items ("vampire fare") are available. *325 Columbus Ave. near Broadway, tel. 415/781–7673. AE, DC, MC, V. Sun. 11–11.*

$ *CH* **Capp's Corner.** Former boxing manager Joe Capp was the founder, and the walls are covered with photos of sports stars and other celebrities who have eaten here. Patrons rub elbows at long tables where hefty five-course dinners are served family-style at rock-bottom prices. A light dinner is also available. *1600 Powell St. at Green, tel. 415/989–2589. DC, MC, V. Sun. 4–10:30.*

$ **Mario's Bohemian Cigar Store Cafe.** This legendary corner café has large windows with views of Washington Square, the best cappuccino around, delicious focaccia sandwiches, and small tables where you can chat with interesting strangers over a plate of ricotta cheesecake. *566 Columbus Ave. at Union, tel. 415/362–0536. Reservations not accepted. No credit cards. Sun. 10 AM–11 PM.*

Mediterranean *$$$* *O* **Enrico's Sidewalk Cafe and Restaurant.** Enrico's is open again and it's better than ever, with prime people-watching and views of the Broadway scene from the sidewalk café, great martinis, and a Steinway grand in the bar where a trio plays every Sunday evening. The changing menu features Italian-influenced specials, such as spaghetti with garlic, olive oil, and deep-fried shrimp; pizza with wild mushrooms and pancetta; and Tuscan-style New York steak with cannellini beans. *504 Broadway at Kearny, tel. 415/982–6223. AE, MC, V. Sun. noon–11.*

Middle Eastern *$$–$$$* **Maykadeh.** Lamb kebabs marinated in a yogurt-based sauce and grilled over mesquite and rose-perfumed ice cream are among the authentic Persian specialties offered at surprisingly reasonable prices in an atmosphere fit for a shah. *470 Green St. between Kearny and Grant, tel. 415/362–8286. MC, V. Sun. noon–10.*

Pizza *$–$$* *CH, L* **North Beach Pizza.** This family-oriented eatery has red-checked tablecloths, candles in wine bottles, a cheerful staff, and fans who claim it serves the best pizza in town. At least 20 varieties are available, along with pastas, subs, and Italian entrées. *1499 Grant Ave. at Union St. (also 1310 Grant Ave. near Vallejo), tel. 415/433–2444. Reservations not accepted. AE, D, DC, MC, V. Sun. noon–1 AM.*

$$ *VG* **Tommaso's.** The inevitable wait is worthwhile at this rustic trattoria, whose wood-burning oven produces perfect, crisp pizza. *1042 Kearny St. at Broadway, tel. 415/398–9696. Reservations not accepted. MC, V. Sun. 4–9:45; closed 3½ wks Dec.–Jan.*

Steak *$$$$* *CH* **Alfred's.** San Franciscans have been getting cholesterol highs here since 1928. Huge steaks are served by experienced waiters in a setting with chandeliers, leather, red flock wallpaper, and flowers. *886 Broadway near Mason (close to Broadway tunnel), tel. 415/781–7058. AE, MC, V. Sun. 5:30–9.*

Pacific Heights

Even the moneyed must eat, and for inhabitants of the mansions in Pacific Heights, the Upper Fillmore has become the top destination when hunger strikes.

American Casual $$ **Harry's.** You can't beat the cheeseburger and fries (or the tender pepper steak) at this popular Fillmore hangout with beveled glass mirrors, an antique mahogany bar, and Italian lanterns. The crowd is older and quieter on Sundays. *2020 Fillmore St. between Pine and California, tel. 415/921–1000. AE, MC, V. Sun. 3:30–10.*

$ **Ella's.** There is already a line waiting outside the door when this bright corner spot opens on Sunday mornings. The early risers can't wait to sit down to a breakfast of buttermilk pancakes, eggs any style, sticky buns, and the other house specialties that fill the menu. *500 Presidio Ave. at California, tel. 415/441-5669. Reservations not accepted. AE, MC, V. Sun. brunch 9–2.*

$ **Trio Cafe.** This simple, cheerful little café serves a range of comforting Continental breakfast and lunch selections to Fillmore shoppers. *1870 Fillmore St. near Bush, tel. 415/563–2248. Reservations not accepted. No credit cards. Sun. 9–5.*

Barbecue $ CH **Leon's Bar-B-Q.** The tender ribs, hot links, and chicken at Leon's are among the best barbecue in town. *1911 Fillmore St. between Bush and Pine, tel. 415/922–2436. AE, MC, V (accepted only for orders over $10). Sun. 11–10.*

Cajun/Creole $$$ CH **The Elite Cafe.** The marble and wood interior has a '20s elegance and private booths. The bar serves fresh oysters and fried calamari, the menu features blackened fish and crab cakes, and dessert includes such sinful treats as bread pudding with bourbon sauce. *2049 Fillmore St. near California, tel. 415/346–8668. DC, MC, V. Sun. brunch 10–3; dinner 5–10.*

Ethiopian $$–$$$ MU, VG **Rasselas.** Live jazz and spicy fare (including great vegetarian selections and a combination platter) are served family-style with *injera* (spongy bread) in a setting that simulates a royal tent. *2801 California St. at Divisadero, tel. 415/567–5010. AE, DC, MC, V. Sun. 5:30–10.*

French $$$$ **The Heights.** When you're craving a Sunday-night splurge, reserve a table in the dining room of this old Victorian and order the six-course tasting menu. Or select from the à la carte card and enjoy an exquisite vegetable pot-au-feu or crispy-skinned duck with braised pears and endive. Both menus change weekly, but both are invariably tempting. *3235 Sacramento St, near Lyon, tel. 415/474–8890. AE, DC, MC, V. Sun. 5:30–9:30.*

Italian $$$–$$$$ **Vivande Porta Via.** Food is the focus of the decor in this European-style deli with exposed brick walls, an open kitchen; Italian ceramic tiles; and displays of gourmet groceries, delicacies, and colorful glass bottles. Take out or eat here: There are house-made sausages and pastas, fresh mussels, and a wonderful array of pastries and sweets. Owner Carlo Middione also has a fancier place near the Opera House (*see* Civic Center, *above*). *2125 Fillmore St. near California, tel. 415/346–4430. AE, DC, MC, V. Sun. 11:30–10.*

$$$ VG **Jackson Fillmore Trattoria.** Regulars pack in here to dig into such specialties as homemade gnocchi or chicken with garlic and vinegar. The setting is casually defined by blue-and-white check tablecloths; works by local artists hang on the walls. *2506 Fillmore St. near Jackson, tel. 415/346–5288. AE, D, DC, MC, V. Sun. 5–10.*

Pacific Rim $$$ VG **Oritalia.** This stylish restaurant is a treasure trove of fusion food: Korean beef tucked into romaine leaves, steak topped with a crown of fried Chinese long beans, chicken *satay* (grilled skewers marinated with peanut sauce), and mu shu chicken with whole-wheat pancakes are among the many dishes to sample from the changing menu. The space is as unusual as the menu, with marble floors, a copper hood over the open kitchen, and a profusion of striking artwork—papier-mâché creations, Chinese gold-leaf paintings, and hand-painted lamps and sconces. *1915 Fillmore St. near Pine, tel. 415/346–1333. AE, DC, MC, V. Sun. 5–10.*

Potrero Hill/China Basin

Potrero Hill is home to a classic SF blend of blue-collar workers, artists, and a range of ethnic groups. A short drive away is San Francisco's best-kept secret: the working waterfront called China Basin, with uncommon views of the bay, easy parking, no tourists, and a couple of unpretentious places serving good food and drinks at reasonable prices.

American Casual
$
MU, O

Bottom of the Hill. For a fun-filled afternoon, hunker down for an all-you-can-eat-for-two-bucks barbecue and free entertainment (several different bands each Sunday play all types of music). The food runs out fast, so get here early and grab a seat outside on the patio, or retreat into a bar dating back to 1910. *1233 17th St. near Missouri, tel. 415/626–4455. Reservations not accepted. MC, V. Sun. barbecue 4–7 (or until food runs out), bar until midnight.*

$
CH, O, VU

Mission Rock Resort. This ramshackle wood building is a waterfront hangout amid the piers and dry docks south of the Bay Bridge. Breakfast and lunch are served upstairs, burgers and sandwiches downstairs. Two outdoor decks offer prime views of a working marina—and a great perch for drinks from a full bar. *817 China Basin St. near Mariposa and 3rd, tel. 415/621–5538. AE, DC, MC, V. Sun. 8 AM–9 PM.*

$
CH, MU, O, VU

The Ramp. This funky waterside restaurant has a patio and deck and a view of the bay from a different perspective, looking west past crumbling piers and pilings. It specializes in serving large portions of home-cooked American fare—barbecue, burgers, fish-and-chips—and mud pie for dessert. On Sundays from April through October, a festive jazz barbecue from 3:30 to 7:30 draws crowds. *855 China Basin St. (foot of Mariposa off 3rd St.), tel. 415/621–2378. Reservations not accepted. V. Sun. 8 AM–10 PM: jazz barbecue 3:30–7:30 April–Oct.*

Chinese
$$

Eliza's. Antiques and orchids adorn this always-full Potrero Hill eatery, where Chinese dishes have been clearly influenced by a California kitchen. Shrimp and snow peas arrive in sweet ginger sauce, and the popular sunflower beef—thin slices of beef in a perky satay sauce—comes with slim enoki mushrooms. *1457 18th St. at Connecticut, tel. 415/648–9999. MC, V. Sun. noon–10.*

Greek
$$
CH

Asimokopoulos Cafe. Wonderful renditions of Greek favorites—moussaka, lamb, phyllo-wrapped treats, and pastries—go for reasonable prices in a light, airy dining room that will remind you of the islands. Expect a wait. *288 Connecticut St. near 18th St., tel. 415/552–8789. Reservations not accepted. AE, MC, V. Sun. 5–10.*

Italian
$$$

Aperto. The quintessential neighborhood eatery, this corner trattoria has a friendly atmosphere and an active open kitchen. On the menu are generously portioned pastas, crisp polenta squares, simple grilled meats, and a slew of tempting desserts. *1434 18th St. near Connecticut, tel. 415/252–1625. MC, V. Sun. 5–9.*

Thai
$$
CH

San Francisco Bar-B-Que. This tiny, no-frills place offers a great introduction to the succulent wonders of Thai barbecue, using a rich blend of exotic spices on duck, chicken, and ribs. Eat here or take out. *1328 18th St. near Missouri, tel. 415/431–8956. Reservations not accepted. No credit cards. Sun. 4:30–9:30.*

Richmond

Running the length of the Panhandle and Golden Gate Park out to the beach, the Richmond District has a series of distinctly different pocket neighborhoods. The restaurants here are famed citywide, but even better is the string of well-loved—and well-kept-secret—eateries: from dim sum bakeries on Clement Street to global fare along Geary Boulevard to upscale cafés in the Laurel Heights District.

American Casual
$$$
CH, MU, VU
The Cliff House. Though it's touristy, tacky, and overpriced, everyone ends up here sooner or later for the spectacular view of Seal Rock and the old Sutro Baths. The offerings range from a buffet brunch (complete with a harpist) in the Terrace Room to afternoon nachos and buffalo wings in the bar to pasta and seafood for dinner. *1090 Point Lobos Ave. (foot of Geary Blvd.), tel. 415/386–3330. Reservations not accepted. AE, DC, MC, V. Sun. 8 AM–9 PM.*

$
CH, O
Bill's Place. Simple but good: Here you'll find milk shakes; hot fudge sundaes; and some of the weirdest, sloppiest, best-tasting burgers around, including children's specials and celebrity items, such as the Carol Doda burger, which simply has to be seen to be believed. Inside there are crystal chandeliers and a presidential plate collection; outside, a garden patio. *2315 Clement St. near 25th Ave., tel. 415/221–5262. No credit cards. Sun. 11–10.*

Burmese
$
VG
Mandalay. There's Chinese fare on the menu at this convivial little eatery, but focus on the Burmese specialties—green-tea salad, Mandalay squid (prepared with hot-and-sour sauce on a bed of tender spinach), coconut chicken noodle soup, and succulent chicken satay. *4348 California St. between 5th and 6th Aves., tel. 415/386–3895. MC, V. Sun. 11:30–9:30.*

Cambodian
$$
Angkor Wat. Revel in the wonders of banana blossoms doused with lime, lemongrass rabbit, superb charbroiled chicken, and green papaya salad in a soothing dining room with pictures of Angkor Wat on the walls. The chef-owner is French-trained. *4217 Geary Blvd. between 6th and 7th Aves., tel. 415/221–7887. AE, MC, V. Sun. 5–10:30.*

Chinese
$$$
CH
Hong Kong Flower Lounge. Food critics and neighborhood fans come here for great Cantonese seafood dishes and picture-perfect dim sum in plush surroundings. *5322 Geary Blvd. between 17th and 18th Aves., tel. 415/668–8998. AE, D, DC, MC, V. Sun. dim sum 10–2:30, dinner 5–9:30.*

$$–$$$
Fountain Court. In a neighborhood crowded with Cantonese restaurants, the Shanghai fare here stands out. At lunchtime on weekends, the kitchen delivers a steady stream of bowls of salty or sweet soy milk, platters of thick stir-fried noodles, steamed dumplings, and fried savory cakes. A variety of fish, meat, and vegetable dishes fill the fine evening menu. *354 Clement St. at 5th St., tel. 415/668–1100. AE, DC, MC, V. Sun. lunch 11–3, dinner 5–10.*

$$–$$$
Hong Kong Villa. Swimming-fresh seafood—shrimp, crabs, lobsters, catfish, geoduck clams, bass—and bushel baskets of fresh vegetables are transformed into stellar Cantonese plates at this two-story restaurant. Lunchtime brings a competent assortment of dim sum. If lobster is being offered on a bed of ribbony noodles, don't pass it up. *2332 Clement St. between 24th and 25th Aves., tel. 515/752–8833. Sun. dim sum 10:30–2:30, dinner 5–10.*

$$
CH
Ton Kiang Restaurant. A good choice for family dining, this place serves the superbly prepared Hakka cuisine of southern China: salt-baked chicken, steamed stuffed bean curd, fish ball and greens soup, meat or seafood cooked in wine sauce. The branch at Spruce offers a full menu of noodles and rice plates at lunchtime, while the larger and fancier branch at 22nd Avenue serves what is arguably the best dim sum in the city. *3148 Geary Blvd. at Spruce, tel. 415/752–4440. 5821 Geary Blvd. near 22nd Ave., tel. 415/386–8530. MC, V. Sun. 11–10:30 (Spruce); 10–10:30 (22nd Ave.), dim sum until 2:30.*

$
CH
Mayflower Restaurant. If you're planning a family dim sum outing, this is a good pick. The array of dumplings and small dishes will delight adult palates, and the rolling carts of endless food will provide enough action to keep children entertained. *6255 Geary Blvd. at 25th Ave., tel. 415/387–8338. MC, V. Sun. dim sum 10–2:30, dinner 5–9:30.*

$ CH, VG **Vegi Food.** Housed in what used to be a pizza parlor, this plain-Jane eatery has an intriguing clientele and equally intriguing Chinese-vegetarian fare: walnuts in sweet-and-sour sauce, crisp vegetables in black-bean sauce, and soybean sheets with greens. *1820 Clement between 19th and 20th Aves., tel. 415/387–8111. No credit cards. Sun. 11:30–9.*

French $$$$ **Alain Rondelli.** There are only four dozen seats in this ascetically appointed restaurant; they are nearly always filled with serious devotees of French-born chef Alain Rondelli. His culinary mastery is evident in first courses of fresh foie gras or delicate soups built on seafood, and the main courses of monkfish and duck. Don't overlook the desserts; they inevitably shine as brightly as what has preceded them. Half glasses of wine make tasting an affordable part of the meal. *126 Clement St. between 2nd and 3rd Aves., tel. 415/387–0408. MC, V. Sun. 5:30–10.*

Japanese $$$ **Kabuto Sushi.** Competent dinner fare is available in the dining room, but head for the black-lacquer bar for great showmanship and artful preparation. It's hard to find better sushi. *5116 Geary Blvd. between 15th and 16th Aves., tel. 415/752–5652. D, MC, V. Sun. 5–10.*

Moroccan $$$ CH, MU **El Mansour.** Dip into savory couscous, lamb, and chicken specialties with Arabic bread and watch the belly dancers while you loll on plush pillows in a tented dining room. *3123 Clement St. between 32nd and 33rd Aves., tel. 415/751–2312. AE, D, DC, MC, V. Sun. 5–10.*

$$$ **Mamounia.** Guests here lounge on pillows or hassocks in a canopied room and scoop up chicken or lamb concoctions with their fingers. Taste sensations range from spicy lentil soup to aromatic mint tea to gratingly sweet Moroccan pastries. *4411 Balboa St. near 45th Ave., tel. 415/752–6566. AE, MC, V. Sun. 5–10.*

Russian $$ **Katia's.** Katia Troosh's small, light-filled restaurant and tearoom is a gathering place for the local Russian community, who come for her house-cured pickles; thin, tasty blini with silky smoked salmon; and flaky baked piroshki encasing beef, cabbage, or mushrooms. Borscht is filled with a gardenful of beets and vegetables and enriched with a dollop of sour cream. Berry-topped meringues and rich Russian cheesecake are among the sweets. *600 5th St. at Balboa, tel. 415/668–9292. AE, DC, MC, V. Sun. lunch 10–3, dinner 5–9.*

Seafood $$$ CH **Pacific Cafe.** With sea-shanty decor, proximity to the beach, and fish so fresh you can almost hear them flopping in the kitchen, this is one of the most genuine, gratifying seafood joints around. Hospitality includes free wine during the wait for a table and free ice cream for the kids at the meal's end. *7000 Geary Blvd. at 34th Ave., tel. 415/387–7091. Reservations not accepted. AE, MC, V. Sun. 5–10.*

Singaporean $$ **Straits Café.** A blend of Chinese, Thai, Malay, Indonesian, and Indian cuisines, Singaporean food is an appealingly exotic culinary journey. At this tropically turned-out restaurant, the banana-leaf brunch promises a varied assortment of national dishes served on banana leaves in the traditional Singaporean manner. The dinner menu includes everything from Hainan chicken rice—a specialty of the island of the same name off the south coast of China—to green beans tossed with peppers and dried shrimp. *3300 Geary Blvd. at Parker, tel. 415/668–1783. AE, MC, V. Sun. 11:30–10.*

Thai $$$ MU **Khan Toke Thai House.** Be prepared to slip your shoes off and savor a great rendition of pad thai noodles and a range of mildly spiced classic fare (they'll honor requests for hotter spicing) in this tranquil candlelit retreat. Temple dancers provide entertainment most Sunday evenings starting around 8:30. *5837 Geary Blvd. near 24th Ave., tel. 415/668–6654. AE, MC, V. Sun. 5–10:30.*

$$ CH **Narai Thai Restaurant.** This neighborhood favorite on the fringe of the Richmond District's Chinatown features familiar Thai favorites as well as some southern Chinese specialties at prices that are easy on the budget. Don't leave without sampling the homemade coconut ice cream with fried bananas. *2229 Clement St. between 23rd and 24th Aves., tel. 415/751–6363. D, MC, V. Sun. 11:30–9:30.*

$–$$ VG **Royal Thai.** The original San Rafael branch (*see* Marin County, *below*) reaped critical acclaim for superlative cuisine. This version is more spacious and has a full bar, costumed waitresses, and lots of greenery, but you'll find the same delicious fare: Thai crepes; barbecued prawns, pork, and catfish; and tasty vegetarian dishes. *951 Clement St. at 11th Ave., tel. 415/386–1795. AE, DC, MC, V. Sun. 5–10:30.*

Vietnamese $$ **Le Soleil.** At midday, patrons of this charming Southeast Asian outpost can be found consuming wonderful noodle soups based on fragrant broths and sampling from a wealth of rice plates topped with succulent barbecued meats. In the evening there are refreshing salads of squid, beef, or chicken; plates of grilled marinated pork; catfish or shrimp in a claypot; beef dipped into a hot vinegary fondue and tucked into a rice-paper wrapper; and dozens of other dishes that reflect the inviting nature of Vietnamese cuisine. *133 Clement St. between 2nd and 3rd Aves., tel. 415/668–4848. AE, MC, V. Sun. 11–10.*

Russian Hill

Neighborhood restaurants on this ritzy peak cater to a sophisticated local clientele; the result is fine food at surprisingly reasonable prices. Parking on the hill can be a nightmare, but the steep hike from downtown does wonders for the thighs. Alternatively, the Hyde Street cable car will haul you to the summit.

Italian $$$ CH, O **Frascati.** Chef-owner Luigi Dominici is the perfect host at this contemporary trattoria with ceramic tile floors, lemon walls, wooden tables, sidewalk dining, and views of the cable cars. The central and northern Italian cuisine features a knockout antipasto plate and some of the most seductive pastas around. *1901 Hyde St. at Green, tel. 415/928–1406. AE, D, MC, V. Sun. 5–10:30.*

$$$ CH **Ristorante Milano.** Risotto, polenta, homemade pastas, tempting appetizers, and top-notch tiramisu make this northern Italian eatery a perpetual favorite. The decor is modern Milano-style, with blacks, grays, and beiges and lots of wood throughout. *1448 Pacific Ave. near Hyde St., tel. 415/673–2961. AE, MC, V. Sun. 5–10.*

$$$ VG **Hyde Street Bistro.** The cuisine is a blend of the owner's Austro-Italian heritage and home-style southern Italian cooking; the menu of pastas, seafood, and roasted meats includes a tasty schnitzel, and the pastries are great. *1521 Hyde St. between Pacific and Jackson, tel. 415/441–7778. AE, MC, V. Sun. 5:30–10:30.*

Seafood $$ CH **Hyde Street Seafood House and Raw Bar.** Better known among locals as simply the "raw bar," this unique restaurant has a nautical theme and sidewalk seating and specializes in traditional *en papillote* baking (in parchment paper). Staples here are julienned vegetables, fresh herbs, butter, white wine, and a selection of fresh seafood baked to tender perfection. *1509 Hyde St. at Jackson, tel. 415/928–9189. AE, MC, V. Sun. 5–10:30.*

SoMa

The stretch of land south of Market Street, known as SoMa, is so extensive and diverse that someone should come up with names to differentiate the various districts. Near the foot of Market Street, the relatively new Rincon Annex sports a range of upscale restaurants. Nearby, the restored South Park area has cafés where designers, architects, and multimedia moguls cluster. The Moscone Convention Center, Yerba Buena Center, and new Museum of Modern Art facility are turning mid-SoMa into an action-packed cultural mecca with a complement of restaurants. Fortunately, the nightclubs, art studios, leather bars, and offbeat eateries that made this area so hip linger on.

American Casual
$$$
VU

Harry Denton's. This happening waterfront hangout is a little more mellow on Sundays, the only day there isn't a live band. But the bar does brisk business, the upscale saloon fare is good, and the bay view is inspiring. *161 Steuart St. between Mission and Howard Sts., tel. 415/882–1333. AE, D, DC, MC, V. Sun. 8–9.*

$$

OPTS Café. There are two parts to this intriguing menu, one dubbed Featured Artist and the other Permanent Collection. The former offers a regularly changing palette of dishes from local restaurant chefs, while the latter features recipes from the kitchen's regular repertoire, from Caesar salad to savory pies to robust sandwiches. Desserts are not to be ignored. *Center for the Arts Galleries and Forum, 701 Mission St. near 3rd St., tel. 415/896–1770. AE, MC, V. Sun. 11–5.*

$
VG

Brain/Wash. This is the best idea to come along in a while and the most popular laundromat in the city. Stuff your clothes in a washer and chow down on burgers, sandwiches, salads, international vegetarian fare, or pizza. Or drop in for a spin and a breakfast of omelets or pancakes, featuring such specials as cappuccino pancakes with chocolate butter. The industrial decor includes a pinball machine and a computer linked to the chatty SFNET bulletin board. *1122 Folsom between 7th and 8th Sts., tel. 415/861–3663. Reservations not accepted. No credit cards. Sun. 7:30 AM–11 PM.*

$
CH, L, VG

Hamburger Mary's. The flea-market decor is wacky, the bar scene is lively, the clientele are a fascinating mix, and the burgers (including meatless selections, such as the tofu Mary) are huge and absolutely fabulous. Create your own omelet or dig into a hefty portion of eggs Benedict for brunch. *1582 Folsom at 12th St., tel. 415/626–1985. AE, D, MC, V. Sun. 10 AM–1 AM.*

American Contemporary
$$$$

Hawthorne Lane. Chefs David and Anne Gingrass are known for their inventive takes on American food, with inspired borrowings from the kitchens of Asia and Europe. Their latest venture is the hottest ticket in town, with dishes that range from grilled fresh anchovies, seared foie gras, and lamb with eggplant risotto to boned quail on a nest of scalloped potatoes. A café menu served in the large bar lists pizzas, small plates of fried squid, tempura-laced vegetables, and a host of other tantalizing choices. *22 Hawthorne La. between 2nd and 3rd Sts., tel. 415/777-9779. MC, V. Sun. 5:30–10.*

Barbecue
$
CH

Big Nate's Barbecue. Homemade sauce and a wood-burning brick oven produce mighty fine barbecue. Ribs, chicken, and links come with sides of homemade potato salad, coleslaw, and cornbread muffins. *1665 Folsom between 12th and 13th Sts., tel. 415/861–4242. MC, V. Sun. noon–10.*

Chinese
$$$–$$$$
CH

Wu Kong Restaurant. This upscale eatery in the airy and attractive Rincon Center atrium features a range of expertly prepared Shanghai specialties and a fine selection of Cantonese dishes. *One Rincon Center, 101 Spear St. between Mission and Howard Sts., tel. 415/957–9300. AE, DC, MC, V. Sun. lunch 10:30–2:30, dinner 5:30–10.*

Deli
$
CH

Max's Diner. This SoMa offshoot of the Max deli chain serves humongous sandwiches in a simulated '50's diner complete with a soda fountain. *311 3rd St. at Folsom, tel. 415/546–6297. AE, MC, V. Sun. 11:30–10.*

French
$$$–$$$$
VU

Bistro Roti. Views of the bay and a boisterous bar set the mood at this popular, noisy waterfront café. Anything from the brick rotisserie (mint-and-garlic chicken, chops, roasts) is great, and the

French onion soup and seasoned onion rings draw raves. *155 Steuart St. between Mission and Howard Sts., tel. 415/495–6500. AE, D, DC, MC, V. Sun. 5:30–10.*

Italian *$$* **Caffè Museo.** San Francisco's stunning Museum of Modern Art houses this smart self-serve caffè. The Italian-inspired menu showcases panini piled high with smoked chicken and eggplant, ham and roasted onions, baked pastas, salads, and irresistible tarts for dessert. *151 3rd St. near Mission St., tel. 415/357–4500. Reservations not accepted. AE, D, DC, MC, V. Sun. 10–6.*

$$ VG **Ruby's.** With faux-marble arches and an upbeat ambience, Ruby's is a popular Sunday gathering place for gays and straights alike. Pizza with cornmeal crust that's topped with such goodies as roasted garlic, gorgonzola, or walnuts is the specialty—but Ruby's crab cakes, Caesar salad, pastas, and house-made cheesecakes and tortes are also worth trying. *489 3rd St. near Bryant, tel. 415/541–0795. AE, D, DC, MC, V. Sun. 5–10.*

Mediterranean *$$$* **LuLu.** This is one of the hippest restaurants to open in recent years. Chef-owner Reed Hearon creates such superb dishes as rotisserie chicken with fennel or whole steamed catfish and serves them family style in a huge dining room with a vaulted ceiling, exposed pipes, and prime views of the wood-burning oven and rotisserie. The martinis, also huge, may be the best in town. Reservations are not easy to come by here, but you can try to grab a table in the bar. *816 Folsom.between 4th and 5th Sts., tel. 415/495–5775. AE, MC, V. Sun. 5:30–10.*

Mexican *$$$* **Cadillac Bar.** With a long bar, ceiling fans, and hot pink decor, this trendy, yuppie watering-hole serves good mesquite-grilled fish, quesadillas, and roasted goat, along with more predictable fare. Birthday bashes here reach a near-hysterical pitch. *1 Holland Ct., off Howard between 4th and 5th Sts., tel. 415/543–8226. AE, D, DC, MC, V. Sun. noon–10.*

$$ CH **Chevys Mexican Restaurant.** The original SF branch of this popular chain has plate glass, neon signs, and the trademark tortilla machine. Mesquite-grilled meats make fajitas a favorite pick. Some say the food at the Cadillac is superior, but Chevys is more popular with family groups—there's always a wait for a table. *150 4th St. between Mission and Howard Sts., tel. 415/543–8060. MC, V. Sun. 11–10.*

Thai *$$ VG* **Cha-Am.** Art hounds will find this an ideal spot to stop in for a spicy pick-me-up after an afternoon at the nearby Museum of Modern Art, the Center for the Arts, or the Ansel Adams Center—or all three. There are fiery and colorful curries, spicy salads, tempting grilled meats, and an appealing array of vegetarian dishes. The spacious and comfortable dining room and friendly staff invite unhurried meals. *701 Folsom at 3rd St., tel. 415/546–9711. AE, MC, V. Sun. 5–10.*

Sunset

The Sunset District, bordered on the north by Golden Gate Park and extending out to the Pacific, is the haunt of people who don't seem to mind the fog. The restaurants provide cuisine from around the globe and ample consolation for the moody weather.

Barbecue *$ CH* **Leon's Bar-BQ.** No wonder this barbecue joint is always jammed: It serves great ribs, chicken, and links, as well as irresistible homemade desserts. *2800 Sloat Blvd. between 46th and 47th Aves., tel. 415/681–3071. Reservations not accepted. AE, MC, V. Sun. 11–10.*

Greek *$$$ CH, O* **Stoyanof's Cafe & Restaurant.** Chef-owner Georgi Stoyanof turns out superb renditions of all the Greek classics from *spanakopita* (phyllo filled with seasoned spinach and cheese) to *pasticcio* (rigatoni and ground lamb casserole, topped with cheese). His baklava is sublime. There are cafeteria service and outdoor seating on an enclosed deck during lunch, full service indoors during dinner. *1240 9th Ave. at Lincoln Way, tel. 415/664–3664. AE, MC, V (dinner only). Sun. 10–9.*

Mexican *$$$* *CH* **Casa Aguila.** This bright, festive place is usually crowded with folks who come far and wide for the sophisticated, expertly executed cuisine, including chicken mole, pork steak Michoacan, and tempting seafood dishes. Split one of the huge appetizers while you wait, and be sure to order the flan for dessert. *1240 Noriega St. between 19th and 20th Aves., tel. 415/661–5593. Reservations not accepted. AE, MC, V. Sun. lunch 11:30–3:30, dinner 5–10.*

Middle Eastern *$$$* **YaYa Cuisine.** Golden Gate Park is only steps away from this Middle Eastern oasis, where the foods of Iraq are influenced by owner-chef Yahya Salih's many years in California. The dining room's blue and sandy hues provide the ideal setting for Salih's imaginative creations—from tender, pilaf-stuffed roast chicken and lamb *biriani*, fragrant with the spices of the Tigris-Euphrates Valley, to date-filled dumplings dotted with nuts. *1220 9th Ave. near Lincoln Way, tel. 415/566–6966. AE, MC, V. Sun. 5:30–10.*

Seafood *$$$* **P.J.'s Oyster Bed.** This neighborhood joint decked out as a sea shanty always wins popularity polls for its seafood in general and its oyster bar in particular. Finish off with its infamous swamp pie (ice cream, pralines, caramel, and chocolate on a chocolate cookie crust). *737 Irving St. between 8th and 9th Aves., tel. 415/566–7775. AE, D, DC, MC, V. Sun. brunch 11:30–3, dinner 4–10.*

Swiss *$$$* **Luzerne Restaurant.** What better way to fight the fog than with fondue? This small, cozy restaurant specializes in Swiss-French comfort food, from Wiener schnitzel to leek-and-potato soup. The prices are comfortably reasonable. *1429 Noriega St. between 21st and 22nd Aves., tel. 415/664–2353. MC, V. Sun. 5–10.*

Thai *$* **Marnee Thai.** This is a consistent favorite for Thai barbecue and such seafood specialties as crabmeat noodles or garlic prawns. *2225 Irving St. between 23rd and 24th Aves., tel. 415/665–9500. AE, MC, V. Sun. 11:30–10.*

Union Square

This area has it all, from cable cars, world-class shopping, and art galleries to theater and grand old hotels. Hotel dining has made a big comeback in San Francisco, and an interlude at one of these San Francisco landmarks can be unforgettable.

American Casual *$$$* *CH* **John's Grill.** As you might expect, this 1908 establishment is chock-full of old San Francisco charm, including a vintage bar, the original wood-paneling, photos of famous patrons, and tuxedo-clad waiters. But the food is what keeps folks coming back: oysters Wellington, T-bone steak, and lamb chops (highly favored by Dashiell Hammett and his famous detective, Sam Spade). *63 Ellis St. at Powell, tel. 415/986–0069. AE, D, DC, MC, V. Sun. 5–10.*

$$–$$$ *CH, L* **Mama's of San Francisco.** A children's menu; around-the-clock breakfast items, such as cinnamon French toast or three-berry omelet; a good choice of sandwiches at lunch; a wide array of Italian dishes at dinner; and late-night hours make this a popular stop. *398 Geary St. near Mason, tel. 415/788–1004. AE, DC, MC, V. Sun. 7 AM–midnight.*

$$ *CH* **The Dutch Kitchen.** This cheery, hotel coffee shop has colorful Dutch decor; crayons for the kids; and morning selections, including a "California natural" buffet of eggs, bacon, and cereals, as well as a more adventurous Japanese spread of miso soup, grilled salmon, rice, and pickled eggplant. *Westin St. Francis, 335 Powell St. at Geary, tel. 415/774–0264. AE, D, DC, MC, V. Sun. breakfast 5:30–11:30.*

$ **Lori's Diner.** Kids get a kick out of the '50s decor, jukebox, and burgers and fries. Adults can settle into a red vinyl booth, down a milk shake, and mull over Elvis and James Dean posters at 5 in the morning. Three locations give you plenty of opportunity to relive your youth. *336 Mason St. near Geary, tel. 415/392–8646. 149 Powell St. between Ellis and O'Farrell, tel. 415/677–9999. 500 Sutter St. at Powell, tel. 415/981–1950. Reservations not accepted. MC, V. Sun. 24 hrs.*
CH, L

$ **Sears Fine Food.** This quintessential coffee shop, founded by a retired circus clown, has been packing them in since 1938. Favorites range from a platter of 18 little Swedish pancakes to sourdough French toast. *439 Powell St. between Post and Sutter, tel. 415/986–1160. No credit cards. Sun. 7 AM–2:30 PM.*
CH

American Contemporary

$$$$$ **The French Room.** High ceilings, glittering chandeliers, and a country-French decor fit for Marie Antoinette provide the backdrop for the ultimate Sunday brunch buffet (also served next door in the equally astounding Redwood Room). Add piano accompaniment, and life doesn't get more luxurious. Other meals are exquisitely prepared and priced to match. The children's menu is a nice touch, as is the vegetable sampling plate at dinner. *Four Seasons Clift Hotel, 495 Geary St. at Taylor, tel. 415/775–4700. AE, D, DC, MC, V. Sun. 6:30 AM–2 PM, 5:30–11.*
CH, MU, VG

$$$$$ **Postrio.** Wolfgang Puck's contribution to the SF culinary scene has a stunning Pat Kuleto decor (modern art, intricate ironwork, textured fabrics, floral arrangements, sculptural light fixtures). A showy open kitchen turns out elaborately clever dishes with seasonings from all corners of the globe. The bar, with its wood-burning pizza oven, is always packed. Those in the know drop in for brunch (same odds of seeing celebrities and prices are lower). *545 Post St. between Mason and Taylor, tel. 415/776–8328. Reservations essential. AE, D, DC, MC, V. Sun. brunch 9–2, dinner 5:30–10, bar menu 11 AM–12:30 AM.*

$$$$–$$$$$ **Campton Place.** This stellar restaurant is renowned for superbly prepared American regional cuisine, meticulous service, and astoundingly high prices. Brunch is especially noteworthy, with peach pancakes and eggs Benedict with orange hollandaise the standouts. Check out the prix fixe early-bird dinners for theatergoers. *Campton Place Kempinski Hotel, 340 Stockton St. near Post, tel. 415/955–5555. Jacket and tie. AE, D, DC, MC, V. Sun. 8–2:30.*
VG

$$$$ **Victor's.** On the 32nd floor of the Westin St. Francis Hotel, this classy place has panoramic views of the city and bay. The lavish Sunday brunch buffet features salmon with scallop mousse, roast sirloin of beef with horseradish sauce, cheese blintzes with macadamia nuts, and much, much more. Dinner includes lobster or rack of lamb, as well as a vegetarian plate. The three-course prix fixe pretheater menu is a relative bargain. *Westin St. Francis, 355 Powell St. near Geary, tel. 415/774–0253. AE, D, DC, MC, V. Sun. brunch 10–2, dinner 6–10, bar menu 5–11:30.*
CH, VG, VU

$$$–$$$$ **Grand Cafe.** Located in the heart of the city's downtown theater district, the Grand Cafe is a welcome sight to anyone headed to or from an afternoon or evening pondering Stoppard or laughing at Molière. The Beaux Arts dining room and bar serve an appreciative crowd of food-savvy patrons from early morning until late at night, with choices ranging from lobster and shrimp ravioli to duck confit to chicken braised in red wine. *Hotel Monaco, 501 Geary St. at Mason, tel. 415/292–0101. AE, DC, MC, V. Sun. 8 AM–11 PM.*
L

$$$–$$$$ **Rumpus.** Tucked in at the end of one of San Francisco's charming downtown alleys, Rumpus is a contemporary retreat for American food that speaks with a hint of a British accent. The dinner menu changes regularly, but you'll often find tender lamb atop a bed of barley, salmon with saffron risotto, and New York steak with bubble and squeak (potatoes and cabbage). Simpler fare, including a good lamb sandwich and an aggressively seasoned Caesar salad, are reg-

ular lunch selections. *1 Tillman Pl. off Grant St. between Sutter and Post, tel. 415/421–2300. AE, DC, MC, V. Sun. lunch 11:30–2:30, dinner 5:30–10:30.*

Burmese *$–$$* *CH* **Burma's House Restaurant.** The decor is nothing special, but the cuisine—Burmese and Chinese—is. Try anything that starts with "Rangoon." Lunch specials here are a real bargain. *720 Post St. near Leavenworth, tel. 415/775–1156. MC, V. Sun. lunch 11–3, dinner 5–10.*

Chinese *$$$* *VG* **China Moon Cafe.** Barbara Tropp works her culinary magic in a Deco-style coffee shop that's embellished with a big silver moon, violet ceiling, and lush floral arrangements. Tropp evidences a poetic California approach to Chinese food in such dishes as golden-baked Buddha buns filled with curried vegetables and pot-browned noodle pillows topped with spicy beef ribbons and a medley of vegetables. Reservations are essential for seating in the not-so-comfy wooden booths. Risk-takers can take a chance on landing a space at the counter. *639 Post St. between Taylor and Jones, tel. 415/775–4789. AE, DC, MC. V. Sun. 5:30–10.*

Deli *$$* *CH, L, VG* **David's Delicatessen.** Since 1952 this has been the spot for blintzes, jelly omelets, potato pancakes, matzo ball soup, stuffed cabbage, corned beef, pastrami, and European pastries baked on the premises. The place is packed during breakfast and brunch. Nosh your way through a prix fixe four-course dinner with lots of options and waddle away content. *480 Geary Blvd. near Taylor, tel. 415/771–1600. D, MC, V. Sun. 7 AM–midnight.*

French *$$$$* **Bistro M.** French-born Michel Richard launched this large, handsome space in 1994 and has been massaging the menu ever since to come up with a formula that will satisfy the fickle San Francisco palate. The result is French food with a strong California component. The first-course onion tart is thin and crisp and loaded with caramelized onions. Simple main courses of pepper-crusted tuna and roast salmon are generally good, but the kitchen continues to refine the choices. *Milano Hotel, 55 5th St. between Market and Mission Sts., tel. 415/543–5554. AE, DC, MC, V. Sun. lunch 11:30–2:30, dinner 5:30–10.*

$$ **City of Paris.** Named after the old department store, this lively bistro dishes up French comfort food (herb-roasted chicken, duck confit, roasted sea bass, red cabbage salad with Roquefort cheese and bacon). The tile-floor bar is where the chic meet to dine on house-cured gravlax and great burgers and to sample the well-selected, surprisingly low-priced wines. *101 Shannon Alley, in Shannon Court Hotel off Geary St. between Taylor and Jones, tel. 415/441–4442. AE, MC, V. Sun. 7 AM–11 PM.*

German *$* *CH* **German Cook.** This small, unpretentious local favorite has been turning out hearty, home-style German food (potato pancakes, German meatballs, stuffed cabbage) since 1960. The Sunday special is an all-you-can-eat turkey dinner for under $10. *612 O'Farrell St. near Leavenworth, tel. 415/776–9022. AE, MC, V. Sun. 4–10.*

Italian *$$$* *CH* **Iron Horse.** This San Francisco classic has dim lighting, white tablecloths, gruffly affable Old World waiters who cater to your every need (and are awfully patient with kids), and sophisticated Italian food. *19 Maiden La., off Union Sq. between Grant and Kearny, tel. 415/362–8133. AE, D, DC, MC, V. Sun. 4–10:30.*

$$$–$$$$ **Kuleto's.** Since it's one of the most gorgeous restaurants in SF, it's little wonder that owner Bill Kimpton named the place after designer Pat Kuleto. There are high Florentine ceilings, cozy booths, a long open kitchen, a garden area with skylights overhead, and a wooden bar transported from the old Palace Hotel, with meats and cheeses dangling overhead. Order anything (antipasto, smoked-salmon ravioli, grilled radicchio, homemade focaccia) and enjoy. *Vil-*

la Florence Hotel, 221 Powell St. between Geary and O'Farrell, tel. 415/397–7720. AE, D, DC, MC, V. Sun. breakfast 8–10:30, lunch and dinner 11:30–11.

$$$
L
Scala's Bistro. When the Sir Francis Drake hotel reopened in 1995 after a thorough rehab, this handsome spot was part of the sparkling new package. It has been a popular gathering place for the cognoscenti and everyone else ever since. The first courses are intriguing—grilled portobellos, beef carpaccio with slivered raw artichokes; the pastas are al dente creations tossed with garden-fresh vegetables; and the main courses range from pork tenderloin to crackly skinned duck confit. Although it rests here in the Italian category, the kitchen stresses a French country component as well. *Sir Francis Drake Hotel, 432 Powell St. between Sutter and Post, tel. 415/395–8555. AE, D, MC, V. Sun. breakfast 8–10:30, lunch and dinner 11:30–midnight.*

$$
CH
New Joe's. A "Joe" restaurant with Italian American food at reasonable prices is an old SF tradition. This is an update with contemporary decor and contemporary cuisine (hamburger on focaccia, involved pasta dishes, intricate salads). The menu is extensive, and prices are reasonable. *347 Geary St. near Powell, tel. 415/989–6733. AE, D, DC, MC, V. Sun. 7 AM–11 PM.*

Pacific Rim
$$$$
CH
Pacific. All is serene, from the setting (adjoining the hotel's atrium-lobby where artist Elbert Weinberg's stunning fountain sculpture stands) to the service to the Pacific Rim cuisine. Chef Takayoshi Kawai, whose last stop was at the legendary Masa's, heads up the kitchen now, and his European food with Asian embellishments is often stunning. Crayfish salad with green beans, seared foie gras, and creamy risottos are among his fine dishes. There's a bountiful brunch at midday, and simpler food is served in the bar all day long. *Pan Pacific Hotel, 500 Post St. near Mason, tel. 415/771–8600, ext. 5687. AE, D, MC, V. Sun. 7 AM–9:30 PM.*

Seafood
$$$
Brasserie Savoy. A turn-of-the-century corner storefront was miraculously transformed into this classic Parisian brasserie with cherry paneling, brass fixtures, and a traditional tin bar. The chef's position here has been a revolving toque, but the food generally remains French with a good dose of Californian. Prix fixe dinners are an economical option, and folks are encouraged to drop in for dessert at the bar. *580 Geary St. at Jones, tel. 415/474–8686. AE, D, DC, MC, V. Sun. 5:30–10.*

Union Street

Once upon a time this area, which is known as Cow Hollow, actually housed a rural settlement complete with farms and dairy herds. Today the gingerbread Victorians along Union Street have been converted into picturesque shops and boutiques. The restaurants here are now upscale grazing grounds for young professionals, media types, and other San Francisco elite.

American Casual
$$$
L
Perry's. Singles continue to mingle at this classic saloon, but those who have given up the search for a significant other can still delight in great breakfasts, some of the best burgers in town, and such hearty fare as London broil or corned beef hash. *1944 Union St. between Laguna and Buchanan, tel. 415/922–9022. AE, MC, V. Sun. 9 AM–midnight.*

$
Doidge's. This is a popular spot for perfect poached eggs (served straight-up or Benedict-style) and for lighter-than-air omelets in a country-kitchen atmosphere. Some feel the waiters have an attitude, but we've always found them friendly. Reservations are a must. *2217 Union St. between Fillmore and Steiner, tel. 415/921–2149. MC, V. Sun. 8 AM–2:45 PM.*

French
$$$–$$$$
L'Entrecôte de Paris. The house specialty at this fashionable bistro is *entrecôte*: eye of New York steak charbroiled and served with a spe-

cial sauce (blended from 12 secret ingredients) that originated at the Café de Paris in Switzerland. The *pommes frites* are acclaimed as the best shoestring potatoes in town. *2032 Union St. between Webster and Buchanan, tel. 415/931–5006. AE, DC, MC, V. Sun. 11:30–10.*

Italian *$$$* **Pane e Vino.** Terra-cotta floors and an open kitchen give this highly popular trattoria a friendly, provincial ambience. A fine selection of pastas and a nice range of uncomplicated second courses—roast sea bass, grilled veal chops, braised rabbit–show up on the changing menu. Tables are positioned close together here, so don't tell any secrets over dinner. *3011 Steiner St. near Union, tel. 415/346–2111. MC, V. Sun. 5–10.*

$$–$$$ *CH, L, VG* **Prego Restaurant.** The dining room is beige, airy, and minimalist, and the bar is always packed with optimistic singles. The free-range roasted chicken and pizza from the wood-burning oven are good picks. Children not yet ready for the dating scene may be offered pencil and paper to while away the time. *2000 Union St. near Buchanan, tel. 415/563–3305. AE, DC, MC, V. Sun. 10–midnight.*

Japanese *$$$* **Yoshida-Ya.** Sample some 20 different yakitori—meat, fish, or vegetables skewered and grilled over charcoal—or order the sushi, sashimi, and teriyaki that make up the balance of the menu. The country-inn decor includes comfortable floor seating with foot wells. *2909 Webster St. at Union, tel. 415/346–3431. AE, D, DC, MC, V. Sun. 5–10:30.*

Southeast Asian *$$$* **Betelnut.** Even on a foggy day, this Asian drinking house-cum-restaurant, with its slowly turning bamboo fans and windows that open onto the sidewalk, will make you think of the tropics. On mild days you can eat outside at an array of tables and chairs that spill out from the bar area onto the sidewalk. The pan-Asian menu lists many small dishes—noodles, dumplings, shrimp with green papaya, satay—and some larger plates: chili crab and tea-smoked duck. The custom here is to enjoy the wealth of beverages—beers, sakes, Chinese liquors, draft rice ale, even martinis—with a table of food that everyone shares. *2030 Union St. near Buchanan, tel. 415/929–8855. MC, V. Sun. 11:30–11.*

Van Ness Avenue/Polk Street

Van Ness Avenue and Polk Street run parallel to each other, forming a corridor across the city from the Civic Center to the bay. The motley collection of car dealerships, movie theaters, and mundane stores along Van Ness could make you overlook some of the best steak houses in the Bay Area. Polk Street, once the most popular gay strip but relegated to second place since the Castro District's rise, plays host to hip theme eateries and bars, ethnic restaurants, and all-night pit stops favored by insomniacs, cabbies, and folks from the city's underbelly.

American Casual *$–$$* **Hard Rock Cafe.** Billed as "the Smithsonian of rock and roll," this is teen heaven: loud music, lots of yelling, rock memorabilia, and a finned Cadillac crashing through one wall. For a real vacation, drop the young and restless off here for burgers, ribs, barbecued chicken, and huge desserts—and go somewhere else. *1699 Van Ness Ave. at Sacramento, tel. 415/885–1699. AE, DC, MC, V. Sun. 11:30–11.*

$ *CH, L* **The Grubstake Restaurant.** A handy budget stop for families during the day, this funky railroad-car diner (complete with jukebox) is best known for full breakfasts, burgers and fries, and homemade apple pie dished up to a weird crowd in the wee hours of the morning. *1525 Pine St. near Polk, tel. 415/673–8268. No credit cards. Sun. 10 AM–4 AM.*

$ *CH, L* **Tommy's Joynt.** There's a startlingly colorful paint job on the outside of this classic cafeteria-style hofbrau, a decor composed of beer-related kitsch within, great corned beef and carved-meat sand-

wiches, and a television that's always tuned to sports. *1101 Geary Blvd. at Van Ness, tel. 415/775–4216. No credit cards. Sun. 11 AM–1:45 AM.*

Indian *$$$–$$$$* *CH, MU, VG* **Maharani Restaurant.** The Moghul-style tandoori and vegetarian cuisine consistently reap rave reviews, and the Fantasy Room, offering candle-lit dinners in plush, peach, cushioned alcoves, is made for romance. The equally elegant banquet room has live jazz music (and a cover charge) during dinner. *1122 Post St. between Polk and Van Ness, tel. 415/775–1988. Reservations essential for Fantasy Room. AE, D, MC, V. Sun. lunch 11:30–2:30; dinner 5–10.*

Italian *$$* *CH, L* **Mario's Bohemian Cigar Store Cafe.** This is an offshoot of Mario's in North Beach (*see above*), but with a lot more space. What hasn't changed is Mario's kitchen: It serves the same focaccia sandwiches stuffed with meatballs or eggplant, polenta and sausages, Italian cheesecake, and Mario's trademark jet-fuel espresso. *2209 Polk St. between Vallejo and Green, tel. 415/776–8226. No credit cards. Reservations not accepted. Sun. 10:30 AM–midnight.*

Pacific Rim *$$$–$$$$* *CH* **Crustacean.** Seafood here, wonderfully fresh and wildly creative, reflects both Vietnamese and California influence. The restaurant's famous Dungeness roasted crab, An's garlic noodles, and royal tiger prawns are all downright addictive. A major renovation was underway at the time of this writing, with promises of a both a new highly distinctive interior and such dishes as roast ginger lobster and seared Norwegian salmon with arugula. *1475 Polk St. (top floor) near California, tel. 415/776–2722. AE, D, DC, MC, V. Sun. 5–10.*

Steak *$$$$* **Harris' Restaurant.** A well-heeled older crowd frequents this handsome Old San Francisco dining room with high ceilings, booths, and a turn-of-the-century bar. The dry-aged steaks (from the Harris ranch) keep winning popularity polls as the best in town, but don't overlook the prime rib, fresh seafood, Maine lobster, or dessert cart of house-made pastries. *2100 Van Ness Ave. at Pacific, tel. 415/673–1888. AE, D, DC, MC, V. Sun. 5–9:30.*

$$$$ *CH* **Ruth's Chris Steak House.** One of the contenders for the best steaks in town, this place serves corn-fed U.S. prime beef broiled to a turn, as well as Maine lobster, housemade desserts, and eight kinds of potatoes. The dining room, with its thick white tablecloths and dark wood paneling, is a classic. *1601 Van Ness Ave. at California, tel. 415/673–0557. AE, DC, MC, V. Sun. 5–10:30.*

$$$–$$$$ **House of Prime Rib.** Perfect prime beef is carved at your table and to your specification in this archetypal meat lover's restaurant. *1906 Van Ness Ave. at Washington, tel. 415/885–4605. AE, DC, MC, V. Sun. 4–2 AM.*

Vietnamese *$$* *VG* **Emerald Garden Restaurant.** The food here has a French flair with occasional forays into Thai and California cuisine and some intriguing vegetarian specials. Papaya salad and satay are favorite picks. *1550 California St. between Polk and Larkin, tel. 415/673–1155. AE, D, DC, MC, V. Sun. 5–10.*

$$ *VG* **Golden Turtle Vietnamese Restaurant.** Superb marinated and grilled seafood and vegetarian specialties are served in an attractive dining room with wall-size wood carvings and Vietnamese art. *2211 Van Ness Ave. near Broadway, tel. 415/441–4419. AE, DC, MC, V. Sun. lunch 11:30–3; dinner 5–11.*

Wharf

The ongoing tourist carnival along the waterfront from Fisherman's Wharf and Ghirardelli Square to Pier 39 may look like Corn Dog Central, and it's true that some waterfront restaurants serve up a spectacular view and mediocre food at inflated prices. But those stands serving take-away crab and shrimp cocktails continue to offer a quintessential San Francisco experience. Moreover, it's still possible to find a good sit-down meal at digestible prices along the Wharf, where the all-star scenery never disappoints.

American Casual
$$
CH, VU

Bobby Rubino's Place for Ribs. There's something for every member of the family in this friendly rib joint: fabulous baby-back ribs, four big screens in the sports lounge, breathtaking views of the bay, and budget-minded children's menus. *Fisherman's Wharf, 245 Jefferson St. between Jones and Taylor, tel. 415/673–2266. AE, D, DC, MC, V. Sun. 11:30–10, until 11 in summer.*

$$
VU

Buena Vista Cafe. The birthplace of Irish coffee has great breakfast fare, a view of Victorian Park and the cable car turnaround, and lots of people waiting for seats. *2765 Hyde St. at Beach near Fisherman's Wharf, tel. 415/474–5044. Reservations not accepted. No credit cards. Sun. 8 AM–2 AM).*

$
CH

Boudin Sourdough Bakery & Cafe. This is the best bargain pit stop on Pier 39, offering clam chowder in a sourdough-bread bowl, along with a range of salads, sandwiches, sweets, and espresso drinks. *Pier 39 (space 5Q) between Grant Ave. and The Embarcadero, tel. 415/421–0185. Reservations not accepted. MC, V. Sun. 8–9. (Other locations open on Sun.: Ghirardelli Square, 900 North Point St., tel. 415/928–7404; Fisherman's Wharf, 156 Jefferson St., 415/928–1849.*

$
O, VU

Eagle Cafe. This turn-of-the-century building full of waterfront memorabilia was transported from its former location two blocks away and plunked atop Pier 39. Since 1928 it's been dishing up trademark corned beef hash, hot cakes, and eggs at rock-bottom prices, and now tourists jam the outdoor deck for Irish coffees, Bloody Marys, eggs Benedict, bay views, and hefty Eagle fare. *Pier 39 at Stockton St., tel. 415/433–3689. Reservations not accepted. No credit cards. Sun. 7:30 AM–10 PM.*

Chinese
$$$
VG, VU

The Mandarin. For more than a quarter of a century this waterfront restaurant has offered bay views, a setting that bespeaks the grandeur of prerevolutionary China, and a spectrum of northern Chinese cuisine from Peking duck and crab Mandarin to glazed bananas. You pay a premium for the elegance, but most feel it's well worth the splurge. *Ghirardelli Square, 900 North Point St. near Polk, tel. 415/673–8812. AE, DC, MC, V. Sun. 11:30–11.*

French
$$$$

Chez Michel. After two decades of operation, Michel Elkaim closed down his famous Chez Michel for seven years. He returned in 1995 to his old address, but it has been given a sleek new look by the same architect who designed the original restaurant. Classic French cuisine with some California touches is what you find here, from duck confit to roasted monkfish to chicken breast stuffed with wild mushrooms. This place is sometimes plagued by uneven service; if that's the case on your visit, cool down with the utterly delectable Grand Marnier soufflé. *804 Northpoint St. at Hyde, tel. 415/775–7036. MC, V. Sun. 5:30–10:30.*

Indian
$$$
VG, VU

Gaylord Restaurant. Top-notch tandoori dishes, curries, vegetarian specialties, and Indian sweets are served in a sumptuous setting. Sample a range of exotic fare amid palms, Indian art, and bay views at the prix fixe Sunday brunch buffet. *Ghirardelli Square (3rd floor of Chocolate Bldg.), 900 North Point St., tel. 415/771–8822. AE, D, DC, MC, V. Sun. brunch noon–2:45, dinner 5–10:45.*

Italian
$$$$
CH, O, VU

Castagnola's Restaurant. Also known as Lolli's Castagnola's, this city classic caters to kids with a loving touch. Adults will appreciate great views from floor-to-ceiling windows and a good version of the San Francisco Italian seafood stew called cioppino. *Fisherman's Wharf, 286 Jefferson St. at Jones, tel. 415/776–5015. AE, D, DC, MC, V. Sun. 8 AM–10 PM, until 11 in summer.*

$$$
CH, VG, O

Cafe Pescatore. This simpatico neighborhood café has cheerful floral tablecloths; wicker chairs; sidewalk seating; coloring-paper menus and crayons for the kids; and a tempting selection of seafood, pasta, and house-made desserts. Both breakfast and brunch are offered on

Sundays. Select from a wonderful array of pizzas, including one with four cheeses, mushrooms, and roasted garlic and another with roasted eggplant, peppers, garlic, and goat cheese. *2455 Mason St. near North Point, tel. 415/561–1111. AE, D, DC, MC, V. Sun. 7 AM–10 PM.*

$$$ *VU* **Nick's Lighthouse.** The decor, a combination of Italian Old San Francisco and nautical motifs, includes a tank of live Maine lobsters and a view of fishing boats outside. The cioppino here is a winner, along with fare ranging from pasta to fresh seafood. *5 Fisherman's Wharf at Embarcadero and Bay, tel. 415/929–1300. AE, DC, MC, V. Sun. 11–10:30.*

Seafood *$$$$* *VU* **McCormick & Kuleto's Seafood Restaurant.** With famed SF restaurant designer Pat Kuleto behind it, this place is predictably spectacular: wood and copper grillwork, dramatic lighting, floor-to-ceiling windows, and stunning bay views. The fare includes 20 to 30 fresh seafood specials daily. In the casual Crabcake Lounge, there's pizza from a wood-burning oven and a full oyster bar. *Ghirardelli Square, 900 North Point St. at Beach and Larkin, tel. 415/929–1730. AE, D, DC, MC, V. Sun. 11:30–11.*

$$$–$$$$ *CH, VU* **Neptune's Palace.** High-priced, view-oriented seafood joints along the wharf are generally scorned by locals, but Neptune's does a good job. The seafood is fresh and well prepared, there are crayons for the kids, and the view from the picture windows is magnificent. *Pier 39 at Beach and Embarcadero Sts., tel. 415/434–2260. AE, D, DC, MC, V. Sun. 11:30–9.*

East Bay

Though Alice Waters and her internationally famous restaurant, Chez Panisse, can be credited with putting the East Bay on the culinary map, they are actually part of a larger phenomenon characterized by specialty markets, "gourmet ghettos," and great little restaurants. Chez Panisse is closed on Sundays, and while pilgrims can still sample Waters's fare at Café Fanny, named after her daughter, the East Bay has become a haven for food fanatics, with scores of other noteworthy restaurants.

American Casual *$$* *CH, O* **Bette's Oceanview Diner.** This trendy '50s-style diner in the fashionable Fourth Street shopping zone lays claim to great breakfasts, the best jukebox in the Bay Area, and its own notorious niche in political history ever since a waitress kicked a customer out for reading *Playboy*. Expect long lines or opt for the take-out branch next door. *1807 4th St. near Hearst (University Ave. exit from I–80), Berkeley, tel. 510/644–3230. Reservations not accepted. No credit cards. Sun. 6:30 AM–4 PM.*

$ *CH* **Fatapple's.** Hand-chopped grilled burgers on housemade rolls are the best in town; corn-chowder soup, spinach salad, down-home pies, cheese puffs (stuffed with baker's cheese and sprinkled with powdered sugar), and thick shakes also draw raves. Buttermilk waffles and wonderful pastries make breakfast a hit. *1346 Martin Luther King Jr. Way at Rose, Berkeley, tel. 510/526–2260. Reservations not accepted. No credit cards. Sun. 7 AM–11 PM.*

American Contemporary *$$$–$$$$* *O* **Bay Wolf Restaurant.** A close second to Chez Panisse in the affections of local food lovers, this tranquil eatery is known for its creative use of exquisitely fresh ingredients on a constantly changing menu. It's in a converted brown-shingle house with a kitchen garden in back; an enclosed deck out front; and artfully simple, soothing decor inside. Inquire about special Sunday brunches on Mother's Day and Valentine's Day. *3853 Piedmont Ave. near Rio Vista, Oakland, tel. 510/655–6004. MC, V. Sun. 5:30–9.*

$$$–$$$$ **Citron.** This place has won consistent raves since its opening in the early '90s. Wicker chairs, tile floors, and cozy banquettes evoke a simple but elegant mood. The menu changes seasonally to include

such eclectic dishes as steamed mussels and fines herbes sausage in spicy red wine broth, roasted squash soup, and braised Peking duck legs on a bed of Savoy cabbage, onions, and roasted parsnips. *5484 College Ave. near Taft, Oakland, tel. 510/653–5484. Reservations essential. MC, V. Sun. 5:30–9:30.*

$$$–$$$$ **Rivoli.** This small two-room eatery turns out intriguing plates that lucky Berkeley residents appreciate and plenty of other people will travel long distances to enjoy. Chef Wendy Brucker, who has cooked in some of San Francisco's best-known restaurants (Square One, Stars), has created such sublime offerings as warm spinach salad with Stilton croutons, braised veal stew with polenta, and grilled bass on a bed of braised greens. A large window in the rear dining room looks out on an inviting flower-and-shrub-filled garden. *1539 Solano Ave. at Peralta, Berkeley, tel. 510/526-2542. MC, V. Sun. 5–9.*

Barbecue
$
L
Flints. Most agree that San Francisco competitors simply can't match the funky atmosphere, fiery sauce, and dynamite ribs, chicken, and links you can score at this classic take-out joint anytime until midnight. *6609 Shattuck Ave. at 66th, Oakland, tel. 510/653–0593. Reservations not accepted. No credit cards. Sun. 11 AM–midnight.*

Burmese
$$
VG
Nan Yang. Chef-owner Philip Chu helped to introduce Burmese cuisine to the Bay Area, and foodies now throng to the Rockridge District of College Avenue to sample his ginger salad, curried chicken noodle soup, and garlic noodles. Book ahead for a prix fixe special gourmet dinner prepared by Chu. *301 8th St. at Harrison, tel. 510/465–6924. 6048 College Ave. near Claremont, Oakland tel. 510/655–3298. Sun. noon–9. MC, V.*

Cambodian
$$
VG
The Cambodiana's. The lighting is too bright and the color scheme a bit jarring, but the nouvelle Cambodian cuisine at this friendly, family-run place is outstanding—the grilled lamb chops and smoky eggplant are out of this world. An extensive vegetarian menu, prepared according to ancient Buddhist tradition, is also available, and the prix fixe Boulevard Dinner is a deal. *2156 University Ave. between Shattuck and Oxford, Berkeley, tel. 510/843–4630. AE, MC, V. Sun. 5–9:30.*

Chinese
$$$–$$$$
CH, VU
Hong Kong East Ocean Seafood Restaurant. The dining room is formal, the views of the bay can't be beat, and the menu is priced accordingly. Indulge in such specials as smoked black cod, seafood and bean thread noodles in a claypot, stir-fried Dungeness crab, or wok-charred calamari. The dim sum service draws a big crowd. *3199 Powell St. (Powell St. exit off I–80), Emeryville, tel. 510/655–3388. AE, V, MC, D. Sun. brunch 10–2:30, dinner 5–9:30.*

$
CH, VG
Long Life Vegi House. Prices are low at this popular vegetarian restaurant, and it's astounding what the cook can do with tofu and gluten. Try the lemon "chicken"; you won't believe it! *2129 University Ave., above Shattuck, Berkeley, tel. 510/845–6072. AE, MC, V. Sun. 11:30–9:30.*

Deli
$
Saul's Delicatessen. This quintessential Jewish deli has everything from corned beef and egg creams to potato knishes and chicken soup. Breakfast is served all day, sandwiches are huge, there's a take-out counter as well as table seating, and you get a complimentary jar of dill pickles at your table. *1475 Shattuck Ave. near Vine, Berkeley, tel. 510/848–3354. MC, V. Sun. 7 AM–9 PM.*

Ethiopian
$
VG
The Blue Nile. Bamboo and basketry decor, reasonable prices, and consistently good fare make this the people's choice. Order combination meat and veggie plates and eat family style for maximum entertainment. *2525 Telegraph Ave. between Dwight and Parker, Berkeley, tel. 510/540–6777. AE, MC, V. Sun. 5–10.*

French
$$$–$$$$
La Brasserie. Tucked away on the shore of Lake Merritt is what many believe to be one of the best French restaurants west of the

Rockies, with the informality of a bistro and a setting made for romance. The filet mignon doused in cognac-Roquefort fondue is sublime. Roger Martin is a wine expert and convivial host; his wife Kimala whips out culinary miracles and phenomenal desserts. Drop by (with reservations) for dessert anytime after 8:30. *542 Grand Ave. near Euclid (Grand exit off I–580), Oakland, tel. 510/893–6206. AE, DC, MC, V. Sun. 5:30–9 (closed 3 wks in Sept.).*

Indian *$$$* *CH, VG* **New Delhi Junction.** Tucked back on the second level of a defunct hippie mall, this serene retreat has linen cloths and a rose on each table. In addition to good tandoori selections and vegetarian dishes, a culinary tour of India features different regional dishes each month. *2556 Telegraph Ave. between Parker and Blake, Berkeley, tel. 510/486–0477. MC, V. Sun. lunch 11:30–2:30, dinner 5:30–9:30.*

$$ *CH, VG* **Ajanta.** Lachu Moorjani, the chef-owner of this handsome dining room on Berkeley's busy Solano Avenue, sends out a newsletter to his regular customers announcing what new dishes are in store for them each month. The classics—chicken tikka, rich lamb curries, and a cache of delicious vegetarian preparations—appear regularly on the menu. Beautiful wall murals depict the art of the caves of Ajanta. *1888 Solano Ave., Berkeley, tel. 510/526–4373. AE, MC, V. Sun. lunch 11:30–2:30, dinner 5:30–9:30.*

$ **Pasand Madras Cuisine.** An extensive selection of south Indian cuisine includes *dosas* (crispy crepes stuffed with vegetables), specialty breads, tasty curries, and soups at prices that even starving students can afford. Live music will soothe your Sunday soul. *2286 Shattuck Ave. between Bancroft and Kittredge, Berkeley, tel. 510/549–2559. AE, MC, V. Sun. noon–10.*

Italian *$$–$$$* *O* **Oliveto Cafe & Restaurant.** The casual downstairs café, serving espresso drinks, pizzas, tapas, and desserts, is always packed with interesting bohemian types. The second floor, with its handsome open kitchen and walls done in warm Mediterranean earth tones, is more formal and is where you will find expertly prepared rustic Italian fare, including risotto, pasta, grilled fish and meats, and an extensive wine list. *5655 College Ave., across from Rockridge BART, Oakland, tel. 510/547–5356 (restaurant), 510/547–4382 (café). AE, DC, MC, V. Sun. café (2$) 8 AM–10 PM; restaurant (3$) brunch 9:30–2, dinner 5:30–9.*

$$–$$$ *CH* **Zza's Trattoria.** There's always a wacko party atmosphere here due to the flashing neon sign on the back wall and the fact that all the waiters seem to be drama students. Butcher-paper tablecloths and crayons provide entertainment for kids and adults, and customers' creations adorn the walls. The fare includes homemade ravioli, lasagna, risotto, and gnocchi. *552 Grand Ave. on Lake Merritt (Grand exit off I–580), Oakland, tel. 510/839–9124. MC, V. Sun.4:30–10.*

$$ *CH* **Venezia Caffe & Ristorante.** Housed in a large, open setting with high ceilings, hanging laundry, a central fountain, and colorful murals creating the feel of a Venetian piazza, the Venezia is an old favorite of Berkeleyites. The grilled house-made chicken sausages and fresh pastas are a consistent hit. Children are offered free antipasti, crayons, and a kids' menu. *1799 University Ave. near Grant, Berkeley, tel. 510/849–4681. AE, MC, V. Sun. 5–9:30.*

Japanese *$$$* *VG* **Yoshi's.** Great Japanese fare (including a vegetarian *bento* box) and top-notch sushi are just the beginning; this is also a world-class jazz club. If you plan to see the show, book a table for the club before you go in to an early dinner. *6030 Claremont Ave., 1 block south of College, Oakland, tel. 510/652–9200. AE, D, DC, MC, V. Sun. 5:30–10.*

Mediterranean *$$$* *O, VU* **Blackhawk Grille.** Near the U.C. Berkeley Museum and the Behring Auto Museum in upscale Blackhawk Plaza, this restaurant is a design fantasy that follows the auto theme, with hubcap sconces and a vintage auto in the middle of the dining room. The menu is surprisingly reasonable, and the pastas, spit-roasted game and fish, wood-fired pizzas, and huge desserts are prepared to perfection. *3540*

Blackhawk Plaza Circle off Camino Tassajara (680 S. from Walnut Creek, Sycamore Valley Rd. E), Danville, tel. 510/736–4295. AE, D, MC, V. Sun. 10:30–9:30.

$
CH, O
Café Fanny. At this trendy stand-up food bar owned by Jim Maser, brother-in-law of the famous Alice Waters, you'll find out just how gourmet a grilled cheese sandwich can get. Sample the pizzette, sandwiches and desserts and judge for yourself whether the inevitable wait in a long line is worth your time. Breakfast items are served all day on Sundays. *1603 San Pablo Ave. at Cedar, Berkeley, tel. 510/524–5447. Reservations not accepted. No credit cards. Sun. 9–3.*

Mexican
$$
CH
Juan's Place. Why does this nothing-special joint in an industrial district serving hefty portions of so-so fare keep winning East Bay popularity polls? We don't know, but the prices are reasonable and the parking's easy, and the tables in the bar may well be the last place in Berkeley where you can eat and smoke at the same time. *941 Carleton at 9th St., Berkeley, tel. 510/845–6904. MC, V. Sun. 2–10.*

$
CH, VG
Cactus Taqueria. A forerunner of the '90s taqueria trend of serving exquisitely fresh ingredients and a wide variety of tempting fillings, this one is reasonably priced and a big hit among families with kids. *5525 College Ave., across from Rockridge BART, Oakland, tel. 510/547–1305. Reservations not accepted. No credit cards. Sun. 11–9.*

$
CH, VG, O
Picante Cocina Mexicana. In a large space in a changing industrial neighborhood, this is a cheerful self-serve spot where you can get Mexican plates made from only the freshest ingredients. The open kitchen allows you to watch the cooks and tortilla makers at work. It's owned by the proprietors of Café Fanny (*see above*), which explains why just about everything here is first-rate, right down to the aguas frescas. *1328 6th St. between Gilman and Camelia, Berkeley, tel. 510/525–3121. MC, V. Sun. 11–10.*

$
CH
Taqueria Morelia. East 14th Street in Oakland has mile after mile of taquerias, Mexican restaurants, and mobile taco vans serving the most authentic Mexican fare you're likely to find this side of the border. Taqueria Morelia has a funky, nothing-fancy ambience and the best *tortas* (Mexican sandwiches), tacos, and burritos around. *4481 East 14th St. near 45th (High St. exit off I–880), Oakland, tel. 510/535–6030. No credit cards. Sun. 10–10.*

Pizza
$
CH, VG
Zachary's Chicago Pizza. These hands-down favorites draw fans from across the bay. While they make the thin-crust New York version, it's the deep-dish, double-crust creation that draws the standing-room-only crowds. The walls are decorated with children's pictures of pizza. Takeout is available, but expect a wait even with phone-ahead orders. *1853 Solano Ave. near the Alameda, Berkeley, tel. 510/525–5950. 5801 College Ave. near Rockridge BART, Oakland, 510/655–6385. Reservations not accepted. No credit cards. Sun. 11–9:30 (Solano), 11–10 (College).*

Seafood
$$–$$$
CH
Spenger's Fish Grotto. Frankly, the quality of the food simply doesn't warrant the crowds that pack this place, particularly on Sundays. It's huge and noisy, with an oyster bar and a big-screen sports bar up front. Still, the prices are fairly reasonable, and the menu has every standard seafood dish under the sun. *1919 4th St. near University (University Ave. exit off I–80), Berkeley, tel. 510/845–7771. AE, D, DC, MC, V. Sun. 7 AM–11 PM.*

Thai
$$
VG
Plearn's Thai Cuisine No. 2. The decor looks like an airport lounge (in L.A., not Bangkok), but fans agree that the extensive selection of spicy Thai cuisine is some of the best around. Parking is difficult, and lines can be long. *2050 University Ave., between Shattuck Ave. and Milvia, Berkeley, tel. 510/841–2148. MC, V. Sun. 11:30–10.*

Vietnamese
$–$$
Le Cheval. Arguably the most popular Vietnamese restaurant in the East Bay, Le Cheval serves the classic French-inspired fare of Viet-

nam. Fresh ingredients, exotic spices, and intriguing sauces are hallmarks here. The selection of domestic and imported beer is staggering. *1007 Clay St. at 10th, Oakland, tel. 510/763–8495. AE, MC, V. Sun. 5–9:30.*

Peninsula

Silicon Valley, Stanford University, the Stanford Shopping Center, and a series of well-heeled bedroom communities stretching along the Peninsula south of the San Francisco Airport have created a ready audience for good restaurants of every variety. There is an increasing number of family-run ethnic eateries, and a number of noted restaurateurs have branched out into the area.

American Casual

$$$ **Barley and Hopps.** This is a busy, busy place. You can hear blues in the basement, play pool or smoke cigars on the top floor, and eat some of the biggest steaks you have ever seen on the level in between. A giant wood-fueled smoker is regularly stocked with chicken, brisket, ribs, hot links, and other meats; you can order the four-meat sampler to test the smoky results. The house salad is an old-fashioned wedge of iceberg lettuce topped with the dressing of your choice, and the baked potatoes are the size of footballs. Desserts, which run the gamut from a root beer float to sweet potato pie, are the real thing. *210 South B St. at 2nd Ave., San Mateo, tel. 415/348–7808. MC, V. Sun. 5 PM–1 AM.*

$$$ O **Empire Grill and Tap Room.** The long bar, big outdoor dining patio, and general conviviality of this place attract young Silicon Valley workers tired after a hard week of pondering the mysteries of the chip. Chic pizzas, healthful salads, and grilled fish dishes are a hit. *651 Emerson St., Palo Alto, tel. 415/321–3030. MC, V. Sun. 11–10.*

$$$ **MacArthur Park.** Go for the oak-smoked, mesquite-grilled ribs; get mud pie for dessert; and indulge in picks from an impressive list of wines and single-malt Scotches. Mesquite-grilled steaks are also good. The crowd inside this historic Julia Morgan building can resemble an old boys' club. *27 University Ave. at El Camino Real, next to Caltrans station, Palo Alto, tel. 415/321–9990. AE, DC, MC, V. Sun. brunch 10–2, dinner 5–10.*

$$ **Buns Restaurant.** The owners' alleged goal for this airy, high-tech eatery was to create the best burger joint in the world. Thick, juicy, and served on toasted onion rolls, they are mighty good, but the menu also includes more unusual fare, such as baked brie and stuffed Anaheim chilies—both of which warrant a visit. *209 Park Rd. between Burlingame and Howard, tel. 415/579–2867. AE, MC, V. Sun. 5–9.*

$ CH, VG **First Watch.** This airy downtown restaurant serves both health-conscious fare (omelets made with cholesterol-free egg substitute, fruit salads, herbal teas, yogurt concoctions) and hearty, hell-bent feasts (eggs Benedict; frittatas; and skillet fries with sautéed potatoes, eggs, mushrooms, cheese, and sausage). The combination is a success. There's always a line, but the wait is reasonable (20 minutes), and you get a fresh pot of strong coffee as soon as you sit down. *201 2nd Ave. at Ellsworth, Palo Alto, tel. 415/342–2356. Reservations not accepted. AE, DC, MC, V. Sun. 7–2:30.*

American Contemporary

$$$$ **Buffalo Grill.** At this upscale take on a classic American grill with a bit of a California spin, favorites include beef brisket with garlicky mashed potatoes and heavenly, maple-cured, double-cut pork chops. *66 31st Ave. near El Camino, San Mateo, tel. 415/358–8777. AE, DC, MC, V. Sun. 5–10.*

$$$$ **Stars Palo Alto.** Peninsulites who relish their good weather appreciate chef Jeremiah Tower's latest gastronomic outpost, where retractable glass walls slip away to create a stunning open-air dining room and bar. Though the kitchen suffered through a number of upheavals in its first six months, the food seemed to suffer surprisingly

little. Roast pork loin, rack of lamb, and thick salmon filets show up on the fluid dinner menu. The lunch menu is simpler: penne tossed with oven-roasted tomato sauce, lemon-thyme risotto, ancho chile chicken sandwiches, and the like. *365 Lytton Ave. between Ramona and Bryant, Palo Alto, tel. 415/321–4466. AE, DC, MC, V. Sun. 10:30–2:30, 5:30–11.*

$$$$ **The Village Pub Restaurant.** The antithesis of your archetypal pub, this airy, spacious eatery in the hills of Woodside near Filoli Gardens has cream walls, a carved oak bar, and contemporary artwork. The fare is strictly California: crab cakes, mussels flavored with chipotle, grilled veal chops. The dessert list is worth lingering over. *2967 Woodside Rd. near Cañada Rd. (Woodside Rd. exit, 3/4 mi west off I–280 or 7 mi west off I–101), Woodside, tel. 415/851–1294. AE, D, MC, V. Sun. 5:30–9:30.*

$$$ *CH, VG* **Flea Street Cafe.** The decor is country European, the ambience is intimate and romantic, there's a toy chest for kids, and the owner is committed to a sustainable environment. Organic, pesticide-free ingredients from local producers, home-baked goods, and seasonal homemade jams are just part of what make the fare so good. Options range from grilled salmon with caviar-dill cream sauce and mashed buttermilk potatoes at dinner to fluffy omelets and homespun pancakes at brunch. *3607 Alameda De Las Pulgas (Sandhill Rd. E exit from I–280, left on Santa Cruz, left on Alameda De Las Pulgas), Menlo Park, tel. 415/854–1226. MC, V. Sun. brunch 9–2, dinner 5:30–9.*

Chinese *$$$* *CH* **Hong Kong Flower Lounge.** After establishing themselves as successful restaurateurs in Hong Kong, the Wongs brought their know-how, Hong Kong chefs, and knockout Cantonese cuisine to the Bay Area. While the SF branch (*see* Richmond District, *above*) is renowned, the Peninsula is where it all started. Expect superb fare, glittering red-and-gold decor, and tanks of live fish. *51 Millbrae Ave. at El Camino Real, tel. 415/692–6666. 1671 El Camino Real, Millbrae, tel. 415/588–9972. AE, D, DC, MC, V. Sun. dim sum 10:30–2:30, dinner 5–9:30.*

$$–$$$ *CH* **Fook Yuen.** This large Hong Kong–style restaurant is often filled with families on Sundays. They come at midday for the dim sum and in the evening for an ocean's worth of seafood and crisp Peking duck. Proceed with caution when ordering the fresh fish and shellfish; the bill can mount quickly. *195 El Camino Real, Millbrae, tel. 415/692–8600. AE, MC, V. Sun. dim sum 10–2:30, dinner 5:30–9:30.*

French *$$$* **La Bonne Auberge.** When you dine by candlelight at this cozy little cottage amid San Mateo's suburban sprawl, you'll feel as if you've escaped to the French countryside. The excellent fare (onion soup, house paté, steak with Madeira sauce, Grand Marnier soufflé, homemade pastries) is surprisingly reasonable; the wine list is expert and extensive. *2075 S. El Camino Real, 2 blocks south of Rte. 92, San Mateo, tel. 415/341–2525. MC, V. Sun. 5–9.*

Indian *$$$* *VG* **Gaylord.** This branch of Gaylord offers a resplendent setting of jade-green banquettes, rose walls, and mahogany Chippendale chairs. The fare includes tandoori specialties from a mesquite clay oven, an extensive list of vegetarian selections, and several prix fixe royal feasts. *317 Stanford Shopping Center off El Camino, Palo Alto, tel. 415/326–8761. AE, DC, MC, V. Sun. lunch noon–2:45, dinner 5–10.*

$$ *CH, VG* **Gandhi Restaurant.** Though this looks like any one of a number of Indian eateries along El Camino Real, excellent breads, samosas, yogurt drinks, and such unique fare as pumpkin curry or carrot pudding make it special. At lunchtime, a reasonably priced buffet is served. *2299 S. El Camino Real near 23rd Ave., San Mateo, tel. 415/345–4366. AE, D, DC, MC, V. Sun. lunch 11–2, dinner 5–10.*

Italian *$$$–$$$$* **Carpaccio.** For those in love with the dish, the name says it all, and the rendition here is perfect: paper-thin beef with lemon and mustard, capers and onions, and a dribble of olive oil. In fact, most dishes at this northern Italian eatery are pretty good, from mozzarella salad to veal piccata to pizza from a brick oak-burning oven. *1120 Crane St. between Santa Cruz Ave. and Oak Grove, Menlo Park, tel. 415/322–1211. AE, DC, MC, V. Sun. 5–9.*

$$$ **Capellini.** If you reserve a table on the loft level, you may escape some of the bruising noise that fills this well-liked Peninsula eatery. As with so many other restaurants in the Bay Area, Pat Kuleto is responsible for the room's casual yet smart good looks, with its yards of rich wood and shiny fixtures. The resulting welcoming atmosphere encourages everyone to enjoy the salads, pastas, and seafood dishes that make up much of the menu. *310 Baldwin at South B, San Mateo, tel. 415/348–2296. MC, V. Sun. 5–9.*

$$$ **Il Fornaio.** One of many in the steadily growing chain of Il Fornaio eateries, this place has the same rotisserie-roasted meats and fowl, varied pastas, and classic pizzas pulled from a wood-burning oven that are found at the other branches. Just inside the door is a retail *panetteria* (bakery) that stocks the breads that are served with meals here, plus dozens of other tempting Il Fornaio bakery specialties that can be purchased on your way out. *327 Lorton Ave. at California, Burlingame, tel. 415/375–8000. AE, DC, MC, V. Sun. 8:30 AM–10 PM.*

$$$
CH, VG **Il Fornaio.** This branch of the deservedly popular chain is on the ground floor of the gorgeous Garden Court Hotel. As usual, the baked goods are fabulous; the antipasti, pizzas, and calzones are irresistible; and the ambience is simpatico. *520 Cowper St. near University, Palo Alto, tel. 415/853–3888. AE, DC, MC, V. Sun. 8 AM–11 PM.*

Japanese
$$$ **Fuki Sushi.** This is a perpetual favorite for its astounding variety of sushi—with as many as six different types of tuna alone and fresh fish flown in daily from around the globe—and for its feather-light tempura. *4119 El Camino Real near San Antonio Rd., Palo Alto, tel. 415/494–9383. AE, MC, V. Sun. 5–9:30.*

Mexican
$$–$$$
CH **Café Marimba.** Not long after chef Reed Hearon opened the instantly popular Café Marimba in San Francisco's Marina district (*see above*), he duplicated the success at this bright blue location in Burlingame. The same heady salsas, potent moles, and chunky guacamole are offered here, and a children's menu keeps the youngsters happy. *1100 Burlingame Ave. at California, Burlingame, tel. 415/347–0111. AE, MC, V. Sun. 11:30–9.*

Pizza
$–$$
CH, VG **Pacific Gourmet Pizza.** Sublime pizza (regular, wheat, or corn crusts), weird appetizers (margarita-marinated prawns on corn pancakes, deep-fried wontons stuffed with jalapeños), and sinful desserts make this place lots of fun. *1080 Shell Blvd., 10 min. from SF airport, Foster City, tel. 415/570–2253. MC, V. Sun. 5–10.*

$
CH, O, VG **Vicolo Pizzeria.** Gourmet pizza, California style, with a crisp cornmeal crust and a staggering range of fresh toppings is the specialty at this alluring eatery tucked into an alley with sidewalk seating. *473 University Ave. between Cowper and Kipling, Palo Alto, tel. 415/324–4877. Reservations not accepted. MC, V. Sun. 11:30–10.*

Seafood
$$$
CH **Duarte's Tavern.** This venerable tavern has been part of the small coastal community of Pescadero for over a century. Once nothing more than a saloon, it's now known as a homey seafood restaurant that serves great bowls of artichoke soup, fine fresh fish, and old-fashioned berry pie. Stop in and take a trip back in time. *202 Stage Rd., Pescadero, tel. 415/879–0464. MC, V. Sun. 7 AM–9 PM.*

$$$ **Kincaid's Bay House.** With striking views of the south bay and a museum-quality display of liquor at the bar, this place is reminiscent of a Cape Cod restaurant. The contemporary California cuisine features countless varieties of fresh fish, but carnivores can sink their teeth into succulent lamb or pork chops. *60 Bayview Pl. at Airport*

Blvd., Burlingame, tel. 415/342–9844. AE, D, DC, MC, V. Sun. 5–10.

Southeast Asian *$$$* *CH, O*
Ginger Club. Celebrated chef Bruce Cost has brought his sweeping knowledge of Asian food to this tropical site in the Stanford Shopping Center. Roast Chinese eggplant with ginger-sesame glaze, Indonesian satay with peanut sauce, wontons filled with pork and chives and served with hot vinegar-ginger sauce, and Thai yellow curry noodles with scallops are among the most popular dishes. The house-made ginger ale is a must. *2A Stanford Shopping Center, Palo Alto, tel. 415/325–6588. MC, V. Sun. 11:30–10.*

Spanish *$$$–$$$$* *O*
Iberia Restaurant. Stumble into a rustic inn amid the trees in the hills above Stanford and lounge on the garden patio in the company of the idle rich for superb Spanish regional cuisine. Sample everything from tapas and lamb, shellfish and paella to homemade dessert tortes. The extensive selection of sherries is a perfect complement. *190 Ladera-Alpine Rd. (¼ mi west of I–280 on Alpine Rd.), Portola Valley, tel. 415/854–1746. AE, D, MC, V. Sun. lunch 11–2, dinner 5:30–10.*

Marin County

You could while away a score of Sundays exploring the culinary delights of Marin County's towns. Starting with Sausalito, the prime destination for day-trippers to Marin County, the possibilities are limitless. Though Marin County suffers from tourist traps serving so-so food at inflated prices, there are plenty of gems that give good value, good views, and good food.

American Casual *$$$–$$$$* *O, VU*
Horizons Restaurant. The building, dating back to 1869, was originally the San Francisco Yacht Club. Today the multitier dining room and deck provide superb vistas, and for a view-oriented place packed with tourists, the kitchen turns out surprisingly good fare. Brunch options include all the classics, as well as steak and eggs. Fresh seafood is broiled, sautéed, or tossed with pasta or salad. The open-faced, hot crab melt sandwich with mushrooms and green onions on rye is a winner. *558 Bridgeway near Princess, Sausalito, tel. 415/331–3232. AE, MC, V. Sun. 10–9. Closed 2 wks in Dec.*

$$$–$$$$ *CH, O, VU*
Mountain Home Inn. This mellow rural hostelry with panoramic views serves American cuisine with plenty of forays into the overseas pantry. During brunch, that can mean anything from classic French toast or a smoked salmon omelet to Indonesian salad with marinated chicken and a spicy peanut dressing, a hefty half-pound burger on a sourdough roll, or curried prawns in cream sauce. You'll have to fight for seating on the outdoor patio. *810 Panoramic Hwy. (off Rte. 1), Mill Valley, tel. 415/381–9000. MC, V. Sun. 8 AM–9 PM.*

$$$ *CH*
Buckeye Roadhouse. A cross between a roadside speakeasy and a hunting lodge, this unusual eatery is decorated with animal parts. The fare, all based on wonderfully fresh ingredients, is hearty and creative—from roast Petaluma duck, barbecued baby-back ribs, and braised lamb shank to a top-notch Caesar salad and onion rings with house-made catsup. Leave room for baked lemon pudding or s'more pie. *15 Shoreline Hwy. (Stinson Beach exit from I–101), Mill Valley, tel. 415/331–2600. D, DC, MC, V. Sun. 10:30–10.*

$$–$$$ *O, VU*
Sand Dollar. It's the only bar in Stinson Beach and the owner is the fire chief, so you'll find a lot of locals hanging out on the outdoor deck of this cheerful pub. The fare includes burgers with homemade fries, sandwiches, and salads, and there's mud pie for dessert. Eat before sundown—the seafood and pastas at dinner are mundane. *Rte. 1, Stinson Beach, tel. 415/868–0434. Reservations not accepted at brunch. MC, V. Sun. brunch 11-3, dinner 5–9:30.*

$$–$$$ *O, VG*
Station House Cafe. It's easy to see why this light, airy café with a garden patio and pictures by local photographers is a favorite. Any-

thing grilled (chicken, salmon, mussels) is great, and there are always a couple of vegetarian dishes. *11180 Rte. 1, Point Reyes Station, tel. 415/663–1515. MC, V. Sun. 8 AM–10 PM.*

$$ *O, VU* **Half Day Cafe.** This former old brick mechanic's garage was converted into a sunny, spacious restaurant with a large open kitchen and a garden patio. There are great omelets, scones, and espresso at breakfast; dinner items (noodles, fresh seafood, salads) range from innovative dishes with an Asian twist to such down-home treats as meat loaf and fruit cobbler. *848 College Ave. near Sir Francis Drake Blvd., Kentfield, tel. 415/459–0291. MC, V. Sun. brunch 8–2:30, dinner 5:30–9:30.*

$ *CH* **Bubba's Diner.** With a checkerboard floor, comfy booths, counter seating, and '50s music, this is a classic diner. Almost everything is homemade—from potato pancakes to fresh roasted turkey, corned beef hash, and chocolate cake—with an updated California flair showing up in such items as orange juice whole-grain pancakes and elaborate salads. Kids get coloring books, crayons, and their own menu. *566 San Anselmo Ave. near Tunstead Ave., San Anselmo, tel. 515/459–6862. MC, V. Sun. breakfast and brunch 7:30–2, dinner 5:30–9.*

$ *CH, O, VG, VU* **Gray Whale Inn.** Home-style pizzas, pastries and coffee, sandwiches, vegetarian lasagna, and a sunny patio with a vista of the bay and the mountains make this a perfect lazy-day pick. *12781 Sir Francis Drake Blvd., Inverness, tel. 415/669–1244. Reservations not accepted. MC, V. Sun. 11–8.*

$ *CH* **Lighthouse Coffee Shop.** This bare-bones coffee shop is a blessed relief to families on a budget, early risers, and anyone looking for good basic food (burgers, sandwiches, omelets, roast turkey) served without hype. *1311 Bridgeway, Sausalito, tel. 415/331–3034. Reservations not accepted. No credit cards. Sun. 7 AM–3 PM.*

American Contemporary *$$$$–$$$$$* *CH, O* **Lark Creek Inn.** Chef-owner Bradley Ogden is the undisputed king of American regional cuisine, and this dollhouse-like Victorian in a grove of redwoods is his showcase. The magnificent interior has a huge central skylight, a stone-floor sun porch, and a wood-burning brick oven. The menu changes daily to feature American favorites, such as masterfully prepared Yankee pot roast, roasted salmon, grilled double-cut pork chops, or grilled rabbit. Portions are huge, the wine list is all-American, and Sunday brunch in the garden (wild berry flapjacks, banana–sour cream pancakes, corned beef or salmon hash) is a delight. *234 Magnolia Ave. (north edge of town), Larkspur, tel. 415/924–7766. AE, DC, MC, V. Sun. brunch 10–2, dinner 5–10.*

$$$$ *VU* **Casa Madrona.** Sunday brunch on the deck is sublime, though dinner in the glass-enclosed dining room runs a close second. The hotel complex includes a stately old Victorian, a white stucco manor, and a scattering of cottages all perched on a steep hillside above Sausalito. Prices are also steep, but in this case the ocean-fresh fish, grilled meats, and seasonal produce are so creatively engineered and presented that you get your money's worth. *801 Bridgeway, Sausalito, tel. 415/331–5888. AE, D, DC, MC, V. Sun. brunch 10–2:15, dinner 6–9:15.*

$$$–$$$$ **Manka's.** Regional cuisine featuring wild game (venison, caribou, elk, quail) and freshly caught fish, as well as vegetarian specials, appear on the bill of fare at this renovated 1917 hunting lodge. A huge fireplace, candlelight, and flamboyant floral arrangements make the dinner hour richly atmospheric. *Corner of Callendar Way and Argyll, Inverness, tel. 4415/669–1034. MC, V. Sun. 5:30–8:30.*

Continental *$$$$* *O, VU* **Alta Mira.** Reservations are mandatory for brunch on the terrace of this vintage Spanish-style hotel with a spectacular view of Sausalito harbor, Angel Island, and San Francisco. Cocktails at sunset are equally popular, and while the place has never gotten raves for its food, such fresh fish entreés as poached Pacific salmon are a fair bet. The glass-enclosed dining room has knockout views. *125 Bulkley*

Ave. off Princess, Sausalito, tel. 415/332–1350. AE, D, MC, V. Sun. brunch 7:30–4:30, dinner 5–10.

$
CH, O **Sweden House.** A sign on the deck of this combination café and take-out bakery says, "Please watch your food or the birds will eat it." The birds are after the pastries, breakfast specialties, sandwiches (avocado, bacon, and sprouts; smoked Pacific salmon; asparagus tips and Danish ham), and desserts (princess cake with Bavarian cream, marzipan, and raspberries). Fortify yourself with an espresso and fight them off; this food is worth defending. *35 Main St. near Tiburon Blvd., Tiburon, tel. 415/435–9767. Reservations not accepted. MC, V. Sun. 8–6 (later in summer).*

Czech
$$$
O **Vladimir's.** Vladimir himself bustles around tending bar, waiting tables, and making bad "check" puns. There are equestrian photos, a fireplace, just a couple of tables, a few choice booths inside, and a large patio out front. The prix fixe dinners (roast pork, veal, sausages) are hearty, authentic, and delicious and are accompanied by feather-light dumplings. *Sir Francis Drake Blvd., center of town, Inverness, tel. 415/669–1021. No credit cards. Sun. noon–9.*

English
$$$
CH **Pelican Inn.** After a tramp through the countryside, down a pint of Harp or Guinness at this English Tudor inn complete with antique decor and dartboard. The Sunday buffet lunch includes roast beef and turkey. At dinner, prime rib, rack of lamb, and grilled fish entrées alternate with lighter California fare, but the British theme is nicely advanced with trifle and bread pudding for dessert. *10 Pacific Way off Rte. 1 (Rte. 1/Stinson exit from I–101 N), Muir Beach, tel. 415/383–6000. MC, V. Sun. buffet lunch 11:30–3:30, dinner 5:30–9:30.*

French
$$$
O, VU **Left Bank.** Pick a sunny day for brunch or lunch and reserve a marble-topped table on the veranda of this utterly French bistro. (Heat lamps allow for outdoor dining on chilly days as well.) The generous, homey fare will make you dream of meals you've enjoyed along the road in the French countryside—salade lyonnaise, coq au vin, steak pommes frites, duck confit with lentils. For those on strike against European food, there is a burger Americain at lunch. *Blue Rock Inn, 507 Magnolia Ave., Larkspur, tel. 415/927–3331. AE, MC, V. Sun. 10–10.*

Italian
$$$ **Frantoio.** The centerpiece of this outsized, high-ceiling restaurant is a massive olive press that crushes some 300 tons of olives each season, creating about fifteen gallons of high-quality extra-virgin oil for every 800 pounds that are fed through the granite grinding stones. You can watch it in action in the late fall as you sample the restaurant's above-average renditions of such classic Italian fare as pizzas, pastas, and grilled meats. *152 Shoreline Hwy., Mill Valley, tel. 415/289–5777. AE, MC, V. Sun. 11:30–10.*

$$$
CH, O, VG, VU **Il Fornaio.** This upscale chain dishes up dynamite Tuscan cuisine. At this branch you'll find softly colored walls, dark mahogany, views of Mt. Tamalpais from the outdoor terrace, and terrific rotisserie meats, pastas, pizzas, breads, and pastries, as well as a tempting bar menu. *223 Corte Madera Town Center (Paradise Dr. exit from I–101 N), Corte Madera, tel. 415/927–4400. AE, D, DC, MC, V. Sun.brunch 9–2, dinner until 10.*

$$$
O, VU **Tutto Mare.** The promise of a panoramic view of the San Francisco skyline from a two-level waterside setting is enough to win anyone over to the Tutto Mare. The first-floor bar and dining area, called La Taverna, is the the more casual of the two, with antipasti, pizzas, and salads as the most popular items. Upstairs at Il Ristorante, there are house-made pastas, an abundance of fresh seafood dishes, meats grilled over wood, and more. Watch the boats on the bay on Sunday mornings as you drink a bloody Mary or Bellini and feast on brioche with eggs, prosciutto, and fontina. *9 Main St. between the Tiburon Ferry and Island Ferry landings, Tiburon, tel. 415/435–4747. AE, DC, MC, V. Sun. brunch 10–2, dinner until 10.*

Japanese *\$\$\$–\$\$\$\$* **Sushi Ran.** This small, lively sushi bar, well off the beaten tourist track, is a key pit stop for local celebrities. The fish are superfresh, the presentations are gorgeous, the portions are generous, and the selection of sake is staggering. *107 Caledonia St., next to Marin Theater between Turney and Johnson, Sausalito, tel. 415/332–3620. Reservations not accepted. AE, D, MC, V. Sun. 5:30–10.*

\$\$–\$\$\$ *CH, VG* **Robata Grill & Sushi.** Enjoy the atmosphere of a Japanese country inn by sharing an excellent sampling of sushi and delicacies from the *robata* (Japanese for "grill") with your table mates. Full dinners and a children's menu are also available. *591 Redwood Hwy. in Shelterpoint Business Center (Seminary Dr. exit from I–101), Mill Valley, tel. 415/381–8400. AE, D, MC, V. Sun. 5:30–9:30.*

Mexican *\$\$\$* *CH, VU* **Guaymas.** This colorful, convivial restaurant with views of Tiburon harbor and the San Francisco skyline offers great margaritas and deliciously different regional Mexican specialties. The combination of seafood, red meat, produce, and poultry with delectable sauces and three different salsas make a meal here special. *5 Main St. at ferry terminal, Tiburon, tel. 415/435–6300. AE, DC, MC, V. Sun. 10:30–9:30.*

\$\$ *CH, O* **Las Camelias Mexican Restaurant.** The colorful artwork on the stucco walls of this family-operated cantina is as lively as the spicing in the lovingly prepared Jalisco specialties. The burrito Mexicana, seafood brochettes, and *pollo en mole* (a chocolate-based chicken dish) will make your taste buds sing. *912 Lincoln Ave. between 3rd and 4th Sts., San Rafael, tel. 415/453–5850. AE, MC, V. Sun. 3–9.*

\$\$ *CH, MU, O, VU* **Margaritaville.** Likened to a Caribbean vacation without the airfare, this upbeat eatery serves tropically hip Mexican cuisine. The large deck overlooking Richardson Bay and Belvedere Island is the place to sit, fajitas are the most popular meal (though the bar appetizers provide a tempting detour), and margaritas are the drink of choice. The proprietors promise "great bands." *1200 Bridgeway, 2 blocks north of downtown, Sausalito, tel. 415/331–3226. AE, MC, V. Sun. 11:30–10.*

Seafood *\$\$\$* *CH, O, VU* **Old Sam's Anchor Cafe.** This popular 1920s watering hole has mahogany wainscoting, old photos, and a deck with great views. The specialty is fresh fish served every which way. Kids get free crayons and a color-in menu, and adults generally get tipsy. *27 Main St. near Tiburon Blvd., ½ block from ferry terminal, Tiburon, tel. 415/435–4527. AE, D, MC, V. Sun. 9:30–10.*

\$\$\$ *VU* **The Spinnaker.** The primary draw is the dramatic bay view from a point beyond the harbor, but homemade pastas and such seafood specialties as fresh grilled salmon provide satisfactory sustenance as well. *100 Spinnaker Dr., off Anchor St. near Bridgeway, Sausalito, tel. 415/332–1500. AE, D, MC, V. Sun. 11–11.*

Thai *\$\$–\$\$\$* *VG* **Royal Thai.** The barbecued chicken, coconut-milk curry, pad Thai noodles, and green papaya salad served at this restored Victorian under the freeway are outstanding. Prices are surprisingly low in view of the comfortable decor and solicitous service. *610 3rd St. near Irwin, San Rafael, tel. 415/485–1074. AE, DC, MC, V. Sun. 5–10.*

The Wine Country

One of the peak sensory pleasures that the Bay Area has to offer is a Sunday drive to Napa or Sonoma County for wine tasting and wonderful food. The range of wineries includes everything from Rutherford's relatively new St. Supery—complete with a comprehensive self-guided tour—to the erudite Hess Collection at Napa, where the tasting room adjoins galleries displaying the fine modern art collection of Swiss-born Donald Hess. To explore the culinary heritage of the area, start with the early settlers from Italy, France, and Mexico; add a new wave of world-class chefs emigrating from the city; draw upon the area's abundance of fresh produce, meats, and prime ingredients; and the result is restaurants that have become destinations in their own right.

American Casual *$$$–$$$$* **Wine Spectator Greystone Restaurant.** At last, the Culinary Institute of America, the nation's premiere chefs' school, has opened a West Coast branch. Open since fall 1995, Greystone capitalizes on West Coast bounty: It's in the heart of the Wine Country, in the former home of Christian Brothers Winery. Staffed by the cooking school's students, the restaurant has gone through ups and downs with its Mediterranean–inspired menu. A large array of small dishes, more like tapas, include roasted sweet peppers, eggplants, and leek-and-chicken terrine with aioli. Nicely roasted poussin or rustic monkfish with fennel and onions are among the better main courses. A large open kitchen stands in the middle of the dining room, and everyone from the pastry chef to the grill master takes part. Handcrafted wood tables, brightly colored chairs, and sleek wall sconces add style to the immense structure. *2555 Main St., St. Helena, tel. 707/967–1010. AE, DC, MC, V. Sun. lunch 11:30–3, dinner 5:30–9.*

$$$ *O* **Calistoga Inn.** Hardwood grilled fish and meats are the draw at this turn-of-the-century inn. The truly mellow will opt for patio seating in the garden. *1250 Lincoln Ave. downtown, Calistoga, tel. 707/942–4101. MC, V. Sun. lunch 11-3, dinner 5:30–9:30.*

$$$ *CH, O, VU* **The Grill.** This casual bistro at the opulent Meadowood resort features soups, garden-fresh salads, sandwiches on homemade bread, a special menu and milk shakes for kids, alfresco dining, and a view of the golf course and croquet lawns. *900 Meadowood La. (turn right on Howell Mt. Rd. off the Silverado Trail), St. Helena, tel. 707/963–3646. AE, D, DC, MC, V. Sun. 7 AM–9:30 PM.*

$$$ **Mustards Grill.** This popular bistro has marble floors, upbeat artwork, a great wine list, lots of customers, and lots of noise. The menu features American food with Asian, Mexican, and Indian embellishments. Onion rings, baby-back ribs, and fresh grilled fish are good bets. *7399 St. Helena Hwy., 1 mi north of Yountville, Yountville, tel. 707/944–2424. D, DC, MC, V. Sun. 11:30–8:30 (winter), 11:30–10 (summer).*

$$–$$$ **Silverado Restaurant & Tavern.** In a setting straight from a spaghetti western, savvy locals and seasoned wine connoisseurs linger over wines priced just above retail. The eclectic menu includes egg rolls, chicken-salad sandwiches, Caesar salad, and great burgers. *1373 Lincoln Ave., Calistoga, tel. 707/942–6725. MC, V. Sun. 8 AM–11 PM.*

$$ *CH* **The Diner.** Banana pecan waffles, local sausages, and house potatoes for breakfast, and a health-oriented menu of Mexican classics and fresh California cuisine make this a popular stop. *6476 Washington St. at Oak Circle, Yountville, tel. 707/944–2626. No credit cards. Sun. breakfast and lunch 8–3, dinner 5:30–9.*

$–$$ *CH* **Los Robles Lodge Dining Room.** This user-friendly eatery has the feel of the '50s, with a burgundy interior, stained glass, and a budget approach to dining that's popular with an older crowd and families with kids. There are complimentary hors d'oeuvres, soup, and salad; featured favorites, such as roast leg of lamb, London broil, and corned beef and cabbage; and a Sunday buffet brunch that's a huge hit. *9255 Edwards Ave. (Steele La. exit west from Rte. 101), Santa Rosa, tel. 707/545–6330. AE, D, DC, MC, V. Sun. brunch 10–2, dinner 4:30–9.*

$ *CH, VG* **Omelette Express.** Choose from a list of 300 different omelets at this friendly eatery in historic Railroad Square. *112 4th St. near Wilson, Santa Rosa, tel. 707/525–1690. Reservations not accepted. MC, V. Sun. 7:00–4 PM.*

American Contemporary *$$$$$* *O, VU* **Auberge du Soleil.** From its site atop a hill in an old olive grove, this place exudes rustic elegance: earth tones, wood beams, an outdoor deck, and panoramic views of Napa Valley bring to mind the aura of Provence. Prices are high, but the food (roasted lobster sausage, braised California pheasant, Dungeness crab quesadillas) is heavenly. *180 Rutherford Hill Rd., off Silverado Trail north of Rte. 128, Rutherford, tel. 707/963–1211. Reservations essential. AE, D, MC, V. Sun. 7–11.*

$$$$$
O, VU **The Grill at Sonoma Mission Inn.** Expect the pinnacle of Wine Country cuisine (and a separate spa menu) in this airy pink stucco dining room with vaulted ceilings, original art, and French windows leading onto a patio. Select from such fare as Sonoma leg of lamb or basil-roasted chicken with garlic-mashed potatoes, or better yet, opt for the prix fixe dinner, which includes the perfect wine to complement each course. *2 mi north of Sonoma on Rte. 12, Sonoma, tel. 707/938–9000, ext. 415. Reservations essential. AE, DC, MC, V. Sun. brunch 10–2, dinner 6–9:30.*

$$$$$
O, VU **The Restaurant at Madrona Manor.** Chef Todd Muir keeps a kitchen garden and uses fresh Sonoma produce, Bay Area lamb, and choice seafood to create such memorable dishes as Dungeness crab mousse or smoked lamb salad. Dinner by candlelight or brunch on the deck of this 1881 Victorian mansion surrounded by 8 acres of grounds is a trip to fantasyland. *1001 Westside Rd. (Central Healdsburg exit from I–101, left on Mill St.), Healdsburg, tel. 707/433–4231. Reservations essential. AE, DC, MC, V. Sun. brunch 11–2, dinner 6–9.*

$$$$–$$$$$
O, VU **John Ash & Co.** Fresh seafood, lamb, wild game, and organic produce from an on-site kitchen garden round out a stellar menu. The setting is a Spanish villa with an outdoor patio in a picture-perfect vineyard. *4330 Barnes Rd. (River Rd. exit off I–101), Santa Rosa, tel. 707/527–7687. D, MC, V. Sun. brunch 10:30–2, dinner 5:30–9.*

$$–$$$$$
O, VU **Silverado Country Club.** This famed resort has three restaurants. Vintner's Court has a brunch buffet on Sundays, with classic morning fare as well as some Pacific Rim touches. Royal Oak specializes in seafood and steak dinners. The Bar and Grill is perfect for those who want to get out on the golf course early or come in at midday for a top-notch salad or sandwich. *1600 Atlas Peak Rd. (follow signs to Lake Berryessa), Napa, tel. 707/257–0200. Reservations essential for restaurants, not accepted for Bar and Grill. AE, DC, MC, V. Sun. brunch at Vintner's Court has 3 seatings, 9:30, 11:30, 1:30 (5$); dinner at Royal Oak (4$) 5:30–10; breakfast, lunch at Bar and Grill (2$–3$) 6:30–5:30.*

$$$$
O **Lisa Hemenway's.** Works by local artists, Mexican tile floors, grape-motif upholstery, and patio seating in a garden setting create a mellow backdrop for chef Lisa Hemenway's culinary tour of Southwest, Thai, and Mediterranean cuisines. Tote Cuisine, Hemenway's take-out operation next door, has great picnic fixings. *714 Village Ct. Mall near Village Mall Gardens, Santa Rosa, tel. 707/526–5111. D, MC, V. Sun. lunch 11:30–2:30, dinner 5–9.*

$$$$
V **Napa Valley Wine Train.** Many American travelers miss the days when train travel meant enjoying a meal in the dining car as they watched the landscape roll by. This Napa Valley express, with its beautifully refurbished vintage Pullman parlor cars, recaptures that classic experience on a 36-mile journey through the state's best-known wine region. Breakfast, lunch, and dinner are served aboard the train. Eggs scrambled with caviar and freshly baked scones and croissants are among the morning items; beef tenderloin, Sonoma lamb with port wine sauce, and broiled salmon are served later in the day. *1275 McKinstry near 1st St., Napa, tel. 707/253–2111 or 800/427–4124. AE, D, DC, MC, V. Sun. departures (call for times).*

$$$–$$$$
CH **All Season's Cafe.** The superb, reasonably priced wine list is just part of the allure of this sunny bistro. The organic greens, home-made bread and desserts, local game birds, and house-smoked strip loin of beef are truly seductive. *1400 Lincoln Ave. near Washington, Calistoga, tel. 707/942–9111. MC, V. Sun. lunch 11–3, dinner 5–9, June–Oct. 'til 10.*

$$$–$$$$
O, VU **Anesti's Grill.** Inside, you can feast your eyes on leg of lamb and duckling roasted on the only French rotisserie in Napa; out on the patio, you can feast them on views of vineyards and hills. The food here has a Mediterranean flair. Rack of lamb from the mesquite grill

is the house specialty. *6518 Washington St., Yountville, tel. 707/944–1500. AE, DC, MC, V. Sun. lunch and dinner.*

$$$–$$$$ *O* **Catahoula Restaurant and Saloon.** Although chef Jan Birnbaum hails from Louisiana and has named his comfortable and lively restaurant for the state dog, the menu here goes far beyond his southern roots. The range of dishes is unabashedly varied: meaty short ribs with mashed potatoes, whole roasted fish seasoned with fresh fennel, hearty chicken gumbo, andouille-topped pizza. Save room for the bread pudding and down-home pies that often turn up on the dessert card. The adjoining saloon offers small plates served at long, communal tables. *1457 Lincoln Ave., Calistoga, tel. 707/942–2275. MC, V. Sun. noon–3:30, 5:30–10.*

$$$ *O* **Stars Oakville Café.** Chef Jeremiah Tower has transplanted some of his big-city Stars Cafe know-how (*see* Civic Center, *above*) to the beautiful Napa Valley. The rear of the pleasantly simple, small restaurant opens onto a lovely garden complete with a dovecote. In the warm months, dining tables are set up overlooking the carefully tended landscape. The kitchen cooks up a nice "light fry" of mixed seafood and a highly respectable burger at lunchtime. Come nightfall the menu goes more upscale, with grilled fresh fish and poultry among the best items. Desserts, as at every Tower enterprise, are top drawer. *7848 Hwy. 29, Oakville, tel. 707/944–8905. MC, V. Sun. noon–3, 5:30–9.*

$$–$$$ **Bistro Ralph.** An exceedingly friendly wait staff and a couple of trees perched on the bar temper the industrial setting here. The food—whether it's Szechuan pepper calamari, a juicy lamb burger, or braised lamb shanks with mint essence—is home-style, and the wine list features picks from small local wineries. Note the unusual, eye-catching wine rack of metal and wood. *109 Plaza St., Healdsburg, tel. 707/433–1380. MC, V. Sun. 5:30–10.*

Continental

$$$$$ *O, VU* **The Restaurant at Meadowood.** Dine in a formal resort setting straight out of a Fitzgerald novel, or perch primly on the patio of the pink-and-gray clubhouse and watch croquet players whacking balls about on the lawns below. The classic French cuisine features Napa produce, game, and meats. *900 Meadowood La. (turn right on Howell Mtn. Rd. off the Silverado Trail), St. Helena, tel. 707/963–3646. Jacket required. AE, D, DC, MC, V. Sun. brunch 11–2, dinner 5–9:30.*

French

$$$$$ *O, VU* **Domaine Chandon.** The menu changes daily, offering lamb, poultry, seafood, and venison deftly prepared and presented in a light French style. The cavernous dining room and tree-shaded patio look out over miles of vineyards and native oak trees. *California Dr. (Yountville exit off Rte. 29 toward Veterans' Home), Yountville, tel. 707/944–2892. Reservations essential. Jacket required. AE, D, DC, MC, V. Sun. lunch 11:30–2:30, dinner 6–9:30.*

$$$$$ *O, VG* **French Laundry.** Although this restaurant is a valley old-timer, chef Thomas Keller breathed exciting new life into the onetime stone laundry in 1993. If you go in the evening, be prepared to spend a relaxing three to four hours nibbling your way through Keller's five-course prix fixe menu, the vegetable-tasting menu, or the nine-course chef's tasting menu. Among the complimentary canapés, you might start off with imaginative salmon-and-caviar ice cream cones or "bacon and eggs," which uses tiny quail eggs. Each of the dinners includes a series of small, exquisite plates of intricately presented foods and an elaborate dessert. At lunch, Keller scales back to three- and four-course menus. In keeping with the spirit of the restaurant's name, white linen napkins are suspended from clothespins at each of the elegant place settings and the check is delivered on a laundry tag. A beautiful garden, complete with a flourishing herb plot, is just out the door. *6640 Washington St. at Creek, Yountville, tel. 707/944–2380. Reservations essential. AE, MC, V. Sun. lunch noon–1:30, dinner 5:30–10.*

$$$–$$$$ *O, VU* **Kenwood Restaurant & Bar.** Open and airy, with French doors opening to patios and vineyard and mountain views, this is where local chefs go on their nights off to indulge in such French country fare as braised rabbit or sweetbread salad. *9900 Rte. 12, Kenwood, tel. 707/833–6326. MC, V. Sun. 11:30–9.*

Italian *$$$$* *CH, O, VG* **Tra Vigne.** San Franciscans consistently vote this striking trattoria a hands-down favorite for its alluring Mediterranean ambience, inviting courtyard, and seductive Tuscan cuisine. Seating is hopeless without a reservation, but drop-ins can sample homemade snacks—breads, pasta, mozzarella, proscuitto—at the bar. In the corner of the courtyard, the Cantinetta offers picnic fare and wine by the glass. *1050 Charter Oak Ave. (off Hwy. 29), St. Helena, tel. 707/963–4444. Reservations essential. D, DC, MC, V. Sun. 11:30–10.*

$$$ **Bistro Don Giovanni.** This casual, Mediterranean-style restaurant offers delectable antipasti; rustic pastas; wood-fired pizzas; and memorable main plates, from roast chicken to braised lamb. The full bar is stocked with plenty of Napa wines. Don't miss the delectable fruit-crisp dessert. *4110 St. Helena Hwy., Napa, tel. 707/224–3300. AE, DC, MC, V. Sun. 11:30–10.*

$$$ *CH, O, VG* **Piatti.** The Sonoma cousin of the Napa Valley Piatti, this place is equally popular for its tempting regional Italian cuisine, including spit-roasted chicken, ravioli with lemon cream, and pizza from a wood-burning oven. It's in the El Dorado Hotel (a 19th-century landmark building) and has a convivial country-Italian decor with bright murals, an open kitchen, and an outdoor patio. *405 1st St. W, facing Sonoma Plaza, Sonoma, tel. 707/996–2351. AE, MC, V. Sun. 11:30–10.*

$$$ *CH, O, VG, VU* **Piatti.** As with its Sonoma twin (*see above*), country Italian ambience and regional Italian pastas and risottos make for a winning combo. Here, alfresco dining on the patio offers a view of the vineyards. *6480 Washington St. (Yountville/Veterans' Home exit from Rte. 29 N), Yountville, tel. 707/944–2070. AE, MC, V. Sun. 11:30–10.*

$$ *CH* **The Cafe.** The open-kitchen café at the Sonoma Mission is renowned for its country breakfasts, pizza from a wood-burning oven, and regional Italian cuisine. *18140 Sonoma Hwy., 2 mi north of Sonoma at juncture of Rte. 12 and Boyes Blvd., Sonoma, tel. 707/938–9000. AE, DC, MC, V. Sun. 7 AM–9:30 PM.*

$ *CH* **Boskos.** Pasta and pizza at reasonable prices in a newly restored sandstone building from the 1800s make this a popular place for carbo-loading between winery tours. *1364 Lincoln Ave. downtown, Calistoga, tel. 707/942–9088. Reservations not accepted. No credit cards. Sun. 11–10.*

Mediterranean *$$$$$* **Terra.** The ambience is warm and cozy in this 1884 fieldstone building with terra-cotta floors, and chef Hiro Sone's culinary waltz through southern French and northern Italian cuisine—with an occasional foray to the Orient—is something to write home about. *1345 Railroad Ave., 1 block east of Main St. between Hunt and Adams, St. Helena, tel. 707/963–8931. Reservations essential. MC, V. Sun. 6–9.*

$$$$ *CH, O, VG, VU* **Brava Terrace.** This casual restaurant boasts a stone fireplace and a terrace and deck—great for alfresco dining—overlooking the Napa Valley and Howell Mountain. A small garden alongside the restaurant supplies some of the lettuces that go into the superb salads, and a long-cooked cassoulet earns rave reviews. *3010 St. Helena Hwy. (Rte. 29), 1½ mi north of St. Helena, Oakville, tel. 707/963–9300. AE, D, DC, MC, V. Sun. noon–9.*

Mexican
$
CH, O, VU
La Casa. Come here for a festive atmosphere, patio dining, and a view of a historic mission next door, along with good fajitas, fish dishes, chimichangas, and margaritas at reasonable prices. *121 E. Spain St. off town square, Sonoma, tel. 707/996–3406. AE, DC, MC, V. Sun. 11:30–10.*

Seafood
$$$
O, VG
Eastside Oyster Bar & Grill. Chef-owner Charles Saunders, former star of the Sonoma Mission Inn, does a great job preparing fresh fish, local meat and poultry, and produce from the organic kitchen garden. There's a marble shellfish bar, fireplace, and intimate bistro atmosphere inside, a wisteria-draped terrace with a picture-window view into the pastry kitchen outside. The hangtown fry gets raves, and you'll also find creative renditions of roast chicken, Sonoma lamb, salads, and vegetarian specialties. *133 E. Napa St. off Sonoma Plaza, Sonoma, tel. 707/939–1266. AE, DC, MC, V. Sun. lunch noon–3, dinner 5:30–9.*

Steak
$$–$$$
CH, VU
Jonesy's Famous Steak House. Steaks weighted with Sacramento River rocks and sizzled on a dry grill are the specialty here, along with roasted chicken and fresh fish. The wall of windows looking onto an airport landing strip have made this a hit with kids of all ages since 1946. *2044 Airport Rd., Napa Valley Airport (between Napa and Vallejo off intersection of Rtes. 12 and 29), Napa, tel. 707/255–2003. AE, D, DC, MC, V. Sun. 11:30–8. Closed Christmas week.*

Sweets and Treats

The Castro
CH, O
Just Desserts. Sample some of the best Danishes, scones, classic American desserts, espresso drinks, and Italian sodas around in this exposed-brick building with wood booths and an intimate back garden. The atmosphere is mellow, the crowd mixed with gays and straights. *248 Church St., 1 block south of Market, tel. 415/626–5774. MC, V. Sun. 8 AM–11 PM.*

CH
The Original Double Rainbow. There are just eight seats, so plan to stroll away with cones, sundaes, shakes, frozen yogurt, and espresso drinks. *407 Castro St. near Market, tel. 415/621–2350. No credit cards. Sun. 11–11.*

CH
Sweet Inspiration. A copacetic hangout with an espresso bar and noteworthy Danish pastries and cheesecake. *2239 Market St. near Sanchez, tel. 415/621–8664. No credit cards. Sun. 8 AM–11:30 PM.*

Chinatown
CH
Eastern Bakery. This is the ideal place to sample black bean, lotus, and melon cake and other exotic Chinatown sweets. *720 Grant St. at Commercial, tel. 415/392–4497. No credit cards. Sun. 8–7.*

CH
Golden Gate Fortune Cookie Factory. It doesn't just sell cookies, it takes you right to the source and lets you see the fascinating Rube Goldberg fortune-cookie machinery in action. *56 Ross Alley, between Washington and Jackson, tel. 415/781–3956. No credit cards. Sun. 10–7.*

Civic Center
CH
Mad Magda's Russian Tea Room and Cafe. In this eccentric hideaway, you can have your tarot cards read as you sip espresso or tea and munch on scones and pastries. *579 Hayes St. between Octavia and Laguna, tel. 415/864–7654. No credit cards. Sun. 9–7.*

The Pendragon Bakery Cafe. This artsy oasis has a rotating selection of cakes, pies, trifles, tortes, and cheesecakes, as well as savory pastries and fresh vegetable and pasta salads. *400 Hayes St. at Gough, tel. 415/552–7017. No credit cards. Sun. 6:30–5.*

A number of eateries in the area, including **Stars, Stars Cafe,** and **Spuntino** (*see* Civic Center in Restaurants, *above*) encourage patrons to drop in for dessert. Stars and Stars Cafe have daily changing menus of such renowned selections as coconut custard pie with mango and blackberry sauces. At Spuntino, you're likely to see a couple of ballerinas at the next table sharing a chocolate mousse cake.

Embarcadero The **Park Hyatt** (*see* **Park Grill,** Embarcadero, *above*) lulls the senses with live piano music, afternoon tea (3–4:30), and caviar service (4:30–8) in the Lobby Lounge, as well as a lethal sampling of four desserts entitled "Death by Chocolate" (11 AM–1 AM). **Il Fornaio, Splendido, Square One, Scott's,** and the **Waterfront** encourage patrons to drop by for dessert any old time, while **Gordon Biersch Brewery** welcomes customers for dessert during off-peak hours. Stop by the bakery at Il Fornaio for superb Italian pastries. Splendido offers warm chocolate gâteau with vanilla ice cream, while dessert specials at Square One change daily. Scott's features cheesecake and a dessert sampler. The Waterfront delivers shortcake with fruit. Gordon Biersch serves homemade ice cream, individual tartlets, and warm fruit turnovers.

Financial District/ Jackson Square Several restaurants in the area cater to those with a craving for sweets (*see* Financial District/Jackson Square in Restaurants, *above*, for details on the following). **Bix** welcomes drop-ins for dessert at the bar. In the **Carnelian Room** lounge, dessert specialties include chocolate decadence cake or Carnelian strawberries and come with a 360° view. At **Cypress Club,** treats range from warm chocolate black-walnut cake to an ice-cream and sorbet sampler. **Clown Alley** keeps serving desserts and shakes till 1 in the morning.

The Haight

CH **Gelato.** Tiny, sinfully rich scoops of Italian ice cream come in a variety of flavors. *201 Parnassus St. near Stanyan, tel. 415/566–9696. No credit cards. Sun. 4–11.*

L **Ground Zero.** There's a rotating display of works by local artists, and a new generation of black-clad bohemians sustaining themselves on pastries and espresso drinks (along with sandwiches, beer, and wine). The *caffè lattes* and brownies are tops. *783 Haight St. at Scott, tel. 415/252–9525. No credit cards. Sun. 8 AM–midnight.*

L **Horseshoe Coffee House.** Bring reading material and a brooding demeanor to this lower Haight hangout for the slacker generation. *566 Haight St. between Steiner and Fillmore, tel. 415/626–8852. No credit cards. Sun. 7 AM–1 AM.*

CH **Tassajara Bread Bakery.** Take your pick from a half-dozen different kinds of freshly baked breads, as well as huge brownies, a range of tempting Danish pastries and cakes, and dynamite black-bean chili and vegetable soup. Bring a book or a daydream. *1000 Cole St. at Parnassus, tel. 415/664–8947. MC, V. Sun. 8 AM–9 PM.*

Japantown **Yamada Seika Confectionery.** Here you'll find a fascinating assortment of traditional Japanese pastries and imported jellied candy. There aren't any seats, but you can grab a bench in the Japan Center and pretend you're in Kyoto. *1955 Sutter St. near Fillmore, tel. 415/922–3848. No credit cards. Sun. 9–5.*

Marina

CH, VG, VU **The Bakery at Greens.** This bakery, operated by the Zen Center, serves some of the best breads, buttermilk scones, and cakes in the Bay Area, as well as vegetarian black-bean chili, soups, salads, and sandwiches. When Greens (*see* Marina in Restaurants, *above*) isn't open, you can settle down in the large, airy dining room and enjoy views of the Golden Gate Bridge. When the restaurant is serving brunch, take your bakery fare out to the parking lot and enjoy equally spectacular views alfresco. *Building A, Fort Mason Center, Marina Blvd. at Buchanan, tel. 415/771–6330. No credit cards. Sun. 9:30–3:30.*

Bepples Pies. Moviegoers from the nearby Century 21 movie theater and well-heeled locals find the place bustling with folks downing cranberry-apple-crunch pie, chocolate mousse pie, savory pies, and classic brunch items in an upscale setting. *2142 Chestnut St. near Steiner, tel. 415/931–6226. No credit cards. Sun. 8 AM–11 PM.*

CH **Just Desserts.** Since 1974, folks have been coming to this *simpatico* neighborhood café. Now that Just Desserts and Tassajara Bakery have merged, you'll find fabulous breads as well as great pastries. *3745 Buchanan St., across from Fort Mason, tel. 415/922–8675. MC, V. Sun. 8 AM–9 PM.*

Mission **Café Beano.** Come here if you want to be part of an emerging cultural scene before it even happens. It's the coffeehouse of choice in the Mission. *878 Valencia St. near 16th St., tel. 415/285–2728. No credit cards. Sun. 9 AM–7 PM.*

CH **Dominguez.** One of those only-in-the-Mission establishments that offers patrons a passport to the wonderful world of Latin American pastries, this is a when-in-Rome type place. Pick out selections with tongs, take your tray to a table, and enjoy. *2951 24th St. at Alabama, tel. 415/821–1717. Sun. 8–8.*

CH **La Victoria.** This popular neighborhood hangout is right across the street from Dominguez and neck-in-neck in the competition for best Latin American bakery in the Mission. *2937 24th St. at Alabama, tel. 415/550–9292. No credit cards. Sun. 7–10.*

CH **St. Francis Fountain.** A San Francisco landmark in operation since 1918, this place has a '50s soda fountain and a classic array of homemade ice creams (with all the toppings), shakes, candies, and sandwiches. *2801 24th St. between York and Bryant, tel. 415/826–4200. No credit cards. Sun. 11:30–8.*

Nob Hill The **Fairmont** (*see* Crown Room, Nob Hill in Restaurants, *above*) serves tea from 1–6 (reservations advised) in the downstairs lobby lounge, including finger sandwiches, French pastries, champagne, port, and sherry.

The **Ritz-Carlton** (*see* The Terrace, Nob Hill in Restaurants, *above*) offers the city's most lavish selection of tea options (2:30–4:30; reservations advised) in the elegant Lobby Lounge. Choices range from a traditional tea with scones, confections, and tea sandwiches to a royal tea that starts with kir royale and concludes with strawberries marinated in Grand Marnier.

You can experience the ambience and/or views of a number of upscale establishments by dropping in for dessert (*see* Nob Hill in Restaurants, *above*). The **Top of the Mark** offers house-baked desserts (4–midnight) and tea downstairs in the lower lobby (2:30–5:30; reservations advised). At **The Big Four,** you're welcome to stop in for dessert anytime from 7 AM to midnight. Perch at the bar at **Vanessi's** and sample some of the best zabaglione and tiramisù in town.

Noe Valley *CH* **Rory's Twisted Scoop.** The fun of this place is choosing from a big assortment of goodies—bits of Reese's peanut-butter cups, M&Ms, fruit chunks, and so on—that you can have mixed into any ice cream flavor. All flavors are homemade, as are the huge waffle cones. You can also get frozen yogurt here. *1300 Castro at 24th St., tel. 415/648–2837. No credit cards. Sun. 11:30–10.*

CH **Spinelli Coffee Company.** This neighborhood café offers a selection of pastries as well as a full range of espresso drinks. Pick up some extra-dark French roast beans before you leave; they will propel you out of any sleep-driven stupor. *3966 24th St. near Noe, tel. 415/550–7416. MC, V. Sun. 7 AM–10 PM.*

North Beach **Caffè Malvina.** Sip espresso here while you watch the goings-on in Washington Square. *1600 Stockton at Union St., tel. 415/391–1290. AE, MC, V. Sun. 8–5.*

Caffè Roma Coffee Roasting Company. Enjoy cappuccino and a pastry beneath whirling ceiling fans in this combination retail coffee store and café. *526 Columbus Ave. between Union and Green Sts., tel. 415/296–7662. MC, V. Sun. 8 AM–10 PM.*

L **Caffè Trieste.** Beat poets, artists, and writers (including Jack Kerouac) hung out and drank coffee here. It hasn't changed much since it opened in 1956. *609 Vallejo near Grant Ave., tel. 415/392–6739. No credit cards. Sun. 6:30 AM–midnight.*

CH **Mara's Bakery.** Italian pastries and cookies you seldom see outside Italy and rich coffee can be savored at three tiny tables, or you can take your sweets to nearby Washington Square. *503 Columbus Ave. near Green, tel. 415/397–9435. No credit cards. Sun. 8 AM–11 PM.*

Tosca Café. This vintage bar is famous for its North Beach atmosphere; its opera jukebox; and its cappuccino with steamed milk, chocolate, and brandy. *242 Columbus Ave. near Pacific, tel. 415/986–9651. No credit cards. Sun. 5 PM–2 AM.*

Vesuvio Café. Packed with memorabilia from the Beat era, this landmark North Beach bar still draws poets, artists, writers, and chess players, as well as cab drivers, longshoremen, and yuppies. *255 Columbus Ave. near Broadway, tel. 415/362–3370. No credit cards. Sun. 6 AM–2 AM.*

True romantics should make late-night reservations for one of the extravagantly wonderful dessert soufflés at **Café Jacqueline,** while folks falling in love with San Francisco should drop by for cappuccino and cheesecake at **Mario's Bohemian Cigar Store Cafe** (*see* North Beach, *above*).

Pacific Heights

CH **Rory's Twisted Scoop.** Every bit as good as its Noe Valley brother (*see above*), this Rory's has creamy homemade ice cream, add-on goodies, and ample-size waffle cones. *2015 Fillmore St. near Pine, tel. 415/346–3692. No credit cards. Sun. 11:30–10.*

CH **Spinelli.** Coffee and pastries are sold amid a variety of beans and intriguing espresso machines. *2455 Fillmore St. at Jackson, tel. 415/929–8808. MC, V. Sun. 7–7.*

CH **Sweet Inspiration.** Sip cappuccino and sample magnificent Danish pastries, tarts, tortes, cheesecake, croissants, and coffee cake in this mellow oasis. *2123 Fillmore St. near California, tel. 415/931–2815. No credit cards. Sun. 8 AM–11 PM.*

For creatively exotic desserts in a designer atmosphere, drop by **Oritalia** (*see* Pacific Heights, *above*) for crème brûlée or banana terrine made with chocolate mousse.

Potrero Hill/China Basin

For dessert on the dock of the bay, head for the outdoor deck at **The Ramp** (*see* Potrero Hill, *above*) and dig into mud pie, key lime pie, or "Chocolate Heart Attack." The friendly folks at **Asimakopoulos Cafe** welcome customers for Greek pastries anytime between 8 and 10 PM.

Richmond

CH **Japanese Tea Garden.** At this exquisite little teahouse in Golden Gate Park, gracious waitresses in kimonos serve green tea and cookies to weary parents and wonder-struck children. *Stow Lake Dr. (off King Dr.) in Golden Gate Park, tel. 415/688–0909. No credit cards. Sun. 8:30–6.*

CH **Joe's.** Here's an ice cream shop that has come up with its own version of the San Francisco treat called "It's It": vanilla ice cream sandwiched between two oatmeal cookies and dipped in chocolate. *5351 Geary Blvd. near 18th Ave., tel. 415/751–1950. No credit cards. Sun. 10:45–10.*

CH, L **Toy Boat Dessert Cafe.** A fantasyland for children and adults alike, this place is packed to the rafters with tin toys (including a mechanical horse kids can ride) and serves a menu of pastries, cakes, yogurts, coffee, and espresso drinks. *401 Clement St. at 5th Ave., tel. 415/751–7505. No credit cards. Sun. 8:30 AM–11:30 PM.*

You haven't really done the Richmond District until you've stopped by **Bill's Place** (*see* Richmond District, *above*) for a huge hot fudge sundae.

SoMa

CH **Eppler's Bakery.** The SoMa incarnation offers the same seductive pastries, Danishes, cakes, croissants, and cookies as the more upscale Union Square branch. *90 New Montgomery St. at Mission, tel. 415/392–0101. No credit cards. Sun. 7–6.*

Drop by the combination laundromat-café at the **Brain/Wash** for an espresso and a homemade brownie or cookie. A huge slice of cake and a shake at **Max's Diner** should keep a sugar rush going for hours. (*See* SoMa in Restaurants, *above.*)

Sunset
CH **Double Rainbow.** Yet another branch serves the deliciously rich ice cream that has made it San Francisco's most popular chain. *2116 Irving St. near 22nd Ave., tel. 415/665–3090. No credit cards. Sun. 8:30–10.*

CH **Just Desserts.** Stop by for black-bottom cupcakes, brownies, cheesecakes, pies, and cookies, as well as ice cream, coffee, and espresso drinks. *626 Irving St. near 9th Ave., tel. 415/681–1277. No credit cards. Sun. 8 AM–11 PM.*

CH **Old Uncle Gaylord's Old Fashioned Ice Cream Parlor.** This place was using natural ingredients before they became hip. The ice cream used to be kosher certified; now it's just certifiably good. The parlor serves a range of desserts and coffee drinks, as well as sandwiches and salads. *721 Irving St. near 8th Ave., tel. 415/759–1614. No credit cards. Sun. 9:30–7.*

Stoyanoff's (*see* Sunset District in Restaurants, *above*) encourages strollers to drop by from 10 to 4 for baklava, Napoleons, fresh fruit tarts, and Grand Marnier cake.

O, L **Tart To Tart.** Just one block from Golden Gate Park and a few blocks from UCSF, you'll find a casual dining area with high ceilings and sidewalk seating. Offerings include mixed fruit, cheesecakes, tarts, cakes, and espresso drinks, as well as salads, lasagna, and the like. *641 Irving St. near 8th Ave., tel. 415/753–2359. D, MC, V. Sun. open 24 hrs.*

Union Square/ Downtown
L, MU **The Compass Rose.** The traditional tea includes sandwiches, scones, petit fours, and berries with Devonshire cream. Evening entertainment includes a caviar cart, frozen vodka, martini service, live piano, and a jazz vocalist. Drop by for dessert anytime (St. Francis cheesecake, signature white-chocolate-mousse cake). *Westin St. Francis Hotel, 335 Powell St. near Geary, tel. 415/774–0167. AE, D, DC, MC, V. Sun. 11:30 AM–midnight.*

CH **Eppler's Bakery.** Its history dates back to 1884; now there are several branches around the city. In this particular glass-enclosed Euro-style bakery and café with a German pastry chef, you'll find great tortes, cakes, eclairs, and cookies, as well as sandwiches, soups, and salads. *750 Market St. at Grant and O'Farrell, tel. 415/392–0101. No credit cards. Sun. 7–6.*

CH **La Nouvelle Patisserie.** French pastries, berry tarts, candies, and petits fours are presented here as eye-catching works of art. Try a flaky croissant with homemade jam for breakfast and a quiche or a gourmet sandwich for lunch. *San Francisco Center, 865 Market near 5th St., tel. 415/979–0553. No credit cards. Sun. 11–6.*

Good choices for informal eateries serving noteworthy sweets include **David's Delicatessen, Lori's Diner, and The Dutch Kitchen** (*see* Union Square in Restaurants, *above*). David's specializes in European pastries (baked on the premises) and, while packed during mealtimes, is a good bet during late afternoon and late evening. Lori's dishes up desserts and shakes 24 hours a day. The Dutch Kitchen offers the opportunity to sample landmark St. Francis sweets in an informal setting.

You can also drop in for late-night desserts or sweets at the bar in one of the area's designer restaurants. The **Pacific** caters to dessert customers all day; Wolfgang Puck's **Postrio** welcomes dessert customers at the bar, as do **Kuleto** and the **Brasserie Savoy**; and the hip, happening **City of Paris** welcomes dessert customers with its famed chocolate cake after 10 PM.

Union Street
L **Bepples Pies.** At this festive, upbeat gathering spot, beautiful people go to eat every kind of pie under the sun—from southern pecan, fresh boysenberry, and double-layer chocolate mousse to such savory picks as chunky chicken. *1934 Union St. near Laguna, tel. 415/931–6225. No credit cards. Sun. 9 AM–midnight.*

CH **Il Fornaio.** Packed to the rafters with freshly baked breads and Italian desserts, this is a gorgeous setting for a cup of espresso and a pastry. Pizzas are available as well. *2298 Union St. at Steiner, tel. 415/563–3400. MC, V. Sun. 8–6.*

CH **La Nouvelle Patisserie.** The Union Street location draws a family crowd for French pastries, light lunches, and irresistible chocolate mousse. *2184 Union St. near Fillmore, tel. 415/931–7655. No credit cards. Sun. 8–7.*

Prego (*see* Union Street in Restaurants, *above*), which concocts a delicious tiramisù, serves desserts from 11:30 AM to midnight.

Van Ness Avenue/Polk Street

Double Rainbow. This Polk Gulch branch serves the ultrarich ice cream that has made the local chain a hit citywide. *1653 Polk St. near Clay, tel. 415/775–3220. No credit cards. Sun. 11–11.*

CH, L **The Grubstake,** the **Hard Rock Cafe,** and **Harris'** (*see* Van Ness Avenue/Polk Street in Restaurants, *above*) all welcome dessert customers. The Grubstake dishes up homemade apple and pumpkin pies until 4 in the morning. The young and hungry battle the crowds for a huge piece of chocolate cake at the Hard Rock. Harris' encourages patrons to drop by the bar, peruse the dessert cart of homemade pastries, and pick out a perfect slice of pecan pie or chocolate cake.

Wharf

CH, O, VU **Ghirardelli Chocolate Manufactory.** Chocolate-making machines, old-fashioned soda fountain, photogenic hot fudge sundaes, and views from the garden terrace make this a favored destination for locals and tourists alike. *900 North Point St. at Larkin, tel. 415/771–4903. MC, V. Sun. 10:30 AM–11 PM.*

The **Boudin Sourdough Bakery & Cafe** is a reasonably priced stop serving espresso drinks and such comforting sweets as chocolate layer cake, with locations on Fisherman's Wharf, Ghirardelli Square, and Pier 39. For a pricier treat and late-night sweets, **McCormick & Kuleto's** offers creative dessert specials along with stunning decor and a view of the bay. **Cafe Pescatore,** back a few paces from the bustling crowds, provides sidewalk dining, a friendly, neighborhood ambience, and dessert calzones. (*See* Wharf restaurants, *above*).

East Bay

CH, L **Au Coquelet.** This favored late-night spot serves an assortment of pastries, cakes, and fresh fruit tarts and a full range of espresso drinks as breakfast and lunch fare. *2000 University Ave. at Milvia, Berkeley, tel. 510/845–0433. MC, V. Sun. 6 AM–1:30 AM.*

O, L **Caffé Strada.** Right across the street from the campus, this place has lots of outdoor seating, an international crowd, espresso drinks, pastries, and great eavesdropping opportunities. *2300 College Ave. at Bancroft, Berkeley, tel. 510/843–5282. No credit cards. Sun. 7:30 AM–11:30 PM.*

Fatapple's (*see* East Bay in Restaurants, *above*) is famed for its pastries and homemade pies.

O **French Hotel Cafe.** Get a load of the European ambience and sidewalk seating in the heart of north Berkeley's gourmet ghetto. *1540 Shattuck Ave. between Cedar and Vine, Berkeley, tel. 510/843–8958. No credit cards. Sun. 8 AM–11 PM.*

The Musical Offering. A café up front offers espresso drinks, simple pastries, an intellectual crowd, and luncheon fare; a music store specializes in classical medleys in back. *2430 Bancroft Way, below Telegraph Ave., Berkeley, tel. 510/849–0211. AE, MC, V. Sun. 11:30–5:30.*

CH, O, L, VG **Edible Complex.** Serving pastries, espresso drinks, and café fare (much of it vegetarian) to students, artists, and neighborhood types, this roomy art gallery café has been a popular hangout since 1975. *5600 College Ave. near Oceanview (a few blocks from Rockridge BART), Oakland, tel. 510/658–2172. No credit cards. Sun. 8:30 AM–midnight.*

CH **Fenton's Creamery.** Here you'll find lots of seating, lavish ice-cream extravaganzas, luncheon fare, and lines out the door on sunny days. *4226 Piedmont Ave. at Entrada (4 blocks west of Pleasant Valley Ave.), Oakland, tel. 510/658-7000. MC, V. Sun. 11:30–11.*

Peninsula *CH, O* **Bravo Fono.** What may be the best gelato in the Bay Area is made here from scratch, and the flavors are sublime. Sorbets are also special, and there's alfresco seating beneath sun umbrellas. *99 Stanford Shopping Center off El Camino, Palo Alto, tel. 415/322-4664. MC, V. Sun. 11–6.*

L **Il Fornaio Cucina Italiana** (*see* Peninsula *in* Restaurants, *above*) has a seductive selection of Italian cookies, cakes, tarts, and pastries, and stays open till midnight.

Marin **Il Fornaio** (*see* Marin County in Restaurants, *above*) is always a sure bet for a wonderful selection of Italian pastries. Drop by during off-hours for tiramisù, fruit tarts, rich Italian cake, or cookies—or get goodies to go from the bakery.

CH **Spanky's.** Classic diner food (including a good BLT) is what you'll find here, as well as an ice cream worth pausing for. *1900 Sir Francis Drake Blvd. (middle of town), Fairfax, tel. 415/456-5299. Sun. 8–9.*

Sweden House (*see* Marin County in Restaurants, *above*) has espresso drinks and European pastries that the birds on the outdoor deck are prepared to fight for.

Sports Bars

Bobby Rubino's (*see* Wharf in Restaurants, *above*) features a sports lounge with four big TV screens, along with great ribs, views of the bay, and a special menu for kids.

L **Dooley's Pub.** This Marina District bar has seven big-screen TVs, two satellite dishes, and an extensive menu of burgers, sandwiches and beers. *2526 Lombard St. near Divisidero, tel. 415/922-0985. AE, D, MC, V. Sun. 10:15 AM–2 AM.*

L **Fourth Street Bar & Deli.** Here's a downtown bar with satellite sports, two big-screen TVs, 22 beers on tap, and pool and shuffleboard for when the game gets dull. *Corner of 4th and Mission Sts., tel. 415/442-6734. AE, D, DC. Sun. 9:30 AM–midnight.*

CH, L, MU **Lefty O'Doul's.** This combination bar and hofbrau-style cafeteria near Union Square is a fun place for kids and adults alike. It's full of baseball memorabilia and photos of Lefty—a hero from the era when the city's hometown team was the minor league Seals—and there's piano music starting at 9 PM. There's a TV at either end of the bar and a big screen in the back dining room. *333 Geary St. near Powell, tel. 415/982-8900. No credit cards. Sun. 7 AM–2 AM.*

MU **Pat O'Shea's Mad Hatter.** This Irish bar in the Richmond District has three satellite dishes, 13 TVs, lots of sports memorabilia, live rock and roll at night, a Sunday brunch, and such solid fare as meat loaf and pot roast. *3848 Geary Blvd. at 3rd Ave., tel. 415/752-3148, D, MC, V. Sun. 10–9.*

Two other hangouts where sports fans will feel at home are **Mad Dog in the Fog** (*see* The Haight in Restaurants, *above*) and **Tommy's Joynt** (*see* Van Ness/Polk Street in Restaurants, *above*). They don't feature high-tech equipment or banks of TV screens, but whenever you drop by, you'll find sports on the tube.

3 Sightseeing

By Kathryn Olney

Updated by Daniel Mangin

So many San Franciscans work late at home that it can feel like as many people are out and about on weekdays as on weekends. (Downtown is the exception.) Nonetheless, something about Sunday brings out a more leisurely side of this already laid-back town. Neighborhoods fill up with loiterers, philosophers, and perambulators; the air feels crisper; and even the sun seems to shine a little brighter—when it decides to come out. It's a day to admire the city's charming architecture, the splendid views from its hills, its parks and wooded areas, and the stately Victorian houses that stand right next to them.

Views

The topography of the Bay Area provides some of the best urban vistas in the world. San Francisco's 42 windswept hills are constantly yielding city views with golden peaks to ponder in the distance. The downtown skyscrapers are fine vantage points, too, but the hills are unsurpassed. On a clear afternoon, when the sun glints off the sea or reflects in the windows of pastel Victorians, there's no finer spectacle. Sundays are busy, and in summer it's a good idea to head for some of the following places early or late—which in any case are the most beautiful times of day.

Skyscraper Panoramas

Bank of America. Sunday brunch (10–2:30) is served in the **Carnelian Room** on the 52nd floor (*see* Financial District/Jackson Square *in* Chapter 2), or you can just have drinks. *555 California St. at Montgomery, tel. 415/433–7500.*

Embarcadero Center. The revolving **Equinox** restaurant in the Hyatt Regency Hotel has constantly changing views of the city and the bay. Breakfast starts at 10, cocktails only after 2, and dinner begins at 6. *5 Embarcadero Center (Market and Drumm Sts.), tel. 415/788–1234.*

San Francisco Marriott. Light lunch is served from 11 AM to 2:30 PM in the **View Lounge** of this Deco-inspired downtown favorite—or eyesore, depending on your architectural tastes. *55 4th St. at Mission, tel. 415/896–1600.*

Other Views

The noteworthy views below are just a beginning, since the city provides views at nearly every turn. The Great Walks listed later in this chapter provide spectacular vistas as well.

Cliff House. Yes, it's touristy, but nothing beats it for views of San Francisco's longest beach and the Marin Headlands, accompanied by the barking of the seals on Seal Rock. For more on dining here, *see* Cliff House *in* Chapter 2. *1090 Point Lobos Ave. (foot of Geary Blvd.), tel. 415/386–3330.*

Coit Tower. This well-loved Art Deco landmark was erected by Lillie Hitchcock Coit as a tribute to the firefighters of San Francisco ; its modern form is derived from a fire hose. (*see* Explorable Neighborhoods: North Beach, *below.*)

Mt. Davidson. This sylvan summit, 16 feet higher than Twin Peaks, is the site of an ongoing court battle. The largest steel-and-concrete cross in the country, which has stood at the top since 1934, was lit every evening until 1989, when a multifaith group challenged its constitutionality. Easter services are still held here (*see* Seasonal Pleasures: Spring *in* Chapter 1), but the cross remains in the dark. To reach the summit, take the steps between 919 and 925 Rockdale Drive, near the dead end; stay on the 5-foot-wide dirt path, keeping to the left at every fork. Those not up for a trek can get fairly close to the top by car. Turn left off Portola Drive onto Evelyn Way, right onto Teresita Boulevard, right onto Reposa Way, and left onto Myra Way. Take Myra Way to its intersection with Dalewood Way. (To get to Rockdale from downtown, take Market Street, which becomes Portola Drive as it ascends past the Castro District. Take a left onto Evelyn Way and a right onto Chaves Avenue, which runs into Rockdale.)

Seacliff. A walk through this exclusive neighborhood, bounded by Lake Street and 25th and 33rd avenues, is only mildly interesting from an architectural standpoint—most of the big, vaguely Mediterranean-style houses went up quickly in the 'teens and '20s. (Willis Polk designed the three stucco residences at 9, 25, and 45 Scenic Way.) But if it's a sunny day, you can catch some of the finest views of the bay by looking in between the houses. Check out the stairway off El Camino del Mar, just west of the end of 32nd Avenue. This will take you down to the Coastal Trail (*see* Great Walks, *below*). Walk out to the circular deck at the beginning of the trail, and you'll catch a wonderful view of the whole Seacliff neighborhood, not to mention the Golden Gate Bridge and the Marin Headlands.

Sutro Heights. This magnificent park overlooking the Cliff House—once the grounds of May Adolph Sutro's mansion—provides a shady perch from which you can look down to the Great Highway and the ocean beyond. For a short but invigorating uphill walk, pick up the trail at Balboa Street across from the end of La Playa and head north up the path to the park.

Twin Peaks. The Empire State Building of the West affords a 360° panorama of the city and beyond. The hilltop is often windy and notoriously chilly, and it can get crowded with tour buses. But the views are magnificent any time of day or night.

Great Walks

Although people do flee on the weekend—to the Marin wilderness, to the mountains, to the bay itself—there's probably no other city in the contiguous states where so many inhabitants stay so happily in town. On Sundays San Franciscans go out to meet once again the incredible natural valentine that awaits them just a bus ride away.

In the City

Embarcadero
Along the Promenade

Thanks to the Loma Prieta earthquake of 1989 and the resulting demolition of the unsafe Embarcadero Freeway, a new city vista has opened up, stretching south from the Ferry Building past the Bay Bridge to Third Street. You can see the whole bridge now as it spans the water to Treasure Island. At twilight, when the lights twinkle on, it's even prettier. Several dozen Great Canary palms (like the ones on Dolores and Market streets) now line the middle of the Embarcadero, and tracks for a streetcar line will connect the area south of the bridge and Fisherman's Wharf by the end of the century. In the meantime the waterfront Promenade is already a great place for a stroll.

The 100 block of the Embarcadero gives a peek into late-19th- and early 20th-century San Francisco. At the beginning of the block the 1889 **Audiffred Building** (11–21 Mission St.) is one of the oldest downtown; the original owner hailed, as the mansard roof suggests, from France. At 166 Embarcadero is the 1926 **YMCA Building,** part of which now belongs to the Harbor Court Hotel. In **Bayside Village** (Embarcadero and Townsend St.) and the Spanish-Italian **Delancey Street Center and Apartments** (602 Embarcadero at 2nd St.), you'll find a neighborhood feeling, along with outdoor cafés. The two contrasting architectural styles define the new waterfront. For more about neotraditional spaces, *see* Secret Places, Secret Spaces, *below*.

Golden Gate Bridge *From the Bridge to Fort Point* Windy, often misty and chilly, but breathtaking nonetheless, the nearly 2-mile-long bridge, constructed between 1933 and 1937, is the country's most popular tourist walk. On weekends the eastern (bay side) walkway is reserved for pedestrians from 5 AM to 9 PM, the western (ocean side) one for cycling. (After 9 PM, no pedestrians are allowed on the bridge, but cyclists are permitted on the east side.) Parking is permitted near the toll stations on the San Francisco side or at Vista Point on the Marin side. Just below the bridge on the San Francisco side is the 19th-century Fort Point (*see* Historical Treasures *in* Chapter 4). A paved path from the toll plaza winds through a grove of eucalyptus and cypress trees to the fishing pier near Fort Point. From there, it's a short walk along the bay to the fort.

Marina *Golden Gate Promenade* This perfectly flat paved trail stretches along the bay for more than 3 miles, from Aquatic Park, past the Marina Green and Fort Mason, to Fort Point. There are superb views of the Golden Gate Bridge, Alcatraz, Tiburon, and Sausalito, and all types of boat traffic to look at. Popular with joggers, stroller pushers, and cyclists, it can get crowded on Sundays. There's parking at Marina Green, Crissy Field, and near the St. Francis Yacht Club (near Lyon St. and Marina Blvd.).

Richmond *Land's End and the Coastal Trail* This magnificent walk offers views of the Marin Headlands, the Golden Gate Bridge, and, on a clear Sunday, the Farallon Islands and Point Reyes National Seashore. Start at Cliff House (*see* Views, *above*); climb up to 48th Avenue via Point Lobos Avenue, turn left on El Camino Del Mar, head down the steps at the end of the road, and turn right onto the Land's End Trail. The trail, set among cypresses and pines, varies between dirt path, sidewalk, old railroad bed, and erstwhile military roadway. If you want the vista without the hike, park near the Palace of the Legion of Honor and walk east on El Camino Del Mar. Roughly 300 feet before you get to the end of 32nd Avenue, you'll see Eagle's Point, a breathtaking stairway with places to sit and ponder. (You can pick up the Coastal Trail halfway down.)

Sunset *Fort Funston* The beautiful paved trails along the ocean cliffs are ideal for people with strollers or wheelchairs, and dog owners can let their pets frolic off-leash, safely away from the traffic. On weekends there's the added plus of hang gliders soaring overhead. As you walk from the parking lot north toward the city, you'll pass Battery Davis, a 1938 gun battery camouflaged to aircraft; a little bit beyond you'll have views of the Sunset District, Lake Merced, and the western hills of the city. You can also climb down the steep ridge to the beach below, a popular picnicking and sand-dollar-collecting spot that's often blissfully uncrowded. To get to Fort Funston, take the Great Highway south past the zoo to Skyline Boulevard and watch for the sign on the coastal side.

Around the Bay

East Bay *Lake Chabot Regional Park* This park near Castro Valley provides a beautiful valley-floor walk along its **Grass Valley Trail,** which bursts with color in the spring but is exquisite any time, since it's framed by the mountains. Start at the Bort Meadow Trailhead on Skyline Boulevard and hike south about 1½ miles to Stone Bridge. *Lake Chabot Regional Park, tel. 510/635–0135, ext. 3402 or 3400. Open daily 5 AM–10 PM.*

Tilden Park The Tilden Nature Study Area has several different trails—some hiking only, others multiuse—that together provide an overview of East Bay vegetation and small wildlife. The gentle **Jewel Lake Trail** is just under a mile; it begins near the park's Environmental Education Center, where self-guiding booklets are available. The more rugged **Wildcat Peak Trail** (1½ miles) leads up to the 1,250-foot Wildcat Peak, which yields panoramic views of Mt. Diablo, Mt. Tamalpais, San Francisco, and the Peninsula. The easy **Sylvan Trail**—

less than a mile in length—leads to the peak trail, then loops through grassland and oak and eucalyptus groves. The moderate **Pack Rat Trail** (just under a mile) contains a cross-section of north-coast vegetation, some quite thick. With hermit thrush, Townsend warbler, and other bird species, it's a magnet for ornithologists. The Pack Rat winds up at Jewel Lake, where more birds (including a lone Great Blue Heron) reside. *See* The Urban Outdoors *in* Chapter 6 for more on Tilden Park. *Environmental Education Center, tel. 510/525–2233. Admission free. Open Sun. 10–5; park open dawn to 10 PM.*

Marin County
Mt. Tamalpais

This Marin County mountain offers a nearly perfect view of the North Bay area from an elevation of more than 2,500 feet. On a clear day you can see all the way from the Santa Clara Valley to Napa County. It can be foggy in San Francisco and even Marin County, yet still sunny on top of "the Sleeping Lady." Several trails begin near the Pantoll Ranger Station (on Panoramic Highway near Pantoll Road). A popular, easy-to-moderate, 8½-mile round-trip hike to Mt. Tam's East Peak includes some groomed trails on the way up and a portion of the **Old Railroad Grade Fire Road** on the way down. In either direction, visitors can stop at the **West Point Inn** (tel. 415/388–9955), which sells cold drinks and has a display of historic photos of the old railroad that wound a very crooked path up the mountain. If you're pressed for time or not up to a long walk, drive up to the parking lot on the East Peak; near the rest rooms you'll see a sign for the **Verna Dunshea Trail.** A pamphlet available at the beginning of the trail describes the local history and flora. Another short walk—this one with sweeping coastal views—is to **O'Rourke's Bench**, set on a knoll at 2,000 feet. To get there, park at Rock Springs and take the short O'Rourke Bench Trail for a mere $^{3}/_{10}$ mile. *Mt. Tamalpais State Park, tel. 415 388–2070. Open daily 7 AM–9 PM.*

Muir Woods National Monument

It's best to come to Muir Woods early in the morning or two hours before sunset to beat the crowds—and to find parking, which is often scarce Sundays from 10 to 4. A constant stream of humanity follows the main, paved wheelchair-accessible trail along Redwood Creek. The redwood and sequoia trees here—some of them nearly 250-feet tall and 1,000 years old—are so majestic the crowds might not even phase you, but a detour onto one of the graded, well-marked dirt paths yields something closer to solitude. The **Hillside Trail** is reasonably easy. The more difficult **Ocean View Trail** winds through forests of redwoods and Douglas fir. The trail joins other paths and forms a loop to Mountain Home Inn (*see* Restaurants: Marin County *in* Chapter 2), where brunch or beverages are available. Take the **Lost Trail to Ferncreek Trail** to loop back to the park's entrance. The Muir Woods paths connect with the extensive network of hiking trails on Mt. Tamalpais, including the **Dipsea** (*see* Explorable Neighborhoods: Mill Valley, *below*). Pick up a trail map at the park's entrance. *Tel. 415/388–2595. Admission free. Open Sun. 8–sunset.*

Peninsula
Purisma Creek Redwoods

It's a 45-minute drive south to this open-space preserve off Skyline Boulevard (Hwy. 35) west of Woodside. The quarter-mile-long Redwood Trail stands on a ridge 2,000 feet above sea level under a canopy of redwood trees, and it's accessible to people with strollers or wheelchairs. Call the Mid-Peninsula Regional Open Space District (tel. 415/691–1200) for information and directions.

Architecture

Downtown San Francisco isn't known for its architecture, but there are a few gems. The city's most beloved buildings—its famous Victorian houses—are mostly out in the neighborhoods, and you don't have to be a student of architecture to appreciate their charm. Lobbies and atriums contain some of San Francisco's grandest, most imposing architecture. Although many buildings are closed Sundays, the guards who admit weekend workers are sometimes willing to accommodate sightseers, too.

The Castro

Castro Theatre. The ornate 1920s movie house, now a neighborhood landmark, was the flagship of a San Francisco cinema baron who also built theaters in Noe Valley. The 1,500-seat auditorium—with an elaborate plaster ceiling cast in the form of a tent, replete with swags, ropes, and tassels—is one of the few from its era that hasn't been demolished or broken up to accommodate a multiplex. *429 Castro St. at Market, tel. 415/621–6120.*

Civic Center

The Beaux Arts complex between McAllister and Grove streets and Franklin and Hyde streets, which includes **City Hall, the War Memorial Opera House, the Veterans' Building,** and the **old Public Library** (slated to become the new home of the Asian Art Museum by the year 2000), is a product of the turn-of-the-century "City Beautiful" movement—the same movement that produced the Mall in Washington, DC. City Hall, a masterly example of French high-Baroque Revival architecture, is the centerpiece, completed first, in 1915. Its dome towers even higher than the Capitol dome in Washington, which was its model. The new main library on Larkin between Fulton and Grove is a modern variation on the Civic Center's architectural theme. (Note: City Hall will be closed well into 1998 for seismic retrofitting. The opera house will reopen in 1997.)

Packard Auto Showroom. This stylish building was designed to showcase one of the 1920s' premier automobile lines. Note the frieze just below the roof and the stately columns, topped by Corinthian capitals. *901 Van Ness Ave. at O'Farrell St.*

Embarcadero

Ferry Building. This structure at the foot of Market Street, completed in 1898, was the gateway to the city before the bridges were built. Until 1958 some 170 ferries disembarked here every day. The 230-foot clock tower was modeled on the Giralda tower of the Seville Cathedral; illuminated at night, it's one of the city's loveliest sights. Some city planners are angling to turn the building into a public market; in the meantime it houses offices.

Hills Brothers Coffee Building. The famous old coffee building is now Hills Plaza, a block-long apartment complex and commercial development incorporating the original 1933 Romanesque arched brick facade. On the south end, under the tower, there's a pleasant garden with a great vantage point of the Bay Bridge. *345 Spear St. at Harrison.*

Rincon Center. The fountain in the skylighted marble atrium of this complex is one of the city's best: Water drips from a flat "pool" suspended 60-feet above the floor. The "Historic Lobby"—the walk-up window area for the post office that once occupied the premises—is an Art Deco setting decorated with Anton Refregier's WPA mural. The 27 panels depict California life from the days when Native Americans were the state's sole inhabitants through World War I. Completion of this significant work was interrupted by World War II and political infighting; the latter led to alterations in some of Refregier's radical historical interpretations. The panels generated a number of controversies; Refregier was considered a radical by conservative groups, and he had to tone down some of his work in order to appease local tempers. The mural was attacked again during the

McCarthy era, but congressmen managed to keep it from being removed. *121 Spear St. at Mission, tel. 415/243–0473.*

Financial District

Mechanics Institute. The first educational institution in California (established in 1854 to train and educate tradespeople) has a 1909 marble lobby with a mural of "The Arts" done in California decorative style by Arthur Mathews. *57–65 Post St. at Montgomery.*

Mills Building. The only Chicago School building that survived the 1906 quake, the 10-story all-steel structure had its own electric plant in the basement. The lobby features a double staircase and plenty of marble, gold, and glass. The tower next door (220 Bush St.), designed by Lewis Hobart, was added in 1931 and blends in superbly with the original building. *220 Montgomery St. at Bush.*

Pacific Stock Exchange Tower. This Art Deco classic, around the corner from the Stock Exchange on Pine Street, was designed by the architects Miller and Pfleuger. Be sure to peek through the door into the 1930 lobby to see the gold ceiling and the black marble-wall entry. *155 Sansome St. at Pine.*

Marina

Palace of Fine Arts. The only survivor of the eight "palaces" built for the 1915 Panama-Pacific International Exposition in the Marina, this is many San Franciscans' favorite Bernard Maybeck building. The deteriorating stucco was replaced with concrete in 1967. Behind the romantic quasi-Roman structure, with its massive columns and great rotunda, the swan-filled lagoon provides one of the city's most charming picnic spots. Inside is the Exploratorium, the city's best science museum (*see* Science and Nature Museums *in* Chapter 4). *Baker and Beach Sts.*

Nob Hill

Grace Cathedral. Former railroad baron Charles Crocker's grandiose mansion stood on this site until it was destroyed in the 1906 earthquake. The steel-and-concrete cathedral is a modern version of a traditional Gothic design. Its doors are casts of the Ghiberti *Gates of Paradise* on the Baptistery in Florence. Added in 1995 were the sweeping eastern staircase and a new $450,000 outdoor terrazzo meditation labyrinth. Cathedral tours are given Sunday at 12:30 PM after the 11:00 AM service. *1051 Taylor St. at California, tel. 415/776–6611.*

Ritz-Carlton Hotel. The elegant Roman-Renaissance lobby (1909), with crystal chandeliers and 18th-century paintings, has seen it all—first as the entrance for the Metropolitan Life Insurance Company, then for Cogswell College, then for Werner Erhard's EST activities—before it became the portal to a luxury hotel. *600 Stockton St. at California, tel. 415/296–7465.*

Pacific Heights

Spreckels Mansion. Architect George Applegarth fashioned this elegant house, formerly known as "the Sugar Palace," for sugar heir Adolph Spreckels and his wife Alma. Apparently, Alma liked it—for she then commissioned Applegarth to design the California Palace of the Legion of Honor in Lincoln Park. *2080 Washington St. at Octavia.*

Stanyan House. Only a few of the prefabricated New England houses that were sent around Cape Horn by boat in 1852 have been identified with certainty; this is one of them. The inside has the usual mid-19th-century detail, but the New England–size rooms are small for the Bay Area. *2006 Bush St. at Buchanan.*

Swedenborgian Church. This unusual 1894 Craftsman-style structure was a product of the California Arts and Crafts Movement. Bruce Porter provided the original design and the stained glass; Bernard Maybeck was responsible for the pegged wooden chairs with seats of woven rushes—said to be one of the inspirations for the California Mission Style. The roof is supported by trunks of madrone trees. You can request a tour after the 11 AM service Sunday. *2107 Lyon St. at Washington, tel. 415/346–6466.*

Richmond

The Beach Chalet. This long-vacant but lovely structure is slated to reopen as a park visitors center and brew-pub restaurant with the help of a federal restoration grant. Murals depict bathers and picnickers at Ocean Beach in the '30s. The exquisite wooden staircase is carved with mermaids and sea creatures. *John F. Kennedy Dr. and Great Highway, Golden Gate Park.*

San Francisco Columbarium. This fine 1898 burial vault holds the cremated remains of some of San Francisco's most illustrious families—Magnins, Folgers, Turks, and Eddys, to name a few—on four ornately decorated stories. In late 1995, plans were approved for a new exterior wall to hold more urns. *1 Loraine Ct., off Anza St. between Arguello Blvd. and Stanyan, tel. 415/752–7891. Open daily 10 AM–1 PM.*

Russian Hill

San Francisco Art Institute. The 1926 courtyard lobby, fashioned in monastery-and-cloister style, includes a tiled fish pond; an adjacent gallery (to your left as you enter; open Sunday 10 to 5) features a Diego Rivera mural and exhibitions of students' work. *800 Chestnut St. at Jones, tel. 415/771–7020 or, for 24-hr event information, 415/749–4588.*

South of Market

Moscone Center. The Esplanade Ballroom lobby in the center's south building features a giant replica (25 feet by 40 feet) of the first known map of San Francisco. Underneath the map are interesting period artifacts. *747 Howard at 3rd St.*

San Francisco Museum of Modern Art. Italian-Swiss architect Mario Botta, known for his skylights, has created a great slanting ellipse for the roof of the new museum in the Yerba Buena Center. By night it lights up the sky, and by day it provides natural light for the art inside. A pedestrian bridge on the fifth floor crosses underneath the central light tower; below it is a huge granite atrium surrounded by a bookstore, restaurant, and coat check. Across 3rd Street is Japanese architect Fumihiko Maki's **Performing Arts Center,** with a huge glass-wall upper lobby that opens onto Yerba Buena Gardens. *3rd St. at Mission.*

Sheraton Palace Hotel. The Garden Court Restaurant (*see* Financial District/Jackson Square *in* Chapter 2) was once a coach house where horse-drawn carriages dropped off passengers. Today it's a grand spot for Sunday brunch, high tea, or dinner. The huge room boasts a four-story skylight of 25,000 panes, which were cleaned and repaired during the hotel's restoration in 1989. The mosaic floors replicate Oriental rug designs. *2 New Montgomery St. at Market, tel. 415/546–5000.*

Union Square

Circle Gallery. As you walk through the archway of this 1949 mini-Guggenheim, you'll enter a quintessential Frank Lloyd Wright lobby: an organic ramp that circles up to the next level, with round corners everywhere. *140 Maiden La. at Stockton, tel. 415/989–2100. Open Sun. noon–5.*

Flood Building. This bold edifice with its round corner was built in 1906 to lend grandeur to the downtown area. The first two floors were gutted during the earthquake that year; the floors above remain essentially as they were constructed. (The Woolworth store on the site used to be the largest in the world, but was recently downscaled to make room for other occupants.) *870 Market at 5th St.*

Neiman Marcus. Although Philip Johnson's 1982 building is unspectacular (to put it kindly), it has a pretty glass dome at the entrance, preserved from the old City of Paris dry goods store that used to stand in its place (and which many San Franciscans battled unsuccessfully to save). *Stockton and Geary Sts.*

Explorable Neighborhoods

Unlike many California cities—Los Angeles, San Diego, San Jose—that matured after the invention of the automobile, San Francisco's design is largely the product of an earlier time. Geography plays a role as well: Despite its population density (among the highest in the nation), the fresh ocean air, bay views, and many green spaces make the city eminently walkable. San Francisco's three-dozen-plus hills have produced a series of discreet neighborhoods, each with its own character. In most cases, the walk from one neighborhood to the next is less than a mile.

San Franciscans take to the streets, cafés, and coffeehouses on Sundays, making it the prime day to meet the locals. Chinatown, Union Square, and North Beach are all popular destinations for out-of-towners, but the less well-known spots just a few blocks away can be just as rewarding and a lot less crowded. Your explorations don't have to stop at the city limits; we've also listed some choice spots around the bay.

In the City

The Castro

Castro Street south of Market forms the heart of one of the best-known gay districts in the world, but it's by no means exclusively gay—partly because the Castro Theatre draws people from all over, partly because gentrification has attracted many straight families, and partly because many residents remain from the era when this was a blue-collar Irish district. The neighborhood's Victorians have been restored to the hilt; there are usually a few open houses being shown Sundays. (Stop in for decorating ideas.) Across Market Street, at no. 2362, are the workshop and offices of **The Names Project,** which has been responsible for the quilt of more than 31,000 panels sewn in memory of lovers and loved ones who have died of AIDS. Farther along, at the junction of Noe and Market, is the **Café Flore,** one of the city's prime people-watching spots.

In the other direction (west) from Castro Street, two blocks over on **Diamond Street** between 18th and Market, you'll find a fine example of community mutual support. You can't miss the three pink buildings: the Holy Redeemer Catholic Church, the Live Oak School and Diamond Senior Center, and the Coming Home Hospice. (The church owns all three buildings, but the organizations are separately administered.) The Hospice cares for AIDS patients in their final days, with support from the church; children at the school help out at the senior center and make cards and gifts for the hospice patients.

A block back toward Castro Street, up steep **Collingwood Street** between 21st and 22nd streets, you can see cobblestones in the foundations of several houses. (Check out no. 480, built in 1932.) They were saved when the old cable-car line that used to run through here was dismantled. A few blocks away at 250 Douglass Street—head west down the staircase at 22nd and Collingwood, then north on Douglass Street to Caselli Avenue—is a beautiful 1892 mansion. The house was known as **Clarke's Folly**—Alfred "Nobby" Clarke was a local water baron—because of the fortune that it took to build it. (It has five stories and 52 closets.) Caselli is a pleasant hidden avenue to hike up; if you make a left on Yukon Street after you pass Clover Street, you'll reach **Kite Hill Open Space,** a small, steep hill surrounded by charming Victorians and their gardens. Continue to the end of Caselli, then take a right onto Eagle Street, loop left up onto the Market Street sidewalk and cross at Clayton Street. Walk up Clayton until you see the sign for the **Pemberton Steps** (*see* Sutro Forest, *below*).

Chinatown Easily San Francisco's most explorable neighborhood, Chinatown has fascinated visitors and locals for a century and a half. Though many Chinese have moved beyond its borders (which are, roughly, Broadway and Stockton and Bush and Kearny streets), it remains the spiritual heart of San Francisco's Chinese community. These days it is home to a sizeable Southeast Asian community as well.

While wandering through Chinatown's streets and alleys, don't forget to look up: Above street level, many older structures—mostly brick buildings that replaced rickety wooden ones destroyed during the 1906 earthquake—have ornate balconies and cornices. The architecture in the **900 block of Grant Avenue** (at Washington Street) and **Waverly Place** (north of and parallel to Grant Avenue between Sacramento and Washington streets) is particularly noteworthy.

Chinatown is lined with herb shops. The **Superior Trading Company** (837 Washington St. at Waverly Pl.) is one of the largest. All day, sellers fill prescriptions from local doctors and herbalists, measuring exact amounts of tree roots, bark, flowers, and other ingredients with their scales. Many add up the bill on an abacus, an ancient calculator.

Hidden away in tiny Ross Alley (north of and parallel to Grant Avenue between Washington and Jackson streets) is the **Golden Gate Fortune Cookies Co.** (56 Ross Alley), where bakers sit at huge motorized griddles. Cookie batter pours onto tiny metal plates, which rotate into an oven and come out cooked and ready for folding. It's easy to peek in for a moment here; a bagful of cookies (with mildly racy "adult" fortunes or more benign ones) costs $3.

A refreshing Chinatown respite is the shop of the **Ten Ren Tea Co. Ltd.** (949 Grant Ave. at Jackson), which offers tastings of aromatic brews. Or stop by the **Golden Gate Bakery** (1029 Grant Ave. at Pacific). One of Chinatown's best, it prepares moon cakes and other pastries for seasonal festivals.

Shrewd chefs from around the city join Chinatown's residents in scouring local markets for the freshest seafood, meat, and produce—along with delicacies that are only found here. It's also fun to window shop. Some of the best markets are on Stockton Street, where a mural on the east side of the block, between Jackson Street and Pacific Avenue, commemorates the Chinese American community's hopes, dreams, and contributions. The **1100 block of Grant Avenue,** between Pacific Avenue and Broadway, is also intriguing. Don't miss the wok-fried pig noses (no need to ask, you'll know when you see them) often in the window of **Four Seas Supermarket** (1100 Grant Ave.). Four Seas also carries armadillo, freshwater turtle, and other surprisingly edible creatures.

Vegetarians may want to slip past **New Hop Yick Meat Market** (1147–49 Grant Ave.), across the street, where huge strips of fried pork rind are usually piled in the window. A few doors up at **Kwong**

Jow Sausage Manufacture and Food Products (1157–61 Grant Ave.) an artistic array of cured sausages hangs behind the counter. The rare duck-liver sausages here are expensive but sublime. Cooks buy the full duck skeletons toward the back for soup stock.

The corner of Broadway and Grant Avenue marks the beginning of North Beach (*see below*), though the Chinese influence continues into that neighborhood. For more of Chinatown, backtrack on Grant to Washington Street. East a half block on Washington is **Portsmouth Square.** This was the sight of Yerba Buena Plaza, where Captain John B. Montgomery first raised the American flag (in 1846).

Portsmouth Square is a multiuse park: In the morning people perform tai chi exercises; all day children play on modern playground equipment; and in the afternoons and evenings, dozens of men huddle over card games, a Chinese version of chess, and mah-jongg as well. If they seem incredibly intent, there's a reason: Most are playing for money.

Dolores Street The Canary Island palms that line the median of this splendid boulevard were planted by John McLaren (the man who, for a half century, supervised the building of Golden Gate Park) for the 1915 Panama-Pacific International Exposition. The street itself was once the beginning of El Camino Real, the road that the Spaniards constructed in the 18th century to connect the 21 missions founded by Father Junípero Serra. **Mission Dolores** (16th and Dolores Sts.), erected between 1782 and 1791, is the sixth one (*see* Places of Worship *in* Chapter 1 and Cemeteries *in* Chapter 6). **Mission High School** (18th and Dolores Sts.), with its ornate tower, was built in 1926, when Colonial Spanish Revival architecture was the rage in the city.

Mission Dolores Park (which most people refer to simply as Dolores Park) stands on the edge of a former Native American burial site. During the late 19th century, the spot became a Jewish cemetery, until a city ordinance banned burials within the city limits. The 18th Street end is popular with dog owners; the 20th Street end, with its dazzling downtown views, attracts sunbathers on sunny days.

The 1906 fires stopped near 20th Street, so at this point the houses change character subtly. (The wood for many of the houses built after the fire came from the East Bay.) A few blocks farther along, between 23rd and 24th streets, magnificent houses line the stretch from **1000 to 1083 Dolores**; old real-estate brochures used to call such blocks "Zones of Better Residence." (Nearby, on Liberty Street between Valencia and Guerrero, eight beautiful Italianate Victorians line another such "zone.")

Mission District A walk on **24th Street** east from Mission Street is like a stroll in a Mexican town—with a few additions. Once known as Butchertown because it was the site of the city's great German and Irish slaughterhouses, it is now a melting pot of Central Americans, Puerto Ricans, Koreans ,Chinese, and Thais. Most Sundays you'll happen on a mariachi band looking for work in one of the many Mexican restaurants along the street. There are also Asian restaurants, along with fresh food markets. If you detour to the left (north) on **Capp Street,** between 23rd and 22nd streets, you'll find a dozen Stick-style¢¢define?¢¢ Victorians, most of which haven't been changed. On **Folsom Street** there's a beautiful strip of Victorian row houses, cozy but far from gentrified, with graceful Chinese elms lining each side of the street. Continuing along 24th Street, a half block farther, mural-lined **Balmy Alley** (*see* Secret Spaces, Hidden Places, *below*) turns off to the south. Your final destination should be the **St. Francis Fountain** (2801 24th St., tel. 415/826–4200) an old-fashioned ice-cream parlor that's been around since 1918 (*see* Sweets and Treats *in* Chapter 2).

Also in the Mission, the **St. Charles School,** a rare 19th-century frame schoolhouse (3250 18th St. at Shotwell), has survived since 1875. The five-block stretch of **Fair Oaks Street** between 21st and 26th, lined most of the way with Chinese elms, is the Mission at its most charming. On **Hill Street,** between Valencia and Guerrero, you'll find Italianate Victorians on the even (north) side of the block and Stick Victorians on the odd (south) side.

The Mission neighborhood along Valencia Street, between 16th and 24th streets, is often called the **Women's Strip,** owing to its many feminist businesses and lesbian bars. Just off Valencia is the **Women's Building** (3543 18th St., tel. 415/431–1180), which for nearly 20 years has hosted workshops, conferences, and entertainment of particular interest to women. Lately the area has also become known as **New Bohemia,** a caffeine capital for students, 20-somethings, and artists by day, and a post-Beat bar scene, replete with poetry readings and local bands by night. There are a half dozen coffeehouses within a one-block radius of 16th and Mission and at least twice that number in the neighborhood altogether. It's also a good place for book browsers, with more than a dozen shops specializing in everything from political tracts to comic books.

Noe Valley

Once a largely Irish and Hispanic working-class neighborhood, the area was gentrified in the '70s, and now its name calls up an image of 30-something parents pushing strollers. Start at Church Street and climb the steep hill, heading west (toward Twin Peaks) on **21st Street.** (You can also come up from the other direction, starting at Sanchez and 19th streets and climbing a series of staircases.) At 21st and Sanchez is a Tudor-style mansion that is said to have belonged to mayor Jim Rolph; the garden was planted by John McLaren. The top of the hill is the site of a former resort spot where Californians came to languish in the healing waters of the area's many springs. The Native Americans who lived near Mission Dolores came up here for water from those springs; the same source helped extinguish fires after the 1906 quake. The dried-up springs left shaky soil that caused some uneven damage during the Loma Prieta quake of 1989. It isn't hard to figure out where nearby **Hill Street,** parallel to and between 21st and 22nd streets, got its name. (It was once known as Nanny Goat Hill for the goats that grazed there.) The views from all these streets are fine. Proceed downhill (south) on Sanchez Street and you'll hit **24th Street,** the neighborhood's shopping artery, with a cornucopia of boutiques, record stores, coffee bars, and gourmet shops.

Church Street provides another nice stroll from the top of Dolores Park. At **1079 Church** (on the east side between 22nd and 23rd streets) you'll see an unusual facade: a house painted with a giant mural of a tropical rain forest. About 10 blocks farther along, at 29th Street, you'll come to **St. Paul's Cathedral,** constructed in a Gothic Revival style unusual on the West Coast. (It appeared in the 1992 Whoopi Goldberg film *Sister Act.*)

About six blocks southwest of St. Paul's, at the intersection of Noe and Laidley streets, is the bottom of the **Harry Steps** (1932), a quiet, pine-enshrouded gem at the junction of Noe Valley, Glen Park, and Diamond Heights. In the right season the steps are a burst of color: lily of the Nile, fuchsia, daisy, and pyracantha.

North Beach and Telegraph Hill

San Francisco's Little Italy, which once boasted 125,000 Italian American residents, is now home to only about 2,000, most of them elderly; much of North Beach is now Chinese. But walk down narrow **Romolo Place** (off Broadway east of Columbus) or **Genoa Place** (off Union west of Kearny) or **Medau Place** (off Filbert west of Grant) and you can feel the immigrant Italian roots of this neighborhood. And it's still the number one place for cappuccino and biscotti before a Sunday morning visit to City Lights Bookstore. The **North Beach Playground** (Lombard and Mason Sts.) is still one of the best spots in town to watch groups of friends play boccie. There's an early Bernard Maybeck building at **1736 Stockton Street.**

A climb up Greenwich Street takes you to **Coit Tower,** home of the finest WPA murals in the city. Artists and writers have traditionally lived along the **Greenwich Steps** on the other side of Telegraph Hill. At the corner where this staircase intersects with the Filbert Steps stands the elegant Art Deco apartment house (1360 Montgomery St.) where the character played by Lauren Bacall lived in the 1947 movie *Dark Passage*. The plentiful roses, fuchsias, irises, and trumpet flowers along the **Filbert Steps** are the legacy of Grace Marchant, who labored for three decades to transform the site into one of San Francisco's hidden treasures. As you descend, watch for **Napier Lane,** one of the city's last surviving boardwalks. No. 21 has an outdoor stairway. Across Union Street, at 31 Calhoun Street, you'll find one of the oldest cottages in the city.

At the bottom of Telegraph Hill are the fountains and grassy knolls of **Levi's Plaza,** a beautifully scaled complex constructed by Levi Strauss and Company to give its employees a laid-back corporate setting. (During the week, you can spot them holding brown-bag lunch meetings in the plaza.) The redbrick facades match those of the site's original buildings (such as the wine cellar whose contents helped douse the 1906 fire).

Russian Hill This picturesque neighborhood has long been a favorite of writers, from Jack London and Bret Harte to Dashiell Hammett, Jack Kerouac, and Herbert Gold. It's currently engaged in a battle over the "little houses" built with $500 Red Cross loans soon after the 1906 earthquake and fire that destroyed 80 percent of the hill's homes. There are now only 40 or so left from a community once two or three times that size. With land at such a premium, few families can afford to purchase half-million-dollar two-bedroom cottages; more and more buyers have added on to them or simply torn them down. The cottages aren't architecturally significant, but they do provide the hill with much of its charm and light, and they stave off urban overdensity. There are more cottages on **Hyde and Leavenworth streets,** between Lombard and Greenwich.

The beautiful Craftsman-style houses on the **1000 block of Vallejo Street** (between Taylor and Jones) have earned it a listing on the National Register of Historic Places. The Craftsman movement, with its emphasis on simple redwood construction, came after (and in response to) the overelegance of Victorian architecture. One of its leading architects, Willis Polk, designed the **Polk-Williams** house at 1013–19 Vallejo Street and lived in part of the structure himself; he was also responsible for the Vallejo Stairway at the end of the block. (There is another Craftsman enclave nearby on **Macondray Lane,** a cobbled pedestrian street with sweeping bay views, off Jones Street between Green and Union streets.)

The **1000 block of Green Street** (between Jones and Leavenworth) boasts several homes that predate the quake, including the octagonal **Feusier House** at 1067 Green. This single block contains a fine array of San Francisco architectural styles: Italianate at 1055 (remodeled by Julia Morgan in 1916); a 1907 firehouse at 1088; a Queen Anne at 1045; and Joseph Esherick apartments, built in 1966, at 1085.

Sutro Forest For a walk through two unique neighborhoods, rambling woods, and a eucalyptus ravine, start at the intersection of Market and Clayton streets. There's a garden near the corner of Clayton Street and Corbett Avenue; to its right you'll see a sign that says "Pemberton." The **Pemberton Steps** were originally planned to go all the way down past Market Street into the Castro, but the land rush after the fire made the property too valuable. The terraced houses along the steps are among the newest in the city, and their owners take great pride in their gardens. The third flight of steps will bring you to Crown Terrace. Head north (right) and follow Crown Terrace to its end. Across Clarendon Avenue, to the right of the house at 192, you'll see the wood-and-concrete steps to **Tank Hill,** a former watershed that has been filled in and a good spot to take in the vistas.

Take a left off Crown Terrace, continue up the hill on Clarendon Avenue, and turn right on Johnstone Drive. About a quarter of a mile down, at no. 66, is the University of California at San Francisco **chancellor's residence,** a beautiful Japanese-style home in a eucalyptus grove. As soon as you enter the driveway, a path forks off to the left; this will take you into the **eucalyptus ravine** that abuts the university. It's a short but splendid hike through the backwoods of Sutro Forest above the Upper Haight, and it's often deserted. (If you prefer pavement, continue about 50 feet past the chancellor's residence and take a right on Medical Center Drive, which also passes through Sutro Forest.)

The main path brings you out at Woodland Avenue and Willard Street. Head left on Willard to Belmont Avenue, turn left, then left again onto magnificent, redbrick **Edgewood Avenue.** In the spring it's a fog of pink plum blossoms; in the summer it's green with shade trees. The beautiful homes are a mix of Arts-and-Crafts and Victorian houses, English cottages, Maybeck-inspired Tudors, and modern designs. On your way back down Edgewood, go past Belmont Avenue and take bewitching **Farnsworth Lane** back down to Willard.

Around the Bay

Marin County
Belvedere

A walk along Richardson Bay, then inland to the lavish houses set along the Belvedere Lagoon, is a pleasant Sunday diversion. Start at the border of Belvedere and Tiburon, where San Rafael Avenue forks to the south off Tiburon Boulevard. If you stay on San Rafael Avenue, you'll pass the splendid houses along the lagoon. Alternatively, if you keep to the shore along Richardson Bay, you have a quieter, more secluded walk on West Shore Road.

Mill Valley

The neighborhoody feel of Mill Valley makes it one of the most inviting Bay Area suburbs. On Sunday, the entire grassy knoll of **Lytton Plaza** (bordered by Throckmorton, Blithedale, Miller, and Sunnyside avenues), is filled with coffee sippers and paper perusers. (It's nicknamed the Caffeine Triangle.) You can get both coffee and a paper at the **Depot Bookstore and Cafe** (87 Throckmorton Ave. between Bernard and Madrona, tel. 415/383–2665), a former (1903) electric-rail depot. The architecture around here, with its Craftsman-inspired use of natural woods that blend in nicely with the surroundings, is unobtrusive but pleasing; note in particular the **Outdoor Art Club** (Throckmorton and Blithedale Aves.), a 1905 Bernard Maybeck Building, and the shops along **El Paseo Court,** a little street nearby. Mill Valley, like Belmont on the Peninsula, was a summer resort area around the turn of the century. Wealthy San Franciscans built weekend cottages here; follow just about any side street from Lytton Plaza and you'll spot the fetching little homes with rose-covered arbors.

Old Mill Park (Throckmorton Ave. and Cascade Dr.) stands on the site of the old sawmill from which the town gets its name. There's a replica of the old mill there, as well as one of the "Gravity Train" cars that used to come down from Mt. Tamalpais. The park boasts a playground and picnic tables surrounded by an astonishing circle of giant redwood trees. The **Dipsea Trail** (which leads all the way to Stinson Beach, 7 miles to the west) begins here. If you take the trail—or Throckmorton Avenue—north, you'll come to **Three Wells Park,** with its set of small, burbling pools, and then to **Cascade Park,**

where Mill Valley's little waterfall splashes under shady redwoods. You can get a free map of the Dipsea Trail from the reference desk of the **Mill Valley Public Library** (375 Throckmorton Ave. at Elma St., tel. 415/388–2190; open Tues.–Sat. only). The library building itself, set among redwoods on the edge of Old Mill Creek, is quintessential Mill Valley in the way it blends in elegantly with its surroundings. Other interesting houses include the 1893 **Coffin House** (15 Tamalpais Ave. at Summit Ave.), designed to look like a ferry boat, and Louis Mullgardt's 1907 **Evans House** (100 Summit Ave. at Lovell Ave.), a country-woods chalet that is one of the architect's few surviving homes.

Peninsula

Stanford—or, properly, **Leland Stanford Junior University**—was founded in 1885 by railroad baron Leland Stanford and his wife Jane in memory of their only son, Leland, Jr., who had died of typhoid fever in Florence the previous year. The campus centerpiece, the **quadrangle,** was designed by the great landscape architect Frederick Law Olmsted of Central Park fame. The Romanesque-cum-Mediterranean sandstone buildings, with red tile roofs and broad verandas, are perfectly suited to the surrounding golden hillsides dotted with live oaks. Other campus highlights include **Palm Drive,** the stately entrance to the university from El Camino Real; the **Stanford family mausoleum,** off Campus Drive; the mosaic-covered **Memorial Church** in the quad; and 285-foot **Hoover Tower** (the country's 31st president was a Stanford graduate), which has a splendid observation deck. The campus has been hit repeatedly by earthquakes; a photo display at the front of the quad shows the devastation the university suffered in 1906. There was damage in the 1989 quake, too, though it wasn't as dramatic.

There are **Visitor Information Booths** at Hoover Tower (tel. 415/723–2053) and at the front of the quad (tel. 415/723–2560). A free hour-long walking tour from the latter, daily at 11 and 3:15, covers the quad and the engineering and law schools but doesn't enter any buildings. Or you can get a map from either booth and conduct your own self-guided walking tour. The pleasant **coffeehouse** (tel. 415/723–3592), on the first floor of Tressider Union off White Plaza, is a good place for refreshments after your walk.

The **Rodin Sculpture Garden** stands outside the Stanford Museum of Art building (closed since the 1989 earthquake, and scheduled to reopen in 1997) on Museum Way. The University has an impressive collection of Rodins; the garden includes *The Age of Bronze*, *The Kiss*, and *The Gates of Hell*. As you wander around campus, you're likely to come upon individual figures from *The Burghers of Calais*. Two other noteworthy sculptures stand just north of the quad: Josef Albers's *Wall* and George Segal's *Gay Liberation*.

To experience the California foothills in all their unadorned simplicity, walk along the **Dish,** the hill that's home to a huge radio telescope on Stanford land behind (west of) the main campus. The Dish itself is now out of commission, a victim of air and noise pollution. You can access the trails either from Junípero Serra Boulevard just after the turnoff to Campus Drive East (you may have to hop over a fence) or from the Stanford Golf Course. All the trails in this area lead to the Dish; along the way there are horses, cows, and lots of birds.

Secret Places, Hidden Spaces

In San Francisco, neighborhoods tumble down the hillsides, leaving areas where blocks could not be filled by neatly planned grids. As you explore each neighborhood, you'll find your own special blocks, alleys, and magical corners—but here are some starters.

Outdoor Stairways

One of the sweetest of San Francisco's idiosyncrasies is its neighborhood stairways. There are steps to the top of local hills, steps connecting one street to another, and stairway lanes lined with houses and gardens that can't be reached by car. They're almost always worth a look. Here are some of the best:

Bernal Heights Take the steps from the corner of Elsie Street and Esmeralda Avenue up to Bernal Heights Boulevard, and from there climb the hill to **Bernal Heights Park.** The hilltop offers magnificent views and is full of indigenous plants.

Forest Hill **Oakhurst Lane.** The steepest set of stairs (and one of the longest) in the city, **Oakhurst Lane** (Warren Dr. down to Crestmont Dr.), cuts through eucalyptus trees and affords a view of the ocean. There's also a palatial set of stairs on **Pacheco Street** between Magellan Avenue and the 200 block of Castenada Avenue and again between the 300 block of Castenada and 9th Avenue.

Land's End For **Eagle's Point,** *see* Great Walks: Land's End and the Coastal Trail, *above.*

Noe Valley For the **Harry Steps,** *see* Explorable Neighborhoods: Noe Valley, *above.* The **Sanchez Steps** (between Liberty and 21st Sts.) are among the most beautiful in the city. There are also stairs on **Liberty Street** (one set near Castro, another near Noe), **22nd Street** (near Diamond), **Cumberland Street** (across from 670 Noe), and **Elizabeth Street** (near Hoffman and Grand View).

North Beach For the **Filbert Steps** and **Greenwich Steps,** *see* Explorable Neighborhoods: North Beach, *above.* The **Grant Steps** between Francisco and Pfeiffer streets farther north are renowned for their gardens.

Pacific Heights The grand steps on **Pierce Street** (between Clay and Washington) lead up into Alta Plaza. The **Baker Stairs** (between Vallejo and Broadway) have lush pines and bay views.

Potrero Hill The **Vermont Steps** (between 20th and 22nd Sts.) offer some wonderful vistas.

Richmond More great views and more beautiful Victorians make the University of San Francisco **Lone Mountain Terrace** (from Parker Ave. to Stanyan St.) an impressive stairway.

Russian Hill Next to Ina Coolbrith Park, a winding stairway lined with grand homes leads down the **Alta Vista Terrace** from Vallejo Street between Taylor and Mason streets.

Upper Market For the **Pemberton Steps** and **Farnsworth Lane,** *see* Explorable Neighborhoods: Sutro Forest, *above.* Nearby **Iron Alley** (from 1499 Clayton to 495 Corbett) is also worth a look. The **Vulcan Stairs** (north of 17th St. between Ord and Levant) offer cobblestone terraces and beautiful gardens, and the steps from 17th Street (between Roosevelt and Clayton) to **Upper Terrace** lead to a beautiful cul-de-sac with hidden houses.

Lanes and Alleys

Among the Bay Area's most charming nooks are the secluded courtyards, tucked-away alleys, and concealed lanes that dot San Francisco. The Filbert Steps (*see* Explorable Neighborhoods: North Beach, *above*), where public-use lands and stairs snake around the homes on the hillside, are the most familiar example of what has come to be known as "neotraditional" planning, an approach that is enjoying new popularity in many surrounding communities. Architect Daniel Solomon is its leading local proponent. He argues that such public spaces create security and privacy, as well as a sense of community, without the use of gates and walls. Neotraditional planning is the inspiration behind such developments as the proposed 313-acre **Mission Bay** area (SoMa below Townsend Street, between I–280 and the bay), which will consist of gardenlike alleys, lanes, and courtyards.

Balmy Alley. The murals up and down this small side street range from trompe l'oeil laundry to socialist realism. Local children started the project in 1973; it has been carried on by an affiliation of artists and community workers. (Beware when visiting here; the south end of Balmy backs into a somewhat dangerous housing project.) *From 24th to 25th Sts. between Treat and Harrison.*

Fulton Grove Townhome Project, Hayes Valley. Daniel Solomon designed this modern midblock tree-lined alley with a pedestrian mall in the project bordered by Gough, Octavia, Fulton, and Grove streets. *440 Grove St. at Gough St., 1 block west of Performing Arts Library and Museum.*

Loma Vista Terrace. If you follow Masonic Avenue south all the way to its end, you'll find yourself in a charming group of narrow streets, pretty houses, and marvelous vistas on the other side of Buena Vista Park—a pleasant area for meandering.

Pier 7. Designed to convey a shipboard ambience, this pier has Victorian wrought-iron lampposts and benches that will make you feel as though you need a parasol and long skirt. Though it's often windy, the pier is a popular spot for lunch. *Foot of Broadway.*

343 Sansome Street. If you ask nicely, the guard may let you up to the rooftop garden on the 15th floor. It doesn't have a far-ranging view, but it's a wonderful vantage point from which to gaze down on the streets below. The building went up in 1908 but was given an Art Deco twist in 1930. *At Sacramento St.*

Wave Organ. Fashioned by stonecutters George Gonzales and Thomas Lipps in 1986 to capture the sounds of the ocean, this unusual instrument gives off harmonic sounds produced by the seawater that passes through its three stone chambers. *Just west of the Golden Gate Yacht Club, near Lyon St. and Marina Blvd. in the Marina.*

Tours

Tours may be designed with out-of-towners in mind primarily, but an excursion on a red double-decker bus can also be a great Sunday outing for jaded locals who have seen it all—especially if you go whole-hog and buy trinkets at all the stops. Sometimes seeing the city through different eyes is a good way to remind yourself what a jewel it is.

Guided Tours

From the Water

Sailing

For more boating activities *see* Sports and Recreation *in* Chapter 6.

Hornblower Dining Yachts. The *Hornblower*, patterned after the classic steamers of the early 1900s, offers weekend brunch cruises (board at 10:30, sail from 11 to 1) in addition to its afternoon and dinner-dance cruises. Departures are from Pier 33 (Embarcadero at Bay St.). *Tel. 415/788–8866 or 415/394–8900, ext. 7.*

Sonoma–Napa Tour. This eight-hour boat-bus excursion leaves from Pier 41 (Embarcadero and Stockton St.) weekends at 10 AM and pulls in at Tiburon, where patrons catch a motorcoach to the Wine Country for a three-winery tour and lunch. *Tel. 415/546–2700.*

Pacific Marine Yachts and Charter and Dining Cruises. Sunday brunch and dinner cruises on the bay depart from Pier 39 (Beach St. and Grant Ave.) *Tel. 415/788–9100*

Motor Cruises

Blue and Gold Fleet sails under both the Golden Gate and Bay bridges. In 1996 the company took over the Red and White Fleet, which offered similar tours plus cruises to Angel Island, Alcatraz, and other bay destinations. (At press time, government and union approval was pending.) Audiotapes on most tours are available in English, German, Japanese, and Mandarin. *Piers 39, 41, 43 1/2, tel. 415/705–5444, 415/546–2628 or 800/229–2784.*

Oceanic Society Expeditions sponsors Farallon Island excursions on an 85-foot boat that leaves the Yacht Harbor at the Marina Green from June through November. You may see dolphins, sea lions, blue and humpback whales, birds, and other marine life. From December through April, the society organizes whale-watching trips. Make weekend reservations well in advance. *Tel. 415/474–3385 or 800/326–7491.*

Walking Tours

Tour times change with the season, so call ahead. Most companies require reservations.

A.M. Walks are so called because they're held at 8 AM—a good traffic-free time to see Union Square, Chinatown, or the so-called Barbary Coast. *1433 Clay St., Suite 4, tel. 415/928–5965.*

Art Deco Society offers walking tours to view the city's great Deco buildings on most Sundays. *100 Bush St., Suite 511, tel. 415/982–3326.*

Chinatown tours are the specialty of Shirley Fong-Torres, the "Wok Wiz," who visits chefs and other personalities and fills her group in on the area's folklore, history, and food. The tour includes a tea ceremony and a dim sum lunch. *750 Kearny St., Suite 800, tel. 415/355–9657.*

City Guides, sponsored by the Friends of the San Francisco Public Library, offer a number of free tours, including the Gold Rush city, Art Deco in the Marina, and Nob Hill. For a list, stop by the main library or at the counter at the Visitors Information Center in Hallidie Plaza, or send a self-addressed stamped envelope to City Guides, Civic Center, Main Library, San Francisco 94102. *Recorded information, tel. 415/557–4266.*

Cruisin' the Castro from an Historical Perspective is what Trevor Hailey calls her tour, which lets you in on how and why San Francisco became a gay mecca. (At present there's a Saturday tour but not a Sunday one.) *375 Lexington St., tel. 415/550–8110.*

Heritage Walks, held by the Foundation for San Francisco's Architectural Heritage, leave from the Haas-Lilienthal House (*see* Restored Houses *in* Chapter 4) every Sunday at 12:30 for a tour of Pacific Heights. The group also conducts walks through Chinatown and the Presidio for any size group, by advance appointment. *2007 Franklin St. at Washington, tel. 415/441–3004.*

Precita Eyes Mural Arts Center offers its tours of Mission murals on Saturday at 1:30, and for $1 they'll give you a mural map for a self-guided tour Sundays. *348 Precita Ave. at Folsom St., tel. 415/285–2287.*

San Francisco African-American Historical and Cultural Society sponsors quarterly downtown walking tours of companies owned and/or run by black businesspeople. They're offered on Saturday, but with advance notice the organization will lead groups of 15 or more on other days. *165 Building C, Fort Mason, tel. 415/441–0640.*

Stairway tours are the specialty of Adah Bakalinsky, author of *Stairway Walks in San Francisco.* She leads small groups by arrangement. Send a self-addressed stamped envelope for information. *Stairway Walks, 101 Lombard St. –606, San Francisco 94111.*

Theme Tours by Van

Cable Car Charters conducts one- or two-hour tours on motorized cable cars that depart from the front of A. Sabella Restaurant (2766 Taylor St. at Jefferson) in Fisherman's Wharf. Customized tours are available. *Tel. 415/922–2425.*

Escape Artist Tours offers unusual adventures in the Bay Area and beyond, including a ranch tour of the Gold Country and a haunted bed-and-breakfast tour. *150 Tiller Ct., Half Moon Bay, tel. 415/726–7626 or 800/728–1384.*

San Francisco Jewish Landmarks Tours are half- or full-day visits to buildings, homes, synagogues, and other sites in the area that figure in Jewish history. Historians lead the tours. *2865 Green St., tel. 415/921–0461.*

Nature Tours **A Day in Nature** offers customized half-day nature tours in Marin County. Reservations are required. *1490 Sacramento St., tel. 415/673–0548.*

Citywide Bus Tours **Gray Line Tours** (Powell and Geary Sts. and the Transbay Terminal at 1st and Mission, tel. 415/558–9400) operates multilingual tours of San Francisco on double-decker buses. Smaller vans and regular buses head to Sausalito, the Wine Country, Monterey, and Carmel. Gray Line also offers helicopter tours. Other options include **Golden Gate Tours** (tel. 415/788–5775), **Great Pacific Tour Company** (tel. 415/626–4499), **Quality Tours** (tel. 415/994–5054), **Super Sightseeing Tours** (tel. 415/550–1717), and **Tower Tours** (tel. 415/434–8687).

Air Tours **San Francisco Helicopter Tours** (tel. 510/635–4500 or 800/400–2404) will pick you up at your hotel for 20- or 30-minute flights. Options include Wine Country and sunset flights. **Scenic Air Tours** (tel. 415/922–2386) conducts one-hour Bay Area tours, as well as Yosemite Valley tours, in single- and twin-engine aircraft. Both companies offer family rates.

Self-Guided Tours

On Tape **Day Ranger Tours on Cassette** offer two San Francisco audio tours—one from Union Square to Washington Square, the other from Coit Tower to the Transamerica Pyramid—that are full of literary, historical, and architectural tidbits. (Send $12.95 each plus $2 shipping). *143B Arundel St., St. Paul, MN 55102, tel. 612/228–9395.*

In Print Some of the following guidebooks and pamphlets may be hard to find. Try **A Clean Well-Lighted Place for Books** or **Cody's Books** (*see* Specialty Stores: Books *in* Chapter 5), and don't forget the library.

The New San Francisco at Your Feet (Grove Weidenfeld, $12.95). The best of *San Francisco Chronicle* writer Margaret Patterson Doss's "Sunday Punch" columns appear in this collection.

The Dashiell Hammett Tour by Don Herron (City Lights, $9.95).

Earl Thollander's San Francisco: 30 Walking Tours (Clarkson N. Potter, $9.95).)

Forty-One Walking Tours of Berkeley and *The Buildings of Berkeley: Phase Two* (Berkeley Architectural Heritage Association; $5 for the first, $15 for the second, tel. 510/841–2242).

The Guide to Architecture in San Francisco and Northern California, by David Gebhardt and Robert Winter (Gibbs Smith, $18.95).

Hidden Walks in the Bay Area and *More Hidden Walks in the Bay Area*, by Stephen Altschuler (Western Tanager Press, Santa Cruz, both $9.95).

Pocket Guide to the Historic Districts of San Francisco (San Francisco Convention and Visitors Bureau, free). Send a self-addressed, stamped legal-size envelope to the Convention and Visitors Bureau, or pick up a copy at the bureau's Visitors Information Center (*see* Visitor Information *in* Essential Information).

San Francisco Architecture: The Illustrated Guide to Over 1,000 of the Best Buildings, Parks and Public Artworks in the Bay Area, by Sally Woodbridge, John M. Woodbridge, and Chuck Byrne (Chronicle Books, $16.95).

Stairway Walks in San Francisco, by Adah Bakalinsky (Wilderness Press, $9.95). If you have difficulty finding a copy, you can order one from the publisher (2440 Bancroft Way, Berkeley, 94704, tel. 510/843–8080).

A Walking Tour of the Black Presence in San Francisco during the 19th Century (San Francisco African-American Historical and Cultural Society, $10). You can purchase a copy at the society's gift shop (165 Building C, Fort Mason, tel. 415/441–0640; open Wed.–Sun. 11–5).

Sightseeing from City Buses and Cable Cars

City buses are a fine—and cheap—way to see the city without developing bunions. We suggest starting with the 42 line, which runs in a circle—both clockwise and counterclockwise—through downtown San Francisco. If you catch it on its clockwise loop on the east side of South Van Ness Avenue just south of Market Street, it will take you up Van Ness, past the great buildings of the Civic Center to Fisherman's Wharf. From there it heads toward Battery Street, through the skyscrapers of the Financial District, to the CalTrain terminal at 4th and Townsend streets, and finally back to Van Ness and Market.

Cable cars are a wonderful—and, of course, uniquely San Franciscan—way to see the city. The most frequented route is the **Powell and Market Line,** which begins at Hallidie Plaza (Powell and Market Sts.), named in honor of the cable cars' inventor, Andrew Smith Hallidie (1836–1900). Buy a ticket at the police kiosk; from there you can take in the street life—jugglers, mimes, musicians, and occasional pickpockets, too, so watch out)—as you stand in line. The cars get pretty cozy, so the choicest spot, if you're feeling brave, may be the exterior ledge, where you can hang out and gaze at the passing scenery. The Powell and Market Line passes Union Square, Chinatown, and Russian Hill and winds up near Fisherman's Wharf. The **Powell and Mason Line** follows the same route but diverges in Chinatown (at the Cable Car Barn, Washington at Mason) and heads into North Beach. The **California Line** begins downtown at Drumm Street, near the Embarcadero Center, and wends its way up California Street, passing Chinatown and Nob Hill, to Van Ness Avenue. *For further information, call Muni (tel. 415/673–6864).*

Best Bets for Children

Children will love any of the sweeping **views** that we've listed in this chapter; skyscrapers are always fun, and the vista from Twin Peaks is a stunner. A walk across the **Golden Gate Bridge** (bundle up) or down to **Fort Point** is a winner, too. The city's nooks and crannies appeal to every age group, and its **outdoor stairways** may be even more appealing to children, who have the energy to climb them. **Ferry rides** are entrancing to kids, and so, of course, are the **cable cars.** (When you disembark, you can pick up a toy cable car in one of the tacky souvenir shops at Fisherman's Wharf, and the kids can drive you crazy for weeks ringing the bell.) **Fisherman's Wharf** and **Pier 39** might be your idea of tourist hell, but older children love them: they're the city equivalent of the mall scene for the junior-high-school set. **Mural-watching** is another good bet: Precita Eyes Mural Arts Center's map (*see* Walking Tours, *above*) will direct you to the city's finest.

San Francisco is kid-friendly in general, but some neighborhoods stand out—**Noe Valley** in particular. It has good playgrounds, and 24th Street, the main shopping drag, has ice cream parlors, burger spots, coffee joints where children can sip steamed milk while their parents go for something stronger, and plenty of children-oriented stores. At 521 Clipper Street, on the south side midblock between Diamond and Douglass, is the **Rainbow House,** which every girl under six dreams of living in. The former owners painted it in honor of their daughter, whom they had named Rainbow. After several years facing the elements, it's finally starting to fade into less gaudy hues.

4 Museums and the Visual Arts

By Daniel Mangin

Rain or shine, Sunday in San Francisco is a prime occasion for cultural outings. The array of weekend choices ranges from natural habitats (the Golden Gate Raptor Observatory, the new Summit Museum at Mt. Diablo) to historical treasures (the Haas-Lilienthal or Dunsmuir houses) to the often jam-packed galleries of the M.H. de Young Memorial Museum and the San Francisco Museum of Modern Art.

As state and municipal contributions to the arts have decreased in recent years, prices at Bay Area institutions have crept upward: a circumstance that makes two discount programs worth pursuing. The **Young Audiences ArtsCard Project** is described in Best Bets for Children, *below.* The $12.50 Golden Gate Park **Explorer Pass** (tel. 415/391–2000) offers adults savings of up to 30% off entrance fees to the Asian Art Museum, the de Young Museum, the California Academy of Sciences, the Conservatory of Flowers (when it reopens after storm-damage repairs), and the Japanese Tea Garden. The passes, good for several months (one admission to each site), are available at the participating sites (except the conservatory); the TIX Bay Area Booth (open Mon.–Sat.) on Union Square; and the Visitor Information Center on the lower level of Hallidie Plaza, near the Powell and Market cable-car turnaround.

There are also plenty of free attractions (many listed below), so don't let money stand in the way of an edifying and entertaining Sunday.

How to Find Out What's Going On

Museum and cultural listings can be found in the "Weekend" pages of the Friday *Examiner* and on the "Art," "Events," and "Exhibits: Nature/Tours/Attraction" pages in the Sunday *Chronicle*'s Pink Section. Of the tourist booklets available at hotels and major sightseeing attractions, the monthly *Bay City Guide* is the best organized and most comprehensive.

Art Museums

The '90s are seeing great changes at San Francisco's major museums. The San Francisco Museum of Modern Art moved to Yerba Buena Center in 1995. The California Palace of the Legion of Honor, which closed for 3½ half years for a $36.5 million seismic upgrade and expansion, reopened to great fanfare in late 1995. Next up for retrofitting is the de Young Museum, though precise plans are not yet in place. The Asian Art Museum plans to vacate its Golden Gate Park home for a turn-of-the-century move into the former Main Library in the Civic Center. In the East Bay, the Oakland Museum has increased its commitment to the research and exhibition of California's multicultural heritage. Berkeley's University Art Museum, whose collection focuses on 20th century art, reorganized its holdings in the early '90s.

Major Museums

M. H. de Young Memorial Museum

Twice in the mid-1990s, the city's most comprehensive museum celebrated its 100th anniversary. Many of its works were originally displayed in the Fine Arts Building of the 1894 California Midwinter International Exhibition, sponsored by San Francisco *Chronicle* publisher M. H. de Young. When the exposition closed, de Young offered the Fine Arts Building and much of the art as the basis for a permanent museum. The new Memorial Museum (renamed for de Young in 1927) opened in March 1895.

Acquisitions during the museum's early years focused on the ancients, the Americas, and Africa. Over the years, as the collection grew, the emphasis on American art continued. In 1979 the museum received a large bequest from Mr. and Mrs. John D. Rockefeller III (augmented by subsequent gifts from Mrs. Rockefeller) from their private collection of American paintings and works on paper. In 1989 the de Young and the California Palace of the Legion of Honor reorganized their collections, with most of the de Young's European holdings moving to the Legion and some of that museum's American works transferring to the de Young. The combined result has been what the latter justly trumpets as one of the world's best survey collections of American art, from Colonial times to the mid-20th century.

Highlights The **American art** wing consists of 22 chronologically organized galleries, lettered A–V, beginning with 17th- and 18th-century decorative arts and paintings. Highlights include John Vanderlyn's *Marius Amidst the Ruins of Carthage*, George Caleb Bingham's *Boatmen on the Missouri*, Georgia O'Keeffe's *Petunias*, and Grant Wood's *Dinner for Threshers*. Albert Bierstadt and John Singer Sargent are well represented in the collection. Among the Rockefeller gifts usually on display are pivotal works by Gilbert Stuart, Susan MacDowell Eakins, Thomas Cole, and Robert Henri. Edward Hicks's *Peaceable Kingdom* is the centerpiece of the museum's collection of American folk art.

Just off the Hearst Court, near the museum's entrance, is the de Young's collection of **ancient art** from Egypt, Greece, Rome, and the Near East.

In 1993 the de Young opened a **textiles gallery** next to the last of the American galleries. An ongoing installation, *Unraveling Yarns: The Art of Everyday Life*, contains more than 60 samples of fiber art from around the world. Of particular note is the collection of Anatolian kilim carpets from Turkey.

The **African art** collection, to the right of the museum's entrance, focuses on the works of sub-Saharan artisans. Of particular note are a power figure from Zaire, a Makonde helmet mask from Mozambique, and an elephant mask from Nigeria.

A large Teotihuacan mural greets visitors to the **Art of the Americas** gallery, just beyond the African art. Works from Meso-, Central, and South America, as well as from the west coast of North America, are on display here. A 10-foot totem pole from Alaska towers over one section.

Sunday Programs The museum's popular **"Third Sunday Brunch Tours"** include brunch, a lecture and/or slide show, and a tour of a gallery or special exhibition. Advanced reservations (tel. 415/750–3638) are advised. There are usually two seatings, at 10:30 and 11:30; the cost is $12.50 ($8.50 for museum members).

Facilities The **Cafe de Young,** which serves coffee, tea, and light lunches, has indoor seating and tables in a pleasant garden setting.

A reminder: Car traffic is not permitted on Sundays in the area of Golden Gate Park near the de Young. Park along Fulton Street or one of the numbered avenues that intersect it, or take Bus 5 (Fulton) from downtown to the Fulton Street and 8th Avenue stop. *Tea Garden Dr. between South Dr. and John F. Kennedy Dr., near Fulton St. and 8th Ave. entrance to Golden Gate Park, tel. 415/863–3330 for 24-hour information. Admission: $6, includes same-day entry for Asian Art Museum and Legion of Honor. Open Sun. 10–4:45.*

San Francisco Museum of Modern Art Even its most enthusiastic supporters were taken aback by the instant popularity of the 225,000-square foot Mario Botta-designed SFMOMA facility. Within just a few months of its 1995 opening, more people had passed through the museum than had done so in the last full year at its former Civic Center location. Several of the initial exhibitions focused on SFMOMA's permanent collection, the breadth of which could not be conveyed at the old site.

In the past few years SFMOMA's curatorial approach has leaned toward a greater emphasis on interdisciplinary art forms, such as sculptural/film-video installations, but the collection of early modernist works remains a centerpiece. Photography and post–World War II California art are among the important holdings. SFMOMA was a prime champion of art cinema until the '70s, and the museum is expected to regain some of its past prominence in this area with two state-of-the-art film- and video-screening rooms.

Highlights The museum's second-floor galleries exhibit selections from the **permanent collection of painting and sculpture, 1900–1980,** in addition to holdings and special exhibitions in architecture and design. Some galleries present the works of individual artists, including the American abstract-expressionist Clyfford Still, Jackson Pollock, Philip Guston, and Richard Diebenkorn. German expressionist, fauvist, Mexican, and Bay Area art is also exhibited. One popular attraction is the Djerassi collection of Paul Klee prints, drawings, and paintings.

SFMOMA's renowned **department of photography** has most of the third-floor gallery space, which also exhibits works on paper. Pivotal photographs by Alfred Stieglitz, Ansel Adams, Edward Weston, Paul Strand, the German avant-garde of the 1920s, and the European surrealists of the '30s are the backbone of the collection. More recent acquisitions include conceptually derived works by Duane Michals, Joel-Peter Witkin, Jo Ann Callis, and others. Rotating selections from the permanent collection provide a historical overview of the medium.

On the fourth floor are galleries for temporary exhibitions, contemporary art from the collection, and media-arts installations. An intimate gallery specializes in the presentation of sound and interactive media art forms, as well as single-channel videotapes and projected imagery. Fifth-floor galleries are set aside for temporary exhibitions in all media. *151 3rd St. at Mission St., tel. 415/357–4000. Admission: $7. Open Sun. 11–6. Closed major holidays.*

California Palace of the Legion of Honor Commissioned by Alma Spreckels, arts patron and wife of sugar magnate Adolph Spreckels, this knockout museum occupies one of the most stunning pieces of real estate in San Francisco—overlooking the ocean, the Golden Gate Bridge, and parts of downtown. The Legion's view and beautiful architecture are worth the trip alone, but its art holdings merit attention as well: Though not large, the collection constitutes an excellent survey of more than 4,000 years of ancient and European art history. INFORM, a new system of handheld wands with educational information, allows patrons to dial descriptions of individual artworks, rather than follow a preset tour.

Highlights Patrons enter the Legion via the Court of Honor, where Auguste Rodin's *The Thinker* (ca. 1880, cast ca. 1904) presides. A recent addition to the court is the Louvre-like glass pyramid, which lets light into the new underground sculpture court.

The permanent collection, which spans medieval to 20th-century art, fills the museum's first floor. Individual galleries showcase religious medieval art, Italian Renaissance art (note in particular the *Last Judgment Triptych*, ca. 1500, attributed to an unknown Tyrolean Master), and French, Italian, and Spanish painting, sculpture, and decorative art from the 17th to 19th centuries.

The skylit Rotunda contains several fine Rodin sculptures. Behind the Rotunda is the museum's 1924 Skinner pipe organ, which has 4,500 wooden and metal pipes. Though indoors, the organ is used for outdoor concerts as well: The plaster frieze above the Legion's main entrance can be opened so that the music reaches the Court of Honor. Sunday recitals were a tradition before the museum closed; they are expected to continue when the restoration of the organ is completed, it is hoped by late 1996.

Other strong suits are a Louis XVI room with period furnishings and decorative art; a British collection from the 18th and 19th centuries, including Thomas Gainsborough's *Market Carts* (1784–85); and Dutch and Flemish art of the 17th century, including Rembrandt's *Portrait of Joris de Caullerii* (1632). Joseph Turner's *View of Kenilworth Castle* (ca. 1830) and Paul Cézanne's *The Rocks in the Park of the Château Noir* (c. 1898–99) are among the noteworthy paintings.

Downstairs are a porcelain gallery, ancient art, the prints and drawings collection, and seven galleries for temporary exhibitions. Works from Legion's renowned Achenbach Foundation for the Graphic Arts, which spans the complete history of printmaking and drawing, are exhibited here as well. On the northwestern side of the lower level are the new **Museum Cafe,** where large windows afford vistas of the Golden Gate, and a gift shop. *100 34th Ave. (on some maps as Legion of Honor Dr.), Lincoln Park, off Clement St., tel. 415/863–3330. Admission $6; $1 discount for visitors with valid Muni transfer or Fast Pass. Note: Admission also grants entrance to de Young Museum and Asian Art Museum on same day. Open Sun. 10–4:45.*

Other Major Museums

In the City

Asian Art Museum. The heart of the Asian Art Museum's collection are the 10,000 sculptures, paintings, architectural elements, and ceramics amassed by Avery Brundage over a period of nearly 40 years. Brundage, who was president of the International Olympic Committee from 1952 to 1972, donated his collection to the city of San Francisco. The two-floor museum to house it, adjoining the de Young Museum in Golden Gate Park, was completed in 1966. Space limitations allow only about 15% of the collection—which now includes more than 12,000 artworks from 40 Asian countries and spans 6,000 years of history—to be on view at any one time. In late 1999 the Asian plans to relocate to the old Main Public Library building in the Civic Center, where its exhibition space will double.

In the meantime, it's business as usual at the Asian's Golden Gate Park home, where rotating exhibits explore facets of the collection. To accommodate a large, late-1996 show of art from Taiwan's National Palace Museum, curators plan to remove most of the permanent works in its first-floor galleries. Many will not be seen again until the museum completes its Civic Center move.

As we headed to press (midsummer 1996) it wasn't clear how the first-floor galleries would be configured after the Taiwan show departs; usually, the art of China and Korea is the focus on this level. Also on the first floor is the Treasure Wall, a cross-section of bronze, wood, jade, ceramic, and other objects. The Asian's large collections of Japanese and Indian art are on the second floor, along with works from Southeast Asia and the Near East.

The Asian's holdings are generally arranged with an emphasis on stylistic evolution, as well as cross-cultural and political characteristics. The oldest known dated Chinese Buddha image (AD 338) is on display, and the museum also houses the largest museum collection in the United States of Japanese *inro* (small, intricate lacquer boxes for carrying personal items). Also of note are the jade collection, ancient Chinese ceramics, silk and paper scrolls, and blue-and-white porcelains. Usually on display on the first floor is the Rhinoceros-Shaped Zun, a Shang dynasty (China) bronze wine container from the late 12th century B.C. A lengthy inscription inside the vessel records the events of a military battle. *Tea Garden Dr. between South*

Dr. and John F. Kennedy Dr., Fulton St. and 8th Ave. entrance to Golden Gate Park, tel. 415/668–7855. Admission: $6; includes same-day entrance to de Young Museum and Legion of Honor. Open Sun. 10–4:45.

Around the Bay
East Bay

The **Oakland Museum** positions itself as "the only museum in the country devoted exclusively to the environment, multicultural history, and art of California." Founded in 1969 and housed in an innovative building near Lake Merritt, the museum presents permanent and changing exhibitions, plus lectures, workshops, festivals, and educational family programs. Don't miss the Hall of California Ecology and Aquatic California Gallery on Level 1, the Cowell Hall of California History on Level 2, or the Gallery of California Art on Level 3. The Great Hall High and Low Bays on Level 2 host temporary multimedia exhibits with California themes.

Some of the museum's most impressive holdings are in California habitat re-creations; Mexican California; the Gold Rush; California Indian basketry and regalia; early California landscape painting, the Arts and Crafts Movement; African American artists; and the beatnik, hippie, and yuppie movements. Docents hold tours on request on weekends (tel. 510/238–3514 for advance arrangements). *1000 Oak St. at 10th St., Oakland, one block from the Lake Merritt BART station, tel. 510/238–3401. Admission: $5. Open Sun. noon–7; hours 4–7 free.*

The **University Art Museum** began with a bequest from abstract painter Hans Hoffman, who donated 50 of his works to the University of California at Berkeley in the '60s, along with $250,000 toward the construction of a museum. Today the museum shares a building on the Berkeley campus with the Pacific Film Archive. Its major strengths are Asian art and 20th-century western painting, sculpture, photography, and conceptual art. *2626 Bancroft Way at Bowditch St., Berkeley, tel. 510/642–0808. Admission: $6. Open Sun. 11–5.*

Specialty Museums, Small Surprises

In the City

Ansel Adams Center. This gallery, which shows historical and contemporary photography, owns an extensive permanent collection of Adams's work. *250 4th St. at Folsom, tel. 415/495–7000. Admission: $4. Open Sun. 11–5.*

Anton Refregier mural. (*See* Architecture, Rincon Center, *in* Chapter 3.)

Cartoon Art Museum. Here's a place that takes the funnies seriously. Rotating exhibits include comic books, plates and sketches from comic strips, animation cels, and computer-generated imagery. *814 Mission at 4th St., 2nd floor, tel. 415/546–3922. Admission: $3.50. Open Sun. 1–5.*

San Francisco Craft and Folk Art Museum. American folk art, tribal art, and contemporary crafts are on exhibit on two levels here. The gift shop (admission free) sells handmade items at reasonable prices. *Bldg. A, Fort Mason, Laguna St. at Marina Blvd., tel. 415/775–0990. Admission: $1. Open Sun. 11–5.*

Around the Bay
East Bay

University of California at Berkeley Museum of Art, Science and Culture at Blackhawk. This multipurpose exhibition space is home to the Behring Auto Museum, which contains more than 120 classic automobiles from the 1890s to the 1970s. Objects from various U.C. Berkeley museums are exhibited regularly as well. *3700 Blackhawk Plaza Circle at Sycamore Valley Rd., tel. 510/736–2280. Admission: $7. Open Sun. 10–5.*

World and Ethnic Cultures

In the City

Jewish Community Museum. Revolving exhibits in this handsome small museum trace important moments in Jewish history. Sunday tours led by members of the College Guides program begin at 2. *121 Steuart St. at Mission St., tel. 415/543–8880. Admission: $3. Open Sun. 11–5, but hours can vary, so call ahead.*

Mexican Museum. Though plans are in the making to move this museum to Yerba Buena Center by the end of the century, for now it's a very small space containing some stunning examples of Mexican and Mexican American art, from pre-Hispanic figures to works by modern masters. The gift shop stocks colorful folk art, posters, books, and exhibition catalogs. *Bldg. D, Fort Mason, Laguna St. at Marina Blvd., tel 415/441–0404. Admission: $3. Open Sun. noon–5.*

Museo Italo-Americano. In this West Coast outpost of Italian culture are permanent exhibits of works by 19th- and 20th-century Italian-American artists. Shows include paintings, sculpture, etchings, and photographs. The museum presents special exhibits, lectures, and films as well. *Bldg. C, Fort Mason, Laguna St. at Marina Blvd., tel. 415/673–2200. Admission: $2. Open Sun. noon–5.*

San Francisco African-American Historical and Cultural Society. The permanent collection includes material on black California and black Civil War history. Temporary exhibits focus on living California artists. *Bldg. C, Room 165, Fort Mason, Laguna St. at Marina Blvd., tel. 415/441–0460 Admission: $5. Open Sun. 11–5.*

Around the Bay
East Bay

Judah H. Magnes Museum. The third-largest Jewish museum in the Western Hemisphere has an impressive collection of art and artifacts, including paintings, sculpture, prints, and drawings, by Marc Chagall, Max Liebermann, and others. Temporary and permanent exhibits focus on Jewish life throughout the world, showcasing rare treasures from synagogues, as well as textiles and holiday objects used in Jewish homes. Volunteer docents conduct tours of the museum on Sunday afternoons. *2911 Russell St. at Pine, Berkeley, tel. 510/549–6950. Suggested donation: $2–$3. Open Sun. 10–4.*

Phoebe Apperson Hearst Museum of Anthropology. Formerly known as the Robert H. Lowie Museum of Anthropology, this research and exhibition space on the U.C. Berkeley campus has an extensive permanent collection and an ambitious temporary-exhibitions program. Strong suits are California ethnography and archaeology, ancient Peru and Egypt, and classical Mediterranean Europe. The museum also houses the collection associated with Ishi, the last Yahi Indian of northern California. *103 Kroeger Hall, Bancroft Way at College Ave., Berkeley, tel. 510/643–7648. Admission: $2. Open Sun. 10–4:30.*

Galleries

All the major galleries in San Francisco—and most of the minor ones—are closed on Sundays, which is one reason the museums do such a brisk Sunday business. One downtown site that is open, the **Circle Gallery,** is worth a peek for its fine collection of limited-edition jewelry by the renowned designer Erté and for its architecture. Said to be a model for the Guggenheim Museum in New York City (note the circular interior ramp and skylights), the gallery is the only San Francisco building designed by Frank Lloyd Wright. *140 Maiden La., tel. 415/989–2100. Open Sun. noon–5.*

A few blocks south of Circle Gallery (walk down Kearny, which becomes 3rd Street after you cross Market Street) is the **Stones Gallery of Contemporary Treasures,** which specializes in contemporary California crafts but also carries works from around the country and Mexico. *55 3rd St. at Mission, tel. 415/777–4999. Open Sun. 11–4.*

Also in the neighborhood is the **Center for the Arts** in Yerba Buena Gardens. Two multiuse theaters, three visual-arts galleries, a film- and video-screening room, and an outdoor-performance esplanade make this a cultural mecca. The focus is on multicultural art, from the community based to the international. *701 Mission at 3rd St., tel. 415/978–2787. Admission: $5. Open Sun. 11–6.*

Near Fisherman's Wharf in Ghirardelli Square, **Xanadu Gallery** and the nearby **Folk Art International Boretti Amber** display museum-quality tribal art from Asia, Africa, Oceania, and the Americas. Xanadu, on the second floor of the Cocoa Building, exhibits a peerless array of antique and ethnic jewelry. Folk Art International, on the level below Xanadu, displays Latin American art and exquisite amber jewelry. *Cocoa Bldg., 2nd floor, Ghirardelli Sq., North Point. at Larkin, tel. 415/441–5211 (Xanadu), 415/441–6100 (Folk Art). Open Sun. 11–6.*

Creative Spirit Gallery. Artists with disabilites showcase their work on the lower level of the Woolen Mill Building, below the main courtyard. The space is sponsored and run by the National Institute of Art and Disabilities. *Lower Plaza level, Ghirardelli Sq., off Beach St. between Polk and Larkin., tel. 415/441–1537. Open Sun. 11–6.*

Historical Treasures

From the fabled Barbary Coast to the peccadilloes of its turn-of-the-century politicians, San Francisco's history has been nothing if not entertaining. It should come as no surprise, then, that the museums and attractions devoted to recounting that history are engaging and upbeat—perfect fare for a Sunday outing. Two centuries of ships, available for boarding each weekend, provide living documentation of San Francisco's love affair with the sea. On shore, the city's cable cars, its firefighters, and key players in the Bay Area's storied past receive their proper due.

Museums and More

In the City

Cable Car Museum. This is a quick but fulfilling stop. On exhibit are photographs, old cars, and other memorabilia dating from 1873—when the system originated—to the present. From an overlook on the main floor, visitors can observe the cables that haul the cars in action. *1201 Mason St. at Washington, tel. 415/474–1887. Admission free. Open Sun. 10–6.*

Fort Point National Historic Site. What was once a 19th-century fort is now a museum filled with military memorabilia under the shadow of the Golden Gate Bridge. National-park rangers offer guided group tours, and there are cannon demonstrations. The top floor affords a superb view of the bay. *In the Presidio, on Marine Dr. off Long Ave., tel. 415/556–1693. Admission free. Open Sun. 10–5.*

Hyde Street Pier. Several historic vessels, two blocks east of the National Maritime Museum, are a delight to explore. The best is the *Balclutha*, an 1886 full-rigged, three-mast vessel that sailed around Cape Horn 17 times. Also available for boarding are the *Eureka*, a side-wheel ferry; the *C.A. Thayer*, a three-masted schooner; and the recently restored *Hercules*, a 1907 oceangoing steam tugboat. *Foot of Hyde St., off Jefferson, tel. 415/556–3002 or 415/929–0202. Admission: $3. mid-May–mid-Sept., Open Sun. 10–6; mid-Sept.-mid-May, 9:30–5.*

Musée Mécanique. Directly behind Cliff House is a quirky collection of (mostly) working antique mechanical contrivances, including peep shows, sports games, and nickelodeons. Play a few, then step outside and take a peek at the Farrallon Islands, 30 miles offshore, through the magical lens of the camera obscura. *1090 Point Lobos at Great Highway, tel. 415/386–1170. Admission free. Open Sun. 10–7.*

Museum of the City of San Francisco. Significant historical items, maps, and photographs here include the 8-ton head of the *Goddess of Progress* statue that toppled from City Hall just before the 1906 earthquake. Other exhibits trace the history of Chinatown, Golden Gate Park, the Sutro Baths, and the earthquakes of 1906 and 1989. There's also an interesting collection of old movie projectors. *Cannery, 3rd floor, 2801 Leavenworth St. at Beach, tel. 415/928–0289. Admission free. Open Sun. 10–4.*

National Maritime Museum. Ship models, photographs, maps, and other artifacts chronicle the development of San Francisco and the West Coast through maritime history. Hyde Street Pier (*see above*), nearby, is associated with the museum. *Aquatic Park, foot of Polk St. at Beach St., tel. 415/929–0202 or 415/556–3002. Admission free. Open Sun. 10–5.*

Pampanito. See what passed for high tech just 50 years ago on this World War II–era submarine. *Fisherman's Wharf, Pier 45 at Embarcadero, tel. 415/929–0202. Admission: $5. Open Sun. 9–8.*

Presidio Museum. Housed in a former hospital built in 1863, this museum chronicles the Presidio's history, the 1906 earthquake and fire, and the Panama-Pacific International Exposition of 1915. Behind the facility are two cabins that housed refugees from the 1906 earthquake and fire. Photos on the wall of one depict row upon row of temporary shelters at the Presidio and in Golden Gate Park following the disaster. *On the corner of Lincoln Blvd. and Funston Ave., tel. 415/561–4331 or 415/561–4323. Admission free. Open Sun. 10–4.*

Ripley's Believe It or Not Museum. The 200 exhibits here include interactive displays, some of which actually are amazing. It's lite history, but—believe it or not—it's diverting. *175 Jefferson St. at Taylor., tel. 415/771–6188. Admission: $8. Open Sun. 10 AM–10 PM; in summer 10 AM–11 PM.*

San Francisco Fire Department Museum. Equipment, photographs, and memorabilia from two centuries of San Francisco fire fighting are on display at this working firehouse. *655 Presidio Ave. at Bush, tel. 415/558–3546. Admission free. Open Sun. 1–4. Closed holidays.*

SS *Jeremiah O'Brien.* This historic World War II Liberty Ship freighter is the last unaltered one of its kind. Cheap and quickly built, these steamers hauled troops, arms, and other cargo. The *Jeremiah O'Brien* sailed to France for ceremonies connected with the 50th anniversary of D-Day. It's open most Sundays for boarding and takes to the water on periodic "steaming weekends" or bay cruises (call ahead for information about this and to confirm that the ship is in port). *Pier 32, Embarcadero across from Brannan St., tel. 415/441–3101. Admission: $5.*

Treasure Island Museum. One of the few buildings remaining from the 1939 Golden Gate International Exhibition now houses a museum commemorating the exposition and the American military's role in the Pacific. Exhibits also document the history of the *China Clipper*. You get a unique sea-level view of San Francisco's waterfront (a great photo opportunity) outside the museum. *Treasure Island exit off San Francisco–Oakland Bay Bridge, tel. 415/395–5067. Admission free. Open Sun. 10–4:30.*

Around the Bay

Marin County

***China* Cabin.** In 1866, toward the end of the era of wood-hull ships, the Pacific Steamship Company commissioned the SS *China*. When it was sold for scrap 20 years later, only its first-class social saloon was salvaged. The *China* Cabin's large stateroom contains elaborately carved wood painted white with gold-leaf highlights, as well as etched-glass windows, oil-burning chandeliers, and period furniture. From the cabin's three decks you'll get sweeping views of San Francisco's skyline and the Belvedere harbor. *52 Beach Rd. at Peninsula Rd., Belvedere, tel. 415/435–1853. Admission free. Open Sun. 1–4 Apr.–Oct.*

San Francisco and North Pacific Railroad Depot. This 1884 structure on the Tiburon waterfront is all that is left of a 40-acre railroad yard. Listed on the National Register of Historic Places, the building is believed to be the only extant ferry-and-railroad terminal in the United States. It's now open as a railroad museum, and the depot is being restored by the Belvedere-Tiburon Landmarks Society. Sunday hours are slated to begin by fall 1996; call ahead. *1920 Paradise Dr. at Main St., tel. 415/435-1853.*

Peninsula

Museum of American Heritage. This entertaining museum's goal is to "educate and inspire people of all ages through displaying the technology of the past." Reconstruction of the museum's new, permanent home, the historic Williams House (351 Homer Ave., Palo Alto), may be completed by late 1996 (call ahead to be sure). In the meantime, organizers are staging changing exhibits of mechanical and electrical artifacts that predate solid-state electronics at a former car dealership. Larger displays, such as a '20s grocery store, a typical '30s kitchen, and a Depression-era law office, are temporarily in storage. *3401 El Camino Real at Ferndando Ave., Palo Alto, tel. 415/321-1004. Admission free. Open Sun. 11-4.*

Restored Houses

The Haas-Lilienthal House is the only restored San Francisco home open to visitors each Sunday (the Octagon House a few blocks away is open one Sunday per month), but an hour's drive (or less) from the city will bring you to several noteworthy 19th-century living spaces. Some, such as the dramatic Dunsmuir House and Gardens in Oakland, are open only during the tourist season; others can be viewed year-round. As for San Francisco proper, although you may not be able to enter the city's most distinguished residences, you can easily observe their exteriors from the street.

In the City

The **Foundation for San Francisco's Architectural Heritage** (tel. 415/441-3000) conducts an informative tour of the eastern part of Pacific Heights each Sunday, starting at the Haas-Lilienthal House, 2007 Franklin St. at Jackson, at 12:30 ($5 adults, $3 seniors citizens and children). **City Guides** (tel. 415/557-4266) offers free 1½- to 2-hour tours of several neighborhoods—including the Haight, Nob Hill, and the "Gold Rush City"—every Sunday. For several years the group has also offered a popular free tour of San Francisco's Victorian houses.

Haas-Lilienthal House. Built at a cost (in 1886 dollars) of $18,000, this grand Queen Anne house survived the 1906 earthquake and fire and is the only fully furnished Victorian in San Francisco open to the public. The carefully kept rooms offer a glimpse into turn-of-the-century taste and lifestyle. A small display of photographs on the bottom floor reveals that this elaborate house was modest compared with some of the giants that fell to the fire. Docent volunteers of the Foundation for San Francisco's Architectural Heritage lead tours every Sunday. *2007 Franklin St. at Jackson, tel. 415/441-3004. Admission: $5. Open Sun. 11-5 (last tour at 4:15).*

Octagon House. A national fad in the 1850s, eight-sided houses were thought to bring good luck. The Octagon House, one of two remaining local examples (the other is a private residence on Russian Hill), bills itself as the only Colonial museum west of Texas. On display from the Federal and American Colonial periods are silver, furniture, portraits, Chinese porcelain, and signatures of signers of the Declaration of Independence. *2645 Gough St. at Union St., tel. 415/441-7512. Admission free. Open noon-3 on 2nd Sun. of each month Feb.-Dec.*

Around the Bay

East Bay

Alvarado Adobe. Built in 1848, this house was the residence of Governor Juan Bautista Alvarado. It contains a Rancho-era bedroom and a Victorian parlor, as well as Native American artifacts and panels depicting local history. The Alvarado Square complex includes the Blume House, a 1905 folk-Victorian-style furnished farmhouse. *1 Alvarado Sq., off San Pablo Ave., San Pablo, tel. 510/215–3096. Admission free. Open third Sun. of month 12–4 and by appointment for groups of 10 or more.*

Camron-Stanford House. The former site of the Oakland Public Museum has five rooms furnished and decorated in the style of 1880. The Italianate house, built in 1875, won one of five grand prizes awarded by the California State Historic Preservation Conference. *1418 Lakeside Dr., near 14th St. at Lake Merritt, Oakland, tel. 510/836–1976. Admission: $2; free 1st Sun. of month. Open Sun. 1–5.*

Casa Peralta. Now owned and operated by the city of San Leandro, this house was erected by a member of the prominent Peralta family, which controlled one of the most famous ranchos during the period when the Spanish and then the Mexicans controlled California. Spanish ceramic tiles in the 1897 home depict the story of Don Quixote. *384 W. Estudillo Ave. at Clarke St., San Leandro, tel. 510/577–3490 (for information weekdays only). Admission free (donations accepted). Open Sun. noon–4.*

Dunsmuir House and Gardens. San Francisco architect J. Eugene Freeman designed this 37-room Colonial Revival mansion for coal and lumber baron Alexander Dunsmuir, who died shortly after its completion in 1899. John McLaren, landscape architect of Golden Gate Park, is said to have assisted in designing the lush gardens. The house is the main point of architectural interest, but the dairy barn, carriage house, and gazebo are worth a look. "Christmas at Dunsmuir" festivities—which include house tours, tea, full meals, caroling, and spectacular decorations—have become an East Bay tradition. *2960 Peralta Oaks Ct. off Peralta Oaks Dr., Oakland, tel. 510/615–5555. Admission to mansion: $4. Grounds open 11–3 on 1st and 3rd Sun. of each month Apr.–Sept.; mansion tours at noon, 1, and 2 on 1st and 3rd Sun. of each month Apr.–Sept. "Christmas at Dunsmuir" open Sun. 10–5 late Nov.–mid-Dec. Call for additional activities and fees.*

McConaghy House. Built in 1886, this estate includes a 12-room farmhouse, a tank house, and a carriage house with a buggy and farm equipment. Period decorations adorn the house for holidays; "Christmas 1886" is the annual December theme. Adjacent Kennedy Park has picnic tables, a merry-go-round, and a train. *18701 Hesperian Blvd. at Bockman Rd., off I–880, Oakland, tel. 510/276–3010. Admission: $3. Open Sun. 1–4 Feb.–Dec.*

George W. Patterson House. The East Bay Regional Parks District maintains this 1889 Queen Anne home, the centerpiece of a 205-acre historic farm operated by the city of Fremont. Farm animals, Victorian gardens, horse-drawn rail and wagon rides, and Victorian crafts demonstrations are among the attractions. *Ardenwood Regional Park, Ardenwood Blvd. at Hwy. 84, Fremont, tel. 510/791–4196. Admission: $6. House open Sun. 11:30–3:30; park open Sun. 10–4.*

Shadelands Ranch Historical Museum. Hiram P. Penniman, who established one of the first farms in the Ygnacio Valley, built his Colonial Revival home in 1902. Nine rooms contain many of the original period furnishings. Changing exhibits document ranch life in Ygnacio Valley. *2660 Ygnacio Valley Rd. near Wiget La., Walnut Creek, tel. 510/935–7871. Admission: $2. Open Sun. 1–4 (call ahead because museum is closed some Sundays).*

Marin County and Beyond

Luther Burbank Home and Gardens. An hour's drive north of San Francisco, this registered National and State Historic Landmark includes the working garden where the horticulturist bred plants during his 50-year career—not to mention many of the home's original furnishings. The carriage house has been converted into a museum and gift shop. *Santa Rosa Ave. at Sonoma Ave., Santa Rosa, tel.*

707/524–5445. Admission to house: $2; garden only free. House open Sun. 10–4 Apr.–Oct., gardens 8–5 year-round. House tours by volunteer docents begin every half-hour.

Peninsula **Filoli.** (*See* Gardens *in* Chapter 6.)

Harris-Lass Historic Museum. The last farm site in now decidedly high-tech Santa Clara is a living history museum that honors the area's rural past. Visitors can tour the two-story Italianate house, as well as a barn, tank house, summer kitchen, and chicken coop. *1889 Market St. at Winchester Blvd., Santa Clara, tel. 408/249–7905. Admission: $3. Open Sun. noon–4.*

Rengstorff House. The oldest home in Mountain View (a 45-minute drive from San Francisco), built by one of the South Bay's most prominent farmers, was moved to the Shoreline at Mountain View park from its original site and converted into a museum. Photos and memorabilia offer a window into the early history of California and the South Bay region. *3070 N. Shoreline Blvd. near Charleston Rd. (take U.S. 101's Shoreline Blvd. exit and head east into the park), Mountain View, tel. 415/903–6392. Open Sun. 11–5.*

Sanchez Adobe. This historic 5-acre estate south of San Francisco was part of an 8,000-acre Mexican land grant to Don Francisco Sanchez, *alcalde* (mayor) of San Francisco. The original home was built in 1846 and was then enlarged as a residence for a U.S. general and his wife. In later incarnations it was a hotel, a hunting lodge, a speakeasy, and an artichoke-storage shed before being restored, in 1953, to its original appearance. An Ohlone Indian midden (compost heap) can be found on the grounds; in the adobe are artifacts of the Ohlones, who lived in the Pacifica valley area at the time the Spanish arrived. *1000 Linda Mar Blvd. at Adobe Dr., Pacifica, tel. 415/359–1462. Admission free (donations appreciated). Open Sun. 1–5.*

Winchester Mystery House. An hour south of San Francisco is one of the kitschiest edifices in the Bay Area (or anywhere). Sarah Winchester, the loopy gun heiress who believed she would die if construction on her estate ever stopped, kept workers busy erecting more than 160 rooms over several decades. The whole affair is *très* touristy and a bit pricey, and the most benign query is likely to upend your guide's carefully scripted rap. The house, though, is so silly and Sarah's story so peculiar (no matter how it's related) that many will find a visit good fun. *Winchester Blvd. at Stevens Creek Blvd., off I–280, San Jose, tel. 408/247–2101. Admission: $12.50. Open Sun. 9:30–4.*

Science and Nature Museums

In the City

California Academy of Sciences. One of the top natural-history museums in the country, the academy also houses the **Steinhart Aquarium** and the Morrison Planetarium. The Steinhart's dramatic 100,000-gallon Fish Roundabout, home to 14,000 swimming creatures and a living coral reef, is always a hit with children. So is feeding time for the Steinhart's many occupants, which include penguins, seals, and dolphins. (For the daily feeding schedule, call 415/750–7145.) The Space and Earth Hall has an "earthquake floor" that simulates a California earthquake. Another major draw is the Far Side Gallery, with more than 150 original Gary Larson cartoons. There is an additional charge for entrance to **Morrison Planetarium,** the largest in northern California. In addition to lectures and shows on astronomical themes, the planetarium also produces Laserium events—krypton- and argon-laser visuals "under the stars." Sunday-afternoon shows include "Inside Laserium," which surveys lasers and their uses in science and entertainment; it's set to all kinds of music, from rock to classical. Two long-running Sunday-evening shows are strictly rock and roll (call ahead to be sure they're still playing). *Music Concourse Dr. off South Dr., Golden Gate Park, tel. 415/750–7145. Admission to academy: $7; $1 discount with valid Muni Fast Pass or transfer. Additional admission to Morrison Planetarium (tel. 415/750–7141 for schedule): $2.50. Laserium tickets (tel. 415/750–7138; $7, available in advance from Bass ticket agency (tel. 510/762–2277); remaining tickets sold at planetarium ½-hr before show time. Open Sun. 9–6 July 4–Labor Day; 10–5 Labor Day–July 3.*

Exploratorium. Learning what makes the world tick is exciting at this hands-on science museum inside the Palace of Fine Arts. The emphasis at the 103,000-square-foot facility, as its title suggests, is on individualized exploration; nearly 700 interactive exhibits appeal to people of all ages and backgrounds. At the highly popular and frenetic Tactile Dome, patrons learn about the sense of touch as they crawl through a pitch-black chamber. Among the quieter but still stimulating exhibits are ones that illustrate how laser beams operate or why water flows the way that it does. The Exploratorium's orange-jacketed "explainers," all high school students, supply further information and answer questions. A range of science-related and other films and multimedia works is shown—sometimes with their creators present—on many Sunday afternoons (usually at 2 PM at the 175-seat McBean Theater. *3601 Lyon St. at Richardson, tel. 415/561–0360 for general information; 415/561–0362 for required reservations for Tactile Dome. Admission: $9. Open Sun. 10–5.*

Around the Bay

East Bay

Lawrence Hall of Science. Interactive exhibits, continuous science-film screenings, children's theater, discovery labs, a 50-foot whale model kids can climb on, and a planetarium number among the attractions at this fascinating museum, a hit with both children and adults. Its octagonal shape represents the eight branches of physical science. *Top of Centennial Dr. near Grizzly Peak Blvd., above U.C. Berkeley campus, tel. 510/642–5132. Admission: $6. Additional fee for planetarium shows: $1.50. Open Sun. 10–5 (cafeteria 11–3:30).*

Summit Museum. Exhibits here explain the culture and natural history of Mt. Diablo, the highest spot in the East Bay. An art gallery and an observation deck provide visual pleasure indoors and out. *Top of Mt. Diablo Scenic Blvd., Walnut Creek, tel. 510/837–6119. Admission free; $5 per car admission to Mt. Diablo State Park.* (See *Parks and Woodlands* in *Chapter 6 for park information.)* *Open Sun. 11–5.*

University of California Museum of Paleontology. This collection of fossils, from tiny bacteria to huge vertebrates—including a complete mounted skeleton of Tyrannosaurus rex—is one of the oldest (it dates back to 1860) and largest in North America. The museum's new galleries opened in 1995; exhibits focus on the process of evolution, fossilization, and biogeography. *1101 Valley Life Sciences Building (near Oxford St. and University Ave.), Berkeley, tel. 510/642–1821. Admission free. Open Sun. 1–5.*

Western Aerospace Museum. Rare aircraft and modern space exhibits here relate to Bay Area and northern California aviation. *Oakland Airport, 8260 Boeing St., across from Hanger 6, North Field, tel. 510/638–7100. Admission: $3. Open Sun. 10–4.*

Peninsula

Coyote Point Museum. Here's a chance to view native mammals, reptiles, and birds in wildlife habitats. The Environmental Hall has games, computers, displays, and films. *Coyote Point Park, 1651 Coyote Point Dr. off U.S. 101 (coming from San Francisco take Poplar Ave. exit, coming from south take Dore Ave. exit) San Mateo, tel. 415/342–7755. Admission: $3. Open Sun. noon–5.*

Best Bets for Children

Children's activities at the de Young and other major art museums are usually held on Saturdays, but there are still plenty of Sunday options. The **California Academy of Sciences, Exploratorium,** and **Lawrence Hall of Science** (*see* Science and Technology Museums, *above*) have Sunday events. Fisherman's Wharf attractions, such as the **National Maritime Museum** and the **Hyde Street Pier,** are also good bets. The best all-around guide to events for children is *Parents Press*, available at most large grocery stores in the Bay Area. Also helpful is the "Young and Restless" column in the "Weekend" section of the Friday *Examiner*.

The **Young Audiences ArtsCard Project** offers a card good for discounts and even free admission to art, science, and historical museums and performing arts centers—from the San Francisco Ballet and Symphony to community-based theaters—for children in kindergarten through grade 12. The ArtsCard costs $5 per family (no matter how many children there are), so the savings can be significant. The project's hot line (tel. 415/863–2549) is an invaluable resource for weekend events, some of which the organization itself sponsors at exhibition spaces around the Bay Area. To receive an application, leave your name and address on the hot line. **Temporary "Visitor" ArtsCards** are available at $2 per child. In or out of town, allow a minimum of two weeks for delivery for the temporary card, four weeks for the regular one (although the friendly staff tries to accommodate last-minute requests).

In the City

Randall Museum. Only its theater is used (occasionally) on Sundays, but this small museum in Corona Heights Park, just north of the Castro district, is open Saturdays. There are hands-on nature and science exhibits and Saturday arts workshops. Young kids especially like the petting corral, where they can stroke rabbits and ducks. *199 Museum Way off Roosevelt Way, tel. 415/554–9600. Admission free. Sat. 10–5.*

Around the Bay

East Bay

Museum of Children's Art. This facility near Jack London Square lets kids see art created by other children, both locally and from abroad. The museum has plenty of art supplies on hand so that kids can produce their own minimasterpieces. *560 2nd St. at Clay St., Oakland, tel. 510/465–8770. Donations accepted. Open Sun. noon–5.*

Marin County

Bay Area Discovery Museum. This is a fun hands-on museum for kids, with plenty of interactive exhibits, such as "San Francisco Bay," which allows children to crew a ship or explore an underground tunnel. *557 E. Fort Baker St., Sausalito, tel. 415/487–4398. Admission: $7. Open Sun. 10–5.*

Peninsula

Children's Discovery Museum of San Jose. An hour's drive from San Francisco is one of the best museums of its kind in the country. Interactive science, history, geography, and other exhibits are clever and informative. *180 Woz Way at Auzerais St., San Jose, tel. 408/298–5495. Admission: $6. Open Sun. noon–5.*

5 Shopping

By Daniel Mangin

From the ultrafine to the ultrafunky, San Francisco offers shopping alternatives rivaled by few places in the world. All the city's best shopping areas keep Sunday hours, and each has an assortment of shops and a distinctive clientele. Need a new (fake, of course) fur? There are options aplenty downtown, where most of the city's great emporiums are open on Sundays and ready for business. Want some ecologically sensitive accessories? Off you go to the Lower Haight, where Used Rubber USA recycles steel-belted radials into purses, belts, and other personal essentials.

Shopping Hours

The following stores, which usually do a full day of business on Saturday, are generally open Sunday from 11 AM or noon to 5 PM. Shops at Fisherman's Wharf and in Chinatown tend to open a little earlier and close a little later, but it's wise to check ahead if you plan on arriving later in the day or on holiday Sundays. Everything listed in this chapter is open at least from 1 to 4.

Shopping Neighborhoods

The Castro Known since the '70s as a gay mecca, the Castro was once a sleepy neighborhood known as Eureka Valley. Though only a handful of businesses from this area remain, the newer, hipper, gayer shopping scene that evolved has retained the casual, friendly ambience of before. Exploring the Castro District's shops and boutiques can make for a pleasurable Sunday afternoon. Gifts—from kitschy to fine—and men's clothing are the main attractions, but you'll also find electronics stores, the city's premier gay bookshop (A Different Light), and a couple of good antiques sellers.

Chinatown The intersection of Grant Avenue and Bush Street marks the gateway to Chinatown. The key here, as with Fisherman's Wharf, is to uncover the singular amid the mass-produced. Jade and pearls predominate in Chinatown's jewelry shops. Elsewhere, you'll find silks, pottery, baskets, and large figures of soapstone, ivory, and jade. For more on Chinatown shops, *see* Explorable Neighborhoods *in* Chapter 3.

Embarcadero Five modern towers of shops, restaurants, and offices, plus the Hyatt Regency Hotel, make up the **Embarcadero Center** at the end of Market Street. Most of the 175 stores and services are open Sunday, and traffic is light, so the shopping here is less hectic than downtown. The center includes such nationally known stores as **The Limited, B. Dalton Bookseller, Ann Taylor,** and the **Nature Company.**

Fisherman's Wharf The Wharf hosts a number of shopping attractions: **Pier 39, the Anchorage, Ghirardelli Square,** and **The Cannery.** Though the first two are top-heavy with tourist-oriented clothing and trinkets, Pier 39 is worth seeing. Its bay-side layout is a visual delight, and the colony of boisterous sea lions commands attention even when the shops—many of which carry items available Anywhere, USA—don't. Pier 39 also includes an amusement area and a double-decked Venetian carousel for shopping-weary tykes. A new attraction opened in 1996: Underwater World at Pier 39, a walk-through look at Bay Area marine life from plankton to sharks. Many San Franciscans let years go by between visits to Ghirardelli Square and the Cannery, which is a shame because each of these historic buildings (a chocolate factory and a working cannery) houses interesting shops. The Cannery's courtyard entertainment (nearly constant on Sundays) is often quite good.

The Haight The Haight's many secondhand clothing stores, all of which are open Sundays, are among the city's finest. Local and even national rock stars can often be found rummaging through the racks looking for additions to their onstage and offstage wardrobes. The street also boasts some good used-book stores and several of the best used-record shops in the Bay Area.

There are really two Haight Streets—the one the hippies made famous in the '60s (from the 1300 block on) and the Lower Haight, an offbeat spot (from Webster to Pierce streets and along Fillmore Street a block north and south)—with one of the best video stores in town, a store full of recycled rubber products, and several other zany and original boutiques.

Japantown The 5-acre **Japan Center** is the social and commercial focal point of Japantown. Sunday is the center's busiest day, as locals and tourists mix and mingle inside and outside the enclosed mall of shops filled with antique kimonos, calligraphic scrolls, and new and old porcelains. The center's westernmost building abuts Fillmore Street; head north on Fillmore to visit the district's fine clothing boutiques and housewares shops.

Marina The Marina's main shopping district, on Chestnut Street from Fillmore Street to Divisadero Street, has been heading inexorably upscale throughout the past decade. Chain stores have wedged their way into the area, along with more coffee sellers per square inch than almost anywhere else in the city. Still, the neighborhood maintains a laid-back feel, and there are some interesting clothing and housewares boutiques among the monoliths.

Noe Valley A walk down sunny, stroller-filled Noe Valley is particularly enjoyable. This is a homey neighborhood, with good clothing, shoe, and children's stores. Various crafts—wearable and otherwise—are well represented here, sometimes at rates less than elsewhere in town. There are plenty of cafés and ice cream shops for those times when you need to take a break.

North Beach The face of the once Italian North Beach is changing, but despite the encroachment of Chinatown and the Financial District, the area has maintained its mix of chic boutiques and secondhand shops. Beat poet Lawrence Ferlinghetti's eccentric **City Lights Bookstore** on Columbus Avenue is the area's intellectual center. **Quantity Postcard,** a perennial favorite on Grant Avenue, stocks 15,000 current and collector's postcards. If your feet get sore or your attention wanes, have an espresso at historic **Caffe Trieste** or any of a dozen other coffee joints nearby.

South of Market (SoMa) In keeping with SoMa's tradition as the city's underside, the area now offers the underside of shopping: discount outlets. Dozens of them, some open seven days, have sprung up along the streets and alleyways bordered by 2nd, Townsend, Howard, and 10th streets. A good place to start is the big **Burlington Coat Factory** clothing outlet, the chief attraction at the **Yerba Buena Square** discount warehouse at 5th and Howard Streets. Here you'll find bargains on toys, shoes, and other items as well. Up the street at the Visitors Information Center at Hallidie Plaza (5th and Market Sts.; open Sun. 10–2), you can sometimes find maps and brochures of SoMa outlet stores. Another SoMa option: Join **Price/Costco** and save money on household, food, and other items—only to spend it on things you don't really need—at the nation's first retail membership discount outlet in an urban area. *450 10th St. at Bryant, tel. 415/626–4288. Open Sun. 10–5.*

Sunset Owing to the paucity of traditional closed-in shopping centers in San Francisco, the city's mall-rat population is the smallest in the nation. They can be found in abundance, though, at **Stonestown Galleria,** a fine collection of shops anchored by Macy's (in the space formerly occupied by the Emporium) and Nordstrom department stores. Such national chains as Eddie Bauer, Imaginarium, and Williams-Sonoma have stores here.

Union Street At the base of the north slope of Pacific Heights, Union Street (not to be confused with Union Square, *below*) is an upscale but still friendly shopping area. A few of Union Street's fanciest boutiques are closed Sunday, as are most of its American and European antiques emporiums, but there is still much of interest to be found—particularly crafts, fine art, home furnishings, and clothing for men and women. On sunny days sidewalk cafés bustle and, as if to prove that nothing changes from one generation to the next, on Sundays many guys stop to take in the game and a brew at one of several neighborhood bars while the gals hit the shops.

Union Square "That's Entertainment!" blared the headline of a newspaper story about the changing face of San Francisco's downtown shopping district. The next few years will see the area evolve into something of a retail theme park as a huge **Nike** store (scheduled to open in mid-1996) joins the **Disney** and **Virgin** "megastores" that opened in 1994 and 1995. The goal: to turn shopping into a mega-adventure—as if it wasn't already. But even before the latest marketing strategies began to unfold, the four-block area of downtown, which includes the city's major department stores and a bevy of small shops and designer boutiques, could lay claim to being one of the world's biggest outdoor shopping malls.

Moving clockwise around Union Square from the Powell Street entrance of the St. Francis Hotel, the larger stores that stay open Sundays include the **Disney** and adjacent **Borders Books and Music** stores, **Saks Fifth Avenue,** the **Nike** outlet, **Neiman Marcus,** and the main **Macy's** buildings. (Macy's men's department is housed across Stockton Street from the main store, next to Neiman Marcus.) Just down Stockton Street, at the corner of O'Farrell, is the gigantic **FAO Schwarz** children's store. The **Virgin megastore** is at the convergence of Stockton, Market, and Ellis streets. Near Union Square are the pricey international boutiques of **Hermès, Gucci, Celine of Paris,** and **Louis Vuitton.**

Across Market Street from the Powell and Market cable-car turntable (three blocks south of the St. Francis Hotel) is the **San Francisco Shopping Centre,** with the fashionable **Nordstrom** department store and the popular **Warner Bros.** memorabilia shop. Spiral escalators in a four-story atrium are the center's focal point. To the east of the atrium is the space formerly occupied by the Emporium department store, which closed in early 1996. The century-old site's next tenant had not been determined at press time.

Back across Market from the San Francisco Shopping Centre is the historic **Flood Building.** The biggest **Gap** store in San Francisco anchors the newly redesigned space, which also includes a record store and a two-level **Urban Outfitters** shop. **Woolworth's** occupies the building's basement.

Department Stores

Over the years, **Macy's,** which already occupied a huge chunk of downtown real estate, has gobbled up the spaces vacated by its former competitors, Liberty House and I. Magnin. What has evolved is a somewhat illogical maze of boutiques, restaurants, and traditional housewares, electronics, furniture, clothing, and shoe departments. Macy's remains the ultimate in one-stop shopping. Half of San Francisco seems to be wandering aimlessly through its aisles on any given Sunday, and though service may suffer, it's a cultural anthropologist's delight. The Cellar is devoted to cooking; buy enough gadgets—bread makers, pasta makers, ice-cream makers, fancy toasters, and meat slicers—and you may turn yourself into a gourmet chef yet. *Stockton and O'Farrell Sts., tel. 415/397–3333. Open Sun. 11–7.*

Eclectic designer clothing (the women's more so than the men's), top-brand cosmetics, fancy household wares, and its trademark, one-of-a-kind merchandising ploys are the draws at **Neiman Marcus.** As you pass through the store's main entrance, look up: The spectacular glass dome is, sadly, all that remains of the fabled City of Paris store that once occupied this site. *150 Stockton St. at Geary, tel. 415/362–3900. Open Sun. noon–6.*

Nordstrom is known for its excellent customer service and well-crafted merchandise. Designer fashions, shoes, accessories, and cosmetics are the specialties. *865 Market St. at 5th St., tel. 415/243–8500. Open Sun. 10–7.*

The West Coast **Saks Fifth Avenue** outpost isn't quite as special—in terms of style or service—as its East Coast sister, but it's still a cut above most local rivals. Designer fashions range from the conservative to the almost trend setting; the jewelry and accessories departments are among the best in the city. *384 Post St. at Powell, tel. 415/986–4300. Open Sun. noon–6.*

Specialty Stores

Antiques/ Vintage Items

The city's best antiques shops, including the members of Antiques Row in Jackson Square, close their doors on Sundays, but if you're dying to purchase a Louis XIV chair or a Japanese screen, there's hope yet:

American and European

The Antique Traders (4300 California St. at 5th Ave., tel. 415/668–4444), known for its fine antique glass (*see below*), always has interesting examples of American and European artisanship.

Beaver Bros. (1637 Market St. at Van Ness, tel. 415/863–4344) sells whatever its owners can get their hands on: Louis XVI furniture, Art Deco clocks, armoires, silver, cut glass, and rugs.

The Bombay Company (2135 Union St. at Webster, tel. 415/441–1591; Stonestown Galleria, 19th Ave. at Winston Dr., tel. 415/753–2955) is a national chain that specializes in affordable reproductions of 18th- and 19th-century American and British furniture and accessories.

Butterfield and Butterfield, (220 San Bruno Ave. at 15th St., tel. 415/861–7500, ext. 888 for weekend events), the city's premier auction house, generally does not hold major sales on Sundays, but it does have some objects available for purchase, and you can sometimes preview upcoming items for auction. *It's open Sunday from noon to 5.*

Butterfield West (164 Utah St. at 15th St., tel. 415/861–7500, ext. 308 or 888), an annex to Butterfield and Butterfield, holds auctions of "intermediate property"—objects and art that are not top-of-the-line but not shlock, either—every other Sunday.

Great American Collective (1736 Lombard St. at Laguna, tel. 415/922–2650) is an antiques minimall in Cow Hollow where you may find anything from an antique purse to a Federal-era chest of drawers. The overall feel is upscale-garage-sale, with prices that range from reasonable to precious.

Legend Antiques (5427 Telegraph Ave. at 55th St., Oakland, tel. 510/658–9123) is a volume dealer selling European furniture directly imported from France, Belgium, and England.

Russian Hill Antiques (2200 Polk St. at Vallejo, tel. 415/441–5561) has a fine collection of American country pine and other furniture. Glassware, pottery, and jewelry are other specialties.

Asian

Fumiki (2001 Union St. at Buchanan, tel. 415/922–0573) offers a fine selection of Asian arts, including antiques, jewelry, Chinese silk paintings, and Korean and Japanese furniture. Two specialties are *obis* (sashes worn with kimonos) and Japanese baskets.

A Touch of Asia (1784 Union St. at Octavia, tel. 415/474–3115) is the place to go for exquisite wood furniture. Also for sale are ceramics, kimonos, and paintings.

20th Century The area around Market St. between Van Ness and Gough (and up Gough to Oak Street) has attracted a number of antiques shops, mostly open Sundays, that feature American Modern (1930s–1960s) furniture.

Another Time (1586 Market St. at Franklin, tel. 415/553–8900) is an Art Deco lover's delight, with furniture and accessories by Heywood Wakefield and others.

Jet Age (250 Oak St. at Gough, tel. 415/864–1950) looks a little dumpy from the outside, but inside are some fine Art Deco and '30s and '40s furniture, plus later pieces designed by Eames, Noguchi, and others.

Retrospect Fine Furniture and Collectibles (1649 Market St. at Gough, tel. 415/863–7414) specializes in 20th-century American furniture, particularly sofas.

Clocks, Watches, and Jewelry **Brand X Antiques** (570 Castro St. at 18th St., tel. 415/626–8908) has a fine assortment of jewelry; cut and blown glass; and European, American, and Asian objets d'art.

Old and New Estates (2181 Union St. at Fillmore, tel. 415/346–7525) specializes in vintage watches. Wedding rings, art glass, jewelry, and lamps are also for sale.

Paris 1925 (1954 Union St. at Laguna, tel. 415/567–1925) is a small but handsome shop specializing in estate jewelry and vintage watches.

Urban Antiques (1767 Waller St. at Stanyan, tel. 415/221–0194) looks minuscule from the street, but it's actually 125-feet deep and filled with clocks and music boxes from America, Great Britain, France, Germany, Austria, and Switzerland. A smaller **Urban Antiques** (Baker and Hamilton Square, 7th and Townsend Sts., Suites 201–202, tel. 415/864–7335) is also open Sunday.

Collectibles **The Antique Traders** (4300 California St. at 5th Ave., tel. 415/668–4444) specializes in stained- and beveled-glass windows and lamps—Tiffany, Handel, Pairpoint, and others.

D. Carnegie Antiques (601 Kansas St. at 18th St., tel. 415/641–4704) has porcelains, bronzes, jewelry, signed paperweights, and other collectibles, plus some furniture.

Frank's Fisherman's Supply (366 Jefferson St. at Leavenworth, tel. 415/775–1165) sells marine lamps, clocks, sextants, and ships in bottles that provide a (salty) taste of seafaring days.

Old Stuff (2325 Clement St. at 24th St., tel. 415/668–2220) resembles your granny's attic: the gems are mixed in with the merely dated.

One-Eyed Jacks (1645 Market St. at Gough, tel. 415/621–4390) offers slices of Americana: country-and-western furnishings, saddles, boots, and a trough full of framed art and knickknacks.

Memorabilia **Pioneer Sports and Collectibles** (2284 Union St. at Steiner, tel. 415/771–1860) sells cards, autographed portraits, and other sports and nonsports memorabilia.

Show Biz (1318 Grant Ave. at Vallejo, tel. 415/989–6744) is where you'll find movie, rock-and-roll, jazz, and theater memorabilia, some of it sensibly priced, some not.

Shows **Art Deco–'50s Sale** (Concourse Exhibition Center, 8th and Brannan Sts., tel. 415/599–3326) holds June and December shows of Art Deco, Moderne, and Streamline Modern furniture, jewelry, and collectibles.

Golden Gate Park Ephemera and Book Fair (San Francisco County Fair Building, Golden Gate Park, 9th Ave. at Lincoln Blvd., tel. 415/753–7089), usually held the first week of June, is a sale of books, prints, postcards, antique advertising, and other items.

Golden Gate Shows (Box 1208, Ross, 94957, tel. 415/459–1998) sponsors a half-dozen antiques and collectors' fairs and eight doll shows in northern California each year.

San Francisco Fall Antiques Show (Festival Pavilion, Fort Mason, Laguna at Marina Blvd., tel. 415/921–1411), a benefit sale, sells furniture and decorative antiques.

US Art (Festival Pavilion, Fort Mason, Laguna at Marina Blvd., tel. 310/455–2886) is an annual exposition of 18th-, 19th-, and 20th-century American fine and decorative arts.

Walter Larsen and Associates (Box 640328, San Francisco 94164, tel. 415/441–4290) produces antiques shows in Hillsborough and other Bay Area locations.

Art Supplies

Amsterdam Art (5221 Geary Blvd. at 16th Ave., tel. 415/387–5354) sells canvas, easels, paints, airbrushes, fine pens and art papers, portfolios, and other supplies at discount prices. There are additional branches in Berkeley and Walnut Creek.

The Art Store (812 Mission at 4th St., tel. 415/777–2787; 5301 Broadway at College Ave., Oakland, tel. 510/658–2787) has fine art, crafts, and graphics supplies at discount prices.

Colorcrane Arts and Copy Center (3957 24th St. at Noe, tel. 415/285–1387) carries a complete line of art, graphics, and office supplies. Fax and color copy services are also available.

Mendel's Art and Stationery Supplies (1556 Haight St. at Ashbury, tel. 415/621–1287), a longtime neighborhood favorite, carries art, graphics, and office supplies. In the back are "far-out" fabrics, particularly of the wild '60s genre.

Bicycles

Avenue Cyclery (756 Stanyan St. at Waller, tel. 415/387–3155) has everything you need to get rolling: bikes, helmets, gloves, bars, pumps, and clothing.

Valencia Cyclery (1077 Valencia St. at 22nd St., tel. 415/550–6600) boasts the largest selection of bikes, parts, and accessories in San Francisco, all priced competitively. Its repair shop is at 1065 Valencia St. (tel. 415/550–6601).

Books

Comics

Comic Relief (1597 Haight St. at Clayton, tel. 415/552–9010; 2138 University Ave., Berkeley, 510/843–5002) is fully stocked with new and used comics, graphic novels, art, movie and TV books, and small press and underground comics.

Comix Experience (305 Divisadero St. at Oak, tel. 415/863–9258) sells comics from the popular to the obscure. There are sometimes in-store signings on Sundays.

General-Interest

B. Dalton Bookseller (200 Kearny St. at Sutter, tel. 415/956–2850) has two floors of new books and remainders at this location. There's also a smaller store (2 Embarcadero Center at Front St., tel. 415/982–4278).

Black Oak Books (1491 Shattuck Ave. at Vine, Berkeley, tel. 510/486–0698) is known for its literature, classics, and poetry sections. It carries quite a few imports as well.

Book Passage (Market Place Shopping Centre, 51 Tamal Vista Blvd. off Lucky Dr., Corte Madera, tel. 415/927–0960 or 800/999–7909) has all kinds of books, including used and remaindered ones, but travel books are the specialty. There are visiting mystery authors and a children's story time on Sundays.

Booksmith (1644 Haight St. at Clayton, tel. 415/863–8688) is a fine neighborhood book shop, chock-full of current releases, children's titles, and literary treasures.

Borders Books and Music (400 Post St. at Powell, San Francisco, tel. 415/837–1145; 5800 Shellmound St. off Christie Ave., Emeryville, tel. 510/654–1633; and 588 W. Francisco Blvd. off the Central San Rafael exit of U.S. 101, tel. 415/454–1400) carries more than 140,000 titles in all fields at each of its branches, all of which have a large selection of children's books.

City Lights (261 Columbus Ave. at Broadway, tel. 415/362–8193) is the city's most famous bookstore—and possibly its most comfortable spot for browsing. It's particularly good for poetry, contemporary literature, and translations of Third World literature. Poet Lawrence Ferlinghetti still owns the place, and his Beat friends still stop by—as do subsequent generations of San Francisco literati.

A Clean Well-Lighted Place for Books (601 Van Ness Ave. at Turk, tel. 415/441–6670; 2417 Larkspur Landing Circle at Sir Francis Drake Blvd., Larkspur, tel. 415/461–0171; 21269 Stevens Creek Blvd. at Hwy. 85, Cupertino, tel. 408/255–7600) provides "a large selection of paperbacks and hardbacks in all fields for all ages." Its city location is particularly strong on books about opera and San Francisco history.

Cody's Books (2454 Telegraph Ave. at Haste St., Berkeley, tel. 510/845–7852) is one of the best general-interest bookstores in the Bay Area, with an information desk for all your literary questions.

Depot Bookstore and Café (87 Throckmorton Ave. between Bernard and Madrona Sts., Mill Valley, tel. 415/383–2665), a pleasant, general bookstore, sits on the edge of Mill Valley's downtown, open-air plaza.

Kepler's Books and Magazines (1010 El Camino Real at Santa Cruz Ave., Menlo Park, tel. 415/324–4321) is a large, friendly, independent bookstore with an especially strong selection of books by regional authors and presses. Kepler's Bargain Annex is two doors down.

Kinokuniya Book Stores (Japan Center, 1581 Webster St. at Post, tel. 415/567–7625) offers all sorts of books and periodicals in Japanese and English. The beautifully produced graphics and art books are major attractions.

Printers Inc. Bookstore (310 California Ave., Palo Alto, tel. 415/327–6500; 301 Castro St., Mountain View, tel. 415/961–8500) carries a good selection of current and backlist titles, as well as foreign newspapers and magazines. Both locations have cafés.

Stacey's (581 Market at 2nd St., tel. 415/421–4687; 219 University Ave. at Emerson St., Palo Alto, tel. 415/326–0681; 19625 Stevens Creek Blvd. at Perimeter Rd., Cupertino, tel. 408/253–7521) specializes in professional books—computer, technical, medical, business, travel, and reference. All except the San Francisco branch are open Sundays.

Mystery

San Francisco Mystery Book Store (746 Diamond St. at 24th St., tel. 415/282–7444) has shelves of new and used detective fiction.

Newspapers/Periodicals

DeLauer Super Newsstand (1310 Broadway at 13th St., Oakland, tel. 510/451–6157) carries international newspapers and is open 24 hours.

Good News (3920 24th St. at Sanchez, tel. 415/821–3694), open late every Sunday, has a selection of out-of-town papers and periodicals.

Harolds International Newsstand (524 Geary St. at Taylor, tel. 415/441–2665) carries many out-of-town papers, most major periodicals, and postcards.

Religious

Shambhala Booksellers (2482 Telegraph Ave. near Dwight Way, Berkeley, tel. 510/848–8443) is devoted to Eastern and Western religious traditions. Also available are books on Jungian psychology, acupuncture, bodywork, astrology, Wicca, and magic.

Vedanta Society Bookshop (2323 Vallejo St. at Fillmore, tel. 415/922–2323), in the entrance to the Vedanta Society Temple, carries books on Eastern and Western religions but specializes in Indian philosophy.

Science Fiction/Fantasy

Dark Carnival (3086 Claremont Ave. at Ashby Ave., Berkeley, tel. 510/654–7323) has the Bay Area's largest selection of sci-fi and fantasy books. Mysteries, crime fiction, and children's books are plentiful as well.

Fantasy, Etc. (808 Larkin St. at O'Farrell, tel. 415/441–7617) is a great source for new and used science fiction, detective, and adventure books. Even though it's tiny, you can't miss this shop, right next to a huge adult cinema.

Specialty **A Different Light Bookstore** (489 Castro St. at 18th St., tel. 415/431–0891), the city's full-service gay and lesbian bookshop, is something of a community center as well. Fiction and studies of lesbian and gay history are its strong suits.

Gaia Bookstore (1400 Shattuck St. at Rose St., Berkeley, tel. 510/548–4172) is a longtime local favorite for New Age books, as well as music, tarot cards, and meditation supplies.

Limelight Film and Theatre Bookstore (1803 Market St. at Guerrero, tel. 415/864–2265) carries new and used titles, plus periodicals.

Mama Bears (6536 Telegraph Ave. at 66th St., Oakland, tel. 510/428–9684) is more than a bookstore: It's a women's community center, with a coffeehouse, crafts, music, bulletin boards, and networking opportunities galore.

Marcus Books (1712 Fillmore St. at Post, tel. 415/346–4222; 3900 Martin Luther King Way at 40th St., Oakland, tel. 510/652–2344) has a fascinating selection of books, periodicals, cards, and gifts celebrating and reflecting upon African and African American reality.

The Maritime Bookstore (Hyde St. Pier, end of Hyde St. at Beach, tel. 415/775–2665) is the place to sail for literature of the sea, boatbuilding books, and maritime histories.

Modern Times Bookstore (888 Valencia St. at 20th St., tel. 415/282–9246) is a large shop that stocks leftist books and periodicals. Its collection of fiction and nonfiction from Latin America, in Spanish and English, is unrivaled in the Bay Area. Multicultural children's books are also in good supply.

Phileas Fogg's Books, Maps and More (87 Stanford Shopping Center, Palo Alto, tel. 415/327–1754 or 800/533–3644) also stocks globes and magazines.

University Press Books (2430 Bancroft Way at Telegraph Ave., Berkeley, tel. 510/548–0585) is devoted to books published by more than 100 university presses, plus academic lines, including Penguin, Routledge, Sage, and Beacon.

Used **Acorn Books** (740 Polk St. at Ellis, tel. 415/563–1736) has a large selection of books in all fields.

Green Apple Books (506 Clement St. at 6th Ave., tel. 415/387–2272) always has bins of sale-priced books out on the sidewalk. New books and remainders are on sale in the front section; in the back and upstairs are fairly well-arranged piles of used books. The store's strong suits are literature and history, but there's a broad selection in nearly every discipline.

McDonald's Book Shop (48 Turk St. off Market, tel. 415/673–2235) isn't open Sunday, but it would be a shame to miss this throwback to the good old days of used-book selling, where everything's a mess, and you suddenly realize you've spent your entire afternoon rummaging around. It has the best, if most disorderly, selection of old magazines in the city.

Sunset Bookstore (2161 Irving St. at 23rd Ave., tel. 415/664–3644) is a solid, general-interest used bookshop with emphases on art, psychology, music, history, literature, and philosophy.

Clothing
Alternative **Ameba** (1732 Haight St. at Cole, tel. 415/750–9368) features what can only be described as nouveau hippie-chick fashions—or, in the words of its manager, "psychedelic dance-culture clothing." Visiting the shop is an amusing step back in time.

Dinostore (1553 Haight St. at Ashbury, tel. 415/861–3933) sells everything from suits for men and women to funky clubwear.

Urban Outfitters (80 Powell St. at Ellis, tel. 415/989–1515) will hip you right up (or down, with a Nerd Shirt by Fink) in no time. The store is calculatedly ratty looking, but fun.

X-Large (1415 Haight St. at Masonic Ave., tel. 415/626–9573) specializes in hip-hop, rave, and other funky threads, including a fashion line overseen by bassist Kim Gordon of the rock group Sonic Youth.

Discount/ Second-Hand **American Rag Cie.** (1305 Van Ness Ave. at Sutter, tel. 415/474–5214) is a large, department store–like collection of men's and women's clothes from the United States and Europe, all in excellent shape. The place also stocks shoes and such accessories as sunglasses, hats, belts, and scarves.

Crossroads Trading Co. (1901 Fillmore St. at Bush, tel. 415/775–8885) is an upscale resale clothing emporium where would-be Annie Halls—female and male—can conjure up the complete look. The prices are a little higher than at other local shops, but so is the quality.

Esprit (499 Illinois St.. at 16th St. off 3rd St., tel. 415/957–2550), the city's first mega-outlet, is no longer as jammed as it was a few years ago, but there are still good buys.

European Menswear Outlet (393 Sutter St. at Stockton, tel. 415/788–0340) sells mostly Italian clothing—suits, shirts, ties, and belts. After discounts, which run up to 60%, the prices seem almost reasonable.

Loehmann's (222 Sutter St., near Union Sq., tel. 415/982–3215), a store that many fashionably dressed women swear by, sells such designer labels as Karl Lagerfeld and Krizia at drastically reduced prices. It helps to know designers, however, because the labels are often removed.

New West (426 Brannan St. at 3rd St., tel. 415/882–4929) specializes in top-notch merchandise for men and women, including Armani, Hugo Boss, and Donna Karan.

Yerba Buena Square (899 Howard St. at 5th St., tel. 415/974–5136), anchored by the Burlington Coat Factory (which has a full range of clothing), is a center for apparel, shoes, and toys. The best bargains don't always jump out at you—take the time to wade through the mundane and you're likely to find items by Armani, Calvin Klein, Girbaud, and Dior.

Leather **East/West Leather** (1400 Grant Ave. at Green, tel. 415/397–2886) has been in North Beach for two decades selling boots, jackets, belts, purses, and backpacks for women and men.

The Coach Store (190 Post St. at Grant Ave., tel. 415/392–1772), a branch of the nationally known purveyor of classically designed leather goods, offers an inventory that includes purses, briefcases, silk scarves, and belts and wallets of all sizes, colors, and weights.

North Beach Leather (190 Geary St., tel. 415/362–8300) is one of the city's best sources for high-quality leather garments—skirts, jackets, trousers, and dresses. With its sculpted walls, the store itself is a work of art. The original Fisherman's Wharf store (1365 Columbus Ave., tel. 415/441–3208) is still in business.

Maternity **Today's Maternity** (Stonestown Galleria, 19th Ave. and Winston Dr., tel. 415/731–8617) emphasizes stylish, comfortable, and affordable designs.

Men's Basics **Armani Exchange** (2090 Union St. at Webster, tel. 415/749–0891) sells the designer's casual lines—jeans, sweaters, jackets, handbags, T-shirts, socks.

Culot (1969B Union St. at Buchanan, tel. 415/931–2413) has the grooviest French underwear in San Francisco.

Emporio Armani (1 Grant Ave. at Market, tel. 415/677–9400) offers culinary and sartorial splendor at the designer's hip San Francisco flagship store, which houses a trendy restaurant on its main floor. His latest jackets, pants, shirts, and accessories, of course, are no mere sideline. Downstairs is more casual apparel.

J. Crew (San Francisco Shopping Centre, 865 Market at 5th St., tel. 415/546–6262), the catalog outfit, sells its nouveau-preppy couture at this bustling retail establishment.

Nomads (556 Hayes St. at Laguna, tel. 415/864–5692) has cornered the market on upscale grunge: shepherd's vests, cowhide pants, and other clever necessities and accessories.

The Outlaw (900 North Point St. at Larkin, tel. 415/563–8986), a shop that bikers and wannabikers won't want to miss, peddles Harley-Davidson fashions, plus leather jackets, T-shirts, swimsuits, and hats.

Rochester Big and Tall (700 Mission at 3rd St., tel. 415/982–6455) has a good selection of suits, sport coats, trousers, sportswear, and shoes.

Rolo (2351 Market St. at Castro, tel. 415/431–4545; 450 Castro St. at Market, tel. 415/626–7171; 1301 Howard St. at 9th St., tel. 415/861–1999) keeps the club set up to date.

Shoes

Bally of Switzerland (238 Stockton St. at Sutter, tel. 415/398–7463) sells high-quality men's and women's dress shoes.

Birkenstock (1815 Polk St. at Washington, San Francisco, tel. 415/776–5225) has footwear that may not be pretty, but it's comfortable—as loyal legions will attest.

Kenneth Cole (San Francisco Shopping Centre, 865 Market at 5th St., tel. 415/227–4536; 2078 Union St. at Buchanan, tel. 415/346–2161) has smart, stylish, designs.

Footwear First (2115 Fillmore St. at California, tel. 415/921–5049) stocks leather and suede boots, high heels, pumps, and handbags, too.

Gimme Shoes (416 Hayes St. at Gough, tel. 415/864–0691) sells hip shoes built to last.

Rabat (4001 24th St. at Noe, tel. 415/282–7861) carries a fine line of women's shoes, from conservative to mildly flashy, plus clothing and accessories.

Shaw Shoes (2001 Union St. at Buchanan, tel. 415/922–5676) is a small boutique with high-quality shoes, mostly from Italy, from designers such as Casadei, Via Spiga, Donna Carolina, and Karl Lagerfeld.

Women's Basics

A few downtown and outer Sacramento Street boutiques close on Sundays, but most women's clothing shops remain open. Haight Street, Fillmore Street, 24th Street in Noe Valley, and Union Street are usually bustling.

Ann Taylor (441 Sutter St. at Powell, tel. 415/989–5381; also at Embarcadero Center, Ghirardelli Sq., Stonestown Galleria), the national chain, carries designer fashions for work or evening.

Avant Premiere (1942 Fillmore St. at Pine, tel. 415/673–8875) sells clothing designed and manufactured by the folks at the shop, using fabric from France and Italy, some of it woven exclusively for them. Belts are a strong suit here.

Bebe (2133 Fillmore St. at California, tel. 415/771–2323; San Francisco Shopping Centre, 865 Market at 5th St., tel. 415/543–2323; 1954 Union St. at Buchanan, tel. 415/563–2323) has contemporary women's suiting that's flexible, multiseasonal, not too conservative, and not too trendy.

Company Store (1913 Fillmore St. at Bush, tel. 415/921–0365) sells designer fashions for women size 14 and up.

Designers Club (3899 24th St. at Sanchez, tel. 415/648–1057) sells contemporary natural-fiber clothing for women, some conservative, some offbeat, from local and national designers.

Georgiou (1725 Union St. at Gough, tel. 415/776–8144; 4 Embarcadero Center, Clay St. at Drumm, tel. 415/981–4845; Anchorage Shopping Mall, 2800 Leavenworth St. at Beach, tel. 415/441–3301) concentrates on clothing for career women—blazers, dresses, separates, and accessories. The top floor of the Union Street store is devoted to sale merchandise, as is all the Anchorage mall shop.

Jim-Elle (2237 Fillmore St. at Sacramento, tel. 415/567–9500) has basic, everyday interchangeable separates by Romeo Gigli, Harriet Selwyn, Peter Cohen, Matsuda, and other well-known designers.

Knitz and Leathers (1429 Grant Ave. at Green, tel. 415/391–3480) is a small North Beach shop with original-design coats, sweaters, and handbags.

Peluche (1954 Union St. at Buchanan, tel. 415/441–2505) specializes in contemporary suits and dresses for a youngish clientele. Since the store carries its own private brands, much of its merchandise can't be found in department stores.

Vintage The unrivaled headquarters for vintage fashions is Haight Street, where rock stars, movie costumers, and just plain folk scour the shops from Masonic Avenue to Shrader Street seeking the best of what's left of the glorious past.

Buffalo Exchange (1555 Haight St. at Ashbury, tel. 415/431–7733, also on Polk St. and in Berkeley, Oakland, and Pleasant Hill), sells both new and recycled clothing and will also trade or buy items.

Held Over (1543 Haight St. at Ashbury, tel. 415/864–0818) has an extensive collection from the '40s, '50s, and '60s.

Old Vogue (1412 Grant Ave. at Green, tel. 415/392–1522) has an inspiring selection of hats and vintage Hawaiian shirts.

Electronics **Discount Camera** (33 Kearny St. at Market, tel. 415/392–1100) sells major brands of cameras, VCRs, camcorders, telephones, and tape recorders. On weekdays it also buys and sells used cameras.

Eber Electronics (2355 Market St. at Castro, tel. 415/621–4332) is well stocked with TVs, VCRs, camcorders, speakers, and the like; it also sells large-screen home-theater equipment. The staff is particularly knowledgeable.

The Good Guys (1400 Van Ness Ave. at Bush, tel. 415/775–9323) is a full-service audio/video showroom. You can almost always get 10% off big-ticket items simply by looking like you mean it when you ask—or by musing about checking out the nearby competitor, Circuit City.

Whole Earth Access (401 Bayshore Blvd. at Flower, tel. 415/285–5244; 2990 7th St. at Ashby Ave., Berkeley, tel. 510/845–3000) has a great selection of cameras, video equipment, electronic devices, computers, and small and major appliances.

Computers **Computown** (756 Market St. at Grant Ave., tel. 415/956–8696) carries desktops, laptops, computers, printers, software, and supplies.

Video **Laser Cinema** (2258 Market St. at Noe, tel. 415/621–8434) has a large selection of domestic and imported laser discs for sale or rent.

Le Video (1239 9th Ave. at Lincoln Ave., tel. 415/566–3606) has far and away the best selection of foreign and independent film titles for sale or rent in the city. Hollywood releases are in no short supply, either.

Naked Eye News and Video (533 Haight St. at Fillmore, tel. 415/864–2985) has the city's most eclectic array of videos—odd foreign and cult titles, plus classic and recent Hollywood films—and an equally eclectic stock of periodicals and newspapers.

Erotica **Carol Doda's Champagne and Lace Lingerie Boutique** (1850 Union St., No. 1, at Laguna St., tel. 415/776–6900) is the new headquarters of North Beach topless dancing legend Carol Doda, who remains as alluring as ever. If she's around, she'll reminisce about her heyday at the Condor Club as she helps you find just the right bra, teddy, bustier, corset, garter belt, slinky dress, or swimsuit.

Good Vibrations (1210 Valencia St. at 23rd St., tel. 415/974–8980; 2504 San Pablo Ave. at Dwight Way, Berkeley, tel. 510/841–8987), a "clean, well-lighted place to shop for sex toys, books, and videos," is a friendly, woman-owned-and-operated enterprise.

Romantasy (199 Moulton St. at Fillmore, tel. 415/673–3137) a "sensual, erotic shop for loving couples and romantic singles" offers such essentials *d'amour* as chocolate body paint, tantric love swings, and chinchilla-lined G-strings.

Food

Bread and Bagels

Bepples Pies (1934 Union St. at Laguna, tel. 415/931–6225; 2142 Chestnut St. at Steiner, tel. 415/931–6226) is a San Francisco legend. Most famous for fruit pies, it also has meat- and vegetable-filled pies to eat in or take out.

Fantasia (3465 California St. at Locust, tel. 415/752–0825) sells decadently sweet cakes, pies, tortes, and cookies, plus croissants, scones, and buns (hot-cross and otherwise).

Greens to Go (Fort Mason, Building A, Laguna St. at Marina Blvd., tel. 415/771–6330), an offshoot of the well-regarded vegetarian restaurant, sells breads, pastries, and cookies, plus sandwiches, salads, and vegetable turnovers—to go, of course.

Noah's New York Bagels (2075 Chestnut St. at Steiner, tel. 415/775–2910; 742 Irving St. at 8th Ave., tel. 415/566–2761; elsewhere around the Bay Area) offers all your favorite kosher flavors, plus a few you've never thought of.

Tassajara Just Desserts (1000 Cole St. at Parnassus Ave., tel. 415/664–8947) sells desserts, plus the Tassajara Zen community's very fine breads (cottage-cheese dill, potato) and other baked goods. There's a café on site.

La Victoria Mexican Bakery and Grocery (2937 24th St. at Alabama, tel. 415/550–9292) is the Mexican cookie capital of the Mission. You'll also find Mexican breads, cakes, and other goodies here.

Victoria Pastry Company (1362 Stockton St. at Vallejo, tel. 415/781–2015) has been serving San Franciscans for nearly 80 years. Its specialties are Italian pastries (try the horseshoes) and St. Honoré cakes.

Coffee

San Franciscans love to debate who roasts the best coffee in town. North Beach's Graffeo Coffee Roasting Company and the Caffé Trieste retail outlet are among the longtime favorites; alas, they're not open Sundays. But there are still options galore:

Castro Cheesery (427 Castro St. at Market, tel. 415/552–6676) has the best cheap coffee in town—for as little as half the price of the stuff at other gourmet java shops.

Peet's Coffee and Tea (2139 Polk St. at Broadway, tel. 415/474–1871; various other locations) has been pleasing San Franciscans with its traditional and creative blends since the '60s.

Spinelli Coffee Company (2455 Fillmore St. at Washington, tel. 415/929–8088; 3966 24th St. at Noe, tel. 415/550–7416; 2255 Polk St. at Green, tel. 415/928–7793; 712 Irving St. at 8th Ave., tel. 415/731–9757) has beans and brew for sale at these and other Bay Area locations.

Union Street Coffee Roastery (2191 Union St. at Fillmore, tel. 415/922–9559) roasts more than 30 different beans and fashions some intriguing blends. A sister operation is at 2331 Chestnut St. (tel. 415/931–5282).

Gourmet Specialties

Andronico's Market (1200 Irving St. at Funston, tel. 415/661–3220) is the best full-service grocery in the Sunset District, with a range of gourmet specialties—jams, crackers, pickles, olives, vinegar, and prepared foods.

Bon Appetit (145 Jackson St. at Front, tel. 415/982–3112), a large gourmet grocery store near Embarcadero Center, has exceptional meat and deli departments.

The Cellar at Macy's (Stockton St. at O'Farrell, tel. 415/397–3333) sells bread (the sourdough-specialist Boudin Bakery has an outlet here), coffee, tea, meats, smoked fish, packaged foods, and wine. Wolfgang Puck's concession has superb gourmet pizzas to eat here or take out.

The Chef (3977 24th St. at Noe, tel. 415/550–7982) carries fresh imported and domestic caviar along with other gourmet specialties from pâté to cheese. The shop's gift baskets and party trays are festive and tasty.

The Chocolate Bear (2250 Union St. at Fillmore, tel. 415/922–5711) sells some great fresh fudge, fruit hand-dipped in chocolate, and Neuhaus Belgian chocolates.

Falletti's Finer Foods (Fulton St. at Masonic, tel. 415/567–0976) is rightly renowned for its produce. Separate deli, meat, fish, poultry, dessert, bread, and liquor boutiques offer mouthwatering delicacies.

Milan International Spices and Foods (990 University Ave. at 9th St., Berkeley, tel. 510/843–9600) is a mellow general store that stocks everything a proper Indian, Pakistani, or Middle Eastern kitchen should have.

Say Cheese (856 Cole St. at Carl, tel. 415/665–5020) consistently ranks among the most popular shops in local polls. Besides a broad selection of cheeses and pâtés, it has superb service.

Trader Joe's (555 9th St. at Bryant, tel. 415/863–1292), a discount gourmet grocery *extraordinaire*, has great values on sauces, wine, coffee, prepared quiches, olives, cookies, pasta, cheese, smoked fish, and other delicacies.

Vivande (2125 Fillmore St. at California, tel. 415/346–4430) has an unsurpassed selection of designer olives. It just may be the best gourmet shop in the city, if also the priciest.

Williams-Sonoma sells gourmet sauces, spices and herbs (San Francisco Shopping Centre, 865 Market at 5th St., tel. 415/546–0171; 150 Post St. at Grant Ave., tel. 415/362–6904; 2000 Chestnut St. at Fillmore, tel. 415/929–2520).

Ice Cream

Ben and Jerry's (1480 Haight St. at Ashbury, tel. 415/249–4685) offers the Vermont duo's fine ice cream for you to take home. Or stick around and bask in the memories at the Haight's most famous intersection.

Gelato Classico Italian Ice Cream (576 Union St. at Stockton, tel. 415/391–6667; other locations throughout the city) has the richest dark-chocolate ice cream in town, plus some unique Italian flavors.

Organic Foods

Real Food Company (2164 Polk St. at Filbert, tel. 415/775–2805; 3939 24th St. at Sanchez, tel. 415/282–9500; other locations) is a full-service organic produce and health-food store. Vitamins and other herbal products are in stock at all the stores; some also have full deli departments selling such delicacies as braised eggplant and vegetarian piroshkis.

Thom's Natural Foods (5843 Geary Blvd. at 23rd Ave., tel. 415/387–6367) is a large Richmond District organic produce and grocery store with bulk herb and grain bins and a deli counter.

Pasta

Auntie Pasta (2139 Polk St. at Vallejo, tel. 415/776–9420; and four other stores in the city) has every type of pasta you can imagine, plus sauces and other necessities.

Produce

Happy Supermarket (400 Clement St. at 5th Ave., tel. 415/221–3195) is the one-stop shop for Chinese groceries, with everything from dried fish, dried mushrooms, pot stickers, soy sauce, preserved tofu, and abalone to Chinese vegetables and pickles, Chinese herbs and medicines, and many varieties of rice. Supplies for Philippine, Thai, and other Asian cuisines round out the mix.

Casa Lucas Market (2934 24th St. at Alabama, tel. 415/826–4334) specializes in Spanish and Latin American fresh produce, in addition to wines and cheeses.

Porter's Produce and Epicurean Giftbaskets (498 Sanchez St. at 18th St., tel. 415/626–1057) sells the most exquisite and sometimes expensive produce, always displayed with elegance and taste. Hard-to-find British victuals are a specialty.

Fun, Games, and Gizmos

Brookstone Company (Stonestown Galleria, 19th Ave. and Winston Dr., tel. 415/731–8046) has oddball hardware, kitchenware, and personal items.

Game Gallery (Stonestown Galleria, 19th Ave. at Winston Dr., tel. 415/664–4263) has thousands of games for adults and young adults: board games, puzzles, fantasy card games, and chess computers.

Gamescape (333 Divisadero St. at Oak, tel. 415/621–4263; 1225 4th St. at B St., San Rafael, tel. 415/457–8698; 465 California St. at El Camino Real, Palo Alto, tel. 415/322–4263) has a splendid selection of new and used board, computer, and role-playing games, from old favorites like Monopoly and Parcheesi to the latest high-tech offerings from Nintendo and Sega.

House of Magic (2025 Chestnut St. at Fillmore, tel. 415/346–2218) has magic sets, magic tricks, antique apparatuses, and how-to books and videos—plus hundreds of gag gifts (backwards clocks, celebrity face masks) and goofy gadgets (hand buzzers, wind-up toys).

Little Frankensteins (3804 17th St. at Sanchez, tel. 415/864–6543) is the kooky shop of underground cartoonists Bruce Helvitz and Flower Frankenstein. The two sell Super Cool Fufu Café People finger puppets, the Miss PMS Fun Action Toy, and prints, ceramics, and T-shirts. Most of the items are made right on the premises. There's also a tiny miniature-golf course, the only one in San Francisco.

Pipe Dreams (1376 Haight St. at Masonic Ave., tel. 415/431–3553) keeps the '60s alive in the form of Day-Glo posters, T-shirts, patches, incense, candles, natural soaps, postcards, bongs, water pipes, and hookahs (the last three only for tobacco, of course). Its neighbor, **Golden Triangle** (1340 Haight St., tel. 415/861–7133) has more of the same (though the clerks are a bit gruff—bad tobacco, perhaps?).

The Sharper Image (532 Market St. at Sansome, tel. 415/398–6472; also at Ghirardelli Sq.), a paradise for gadget lovers, has everything from five-language translators and super-shock-absorbent tennis rackets to state-of-the-art speaker systems and Walkman-size computers.

Star Magic Space Age Gifts (4026 24th St. at Noe, tel. 415/641–8626) looks to the future with a New Age perspective. From crystals to kaleidoscopes, star appliqués to spaceship models and solar-system mobiles, it's a cheery window into the space(y) age.

Uncle Mame (2193 Market St. at Sanchez, tel. 415/626–1953) bills itself as a "haven of fun and kitsch." And it is: Big Boy statues, vintage Barbie dolls, snow-globe souvenirs from around the world, vintage cereal boxes, Pez dispensers, and candy from America and Europe attract a fun-loving clientele.

Handicrafts and Artifacts

African Outlet (564 Octavia St. at Hayes, tel. 415/864–3576) holds a trove of mostly handmade goodies—contemporary and antique—from all over Africa: Brilliant fabrics from West Africa, Zulu spears and shields, Cowri shells, Mud Cloth from Mali, Berber and Tuareg jewelry, and a great array of other adornments for the head, neck, arms, and feet. The store also does henna hand and feet painting—very intricate, often Muslim-influenced designs that African women (and sometimes men) wear for ceremonies and events. The process takes 45 to 90 minutes; paintings last about two to three weeks.

Asakichi (Japan Center, on the bridge between the Kinokuniya and Kintetsu Buildings, tel. 415/921–3821) is a tiny space full of such treasures as wind chimes, teapots, and beautifully crafted small furniture.

Enchanted Crystal (1895 Union St. at Laguna, tel. 415/885–1335) has dozens of crystal balls, candleholders, vases, and Art Deco sculptures. There's also a bridal section at this friendly shop.

F. Dorian (388 Hayes St. at Gough, tel. 415/861–3191) specializes in cards, jewelry, and other crafts from Mexico, Japan, Italy, Peru, Indonesia, the Philippines, and Sri Lanka, as well as items from local craftspeople.

Folk Art International Boretti Amber (*see* Galleries *in* Chapter 4).

Global Exchange Fair Trade Center (3900 24th St. at Sanchez, tel.

415/648–8068), a nonprofit store, aims to "foster economic self-sufficiency for Third World communities." It stocks an array of crafts from around the globe.

Light Wave Holography Gallery (The Cannery, 2801 Leavenworth St. at Beach, tel. 415/474–0133) showcases one of America's newest crafts forms, 3D-like photorealistic imagery—from the cute and cuddly (kids, bunny rabbits) to the downright scary (a leaping panther).

Ma-Shi'-Ko Folk Craft (2nd floor, Kinokuniya Building, Japan Center, 1581 Webster St. at Post, tel. 415/346–0748) carries handcrafted pottery from Japan, including Mashiko, the style that has been in production longer than any other. There are also masks and other handcrafted Japanese goods.

The Nature Company (4 Embarcadero Center, ground floor, Front St. at Sacramento, tel. 415/956–4911) is a new-age nature-lover's delight. The store sells amethyst bookends, recycled-paper datebooks and address books, petrified wood, birdbaths, wind chimes, and collector-quality minerals and fossils. If you're looking to cultivate a higher consciousness, pick up a crystal-growing kit.

Planetweavers Treasure Store (1573 Haight St. at Ashbury, tel. 415/864–5526) carries crafts, clothing, masks, some UNICEF-sponsored gifts and cards, drums, music books, and toys from around the world.

Polanco (393 Hayes St. at Gough, tel. 415/252–5733), a colorful gallery of Mexican art, carries Oaxacan woodcarvings, fanciful plates, prints and paintings, religious statuary, and other handmade objects.

Toko Imports (1314 Grant Ave. at Vallejo, el. 415/397–2323) stocks new and antique furniture, folk art, jewelry, and other handicrafts, much of it from Bali and most of it reasonably priced. The accent is on whimsy: brightly painted handcarved banana trees, fanciful wooden puppets, and the like.

Xela (3925 24th St. at Sanchez, tel. 415/695–1323) is a wonderful shop selling ancient and contemporary art from Africa, Asia, Latin America, and elsewhere. The jewelry is quite fine.

Home Furnishings

Accessories

Abitare (522 Columbus at Union St., tel. 415/392–5800) features a quirky mix of artsy furnishings—mirrors, candleholders, frames, and original furniture and decorations.

The Captain's Wharf (125 Powell St. at Ellis, tel. 415/391–2884) is a gift shop specializing in brass ware—doorknobs, door knockers, hooks, towel bars, lamps, candleholders, and clocks.

Kris Kelly (174 Geary St. at Stockton, tel. 415/986–8822) sells imported and domestic handcrafted tablecloths, bed linens, and bath accessories. Handmade quilts from China are the specialty here.

Lamps Plus (4700 Geary Blvd. at 11th Ave., tel. 415/386–0933) has a multitude of lamps by leading manufacturers.

The Plant Warehouse (1355 Bush St. at Polk, tel. 415/885–1515) peddles plants, from the common to the obscure.

Red Desert (1632 Market St. at Franklin, tel. 415/552–2800) is cactus headquarters, with all species and sizes, indoor and outdoor.

Revival of the Fittest (1701 Haight St. at Cole, tel. 415/751–8857) is the place to find telephones, dishes, and assorted collectibles, as well as vintage and reproduction jewelry, clocks, lamps, vases, and furniture.

Standard Brands Paint and Home Decorating Centers (3 Masonic Ave. at Geary Blvd., tel. 415/922–4003), a do-it-yourself store, offers decorating consultations.

Townhouse Living (Japan Center, 1825 Post St. at Fillmore, tel. 415/563–1417) is a homey little shop selling futons, pillows, lamps, frames, Japanese fabrics, tatami mats, vases, and other household accessories.

Worldware (336 Hayes St. at Franklin, tel. 415/487–9030) raises recylced merchandise to higher forms. Here you'll find picture frames and candlesticks made out of old aluminum cans (made to look like silver) and purses fashioned from discarded inner tubes and license plates. If the shop sounds strictly downscale, it's not: owner Shari Sant, who designs her own line of clothing made from organic hemp, wool or cotton, has a discerning eye as she picks among life's ruins. Among the new goods, bedding and linens come from Belgium's The Purist and other high-end, all-natural producers. Worldware also sells essential oils, skin care products, aromatherapy candles, and antique furniture.

Z Gallerie (2071 Union St. at Webster, tel. 415/346–9000; Stonestown Galleria, 19th Ave. at Winston Dr., tel. 415/664–7891, other stores in the San Francisco Shopping Centre and on Haight Street) specializes in home furnishings in black: butterfly chairs, dinnerware, desks, chairs, lamps, and a variety of high-tech accessories. It's also good for posters.

Bed, Bath, Kitchen

Bed and Bath Superstore (555 9th St. at Bryant, tel. 415/252–0490) has two floors of bed, bath, and kitchen necessities, plus picture frames, sculptures, and other decorative items.

Crate and Barrel (125 Grant Ave. at Post, tel. 415/986–4000) sells affordable but stylish kitchen and dining utensils.

Judith Ets-Hokin Homechef Kitchen Store (3525 California St. at Locust, tel. 415/668–3191) has just about every low- or high-tech cooking utensil you may need, from whisks to Cuisinarts. Sign up for weekday and weekend cooking classes while you're there.

The Futon Shop (3545 Geary Blvd. at Jordan, tel. 415/752–9908; for other Bay Area locations tel. 415/920–6800, ext. 3) is a large retailer carrying a full line of futons and frames. Its outlet (2150 Cesar Chavez St. near Evans, tel. 415/920–6800) offers some outstanding bargains.

Williams-Sonoma (San Francisco Shopping Centre, 865 Market at 5th St., tel. 415/546–0171; 150 Post St. at Grant Ave., tel. 415/362–6904; 2000 Chestnut St. at Fillmore, tel. 415/929–2520), the retail outlet of the famous mail-order catalog house, has stylish cooking equipment, tabletop items, and knickknacks.

Set Your Table (2258A Market St. at Castro, tel. 415/626–7330) specializes in Fitz and Floyd fine china and Sasaki crystal. Dinnerware lines and flatware are also for sale.

Carpets/Rugs

Carpet Connection (390 Bayshore Blvd. at Cosgrove, tel. 415/550–7125) boasts San Francisco's largest inventory of new name-brand carpeting at warehouse prices. Rugs and remnants, draperies, miniblinds, and vinyl flooring can all be found here.

Omid Oriental Rugs (590 9th St. at Brannan, tel. 415/626–3466) has a large showroom of Persian, Turkish, Pakistani, Indian, Chinese, Nepalese, and other new, used, and antique rugs.

Fabrics

Discount Fabrics (1432 Haight St. at Masonic Ave., tel. 415/621–5584; two other city locations) has a broad range of satin, wool, and cotton fabrics. The shop sells Simplicity, Butterick, and McCall patterns.

Fabric Factory Outlet (101 Clement St. at 2nd Ave., tel. 415/221–4111) not only has good bargains, it also carries a fine array of fabrics, in addition buttons, lace, appliqués, and other sewing accessories.

Far East Fashion (953 Grant Ave. at Washington, tel. 415/362–8171 or 415/362–0986) has one of Chinatown's better selections of Chinese embossed silks and lace.

Fabric Outlet (2109 Mission at 17th St., tel. 415/552–4525) discounts fashion and decorator fabrics, notions, patterns, and crafts.

Furniture

Ambiente (390 Kansas St. at 17th St., tel. 415/863–9700) offers mildly trendy and reasonably priced contemporary home furnishings: dining room sets, dressers, sofas, and chairs.

Galisteo Home Furnishings (590 10th St. at Division, tel. 415/861–5900) carries furniture and accessories of the American West and Southwest.

Ioma Furniture (1799 Union St. at Octavia, tel. 415/885–2000) imports stylish, unpainted, handworked wicker-and-wrought-iron furniture and fossil-stone coffee and cocktail tables from the Philippine island of Cebu.

Mike Furniture (2142 Fillmore St. at Sacramento, tel. 415/567–2700) has stylish upscale custom furniture that's conservative but with a flair.

Next Interiors (50 Van Ness Ave. at Fell, tel. 415/255–7662) sells trendy furniture. The closeouts at their **Next Express** outlet store (1315 Howard St. at 9th St., tel. 415/255–1311) are often real buys.

Jewelry

Gallery of Jewels (1400 Haight St. at Masonic Ave., tel. 415/255–1180; 4089 24th St. at Castro, tel. 415/285–0626) has a fine assortment of designer costume jewelry, some of it locally produced.

Gargoyle Beads (1310 Haight St. at Central, tel. 415/552–4274) sells exotic beads and other fixin's. Why buy jewelry when you can make your own?

Jade Empire (832 Grant Ave. at Clay, tel. 415/982–4498), one of the many fine jewelry stores in Chinatown, has good jade, diamonds, and other gems.

Union Street Goldsmith (1909 Union St. at Laguna, tel. 415/776–8048) is a traditional jeweler specializing in custom work.

Luggage

El Portal Luggage (San Francisco Shopping Centre, 865 Market at 5th St., tel. 415/896–5637) is a one-stop travel shop, with top-line luggage, briefcases, shaving kits, and other necessities.

The Luggage Center (828 Mission at 4th St., tel. 415/543–3771) sells luggage and travel accessories at a discount. Additional outlets are in Berkeley, Burlingame, Emeryville, and San Rafael.

Malm Luggage (222 Grant Ave. at Sutter, tel. 415/392–0417; Stonestown Galleria, 19th Ave. and Winston Dr., tel. 415/753–2097) has fine luggage, leather goods, and accessories.

Records/CDs

General

Discolandia (2964 24th St. at Alabama, tel. 415/826–9446) is far and away the city's best bet for current and vintage Latin music.

Hear Music (1809B 4th St. at Delaware, Berkeley, tel. 510/204–9595) has 50 listening stations where you can sample any CD before you buy.

New Sandy Music (1126 Grant Ave. at Pacific, tel. 415/989–4964) stocks the latest in Asian pop music.

Star Classics (425 Hayes St. at Gough, tel. 415/552–1110) carries classical, opera, symphonic, ballet, New Age, and jazz tapes, CDs, videos, and laser discs.

Tower Records (Columbus Ave. and Bay, tel. 415/885–0500; Market and Noe Sts., tel. 415/621–0588; for other Bay Area locations, tel. 800/275–7693) is open daily until midnight, with full selections of all types of music. An outlet store (660 3rd St. at Townsend, tel. 415/957–9660) has great video, audio, and book bargains. It's open Sundays 10 to 5:30.

Virgin Megastore (2 Stockton St. at Market, tel. 415/397–4525) has a huge selection of current releases; backlist classical, rock, jazz, world, specialty, country, and other music; and videotapes, laser discs, books, and multimedia products. In-store artist appearances are frequent. Its listening walls allow customers to preview CD releases.

Dance Music

BPM Music Factory (1141 Polk St. at Bush, tel. 415/567–0276) is where Bay Area club DJs shop for imports and domestic products. The store's 12-inch collection includes house, techno, acid jazz, and progressive.

Star Alley (322 Linden St. at Gough, tel. 415/552–3017) features a range of dance music: house, rave, hip-hop, techno, trance, soul,

Euro-HiNRG, and modern. The shop also sells CD singles, and T-shirts.

Rarities **Amoeba** (2455 Telegraph Ave. at Haste St., Berkeley, tel. 510/549-1125), which always wins or places high on local "best of" lists, stocks more than 100,000 new and used CDs, LPs, and tapes.

Reckless Records (1401 Haight St. at Masonic Ave., tel. 415/431-3434) is one of several used record shops that make Haight Street a must-stop for music lovers. The store stocks new recordings along with music-related T-shirts and posters.

Recycled Records (1377 Haight St. at Masonic, tel. 415/626-4075) doesn't have anything new—just an exquisite collection of vintage rock, jazz, soul, pop, blues, reggae, folk, and international CDs, LPs, 45s, and tapes.

Rough Trade (695 3rd St. at Townsend, tel. 415/543-7091), "the alternative music source," specializes in jazz, R&B, rock, and the latest in dance music on independent labels from around the world. It's so good the stars—local and national—shop here, too.

Streetlight Records (2350 Market St. at Castro, tel. 415/282-8000; 3979 24th St. at Noe, tel. 415/282-3550) buys and sells a full range of music, from rave to classical.

Village Music (9 E. Blithedale Ave. at Throckmorton Ave., Mill Valley, tel. 415/388-7400) is well worth a trip to Marin County. John Goddard's world-renowned shop carries new and used LPs, 45s, 78s, tapes, and CDs. Rock, jazz, big band, reggae, classical, movie and Broadway soundtracks, gospel, bluegrass, and folk are well represented in the store's collection.

Paper Goods

Office Supplies **Gables Office Supplies and Stationery** (5636 Geary Blvd. at 21st Ave., tel. 415/751-8152) has an old-time feel, with serious business supplies in the back and gifts, stationery, and cards as you enter.

McWhorters Stationers (Stonestown Galleria, 19th Ave. and Winston Dr., tel. 415/681-1014) carries office products, rubber stamps, pens and gifts, stationery, wedding invitations, legal forms, and artists' materials.

Office Depot (2675 Geary Blvd. at Masonic, tel. 415/441-3044; 855 Harrison St. at 5th St., tel. 415/243-4128) provides a full range of office supplies, plus furniture and business machines.

Papers and Postcards **Oggetti** (1846 Union St. at Octavia, tel. 415/346-0631) carries Italian marbleized papers and other stationery items.

Quantity Postcard (1441 Grant Ave. at Green, tel. 415/986-8866) is a cornucopia of vintage, celebrity, geographic, artistic, campy, and just plain silly postcards.

Party Supplies **The Party Warehouse** (2121 Harrison St. at 17th St., tel. 415/863-0912) provides all the balloons, horns, hats, and piñatas you'll need to create a party in no time.

Seasons Cards and Gifts (2061 Chestnut St. at Steiner, tel 415/923-9400) has party favors, supplies, gift wrap, cards, balloons, and ribbons.

Pets and Paraphernalia **The Animal Connection** (2550 Judah St. at 31st Ave., tel. 415/564-6482) has reptiles, amphibians, birds, tropical fish, and all the exotic creatures and critters you'd ever dream of having in your house.

My Best Friend (4455 18th St. at Douglass, tel. 415/864-0661) carries pet supplies, accessories, and discount bulk pet foods.

Pet Food Express (1798 19th Ave. at Noriega, tel. 415/759-7777; 371 West Portal Ave. at 15th Ave., tel. 415/759-1400) has everything you need to keep birds, bunnies, cats, and dogs chirping, squeaking, purring, and barking with delight. Also in stock: shampoos, stain removers, flea control, and other pet accessories.

Top Dog (1776 Mission at 14th St., tel. 415/626-6610) sells dogs, cats, birds, fish, hamsters, and rabbits and offers pet boarding, too.

Posters **The Artisans of San Francisco** (1964 Union St. at Buchanan, tel. 415/

921–0456) specializes in historical posters and photos of San Francisco. It also does custom framing.

Postermat (401 Columbus St. at Vallejo, tel. 415/421–5536) carries original and reproduction rock posters.

Poster Source (Pier 39, the Embarcadero, tel. 415/433–1995) stocks a wide range of contemporary posters: art, rock, sports, and celebrity.

Sporting Goods/ Athletic Wear

Don Sherwood Golf and Tennis World (320 Grant Ave. at Sutter, tel. 415/989–5000) showcases all the major brands of pro-line golf and tennis equipment and fashions.

G & M Sales (1667 Market St. at Gough, tel. 415/863–2855) carries hiking and ski equipment, barbells, clothing, boots, backpacks, and other sporting goods.

Lombardi's (1600 Jackson St. at Polk, tel. 415/771–0600) has equipment for skiing, camping, golf, and other sports, as well as athletic wear. It also stocks complete lines of exercise equipment—machines, barbells, and stationary bicycles.

The North Face (180 Post St. at Grant Ave., tel. 415/433–3223), a Bay Area-based company, is famous for its top-of-the-line tents, sleeping bags, backpacks, skis, and outdoor apparel, including stylish Gore-Tex jackets and pants. There's also a discount outlet store (1325 Howard St. at 9th St., tel. 415/626–6444).

Toiletries

Beauty Store (2085 Chestnut St. at Steiner, tel. 415/922–2526, others in Pacific Heights, the Haight, Embarcadero Center, Stonestown, and the Castro District) has a full line of traditional and organic beauty supplies.

Body Time (2072 Union St. at Webster, tel. 415/922–4076) sells some of the best concoctions around for the face and body; it makes its own soaps, lotions, creams, perfumes, and body oils.

Crabtree & Evelyn (Stonestown Galleria, 19th Ave. and Winston Dr., tel. 415/753–8015; also at Embarcadero Center and Ghirardelli Sq.) has English and French soaps, shampoos, lotions, creams, shaving supplies, and grooming implements—as well as jams, assorted condiments, and specialty gifts.

M.A.C. (1833 Union St. at Octavia, tel. 415/771–6113) sells its own line of facial cosmetics in addition to brushes and accessories. The shop does makeovers and gives 90-minute lessons to help women (and cunning drag queens) achieve their ideal look.

Best Bets for Children

Books

Charlotte's Web Children's Bookstore (2278 Union St. at Steiner, tel. 415/441–4700) has fiction and nonfiction for kids, plus tapes, videos, and art supplies.

Clothing

Citikids Baby News Store (152 Clement St. at 3rd Ave., tel. 415/752–3837) is a veritable kiddie department store, selling clothing, nursery furniture, diapers, books, games, and toys.

Dottie Doolittle (3680 Sacramento St. at Spruce, tel. 415/563–3244) carries domestic and imported clothing from infant size to 14, plus some baby furniture.

Kids Only (1608 Haight St. at Clayton, tel. 415/552–5445) has a little bit of everything, from the functional (clothing) to the amusing (games and toys).

Little Bean Sprouts (3961A 24th St. at Noe, tel. 415/550–1668; Ghirardelli Sq., 900 North Point at Larkin, tel. 415/346–1662) specializes in fanciful children's playwear and accessories, infants to size 6X-7.

North Beach Baby (468 Green St. at Grant Ave., tel. 415/956–0426) sells new and recycled cotton clothing and books, toys, and games.

Toys

FAO Schwarz (148 Stockton St., tel. 415/394–8700), the San Francisco branch of an American tradition, features a little of everything, from games and stuffed toys to motorized cars and trains.

Sanrio (39 Stockton St. at Market, tel. 415/981–5568) stocks the most complete array of Hello Kitty paraphernalia in the city. Adults are as enamored of the goodies here as the kids.

Toys R Us (555 9th St. at Bryant, tel. 415/252–0607; 2675 Geary Blvd. at Masonic Ave., tel. 415/931–8896) has lots and lots of toys.

6 Sports, Games, and the Urban Outdoors

By Kathryn Olney

Updated by Daniel Mangin

San Francisco is a great city—and a great location—for people who love the outdoors. Every weekend, city denizens head for the parks, the bay, the mountains, and the many forested areas sandwiched in between. City residents who work nights head for spots of green and blue even on weekdays, to hike, bike, sail, and surf—in between café crawling, of course.

The Urban Outdoors

There may not really be farms in Berkeley, but the outdoors beckons from every hill and valley in the Bay Area. The 450 square miles of water known as the San Francisco Bay is indeed a thing of wonder. More than 406 trillion gallons pour through the Golden Gate strait with each tidal shift; depending on drought conditions, another 5- to 27-million acre-feet of fresh water pour in from valley rivers. Owing to landfill and development, only about 15% of the 200,000 acres of tidal wetlands that the bay once harbored remains intact today. Luckily, public support has at last shifted toward preservation.

Beaches

Bay Area beaches offer year-round pleasures from sailing to swimming to shelling to strolling. But the water is very cold, and some of the most beautiful beaches have dangerous surfs. Only two city beaches—Aquatic Park and China Beach—are considered safe for the average swimmer. If you want to swim elsewhere, either stick to the beaches on the bay, where the waves are mild, or head out of the city to one of the ocean beaches or lakes.

In the City

Aquatic Park (tel. 415/556–1659) stands at the north end of Van Ness Avenue, nestled between the Hyde Street and Municipal Piers. It's cold, but if you're serious about swimming, you can rent or buy a wetsuit from one of the surf shops listed in the Yellow Pages. Aquatic Park is the site of many an impromptu sand-castle competition.

Baker Beach (end of Gibson Rd. off Bowley St., near Lincoln Blvd. and 25th Ave., no phone), with its marvelous views of the Marin Headlands and the Golden Gate, sits on some of the most dangerous surf around, so it's just for strolling, picnicking, and wading. You can sunbathe nude on the north end, though it isn't strictly legal.

China Beach (415/556–0560) is a little beach at the entrance to the Golden Gate where Chinese fishermen used to camp during Gold Rush days. (It's sometimes listed on maps as Phelan Beach.) To get here, take the coastal trail from the Cliff House toward the city or park on the bluff off Seacliff Avenue at the end of 28th Avenue and take the steps down. There are rest rooms on site.

Fort Funston Beach (Hwy. 35/Skyline Blvd., about 1 mi south of Sloat Blvd., tel. 415/556–8371). Clamber down from the magnificent lookout at the top of the cliff—the city's prime spot for hang gliding and a popular dog-walking area (*see* Hang Gliding under Sports and Recreation, *below*, and Great Walks *in* Chapter 3)—to reach another walkable beach. It's not for people who can't climb!

Land's End. (*See* Great Walks *in* Chapter 3.)

Ocean Beach (no phone), the longest expanse of beach in the city, starts at Cliff House (end of Geary Blvd.) and stretches south 3 miles to the beautiful bluff at Fort Funston. A paved jogging/biking path runs just east of the Great Highway, and bikes (including baby wagons that hook onto the back) can usually be rented from outdoor vendors along the way (*see* Bicycling under Sports and Recreation, *below*). In winter expert surfers scale the mighty waves, and in summer the place is second only to the Marina Green for kite flying. Don't go in any deeper than your toes unless you're an experienced surfer and you have fins.

Around the Bay

East Bay

Crown Beach (tel. 510/521–6887) is one of the prettiest and sunniest on the bay, and it's safe for swimming. The 2-mile beach runs next to Crab Cove on Alameda, an island just off Oakland, accessible only by tunnel or bridge. (Take the Broadway/Alameda exit off I–880.) Bring boots to hike the mud flats at Crab Cove Marine Reserve, at the west end of the beach. Also visit the visitors center, where a saltwater aquarium holds various creatures from the bay. At the Roemer Bird Sanctuary, on the south side of the beach, you'll spot egrets and more.

Lake Temescal Regional Recreation Area (tel. 510/652–1155) is often warm even when it's cold and foggy in San Francisco. Kids love swimming (May–Oct.); there are also hiking paths, playgrounds, and fishing spots (permits available at the bathhouse). Take the Broadway exit from Route 24 and follow the signs to Route 13; you'll spot the parking area on the right.

Marin County

Paradise Beach (tel. 415/435–9212 or 415/499–6387) is a great place for fishing and swimming in the bay; afterward you can hike the Tiburon Uplands Nature Trail. To get here, take the Belvedere/Tiburon Boulevard exit from U.S. 101, follow Tiburon Boulevard east to Trestle Glen Boulevard, and turn right onto Paradise Drive. The beach is 3 miles farther along. Arrive early, since this is one of the summer's balmiest spots.

McNear's Beach County Park (tel. 415/499–7816) is one of the few with both a bayside beach and a swimming pool (open summer and early fall). To get there, take the Central San Rafael exit from U.S. 101. Turn right (east) on 2nd Street, which eases into 3rd and eventually becomes San Pedro Road. Turn right on Cantera Way; the gate to the beach is about 100 yards farther along. Note: No pets are allowed.

China Camp State Park (tel. 415/456–0766) was a Chinese shrimping and fishing village at the turn of the century; it's still fairly well preserved. Activities here include hiking, picnicking, swimming, boating, and camping; there's also a small historical museum and a café. Call Destinet (tel. 800/444–7275) to reserve a campsite. To get there, take the North San Pedro Road/Civic Center exit from U.S. 101; go east on North San Pedro for about 4 miles, and you'll see the park entrance.

Stinson Beach (tel. 415/868–0942), an ocean beach 45 minutes north of San Francisco off Highway 1 (take the Stinson Beach exit from U.S. 101 and follow the signs), overflows with bathers and beach walkers on Sundays. Stay for the evening if you want to avoid traffic back to the city, and call the weather line (tel. 415/868–1922) first; conditions can range from glorious to foggy.

Muir Beach (no phone), just west of Marin City, is a small but rugged stretch with beautiful dunes and a small lagoon. It's about 25 minutes from the city on Highway 1; you'll see the signs. (You can also hike the 5 miles from the Marin Headlands Visitors Center if you're feeling fit.) Just north of the public beach is one of the best nude beaches in the area; stroll a short distance, hop a few rocks, and you're there. Call the Stinson Beach weather line (*see above*) for the latest on the climate.

Peninsula

Coyote Point Beach (tel. 415/573–2592) is one of the few saltwater beaches on the bay in San Mateo County (*see also* Zoos and Wildlife Centers *and* Best Bets for Children, *below*). It's a convenient beach, with showers; rest rooms; and, in summer, lifeguards; it's also a six-minute walk from the Coyote Point Museum (*see* Science and Technology Museums *in* Chapter 4). To get to Coyote Point Park, take the Poplar Avenue exit from U.S. 101 and stay to the left, turn right on Humboldt Road, and right again on Peninsula Avenue. Note: No pets are allowed.

San Gregorio State Beach (tel. 415/879–2170), with its high bluffs and long stretch of white sand, offers a public beach and, to the north (on private property), one of the Bay Area's most popular nude beaches. It's just under an hour's drive south of the city on Highway 1.

Pescadero State Beach (tel. 415/879–2170) is divided in two. Pescadero North has long dunes and the Pescadero Marsh Natural Preserve. Pescadero South has a natural jetty and tidepools; ranger-led tidepool tours take place Sundays at 1 PM, no reservations necessary. Take I–280 south to Highway 92, then head west to Highway 1; the beach is 20 miles south of this intersection.

Pigeon Point (tel. 415/879–0633) has the second-tallest freestanding lighthouse in the country. It's open for tours on Sundays. Follow the directions to Pescadero State Beach; Pigeon Point is about a half-hour farther south.

Parks and Woodlands

The region's parks are filled with contrasts: historic buildings with modern uses, wide spaces butting up against dense woodland, lowlying waterland next to arid scrub. Inside these spaces you'll find everything from lighthouses to shipwrecks to windmills to bobcats to pelicans, not to mention stunning vistas and miles and miles of trails. Enjoy them!

Golden Gate Park

Golden Gate Park, 3 miles long and ½ mile wide, stretches from the Pacific Ocean into the geographic heart of the city. In 1870 when William Hall, who became the first supervisor, was retained to prepare a topographic map, the land was sand dunes and scrubby fauna. By 1943 when the fourth supervisor, John McLaren, ended his tenure at the age of 97, it was a shady paradise. The planting continues: Starting in 1969, some 2,000 cherry trees were laid, providing wonderful pink-clouded spring walks along Martin Luther King, Jr. Drive.

Owing to the prevailing westerly wind, the area is generally smogfree and cool. On any given Sunday, San Franciscans head for one of the park's microenvironments. Rollerbladers bop around John F. Kennedy Drive; on Sundays it's closed off to automobile traffic. Joggers pant up the gentle hills, while cyclists whiz past. Free **guided walking tours** are offered by Friends of Recreation and Parks (tel. 415/221–1311) on weekends May–October: a Strawberry Hill Tour on Saturdays and, on various Sundays, the popular Japanese Tea Garden tour, "McLaren's Walk" through the park's east end, and the "Windmill Tour" of its west end—including a walk around Lloyd Lake and some "hidden" secrets of the park. The walks last from 45 minutes to two hours.

Skate and bike rentals are available along the perimeter of the park at shops on Stanyan, Fulton, and Irving streets and from trucks parked near all these locations. A popular new place for vendors is the southern end of the park along the Great Highway, where John F. Kennedy Drive ends. (*See* Bicycling and Roller-Skating and Rollerblading under Sports and Recreation, *below*, for vendors' names.)

Park headquarters is at the 1897 McLaren Lodge (John F. Kennedy Dr. at Stanyan); you can pick up a map here weekdays 9 to 5. For **general park information,** call 415/666–7200, weekdays 9 to 5. The following list of sights in the park moves from east to west:

Fuchsia Garden, surrounded by cypresses, pines, and redwoods, is in full bloom summer and fall. *Near Arguello Blvd. south of Conservatory Dr. East.*

Children's Playground, the best and biggest in the city, went up in 1887. In addition to an antique carousel, it has swing sets and a modern jungle gym with a corkscrew slide. A wide lawn nearby is perfect for Frisbee-tossing and relaxing. *Near Kezar Dr. Antique carousel operates Sun. 10–4.*

Tennis Courts and Bowling Green stand northwest of the Children's Playground. The tennis courts are lighted. *Tel. 415/753–7101 for weekend reservations at the courts, 415/864–1843 for information about lawn bowling.*

Conservatory of Flowers, a bewitching Victorian glass house, modeled on the hothouse at Kew Gardens, London, was shipped here around Cape Horn in 1879. A December 1995 storm caused several million dollars worth of damage to the structure, which will remain closed until repairs are completed. *John F. Kennedy Dr., tel. 415/666–7200 for updates on the building's condition.*

Tree Fern Grove is an enchanting grove for fern aficionados. It's across from the Conservatory of Flowers, just east of the Rhododendron Dell.

Rhododendron Dell, first planted in 1942, contains the greatest collection of varieties (850) in the country. It's especially beautiful in March and is famous as a Mother's Day picnic spot. *John F. Kennedy Dr. near 6th Ave.*

California Academy of Sciences sits directly across the Music Concourse from the M. H. de Young Museum in the center of Golden Gate Park (*see* Science and Technology Museums *in* Chapter 4.

Shakespeare Garden, southwest of the California Academy of Sciences, is planted with flowers immortalized by the bard.

Bandshell, formally called the Spreckels Temple of Music, has been the site of free Sunday concerts since 1882. *Between Music Concourse and Tea Garden Drs., tel. 415/666–7035. Open 1 PM, Apr.–Oct., weather and funding permitting.*

Strybing Arboretum specializes in plants from climates similar to that of the Bay Area. Among its 6,000 species are specimens from Australia, South Africa, and the Mediterranean. There's a section of native California plants, a small redwood forest, a fragrance garden (with Braille labels), a Japanese moon-viewing garden, and incredible magnolia and rhododendron collections. Free weekend tours leave the Strybing Arboretum Bookstore (just inside the main entrance at 9th Ave. and Lincoln Way, tel. 415/661–5191) at 10:30 and 1:30. *Near 9th Ave. and Lincoln Way, tel. 415/661–1316. Open Sun. 10–5.*

Japanese Tea Garden is a peaceful place for tea and cookies on a cool, foggy day. The bonsai are exquisite, and in spring the cherry blossoms are ravishing. The Drum Bridge is always a hit with kids, who love to scramble up it. *Tea Garden Dr. next to Asian Art Museum, tel. 415/752–1171. Garden admission: $2.50 adults, $1.50 senior citizens and children 6–12; tea: $2.50. Open Sun. 8:30–6:30 (8:30–5 or 5:30 in winter).*

Stow Lake, in the middle of the park near 19th Avenue, was constructed with clay from a quarry on Divisadero Street—it is basically a huge bowl with 6-inch-thick walls. You can stroll around the perimeter and feed the ducks or cross one of the bridges to the island in the center and climb Strawberry Hill for a view down to Huntington Falls and out to the city. Or you can rent boats (motor-, row-, or paddleboats), as well as bikes (tel. 415/668–6699), from the boathouse at the northwest corner. *Off John F. Kennedy Dr., first left after exit for museum and teahouse; boathouse tel. 415/752–0347. Open Sun. 9–5 summer, 9–4 rest of year.*

Portals of the Past are an evocative relic of a Nob Hill mansion that was wrecked by the 1906 earthquake and fire. Ionic columns that once framed the mansion's entryway now stand in solitude on the edge of Lloyd Lake. *Beside Lloyd Lake off John F. Kennedy Dr., south of 25th Ave.*

Golden Gate Park Stadium (Polo Field) is used by the public for jogging and other sporting activities, as well as for such special events as rock concerts, soccer, and the finish of the San Francisco Marathon. This was the site of the great 1967 Be-In, where Allen Ginsberg and hordes of flower children meditated and chanted together in a mass effort to alter consciousness. *Between John F. Kennedy and Middle Drs. west of 30th Ave.*

Spreckels Lake is the spot for radio-controlled yachts and miniature sailboats, especially on Sundays. Many senior citizens gather here, since the park's senior activities center (tel. 415/666–7015) is nearby. *36th Ave. south of Fulton.*

Golden Gate Park Stables is the place for equestrians. Lessons are available here on a onetime or ongoing basis (minimum age: five); there are no hourly rentals, however. Guided trail rides along any one of the park's 27 miles of bridle paths usually take place Sundays at 1 and 3; advanced reservations are advised. *36th Ave. and John F. Kennedy Dr., tel. 415/668–7360. Open Sun. 8–6.*

Buffalo Paddock is the home of a Wyoming herd that was acquired in 1984. The original denizens were brought to the park in 1894. *John F. Kennedy Dr. west of Spreckels Lake.*

Golf Course, small but devious, offers nine par-3 holes and is open all year. *(See* Golf under Sports and Recreation, *below.) Off Fulton St. opposite 47th Ave., tel. 415/751–8987.*

Archery Field has targets set up for practice year-round; bring your own bow and arrows. *(See* Archery under Sports and Recreation, *below.) 47th Ave. and Fulton St.*

Dutch Windmill, built in 1902 and recently restored, once pumped 20,000 gallons of well water per hour to the reservoir on Strawberry Hill. *John F. Kennedy Dr. near Great Hwy.*

Queen Wilhelmina Tulip Gardens, in the northwest corner of the park next to the Dutch Windmill, bursts into full bloom in February and March. *John F. Kennedy Dr. at Great Hwy.*

Murphy Windmill was the world's largest when it was built in 1905. It, too, pumped water to the Strawberry Hill reservoir. *South Dr. near Great Hwy.*

The Presidio

This breathtaking 1,480-acre expanse, which until very recently housed 6,000 military personnel, is on its way to becoming one of northern California's greatest parks. It's more than twice the size of New York's Central Park, and a good 50 percent of its buildings are listed on the National Register of Historic Places. Some of the Presidio's properties—its golf course, bowling center, and some office buildings—have been leased out, but the National Park Service (tel. 415/561–4323) is in charge of most of the activities within its confines.

Hikes

The Golden Gate National Recreation Area offers a number of free ranger-guided walks through the Presidio. These include the "Back to the Future" program, a walking tour of the heart of the Presidio; the two-mile Ecology Walk that covers the area's natural history and development; and the two-hour Coastal Defense Walk, which includes Fort Point and examines the area's military history. Hikes range from 45 minutes to 3 hours, with the average being about 2, and are usually on Saturdays or Sundays. The visitor information center (Presidio Project Office at the Main Post, Montgomery St. at Lincoln Blvd., tel. 415/561–4323) can tell you more about them. In addition there are several hikes you can do on your own, including

The **Main Post Tour** begins at the visitors center and outlines the Presidio's military past, architecture, cultural landscape, natural history, and future plans. Pick up the self-guided tour brochure at the center.

The **Coastal Trail,** which actually begins south of Ocean Beach at Fort Funston, winds into the Presidio at Baker Beach. Head toward the Golden Gate Bridge; just before the end of the beach, climb the wooden steps over the dunes, and continue following the trail on the ocean side of Lincoln Boulevard. You'll eventually connect with the paved bike path that goes under the Golden Gate Bridge. Follow it to the Civil War–era Fort Point (the spot in Hitchcock's *Vertigo* where

Kim Novak jumps into the bay). If you're still in the mood to stroll, you can continue along the Golden Gate Promenade on the edge of Crissy Field, past Marina Green into Fort Mason and over to Aquatic Park and Fisherman's Wharf.

The **Ecology Trail** winds for 2 miles through the center of the Presidio. Start at Funston and Moraga avenues; the hike will take you through groves of eucalyptus, cypress, redwood, and pine conceived by an industrious Major Jones late in the last century. Complete the loop by returning to the Main Post along the **Lover's Lane Trail,** a paved path continuing through the Presidio Forest.

Elsewhere in the City

Alta Plaza. This pleasant Pacific Heights park offers superb vistas in all directions. Dog lovers may appreciate the Dog Park Walk of Fame—two long cement gutters on the north side of the park, in which dog owners have carved the names of their beloved beasts. *Between Clay, Steiner, Jackson, and Scott Sts.*

Buena Vista Park. As the name suggests, the views north and west from this hilly spot are among the finest in the city. It used to be famous as the site of gay trysts. *Haight St. between Baker and Central Sts.*

Dolores Park. This grassy expanse fills up on sunny days. The north end offers splendid views of downtown; at the south, near the tennis courts, there's a popular dog run. (*See* Neighborhood Walks *in* Chapter 3.)

Fort Funston. *See* Beaches, *above,* and Great Walks *in* Chapter 3.)

Lake Merced. The San Francisco Water Department's emergency reservoir was once a brackish lagoon on the ocean. Eucalyptus, cypress, pine, and silk trees; wildflowers; ferns; and ice plants line the encircling 5-mile jogging/biking path. *John Muir Dr. between Skyline and Lake Merced Blvds. (See* Boating, *below.)*

Stern Grove. Most San Franciscans think of this as the spot for summer Sunday concerts, but during the rest of the year it's an enchanting place for a walk through eucalyptus solitude. There's also a little putting green and a wonderful playground just to the left of the 19th Street entrance. *19th Ave. and Sloat Blvd.*

Sidney G. Walton Square. This pretty downtown park—a sylvan blend of red brick and grass under willows and pines, with a lovely fountain as its centerpiece—is a quiet gem. You can grab a snack at Bon Appetit, the big gourmet grocery store and deli across Jackson Street. *Bounded* by *Jackson, Front, Pacific, and Davis Sts.*

Transamerica Redwood Grove. This cool, shady park is one of four places in San Francisco (besides Golden Gate Park) where redwood trees grow. The statue of children playing leapfrog is named "The Puddlejumpers," and the sculptor is Glenna Goodacre, who was also responsible for the Women's Vietnam War Memorial in Washington, DC. *Washington and Montgomery Sts., east of the Transamerica Pyramid.*

Around the Bay
East Bay

Charles Lee Tilden Regional Park is the East Bay's equivalent of Golden Gate Park—but bigger, with a whopping 2,000 acres. One of a string of lovely parks along the Hayward fault, it has fine trails for serious hikers, swimming in Lake Anza, an excellent botanical garden (*see* Gardens, *below*), an 18-hole golf course *(see* Golf under Sports and Recreation, *below*), and all kinds of attractions for kids. *Tel. 510/843–2137 for recorded information. Visitor Center/Environmental Education Center/Tilden Nature Area: Central Park and Cañon Drs., tel. 510/525–2233.*

The following are Charles Lee Tilden Regional Park highlights:

Botanical Gardens. (*See* Gardens, *below.)*

Inspiration Point. You can get close to this breathtaking lookout by taking Wildcat Canyon Road, or you can hike up the moderately strenuous Curran Trail from just north of Lake Anza. The point provides an excellent view northeast to the Briones and San Pablo reservoirs.

Jewel Lake. The fairly short loop that passes by hidden Jewel Lake is shaded with a canopy of trees. The trail starts near the Visitor Center and the Little Farm and takes you on a boardwalk through woods, around the peaceful lake (visited occasionally by blue heron), and up a brambled ridge that overlooks the valley.

Lake Anza. Less urban than Lake Temescal, Lake Anza feels like a retreat in the Sierra foothills, yet it's only 10 minutes from Berkeley. Swimming is allowed year-round (8:30–5), though the lake is staffed and lifeguarded May through October only. *Take Wildcat Canyon Rd. to Central Park Dr., tel. 510/848–3385.*

The Little Farm. Children can pet and feed cows, pigs, sheep, chickens, and donkeys at this section of the Nature Area next to the Visitor Center. *Tel. 510/525–2233 (visitor center) for information. Barn open Sun. 8:30–4:30; farm area sunrise–10 PM.*

Pony rides. In this favorite corner of the park, two- to five year olds ride ponies hitched to a turning wheel while 5- to 12 year olds are led around a larger corral. Minimum and maximum weight and height limits apply, so it's wise to call ahead. *Just south of the Visitor Center, tel. 510/527–0421. Open Sun. 11–5; closed winter in inclement weather. $2 per ride.*

The Steam Train. This miniature version of a steam train—pulled by three different turn-of-the-century narrow-gauge engine replicas—is maintained with great affection by the Golden Gate Live Steamers. For $1.50 it will take you on a 10-minute ride through the south end of the park. *2500 Grizzly Peak Dr., tel. 510/548–6100. Sun. 11–5, 11–6 in summer.*

Wildcat Peak. For a more strenuous hike, take the Jewel Lake path; when you reach the lake, take the Peak Trail, heading right (east) away from the lake. From here it's a steep, 1½-mile climb framed by live oaks. Along the way you're likely to glimpse coyote, deer, gray fox, red-tailed hawks, canyons—and poison oak. You've reached the peak when you see the giant sandstone formation that overlooks the entire North Bay. Count on about an hour up and back. You can also make a gentler trek from Inspiration Point along the paved Nimitz Way—a route that will take you past the Rotary Peace Grove of Sierra redwoods and giant sequoias.

Tilden Park is the centerpiece of the **East Bay Regional Park District.** Other notable parks under its administration are

Redwood Regional Park/Roberts Regional Recreation Area. Redwood canyons, fern-lined pools, and wonderful hilly trails make this a magical place to visit. The shade makes it especially appealing on hot days. *Redwood Rd. about 2½* mi east of Skyline Blvd., Oakland, tel. 510/635–0135. Admission: $3 per car. Open Sun. 8 *AM*–6 *PM*, summer, 8–9.

Mt. Diablo State Park. On a clear day, from the 3,849-foot summit, you can see from the Farallon Islands to the Santa Cruz Mountains to the Central Valley Delta and sometimes even out to the Sierras. (It's said that only Mount Kilimanjaro grants a farther view.) Exit Diablo Road in Danville from I–680; turn left, heading toward the mountain, and drive about 3½ miles; then turn left on Mt. Diablo Scenic Boulevard (watch the odometer, since the turnoff isn't always clearly marked). From there it's an 11-mile climb to the museum. There are campgrounds and picnic spaces along the ride to the top. *Summit Museum and Visitor Center, tel. 510/837–2525. Admission: $5 per car. Open Sun. 11–5.*

Sunol Regional Wilderness. The "little Yosemite" of the Bay Area affords piles of boulders to climb on, creeks to wade in, wild and rugged hill and canyon views, natural pools, and even waterfalls. To get there, take the Calaveras Road exit from I–680 south and turn left on Geary Road, which will take you right into the park. Pets are allowed at a cost of $1 per animal. (*See* Orienteering, *below.*) *Sunol (east of Fremont), tel. 510/862–2244. Admission: $3 per car. Open 7 AM–sunset.*

Marin County

The major Marin County parks are run by the state or federal government. Individual park numbers are given below. The main state-park information number is 916/653–6995. Two sources for information about ranger-led tours and hiking, biking, and pet trails in the **Golden Gate National Recreation Area** (which includes the Presidio, Marin Headlands, and other federally maintained wildlife regions, plus some parks under county or state control) are the GGNRA's Marin Headlands office (tel. 415/331–1540) and its office at Fort Mason Center (tel. 415/556–0560).

Angel Island State Park. The ferry ride to this island on the bay is a beauty, and the park is a perfect spot for a Sunday picnic. There's an easy 5-mile hike around the perimeter; from there, you may see deer, raccoons, harbor seals, and many species of birds. Some of the 12 miles of trails pass by ruins from its previous incarnations: as a camp for quarantined immigrants, a POW camp, and a prison for Native Americans. Docent tours (Apr.–Oct.) and camping can also be arranged. *Tel. 415/435–1915 for information, 415/546–2628 for ferry information from San Francisco, 415/435–2131 from Tiburon.*

Marin Headlands. It's a world apart from San Francisco—but it also has some of the best views of the city. Conzelman Road offers the finest of the Golden Gate; Hawk Hill (about 2 miles up Conzelman Road) is a prime spot to watch the migration of eagles, hawks, and falcons, mid-August to mid-December. (*See* California Marine Mammal Center under Zoos and Wildlife Centers, *below.*) *Visitors Center (take Conzelman Rd., turn right on McCullough Rd., left onto Bunker Rd.) tel. 415/331–1540.*

Mt. Tamalpais State Park. This favorite of hikers (*see* Great Walks *in* Chapter 3) with 50 miles of trails from easy to rugged, is another spot for spectacular views. There are numerous parking areas along the road, and you can get trail maps at the ranger station. *Tel. 415/388–2070. Open daily 7 AM–sunset.*

Muir Woods National Monument. This stunning redwood grove, with 6 miles of easy trails, is just 17 miles northwest of the city (*see* Great Walks *in* Chapter 3). *Mill Valley–Muir Woods Exit from U.S. 101 north, tel. 415/388–2595. Open Sun. 8 AM–sunset.*

Point Reyes National Seashore (tel. 415/663–1092). Highlights here include the half-mile Earthquake Trail, which passes by what is believed to be the epicenter of the 1906 quake; the 4-mile-plus Bear Valley Trail, which covers all four of the park's ecosystems (forest, meadow, coastal scrub, coastline); the late-19th century Point Reyes Lighthouse (a good spot to watch for whales late-December through March); and the reconstructed Coast Miwok Indian Village near the visitor center. Horses and mountain bikes are permitted on some trails. The turnoff for the visitor center is on Highway 1 about ⅓ mile past the town of Olema.

Tennessee Valley. The valley gets its name from the S.S. *Tennessee,* which ran aground in 1853 when the captain missed the Golden Gate in the fog. The boat now lies buried under the waves of the cove. Trails meander for about 2 miles down to the beach. You're likely to see deer as well as coots and mallards along the lagoon.

Peninsula

James V. Fitzgerald Marine Reserve. Rangers here lead weekend lecture tours to the beach and to some of the best tide pools in northern California. A few blocks north, the **Moss Beach Distillery** (Beach Way and Ocean Ave. off Hwy. 1, tel. 415/728–5595), an old moonshiners' spot turned restaurant/bar, has breathtaking views of the beach. *California Avenue off Hwy. 1, Moss Beach, tel. 415/728–3584). Open sunrise–sunset.*

Gardens

In addition to its splendid parks, the Bay Area offers a more perfectly pruned version of nature in its fine gardens. Sunday is a great day for strolling, sniffing, and admiring the beauty of the blossoms.

In the City

Filbert Steps Gardens (*See* Great Walks *in* Chapter 3.)

Garden for the Environment. This low-tech, high-growth greenhouse—a project of the San Francisco League of Urban Gardeners (SLUG)—shelters drought-tolerant plants, teaches gardeners which ones thrive in the area, and demonstrates the positive effects of composting. All the food grown is distributed to the homeless. *West side of 7th Ave. north of Lawton, tel. 415/285–7584. Admission free. Garden open daylight hours; staff members present Sun. 1–4 only.*

Golden Gate Park. The park is a flower buff's dream. For descriptions of the Fuchsia Garden, Rhododendron Dell, Tree Fern Grove, Shakespeare Garden, Strybing Arboretum, Japanese Tea Garden, and Queen Wilhelmina Tulip Gardens (*see* Parks, *above*).

Yerba Buena Gardens. This new garden atop the Moscone Center's north hall is a blend of art and plantlife. Under the grass are bricks of Styrofoam that add support without adding weight. One section features beds with the native plants of San Francisco's sister cities: carpet bugle (a ground cover) from Haifa, Israel; orchid rockrose (a shrub) from Assisi, Italy; and white and yellow marguerite chrysanthemums from Osaka, Japan. A waterfall cascades down 18 feet in front of an etched-glass Martin Luther King, Jr. Memorial. There are also saucer magnolias, maples, and flowering crab apples; a butterfly garden of wildflowers; and, inside the Center for the Arts building, a two-story atrium protecting a forest of black bamboo. *Admission free. Open daily dawn–10 PM.*

Around the Bay

East Bay

Berkeley Rose Garden. In late spring and summer this multilevel garden offers splendid views and fragrant roses. *Euclid St. between Bayview Pl. and Eunice St., Berkeley, tel. 510/644–6530. Admission free.*

Dunsmuir House and Gardens. Visitors can stroll among the rhododendrons, roses, lavender, and impatiens on nearly 40 acres of grounds. (*See* Restored Houses *in* Chapter 4.)

Lake Merritt. The park surrounding this Oakland lake, created in 1860 when a tidal saltwater lake was dammed, offers a variety of attractions to plant lovers. The **Rose Amphitheater** (Grand Ave. and Jean St.) displays 5,000 plants on 4 acres in grand formal-garden style. About a mile away, on the peninsula that juts out into the lake (near Grand and Bellevue Aves.), the **Lakeside Show Garden** houses a show garden, in addition to a community garden resource center and a palm grove. For more information about the gardens and clubs, contact the park administrator (tel. 510/238–3208).

Tilden Park Botanical Gardens. One hundred sixty thousand square miles of California vegetation have been compressed into 10 acres of parkland. Cacti from the desert grow within feet of pines from the Channel Islands. Docent tours are given most Sundays at 2 PM. *Wildcat Canyon Rd. and South Park Dr., Tilden Park, Oakland, tel. 510/841–8732. Open Sun. 8:30–5.*

University of California Botanical Garden. Every season brings a different bloom to these 34 acres growing 13,000 species. The cactus and succulent garden is marvelous, but so are the Rhododendron Dell, New World Desert, California annuals, Garden of Old Roses, and Mather Grove of redwoods. During rainy winters, the creek that runs through rushes with water. *Centennial Dr. in Strawberry Canyon, tel. 510/642–3343. Admission free; free tour weekends at 1:30. Open Sun. 9–4:45.*

Marin County and Beyond

Luther Burbank Home and Gardens. The working garden where the legendary horticulturist developed more than 800 varieties of plants is now part of a National Historic Landmark in Santa Rosa. (*See* Restored Houses *in* Chapter 4.)

Old St. Hilary's Historic Preserve. The Belvedere-Tiburon Landmarks Society operates this Victorian-era church as a historical and botanical museum. Marin County Open Space District tends to the several-acre surrounding preserve, where such wildflowers as the rare indigenous black jewel (which blooms in May and June), Tiburon morning glory (spring and autumn), and Marin dwarf flax (May and June) can be seen. *Esperanza Rd. off Beach Rd., Tiburon, tel. 415/435–1853. Admission free. Preserve open year-round; church open Sun. 1–4 Apr.–Oct. or by appointment.*

Peninsula

Acres of Orchids. The Rod McLellan Company, a thriving commercial nursery, has more than a million square feet of greenhouses available for inspection. *1450 El Camino Real at Hickey Blvd., South San Francisco, tel. 415/871–5655. Admission free. Open Sun. 9–6; free tours at 10:30 and 1:30.*

Filoli. The mansion featured in the opening credits of *Dynasty* has also made it into many a movie. But its 16 acres of gorgeous gardens are just as big a draw. The daffodils, hyacinths, and tulips are at their peak in February and March; the tulips continue, along with ranunculi, through April. One downer: it's all closed on Sundays. *Cañada Rd. near Edgewood Rd., Woodside (Edgewood Rd exit. from I–280), tel. 415/364–2880. Admission: $8; $4 children. Open for tours (reservations necessary) Tues.–Sat. mid-Feb.–Oct. Call for information on unguided visits and nature hikes.*

Hakone Gardens. Along with the largest collection of bamboo in the west, there's also a Pond Garden, a Zen Garden, and a Japanese-style house constructed without nails or other adhesive materials. The gardens were designed in 1918 by a former imperial gardener of Japan. *21000 Big Basin Way, Saratoga, tel. 408/741–4994. Admission: $5 per car. Open Sun. 11–5.*

Wildflowers

Gardens aren't the only place to see flowers in California. Every spring—especially since the drought ended—the hills, woods, and even city sidewalks and median strips come alive with wild irises, blue lips, California poppies (the state flower), ceanothus, columbine, Chinese houses, arroyo, lupines, and skyrockets—to name just a few. (There are a thousand varieties of wildflower in the Bay Area.) Here are a few top spots to view them, starting around April:

In the City

There are violets scattered around Golden Gate Park. The median strip outside Stern Grove is famous for its summer poppies. Look for lupines at Land's End, ceanothus (wild violet) at Mountain Lake Park (12th Ave. and Lake St.), and California poppies along roads throughout the city.

Around the Bay

East Bay

Look for violets, owl's clovers, lupines, checker blooms, and brodiea at Sunol Regional Wilderness (*see* Parks, *above*) and at Black Diamond Mines (in Antioch, tel. 510/757–2620) and Mission Peak (in Fremont, tel. 510/862–2244) Regional Preserves. Mount Diablo is also a good bet. The East Bay Regional Park District (tel. 510/562–7275) will give you a wildflower update and directions to the sites (call during weekday office hours only).

Marin County

Tennessee Valley Road is a prime place for poppy and lupine viewing in the spring. Point Reyes has wild irises at the south end.

Peninsula

Skyline Drive is always a good viewing area. The Mid-Peninsula Regional Open Space District (tel. 415/691–1200 weekdays) will let you in on the best blooms of the moment and tell you how to get to the following sites: the Pulgas Ridge (west of Redwood City), Los

Trancos Open Space (on Page Mill Road west of Palo Alto), and the Russian Ridge (at Skyline and Alpine Drives).

Zoos and Wildlife Centers

At these facilities the Bay Area plays host to birds, mammals, reptiles, amphibians, and fish from every continent. They're also the place to find some of the best playgrounds and educational activities for kids.

San Francisco

San Francisco Zoo. Among the thousand species that make their home here, more than 130—including the snow leopard, Bengal tiger, jaguar, and Asian elephant—have been designated endangered. A favorite attraction is the greater one-horned rhino, next to the African elephants. Another popular resident is Prince Charles, a rare white tiger. **Gorilla World** is one of the largest and finest gorilla habitats of any zoo in the world. The exceptional **Primate Discovery Center** houses 15 endangered species in atriumlike enclosures. *Feeding times: big cats, 2 PM; penguins, 3 PM.*

The **Children's Zoo,** with about 300 animals, includes a wonderful **Insect Zoo.** Tots love feeding the goats in the **Petting Barn.** They also love the playground just inside the zoo's entrance. (*See* Best Bets for Children, *below.*) *Sloat Blvd. and Great Hwy., tel. 415/753–7080. Admission: $7 adults, $3.50 senior citizens and children 12–15, $1.50 children 3–11, under 3 free. Children's Zoo admission: $1; children under 3 free. Open Sun. 11–4.*

Steinhart Aquarium. (*See* Science and Technology Museums *in* Chapter 4.)

Underwater World at Pier 39. You'd have to be a diver to get any closer to northern California marine life. Scheduled for a spring 1996 opening, the two-story Underwater World is on the cutting edge of aquarium technology. A simulated dive takes visitors "underwater," where a transparent, closed-loop acrylic tunnel allows them to travel, via a moving footpath, among fish, sharks, stingrays, and other species. Interactive displays and exhibits outline the life cycles of local sea creatures. *Pier 39, the Embarcadero near Jefferson, tel. 415/705–5500. Admission: $12.50. (San Francisco residents may buy off-peak passes at reduced prices.) Open Sun. 10–10.*

Around the Bay
East Bay

Children's Fairyland. This park is especially good for preschoolers. There are pony and llama exhibits, seals, and smaller critters like rabbits, geese, and guinea pigs (some in a petting zoo), plus storybook mazes, tree houses, and creative rides and slides. The Fairytale Personalities, tell tales at 12:30 and 3 on the Emerald City Stage; changing puppet shows are at 11, 2, and 4. *Grand and Bellevue Aves., at Lake Merritt, Oakland, tel. 510/452–2259. Admission: $3 adults, $2.50 children 1–12, under 1 free. Open Sun. 10–5:30 in summer (hours vary rest of year; call ahead).*

Lindsay Museum. The centerpiece of this sparkling facility is the oldest and largest wildlife rehabilitation center in the country. The museum, which takes in 8,000 orphaned and injured animals yearly, offers a range of programs that employ "nonreleasable" wild animals to teach respect for nature and the environment. There's also a children's petting zoo, as well as classes geared to various age ranges. *Larkey Park, 1931 1st Ave. at Buena Vista Ave., Walnut Creek, tel. 510/935–1978. Admission: $3. Open Sun. 1–5.*

The Little Farm. (*See* Parks and Woodlands: Tilden Park, *above.*)

Oakland Zoo. It's smaller than the San Francisco Zoo, but it still provides spacious natural habitats for the animals and gorgeous hilltop views for the visitors. Special educational events are often held on Sundays. *Knowland Park, 9777 Golf Links Rd. (1/2 block east of I-580 Golf Links exit), Oakland, tel. 510/632–9523. Admission: $5; parking $3. Open Sun. 10–4.*

Marin County and Beyond

California Marine Mammal Center. Volunteers here work with sick or injured seals and sea lions that have been found on the northern California coast. The goal is to return them, healed, to their habitats. Visitors are free to meander, observing the animals and learning about each species from posted information; docents are on hand on weekends to answer questions. *Fort Cronkhite, Marin Headlands, tel. 415/289–7325. Admission free (donations welcome). Open Sun. 10–4.*

Golden Gate Raptor Observatory. The National Park Service runs this splendid spot, where you can see migrating birds of prey circling above the Marin Headlands. In September and October, during the height of the raptors' migrating season, the park service conducts lectures and banding demonstrations. *Hawk Hill, crest of Conzelman Rd., Marin Headlands, tel. 415/331–0730.*

Marine World Africa USA. Animals of the land, sea, and air perform in shows, roam in natural habitats, and stroll among park visitors with their trainers at this popular 160-acre wildlife theme park. Among the "stars" are killer whales, dolphins, camels, elephants, sea lions, and a troupe of human waterskiers (April–October). You can take a high-speed ferry (tel. 415/705–5444) from Pier 39 at Fisherman's Wharf. *Marine World Pkwy., Vallejo, tel. 707/643–6722. Admission: 25.95; parking $4. Open Sun. 9:30–5 (sometimes later in summer).*

Peninsula

Coyote Point Park and Museum. Native peninsula animals—coyotes, bobcats, raccoons, foxes, river otters, badgers, squirrels, mice, ravens, vultures, owls, hawks, songbirds, snakes, frogs, and bees—are on display. There's also a good beach and a great playground (*see* Best Bets for Children, *below*), plus hiking trails. For directions, *see* Beaches: Peninsula, *above. Tel. 415/342–7755. Admission: $3, plus $4 per carload to enter the park. Open Sun. noon–5.*

Cemeteries

If you're feeling reflective and want greenery without the noise and bustle of a Sunday in the park, a cemetery can be just the place for a stroll. There aren't many graveyards in San Francisco proper, but a short drive south of the city will take you to several. **Near Escapes** (tel. 415/386–8687), a local tour company, offers a graveyard tour to the Colma cemeteries; it visits the graves of Wyatt Earp, Levi Strauss, and sculptor Beniamino Bufano—who lies at the foot of one of his own works)—as well as a pet cemetery. They also offer a Mortuary Tour. (*See* Group Outings, *below.)*

San Francisco

Mission Dolores Cemetery. Small and bewitching, this small graveyard is full of history. Among the San Francisco notables buried here is José Noe (1805–1872), the last chief magistrate of San Francisco under Mexican rule, whose name survives in Noe Street and the neighborhood of Noe Valley. Kim Novak makes a memorable visit here in the 1958 Alfred Hitchcock movie *Vertigo. Mission Dolores, Dolores and 16th Sts., tel. 415/621–8203. Admission: $1. Open Sun. 9–5.*

San Francisco National Cemetery. Some 30,000 servicemen and -women lie interred in this lovely Presidio setting, dotted with pine and cypress and looking out toward the Golden Gate Bridge. Cemetery tours (tel. 415/561–4323) are sometimes conducted on Sundays. *Lincoln Blvd. and Sheridan St., tel. 415/561–2008.*

Peninsula

South of the city, in **Colma,** where the dead outnumber the living by 2,000 to 1, some 1,500,000 people lie buried in a 2-square-mile area. For a complete list of Colma's 17 cemeteries, contact the Daly City/ Colma Chamber of Commerce (244 92nd St., Daly City 94015, tel. 415/755–8526). To get to Colma, take the Junípero Serra Boulevard exit from I–280 and head east, away from Serramonte Center. When you reach El Camino Real, you'll see cemeteries on both sides of the road. You can drive through many of them if you prefer, but most have large lots for visitors to park in. If you're in the mood for local lore and a brew, stop by **Molloy's Bar** (1655 Mission St. across from Holy Cross Cemetery, tel. 415/755–9545).

Cypress Lawns. Beautifully appointed, with rare trees, lagoons, and exquisitely carved monuments, this century-old cemetery became the final resting place of such notable San Franciscans as philanthropist Lillie Hitchcock Coit, entrepreneur James Flood, and batting champion Lefty O'Doul, as well as, more recently, newspaper magnate William Randolph Hearst, Jr., and conductor Calvin Simmons. The grave sites are pricey, the mausoleums are large, and there's a huge collection of stained glass (it's currently in the midst of being restored). The cemetery's story is well told in *Pillars of the Past,* by Michael Svanevik, available free at the cemetery office. *1370 El Camino Real, Colma, tel. 415/755–0580. Open Sun. 8–5.*

Greenlawn Cemetery. The deceased from San Francisco's Odd Fellows Cemetery were moved here in the '30s. *1100 El Camino Real, Colma, tel. 415/755–7622. Open Sun. 9–5:30.*

Hills of Eternity Memorial Park. This Jewish resting ground contains the remains of lawman Wyatt Earp, who shot it out at the OK Corral. His wife was Jewish; he lies buried beside her. *1301 El Camino Real at Serramonte Blvd., Colma., tel. 415/756–3633. Open Sun. 8–2:30.*

Home of Peace and **Emanu-el Mausoleum.** Another Jewish cemetery, this one is the final resting place of blue-jeans pioneer Levi Strauss and department-store magnate I. Magnin. *1299 El Camino Real at Serramonte Blvd., Colma, tel. 415/755–4700. Open Sun. 8–2:30.*

Pets Rest Cemetery. Dogs (including a poodle of Tina Turner), cats, ocelots, snakes, an iguana, a cheetah, and even a horse are interred here. The office is closed on Sundays, but you can still stroll the grounds. Staffers will show you around on Saturdays from 9:30 to 1. *1905 Hillside Blvd. near Serramonte Blvd., Colma, tel. 415/755–2201.*

Woodlawn. San Francisco's first famous street person, the self-proclaimed Emperor Norton (1819–80), lies buried here, in addition to John Daly—namesake of nearby Daly City—and the *San Francisco Independent* publisher John Fang. *1000 El Camino Real at F St., Colma, tel. 415/755–1727. Open Sun. 10-4.*

Group Outings and Tours

For a listing of what's coming up, check the "Weekend" section of the Friday *Examiner* and the Pink Section of the Sunday *Chronicle.* Most of the groups below publish their own calendars or have their own upcoming-events hot line. For city and county park tours, *see* Parks and Woodlands, *above.*

Club and Commercial Outings

Audubon Society (2530 San Pablo Ave., Suite G, Berkeley 94702, tel. 510/843–2222) organizes bird-watching expeditions—usually half days at one of the area parks.

Cal Adventures (2301 Bancroft Way at Telegraph Ave., Berkeley, tel. 510/642–4000) offers outdoor adventure trips—rock climbing, backpacking, cross-country skiing, river rafting, kayaking, sailing, windsurfing—for adults. The university outfit also offers classes in several of those activities, as well as a spring- and summer-break day camp for children in grades 3–12. The office is open for sign-ups on weekdays.

Coastwalk (1389 Cooper Rd., Sebastopol 95472, tel. or fax 707/829–6689) organizes four-to-six-day hiking and camping trips exploring the California coastline and Coastal Trail. The emphasis is on natural and human history and coastal issues.

Near Escapes (Box 193005, San Francisco 94119, tel. 415/386–8687) specializes in such unusual activities for adults as cemetery and mausoleum tours, a behind-the-scenes look at the fish roundabout in Steinhart Aquarium, and an afternoon at a criminal trial.

Outdoors Unlimited (530 Parnassus Ave. at 3rd Ave., underneath the UCSF library, tel. 415/476–2078) sponsors a resource center for trip planning, rents equipment, gives classes, and offers cooperative outdoor adventures. Activities, such as whitewater rafting, sea kayaking, and backcountry and telemark skiing, take place on weekends, but the office is only open weekdays, so plan ahead.

Point Reyes Field Seminars (c/o Pt. Reyes National Seashore Assn., Pt. Reyes 94956, tel. 415/663–1200), is nonprofit and offers day and overnight trips—many of them excellent for families—in conjunction with the park service. Subjects include natural arts and crafts (wildflower drawing, basket making, etc.), nature and natural history, bird-watching, and Native American culture at Point Reyes National Seashore.

Sierra Club (5237 College Ave., Oakland 94618, tel. 510/653–6127) sponsors activities ranging from canine walks to hikes to bike rides. You don't have to be a member to join in. The club publishes a thrice-yearly activities schedule ($4.50 for a subscription, $3.50 if you pick up a copy at the Sierra Club Bookstore, 730 Polk St. at Ellis in San Francisco).

Especially for Families

California Academy of Sciences (tel. 415/750–7098) sponsors day and weekend nature-study trips—some appropriate for children as young as five—with members of the academy staff. Half-day weekend trips head for destinations within a 100-mile radius; longer trips may range as far as the Channel Islands in southern California.

Slide Ranch (2025 Shoreline Hwy., Muir Beach 94965, tel. 415/381–6155) offers day and overnight trips designed to give city families hands-on experience with wildland, coastal, and farm life. Activities include nature hikes; ranch chores (including milking a goat); and cheese, bread, and paper making.

Sports and Recreation

The Bay Area's parks provide super spaces for many a Sunday game. You may need a permit at many of these facilities if you want to be guaranteed a space, but pickup games also abound. For information about where to join in just about any game in the city, look on the bulletin board or ask the friendly folks at **Gamescape** (333 Divisadero St. at Oak, tel. 415/621–4263; 1225 4th St. at B St., San Rafael, tel. 415/457–8698; 465 California St. at El Camino Real, Palo Alto, tel. 415/322–4263)—where you can also purchase board games, new and used software, puzzles, collectible trading card games, family games, and used games. The San Francisco and San Rafael stores are open Sunday 11 to 5, Palo Alto 10 to 5.

Archery

San Francisco

Center Shot (4429 Cabrillo St. at 45th Ave., tel. 415/751–2776) stands a few blocks from the Golden Gate Park Archery Field. It's only open Monday–Saturday, so rent your equipment a day early if you plan to use it on Sundays.

Peninsula

San Francisco Archer's Trail (Rifle Range Rd. off Lundy Way, Pacifica, tel. 415/355–9947) maintains two golf course–like ranges that you walk, plus practice bales and other targets.

Backgammon

In recent years backgammon has moved to the cafés. One place to find players aplenty is **Cafe Fanari** (2773 24th St. at York, tel. 415/285–1467). There's a board available to customers of the **Horse Shoe Coffee House** (566 Haight St. at Steiner, tel. 415/626–8852), too.

Ballooning

Napa Valley

American Balloon Adventures (Box 795, Calistoga, 94515 tel. 707/942–6541 or 800/333–4359), at the north end of the Napa Valley, provides a scenic hour-long flight southward over the vineyards, followed by brunch. Price ranges from $125 to $175 per person, depending on time of year and other factors.

Baseball
San Francisco Small parks throughout the city are available for games; for reservations and availability, call the San Francisco Recreation and Park Department (tel. 415/753–7024). You can often find a pick-up game in Golden Gate Park at the **Big Rec Ball Field,** close to 7th Avenue and Lincoln Way. For softball, try the **Little Rec Ball Field** at Sharon Meadow in the east end of the park, north of the Children's Playground.

East Bay **Grand Slam USA** (5892 Christie Ave. at Powell St., Emeryville, tel. 510/652–4487), an indoor baseball and softball batting range, is the place to hit a few. It offers lessons, too.

Basketball Pick-up games abound all over the city. For some low-key action, try the **James Lick School Playground** at Castro and 25th streets. The two full-length courts are often taken up with four half-court games by a talented pool of weekend warriors—lawyers, artists, and other professionals in the 20-to-40 category who still enjoy a game of hoops. Other good spots are the **Upper Noe Playground** (Day and Sanchez Sts.), **Grattan Playground** (Grattan and Stanyan Sts.), **Rochambeau Playground** (24th Ave. between Lake and California Sts.), and the **Moscone Recreation Center** in the Marina (near the tennis courts at Laguna and Chestnut Sts.) For serious street games, try the Potrero Hill Recreation Center (22nd and Arkansas Sts.), but unless you're really good, they'll mop up the court with you. The same goes for the courts in the **Golden Gate Park Panhandle** in the Haight (Masonic Ave. between Oak and Fell Sts.).

Bicycling On Sunday packs of bicyclers flock west to Golden Gate Park, north to Marin County, or across the bay to Angel Island. The California Department of Transportation publishes transbay crossing information for bicyclists; telephone 510/680–4636 for a schedule.

San Francisco On a fogless day, the **Sunset Bike Path** along the Pacific Ocean (one block east of the Great Highway) can be breathtaking. Plenty of vendors along the way rent bicycles and even trailers for pulling kids. It's a 5-mile ride from Lincoln Way to Lake Merced Boulevard (via Sloat Boulevard). Once you're there, you can extend your ride by another 5 miles on the **Lake Merced Bike Path,** which loops around the lake and the golf course. Alternatively, you can turn up South Drive, just past Lincoln Way, and cycle through the center of **Golden Gate Park;** Sunday is a great day for it, since John F. Kennedy Drive east of Transverse Drive and the connecting streets are closed to automobile traffic. (It's a gradual uphill ride traveling east from the ocean.)

Another favorite biking area is the **Presidio.** Ride in on Presidio Avenue and follow Presidio Boulevard until it turns into Lincoln Boulevard, which you can take all the way to Baker Beach. If you want a flatter ride, turn right onto Long Avenue (a Y in the road after Lincoln passes under U.S. 101) and follow it to Marine Drive. Along the first 1/10 mile of the **Golden Gate Promenade** hiking and biking trail, there's a strip that separates bikes from cars; it's often wet here from the crashing waves, so it's best to walk your bike to the corner where Long and Marine separate. Then you can begin your ride again, heading east.

Angel Island This hilly 5-mile trip past some great views, fine picnic spots, uncrowded beaches, and historic points of interest is the mother of all Bay Area bike rides. Take the ferry (tel. 415/546–2628) from Pier 43½ at Fisherman's Wharf (foot of Jefferson St.); only the first 25 bikes are allowed on board. (You can also ferry over from Tiburon or Sausalito; tel. 415/546–2700 or 800/229–2784. Or you can take the Angel Island–Tiburon Ferry, which leaves hourly from Tiburon; tel.

415/435–2131.) It's a fairly steep climb to the bike path, which you pick up behind the Visitor Center where the ferry docks. The path follows the perimeter of the island; for the most part it's paved, with one difficult hill.

Marin County You can bike across the Golden Gate Bridge or drive over on U.S. 101 into Sausalito. Take a left off Bridgeway past Margaritaville; behind the office buildings past Dunphy Park, you can pick up the **Sausalito Bike Path,** which takes you along the bay through Mill Valley and around the North Bay to Tiburon—an easy ride of about 12 miles. If you want more, continue another 4 or 5 beautiful miles, and you'll reach the narrow path that leads around Larkspur Point. You can take a ferry back to the city.

Serious bikers will want to explore the rugged **Marin Headlands** paths just across the Golden Gate Bridge. You can get a map at the Marin Headlands Visitor Center (tel. 415/331–1540) at Fort Barry, in the Old Chapel. For a description of the paths, which are also used by runners, *see* Running and Walking, *below.*

Peninsula The **Sawyer Camp Trail** (*see* Running and Walking, *below*) is as popular with cyclists as it is with runners. Two other favorites are **Cañada Road,** north from Edgewood Road to Route 92 and back, past the Filoli estate (8 miles), and the **Bayfront Trail,** from the old San Mateo Bridge—now the Werder Fishing Pier—off Hillsdale Boulevard, south along the fire road through Foster City, to the end of Belmont Office Park, which used to be Marine World (3½ flat and easy miles). For a longer ride, take the bike path north from the pier all the way up to Coyote Point Park in Burlingame (about 10 flat miles).

Rentals The **Great Highway** along Ocean Beach has more and more vendors renting regular bikes, tandem bikes, bikes with children's buggies that hook onto the back, and roller skates. (Prices are about the same as in shops or marginally cheaper.) Look for them from 10 till dark at the end of Golden Gate Park near Lincoln Way; you'll see the bikes parked in groups along the highway.

Golden Gate Park Skate and Bike at Golden Gate Park. (3038 Fulton St. near 6th Ave. at Golden Gate Park, tel. 415/668–1117) rents bikes on Sundays from 9 to 5:30 most of the year, 10 to 7 in the summer.

Mike's Bikes and Blades (tel. 415/668–6699) in Golden Gate Park (at the northwest corner of Stow Lake) rents out bicycles every day from 9 AM until one hour before sunset. Many types are available, from regular adult bikes to "stretch limo" quadricycles, contraptions that allow up to six people to participate. Prices range from $5 to $33, depending on which bike you choose and for how long.

Start to Finish Bicycles (672 Stanyan at Haight St., tel. 415/221–7211, open Sun. 10–5; 599 2nd St. at Brannan St., tel. 415/243–8812, open Sun. 11–5; 2530 Lombard St. at Divisadero, tel. 415/202–9830, open Sun. 10–5; 1820 4th St. at H St., San Rafael, tel. 415/459–3990, open Sun. 10–5) offers rentals, sales, and tours.

Wheel Escapes (30 Liberty Ship Way, Suite 2, at Bridgeway, Sausalito, tel. 415/332–0218) rents regular and off-road bikes and conducts group bicycle trips all over the Bay Area and beyond. You can take the Sausalito ferry from the city and rent a bicycle here.

For more rental information, *see* Roller Skating and Rollerblading, *below.*

Mountain Biking This increasingly popular activity has become ever more controversial, with hikers and conservationists complaining that mountain bikes tear up the hiking trails and disturb the terrain too severely. The friction has spawned a few rules that are now in effect at **Mt. Tamalpais State Park** (*see* Parks and Woodlands, *above*), which has become the favorite place to ride close to San Francisco: Riders must stay on fire roads and travel no faster than 15 mph, 5 mph when passing hikers or other bikers.

Also well traveled are the trails in **Tennessee Valley.** The Golden Gate National Recreation Area headquarters at Fort Mason (tel. 415/556–0560) can provide maps of trails under their auspices. The **Bicycle Trails Council of Marin** (415/456–7512) offers a Saturday-morning course on mountain-biking basics.

Group Trips **Backroads** (tel. 510/527–1555 or 800/462–2848) offers tours of the Wine Country and a Brew Pub Bike Tour that covers the Anderson Valley, the Napa Valley, and Sausalito.

Publications *Bay Area Bike Rides* by Ray Hosler (Chronicle Books, $10.95) includes rides from the gentle to the strenuous. Also useful are *Mountain Biking in the Bay Area: A Nearly Complete Guide* by Michael Hodgson and Mark Lord (Western Tanager Press, $12.95); *Cycling the San Francisco Bay Area: 30 Rides to Historic and Scenic Places* by Carole O'Hare (Bicycle Books, $12.95; *Marin County Bike Trails: Easy to Challenging Bicycle Rides for Touring and Mountain Bikes* by Phyllis L. Neumann (Penngrove Publications, $11.95); and *East Bay Bike Trails: Road and Mountain Bicycle Rides Through Alameda and Contra Costa Counties* by Conrad J. Boisvert (Penngrove Publications, $11.95). *City Sports* Magazine (available free at fitness centers and athletic supply stores) lists local and regional biking activities in its Calendar section.

Billiards and Pool Once a strictly blue-collar pastime, billiards has gone upscale. Sunday afternoons, it's family entertainment as well.

Chalkers Billiard Club (Rincon Center, 101 Spear at Mission St., tel. 415/512–0450) is the cream of the crop, with custom tables and a full restaurant. Kids over eight are welcome (with their parents) on weekend afternoons.

South Beach Billiards (270 Brannan St. at 1st St., tel. 415/495–5939), a hip south-of-Market joint, also has a café and a boccie court.

East Bay **Chalkers Billiard Club** (5900 Hollis St. at 59th St., Emeryville, tel. 510/658–5821), like its sister club across the bay, is a class act. This one attracts a younger crowd, 21 and older.

Bird-Watching If you think San Francisco bird life is limited to sea gulls and pigeons, you may be surprised to learn that the Bay Area has more than 200 species of birds, many of which can be spotted by the not-so-trained eye in the region's many parks. The Audubon Society's **rare-bird alert line** (tel. 510/524–5592) fills callers in on the latest sightings.

Farallones National Wildlife Refuge, on the Farallon Islands 25 to 26 miles off the Pacific coast, is one of the largest sea-bird nesting sites in the country, with some 300,000 murres, puffins, petrels, and gulls building nests there annually. The 948-square-mile sanctuary sits over a continental shelf that attracts fish, humpback whales, harbor porpoises, elephant seals, salmon, herring clams, and crabs; the sea creatures, in turn, attract pelicans and other fish-eating birds. Call the **Oceanic Society** (tel. 415/474–3385 or 800/326–7491, fax 415/474–3395) to arrange for a tour.

East Bay **Don Edwards San Francisco Bay National Wildlife Refuge** (tel. 510/792–0222), west of Newark near the Dumbarton Bridge, is a 21,500-acre preserve named for the California congressman who worked to save much of the wetlands. A mile-long trail through tidal sloughs, grasslands, and marshes begins opposite the visitor center. You're likely to see willets, curlew mallards, egrets, and nesting avocets year-round and grebes in the winter.

Marin County **Audubon Canyon Ranch** (4900 Hwy. 1, just north of Stinson Beach, tel. 415/868–9244) is open for courting and mating season, mid-March through mid-July. Among the 60 species that make their home on the 1,000-acre ranch are great blue herons and egrets. (The latter nest in the redwood trees in Schwarz Grove.) There are also telescopes and observation posts for easier viewing.

Richardson Bay Audubon Center and Sanctuary (376 Greenwood Beach Rd. at Tiburon Blvd., Tiburon, tel. 415/388–2524) boasts 900 acres of water that attract 80 species of waterfowl, land birds, and migrants, as well as harbor seals. There's also a ⅓-mile self-guided nature trail that passes various habitats. The headquarters is an 1876 Victorian home. It's open Sunday 9–5. (Take the Tiburon exit off U.S. 101; turn right at the third light.)

Peninsula

Baylands Nature Center (2775 Embarcadero Rd., Palo Alto, tel. 415/ 329–2506) features a wheelchair-accessible boardwalk out to a platform where you can observe ducks, egrets, herons, and pelicans. The nature center offers films, lectures, and bird-related exhibits. There are also hiking, biking, and running trails. Take the Embarcadero Rd. exit from U.S. 101 and drive east until you reach the bay. The center is open weekends 1–5.

Candlestick Point State Recreation Area (tel. 415/557–2593) has 3 miles of shoreline trails from which you can spot red-tailed hawks, kestrels, and brown pelicans, not to mention egrets and herons.

Boating and Sailing

Boating

At the **Lake Merced Boat and Fish House** (1 Harding Blvd., tel. 415/ 753–1101) you can rent rowboats, paddleboats, motorboats, canoes, and windsurfing equipment. It's open Sunday 9–5:30.

Stow Lake Boathouse (Golden Gate Park, northwest corner of Stow Lake near 19th Ave., tel. 415/752–0347) rents rowboats, paddleboats, and gentle battery-run motorboats that kids love to steer. You can also get snacks here. *Open Sunday 9 to 5 in the summer, 9 to 4 the rest of year.*

Sailing

On sunny days crafts of all sizes dot the bay. For those who can afford their own dock, the Marina is the place to be. For the rest of us, sailing companies fill the piers in San Francisco and Sausalito, so you can take your pick. For more boating information, *see* Fishing: Party Boats, *below*.

Adventure Cat Sailing (South Beach Harbor, Pier 40 along the Embarcadero , tel. 415/777–1630), San Francisco's only catamaran sailing vessel, has Sunday excursions at 2:30 and 6:30 (closed December through February).

Cal Adventures (2301 Bancroft Way at Telegraph Ave., Berkeley, tel. 510/642–4000), a university-connected outfit, teaches just about every outdoor activity, including sailing, sculling, windsurfing, and sea kayaking. Once you're certified you can rent its 15-foot Coronados. The offices are open only during the week, so you must rent gear or sign up for weekend classes in advance.

Cal Sailing Club (University Ave. at the Marina, tel. 510/287–5905) runs an affordable sailing school, offering both private and group instruction, where youths and adults can learn how to operate 20-foot sloops. Members, once certified, can use the club's boats. Prospective students can visit and enjoy a free ride on the bay on the first Saturday and Sunday of each month between 1 and 4.

Cass' Marina (1702 Bridgeway at Napa St., Sausalito, tel.415/332–6789) has 22- to 65-foot sailboats (as well as yachts) and a licensed skipper to navigate them—unless you prefer to. Lessons are available.

Let's Go Sailing (Pier 39, foot of Beach St., tel. 415/788–4920) takes a MacGregor 65 sailboat out on the bay for 90-minute rides.

Schooner Expeditions (Marina Plaza Harbor, Marineship Way off Bridgeway, Sausalito, tel. 415/331–1282) sails small groups around the bay on the *Maramel*, a restored 54-foot wooden schooner built in 1929. Overnight and dinner cruises are other possibilities.

Boccie

The city's Italian heritage assures that there's plenty of boccie around. You'll find courts at

Aquatic Park (Larkin and Beach Sts., tel. 415/556–1659).
Crocker Amazon Playground (Italy Ave. and Moscow St., off John McLaren Park, tel. 415/337–4708).
North Beach Playground (Lombard and Mason Sts., tel. 415/274–0201).
South Beach Billiards (270 Brannan St. at 1st St., tel. 415/495–5939) is a happening SoMa spot with an indoor court as well as a café and billiards.

Chess You may find a game at any number of coffeehouses, including **Cafe Macando** (3169 16th St. at Valencia St., tel. 415/863–6517), the **Horse Shoe Coffee House** (566 Haight St. at Steiner, tel. 415/626–8852), and **Jammin Java** (1395 9th Ave. at Judah, tel. 415/566–5282). Games occur regularly at **The Coffee Zone** (1409 Haight St. at Masonic, tel. 415/863–2443), but you'd better be good—some of the Bay Area's best players drop by. Finally, the **Mechanics Institute** (57 Post St. at Kearny, tel. 415/421–2258) offers lessons, tournaments, and a chess library; membership costs $60, and there's a one-day pass for visitors from outside the Bay Area.

Croquet The **San Francisco Croquet Club** (tel. 415/928–5525) is one of the strongest in the country. Telephone to schedule games on the Croquet Lawn (near 19th Ave. and Wawona) in **Stern Grove.** In the East Bay you can play at the **Lakeside Park Bowling Lawns** (Bellevue and Grand Aves., Lake Merritt, tel. 510/834–6293).

Darts For a listing of pubs with teams and competitions, send a self-addressed, stamped envelope to the **San Francisco Dart Association** (Box 192085, San Francisco 94119, tel. 415/452–2722). To find out about other games, try the three **Gamescape** stores listed in the introduction to this section, which also sell darts and boards. Other venues include **Edinburgh Castle** (950 Geary Blvd. at Larkin, tel. 415/885–4074), **The Gavel Pub** (15 Boardman Pl., off Bryant between 6th and 7th Sts., tel. 415/863–5787), and **The Great Entertainer** (975 Bryant St. at 7th St., tel. 415/861–8833).

Dog Walking Popular areas include the dog runs at Golden Gate Park (for a map, send a self-addressed, stamped envelope to Golden Gate Park, McLaren Lodge, San Francisco, 94117), Dolores Park (18th St. end), and Fort Funston. The Golden Gate National Recreation Area (415/556–0560) has a map of off-leash park areas under its jurisdiction from San Mateo to Marin counties. *The Bay Area Dog Lovers Companion*, by Lyle York and Maria Godavage (Foghorn Press, $13.95, tel. 415/241–9550), available in most Bay Area bookstores and pet shops, provides an extensive listing (with ratings) of canine-friendly parks, trails, and beaches, as well as special dog hikes, lodgings that accept pets, restaurants that serve meals outside, and other welcome tidbits.

Elephant-Seal Watching *Peninsula* At Año Nuevo State Reserve (Hwy. 1, 22 miles north of Santa Cruz, tel. 415/879–0227), a 1½ to 2 hour drive south of San Francisco, you'll get close-up views of the huge creatures resting on rocks; during the mating season (mid-Dec.–Mar.), you'll see more energetic activity. (Births start in January.) You can visit during mating season only on a 2½-hour tour, for which you *must* make a reservation (tel. 800/444–7275) at least 10 days (preferably a month) in advance. The tour costs $4 per person (under 3 free); parking is $4. Beginning around January, SamTrans offers weekend bus service; the fare includes park admission. Reservations (tel. 415/508–6441) are essential.

Exercise Classes **Rhythm and Motion** (1133 Mission at 7th St., tel. 415/621–0643), offers classes in, variously, hip-hop, R&B, jazz, ballet, and ethnic music, all taught by professional dancers. Other venues include Glen Park Rec Center, the Harvey Milk Rec Center at Duboce Triangle, the Women's Building at 18th Street and Valencia, and the Koret Health Center at the University of San Francisco.

Gliding
Napa Valley

Calistoga Gliders (1546 Lincoln Ave., Calistoga, tel. 707/942–5000) offers flights year-round. Prices start at $79 for one person ($110 for couples) for 20 minutes.

Fishing
Party Boats

Myriad boats leave **Fisherman's Wharf** at 6 AM and 7 AM daily. You can simply show up at the lagoon on Jefferson Street (between Jones and Taylor Sts.) and try your luck, but it's wiser to reserve. There are also departures from a number of communities along the bay. Among the options:

Bay and Delta Charters (3020 Bridgeway, Suite 271, Sausalito, tel. 415/332–7187, tel. 800/762–6287) offers departures from Fisherman's Wharf and from Sausalito, Oakland, Alameda, and Emeryville.
Capt. John's (tel. 415/726–2913) leaves from Princeton's Pillar Point Harbor, off Highway 1, 4 miles north of Half Moon Bay.
Emeryville Sport Fishing (3310 Powell St., Emeryville, tel. 510/654–6040 or 800/575–9944) leaves from the Emeryville Marina at the foot of Powell Street off I–80.
Hot Pursuit (tel. 415/965–3474), which specializes in salmon and rock cod fishing, has turbo-charged departures from Pier 47 (Jones and Jefferson Sts.).
San Pablo Reservoir (San Pablo Dam Rd. north of Orinda, tel. 510/223–1661) offers trout and bass fishing as well as rowboat, paddleboat, and motorboat rental. It's closed mid-November through mid-February.

Shore Fishing

Berkeley Marina Pier (far west end of University Ave., Berkeley), is the place to catch tiny sharks and, once in a while, bass.
Fort Point (in the Presidio directly under the Golden Gate Bridge) has fishing areas along the seawall and the pier. You need a license (available at any bait and tackle store) to fish from the seawall, but not from the pier.
Muni Pier (just east of Aquatic Park at the north end of Van Ness Ave.) is one of the city's best fishing spots. You can catch flounder, sand dabs, cod, bass, and perch, and you can also net crabs.
Old Borges Ranch (1035 Castle Rock Rd., Walnut Creek, tel. 510/934–6990) has a children's catch-and-release fishing pond. It's open Sun. 8 AM–dusk.

Fly-Fishing

As the site of the 1993 National Flyfishing Championships, **Golden Gate Park** is a tried-and-true spot for fly-fishing. You can hone your skills at the park's **Fly Casting Pools** (across John F. Kennedy Dr. from the Buffalo Paddock, midpark just west of 36th Ave.), which are among the finest ponds of this sort in the country. The **Anglers Lodge** beside them was built during the Great Depression as a WPA project; it's a venue for meetings and social events as well as fly-tying and rod-building seminars. You can pick up tips by stopping by the free casting clinics at the ponds. For information, phone the **Golden Gate Casting Club** (tel. 415/386–2630) on Saturday.

Ocean Fly-Fishing is also possible in San Francisco. At Ocean Beach anglers catch perch and stripers. Phone or stop by the **Orvis Fly Shop** (*see below*) for more information.

Instruction

Fly Fishing Outfitters (463 Bush St. at Grant, tel. 415/781–3474; 3533 Mt. Diablo Blvd., Lafayette, tel. 510/284–3474), **Mel Krieger School of Flyfishing** (790 27th Ave. at Cabrillo, tel. 415/752–1013), **Orvis San Francisco** (300 Grant Ave. at Sutter, tel. 415/392–1600), **San Francisco Flyfisher Supply** (2526 Clement St. at 26th Ave., tel. 415/668–3597.

Frisbee

Drop-in Frisbee tosses can often be found on **Hippie Hill** in Golden Gate Park, north of Sharon Meadow near Stanyan and Fell streets.

Fruit Picking
East Bay

Brentwood, a delta farming community about an hour from San Francisco (take I–80 to Hwy. 4 and follow it east), has several pick-your-own farms (apricots, peaches, nectarines, cherries, pears, corn, etc.). Send a self-addressed, stamped envelope to the Harvest Time farm coalition (Box O, Brentwood, 94513) for a brochure and a map, or phone the Brentwood Chamber of Commerce (tel. 510/634–3344).

Peninsula **Coastside Harvest Trails** (765 Main St., Half Moon Bay 94019, tel. 415/726–4485), run by the San Mateo County Farm Bureau, will send you a map of pick-your-own orchards and farms on the Peninsula and the south coast.

Coastways Ranch (640 Hwy. 1, tel. 415/879–0414), 30 miles south of Half Moon Bay, offers olallieberries, kiwis, pumpkins, and Christmas trees, depending on the season. Bring garden gloves. The ranch is closed January–May and August–September.

Golf Many of the area's courses lie in breathtaking spots with great views of the city—and they're usually jammed. Call ahead for tee times.

Municipal Courses San Francisco has four public golf sites. At **Harding Park** (Lake Merced and Skyline Blvds., tel. 415/664–4690), you can choose between an 18-hole par 72 course and a nine-hole par 32 course; there's also a driving range. Short and hilly though it may be, the 18-hole par 69 **Lincoln Park** course (34th and Clement Sts., tel. 415/221–9911) has magical views of the city skyline and the Golden Gate. At the west end of **Golden Gate Park** (47th Ave. and Fulton St., tel. 415/751–8987) is a small but tricky "pitch and putt" nine-holer. **Glen Eagles Golf Course** (2100 Sunnydale Ave., tel. 415/587–2425) in McLaren Park is a full-size nine-holer.

The **Presidio Golf Course** (tel. 415/561–4653), which opened to the public in 1995, is managed by Arnold Palmer's company.

Tilden Golf Course (Tilden Park, Golf Gate and Shasta Rds., tel. 510/848–7373) is an 18-hole, par 70 course.

Sharp Park (Sharp Park Rd. and Hwy. 1, Pacifica, tel. 415/355–8546) is an 18-hole, par 72 course.

Miniature Golf **Malibu Castle** (320 Blumquist St., Redwood City, tel. 415/367–1905). This is kiddie heaven: three 18-hole putt-putt courses; sprint cars; race cars; batting cages; and plenty of kid-friendly hot dogs, hamburgers, and pizza. Take the Harbor Boulevard exit off U.S. 101.

Handball There are two outdoor and two indoor courts behind Steinhart Aquarium (across Middle Dr. E) in **Golden Gate Park,** and neither require reservations. The park department's indoor courts are at the **Mission Recreation Center** (2450 Harrison St. at 20th St., tel. 415/695–5012).

Hang Gliding On sunny weekends you can watch brightly colored hang gliders swooping along the cliffs at **Fort Funston,** a site for experienced pilots only. Pilots with at least 50 hours behind them can rent equipment from **Airtime** (3620 Wawona St. at 47th Ave., tel. 415/759–1177; closed Sunday except for prearranged lessons, given at a location south of the city). Airtime also sells stunt kites and rents rollerblading equipment. **Chandelle Hang Gliding Center** (1595 E. Francisco Blvd. off U.S. 101, San Rafael, tel. 415/454–3464), which provides sales, service, and instruction in both hang gliding and paragliding, has Saturday outings only.

Ice Skating

San Francisco **Yerba Buena Gardens** (Howard St. at 3rd St.) is slated for a full hockey-size rink above the main entrance to Moscone Center. From late November into January, two small rinks—one for children, one for adults—are set up east of the Embarcadero Center at **Justin Herman Plaza,** and sometimes a single one is erected in Union Square.

East Bay **Berkeley Iceland** (2727 Milvia St. at Derby St., Berkeley, tel. 510/843–8800).

Peninsula **Belmont Iceland** (815 Old County Rd. at Ralston Ave., Belmont, tel. 415/592–0532).

Ice Capades Chalet (Fashion Island Mall, off U.S. 101 near Hwy. 92, San Mateo, tel. 415/574–1616) is a great place for kids to skate (they don't seem to mind the noise level) while their parents shop. There's a food court and a video arcade at rink side.

Winter Lodge (3009 Middlefield Rd. six blocks south of Oregon Expressway, Palo Alto, tel. 415/493–4566) is the only outdoor ice rink in the Bay Area. Open September–April, it's intimate and family oriented. An overhang protects skaters in rainy weather.

Kayaking **Sea Trek** sponsors ecologically responsible kayak tours from Sausalito or Ayala Cove on Angel Island, where groups of eight take single- and double-hole kayaks out on the water. Introductory classes are available on Sundays in Sausalito and on warmer Tomales Bay. Call Sea Trek (tel. 415/488–1000) for information on other kayaking activities as well.

Several sailing outfitters also offer kayaking programs. **Cal Adventures** (*see* Boating and Sailing, *above*) offers weekend lessons and outings, but you must register weekdays when the office is open.

Kite Flying Kites have been growing in popularity here since the late '60s, and the **Marina Green** is the king of the scene. There you'll see everything from homemade rice-paper jobs to expensive numbers that need 10 people to get airborne. Other popular spots include **Ocean Beach, Bolinas Ridge** on Mt. Tamalpais, the **Berkeley Marina, Candlestick Point, Coyote Point** in San Mateo, and **Shoreline Park** in Mountain View.

In July the **Berkeley Kite Festival/West Coast Kite Championship** features national competitions and children's kite flying at the Berkeley Marina; for information, contact **Hi Line Kites** at the Berkeley Marina's North Waterfront Park (tel. 510/525–2755), weekends 1 PM till sundown. Hi Line also sells all types of kites as well as three-wheeled, wind-powered "kite buggies." The company gives lessons and advice and can put you in touch with local kite clubs.

Mah-Jongg You're bound to find a game at **Portsmouth Square** in Chinatown or at **Mountain Lake Park** (12th Ave. and Lake St.).

Orienteering This increasingly popular sport involves navigating a large area, using only a contour map and a compass, to forge a path from one "control point" to the next as quickly as possible. Events are held all over the Bay Area, in such places as the Presidio, China Camp in Marin County, Sunol Regional Wilderness and Montclair Recreation Center in the East Bay, and Emerald Hills Open Space in Redwood City. Some contenders up the ante by orienteering on horseback or mountain bike or by moonlight. For more information, send a self-addressed, stamped evelope to the **Bay Area Orienteering Club** (3015 Holyrood Dr., Oakland 94611).

Riding Bay Area stables are busy on Sundays. Go early—horses are freshest in the morning. It's always best to call ahead and reserve to be safe.

Golden Gate Park Stables (John F. Kennedy Dr. at 36th Ave., tel. 415/668–7360) offers individual or group guided trail rides, pony rides, and lessons (but no hourly rentals) at the Park's west end. The stables are open Sundays 8–6.

Marin County and Beyond At **Five Brooks** (8001 Hwy. 1, Olema, tel. 415/663–1570), paths wind along the beach and through the woods at Point Reyes. Take the San Anselmo exit from U.S. 101.

Miwok Livery (701 Tennessee Valley Rd., in the Golden Gate National Recreation Area, Mill Valley, tel. 415/383–8048) has guided trail rides and lessons. Reservations are required.

Sonoma Cattle Company (Sugar Loaf Ridge State Park and Jack London State Park, Glen Ellen, tel. 707/996–8566) offers everything from two-hour rides to all-day rides, all with great views that make it worth the one-hour trip north.

Peninsula At **Palo-Mar Stables** (2116 Skyline Blvd., Daly City, tel. 415/755–8042), just south of the city, there are ponies for children, horses for grown-ups, and miles of beach and trail riding.

Rifle Ranges The range at **Lake Merced** is sponsored by the Pacific Rod and Gun Club (tel. 415/239–9750 or 415/586–8349). There is also an indoor range south of the city at **Jackson Arms** (710 Dubuque Ave., South San Francisco, tel. 415/588–4209).

Rock Climbing

Indoor Classes Kids as young as six can learn to judge what is climbable and what is foolhardy at the following indoor-climbing spaces (where you can also buy guidebooks): **Cityrock Gym** (1250 45th St. at Doyle St., Emeryville, tel. 510/654–2510) and **Class V Fitness** (25 Dodie St. at Simms St., San Rafael, tel. 415/485–6931).

Outdoor Classes and Outings **Cal Adventures** (2301 Bancroft Way at Telegraph Ave., Berkeley, tel. 510/642–4000) runs classes and Bay Area climbing trips and also rents equipment.

Climbs Once you learn the ropes, you can hit the Bay Area's greenstone and sandstone before you head for the granite at Yosemite. Beginners may want to head for north Berkeley, to **Pinnacle Rock** (Poppy Rd.), **Cragmont Rock** (Regal Rd.), or **Indian Rock** (Indian Rock Ave.); for more information, contact the East Bay Regional Park District (tel. 510/562–7275). More advanced climbers have a wider range of choices:

The sandstone at **Mount Diablo State Park** makes for some of the region's most challenging climbs, with difficulty levels from 5.6 to 5.13. (*See* Parks and Woodlands, *above.*)

Mickey's Beach, with its large greenstone outcropping, offers climbs with difficulty ranges from 5.8 to 5.13. Follow Highway 1 south from Stinson Beach for about a mile, take the first turnout, and follow the trail down to the beach for right-above-the-surf climbing.

Castle Rock State Park (tel. 408/867–2952) is down on the Peninsula, west of Saratoga, 2½ miles south of the junction of Routes 35 and 9. Routes range from 5.1 to 5.4 in difficulty.

Outfitters **Marmot Mountain Works** (3049 Adeline St. at Ashby Ave., Berkeley, tel. 510/849–0735) rents climbing shoes and sells most types of climbing gear.

Roller Skating and Rollerblading **Golden Gate Park** is the place. Rollerbladers almost outnumber cyclists there now. You can often join a game of **Rollerblade hockey** near the park's tennis courts on John F. Kennedy Drive, at James Lick Middle School at 25th and Castro streets, or at **Bladium In-line Hockey Rink** (1050 3rd St. at 4th St. in China Basin, tel. 415/442–5060). For rollerblading and hockey-team information, **Skate Pro** (*see below*) runs a slalom course in Golden Gate Park. Skate stores line Golden Gate Park on every side.

Among the most dependable places to rent or buy are **Skates on Haight** (1818 Haight St. at Stanyan St., tel. 415/752–8376) and **Skate Pro** (2549 Irving St. at 27th Ave., tel. 415/752–8776).

The **Embarcadero Promenade** (*see* Great Walks *in* Chapter 3) is another good spot for in-line skating. **Delancey Wheels** (600 Embarcadero at Brannan St., tel. 415/957–9800) rents equipment.

Peninsula The indoor roller rink closest to San Francisco is **Rolladium** in San Mateo (363 N. Amphlett Blvd., Poplar Ave. exit from U.S. 101, tel. 415/342–2711).

Rowing **Lake Merritt Rowing Club** (tel. 510/273–9041) in Oakland offers crew or team rowing classes and events for teens and adults. The **Dolphin** and **South End** swim clubs (*see* Swimming, *below*) also have rowing clubs.

Running and Walking San Francisco, one of the most beautiful cities to jog in, can also be one of the most frustrating—depending on how you feel about hills. If you've had enough of the city streets, hit the parks. Here are a few favorite runs:

The short but spectacular **Baker Beach Run** starts on Baker Beach near 25th Avenue and continues to the rocks under the Golden Gate Bridge. At the rocks, turn around and run to the other end, next to the stairs up to Seacliff's houses, then back to your starting point. The entire loop covers 1½ miles.

The **Golden Gate Park Run** (5 miles) starts south of the Polo Field and runs east on Middle Drive (the Polo Field should be on your left). Veer left on Overlook Drive; when it ends, take two lefts to get onto Kennedy Drive. After you pass the golf course, turn left onto South Drive (you'll be heading east again). On the home stretch you'll run into another fork: the left one will put you back on Middle Drive.

You can make a substantial run out of the loop around **Stow Lake,** in Golden Gate Park. First circle the lake, then cross the bridge and run up the path to the top of Strawberry Hill. This is a 2½-mile workout.

East Bay A run around the perimeter of **Lake Merritt** will give you a 3.2-mile workout. Start on the bike path close to the Rotary Natural Sciences Center (near Grand and Bellevue Aves.).

The loop in **Coyote Hills Regional Park** (tel. 510/795–9385) in Newark, starting at the visitor center and traveling along the Bayview Trail takes you past salt marshes and Ohlone Indian mounds. It's a little over 3 miles long.

Marin County The **Marin Headlands,** just north of the Golden Gate, will take your breath away—figuratively and literally, since they make for a strenuous run. Starting at the end of Rodeo Lagoon, down by the ocean, a run up the Miwok Trail and back again comes to about 4 miles. If you leave the Miwok Trail when you hit the Wolfridge Trail and continue onto the Pacific Coast Trail, you'll pass bunkers, beaches, and old forts, and you'll probably spot hawks, turkey vultures, and golden eagles. If you want an even longer workout, run across the Golden Gate Bridge instead of driving.

Peninsula Sunday joggers (as well as bikers, hikers, and stroller pushers) may try the 6-mile **Sawyer Camp Trail,** which encircles the San Andreas and Crystal Springs watershed. It's the former highway to Half Moon Bay, so it's paved, and it passes through woodlands and alongside the water. Take the Larkspur Drive exit off I–280 and go south on Skyline Boulevard to Hillcrest Boulevard, then west under the freeway to the trail entrance, which you'll see on the right. Or take CalTrain to the Millbrae station and catch SamTrans Bus 33B.

Running Clubs **Dolphin** and **South End** swim clubs both sponsor running clubs as well. (*See* Swimming, *below.*)

Pamakid Runners (tel. 415/333–4780) emphasizes competitive track work.

San Francisco FrontRunners (tel. 415/978–2429), a mostly gay and lesbian club, sponsors runs (usually Saturday, but sometimes Sunday) followed by a restaurant or pot-luck brunch.

Walking Clubs **Golden Gate Race Walkers** (tel. 415/863–0479) has four Bay Area chapters that hold weekend walks and periodic competitions, as well as free clinics.

Scuba Diving The coast from San Francisco down to Santa Cruz and Monterey is rich with explorable reefs, wrecks, and marine life.

Divequest (2875 Glascock St., Oakland, tel. 510/533–3483 or 800/675–2628), in addition to renting equipment and arranging for lessons, offers dive-boat trips and can hook you up with underwater photo and video experts.
Scuba Unlimited (651 Howard St. at New Montgomery, tel. 415/777–3483; 965 Brewster Ave., Redwood City, tel. 415/369–3483; 4000 Pimlico Dr. at Santa Rita off-ramp of I–580, Pleasanton, tel. 510/734–8343) offers lessons, equipment, and repairs. It will also plan scuba vacations for you.

Skateboarding and Snakeboarding With skyrocketing insurance costs closing more and more suburban "bowls," kids have taken over places like **Justin Herman Plaza** at the Embarcadero and Market Street. On Sunday mornings you'll find hundreds of them negotiating the ramps, the steps, and the dry fountain. Elsewhere the long, sloping city streets make for a skateboarder's heaven—especially on Sundays, when traffic is light.

A **snakeboard** has two footboards—one for each foot—that pivot independently; because you create momentum by twisting your upper body and rotating the plates simultaneously, it gives you more of a workout than a skateboard. **Bruce Duncan** (tel. 415/566–2885) offers free Sunday snakeboarding clinics near 6th Avenue and Irving Street in Golden Gate Park. You'll need your own board; you can purchase one at **Skate Pro** (*see* Roller Skating and Rollerblading, *above*) or at **Battens and Boards** (1200 Bridgeway at Pine St., Sausalito, tel. 415/332–0212).

Soccer You can catch a Sunday pick-up game at the **Polo Field** in Golden Gate Park or at the **Crocker Amazon Playground** (Italy and Moscow Sts.). **Portola Playground** (Felton and Hamilton Sts.) is another good bet.

Surfing Ocean Beach, once a quiet city secret, has become a world-class surfing beach, but riptides and undertow make it a spot for experts only. **Half Moon Bay** has also become a hot spot for expert surfers because of a monster wave in a place known as Maverick's, about ½ mile off Pillar Point Beach at the north edge of Half Moon Bay (near the radar tower). Surfers are heading here from all over the globe, especially in winter. Beginners, though, should stick to Pedro Point at **Linda Mar Beach** in Pacifica or, farther south, **Cowell State Beach** in Santa Cruz.

For surfing information and equipment, visit **Wise Surfboards** (3149 Vicente St. at 43rd Ave., tel. 415/665–7745) in the Sunset. Wise also runs a **surf-conditions hot line** (tel. 415/665–9473). Foam boards (for beginners) and wetsuits can be rented at **Outdoors Unlimited** (530 Parnassus Ave. at 3rd Ave., underneath the UCSF library, tel. 415/476–2078). The office is open only on weekdays, so plan ahead.

Swimming Sundays at 7 AM you'll find a regular crowd of 10 to 100 hardy souls outfitted in nothing more than bathing suits, headgear, and earplugs to brave the chilly waters of the bay. They are members of the **South End Club** (500 Jefferson St., tel. 415/441–9523). Its next door neighbor, the **Dolphin Swim and Boat Club** (502 Jefferson St. at Hyde, tel. 415/441–9329) also schedules Sunday swims. Both clubs have been in existence since the 1870s. When there's an *official* swim—usually on Sunday mornings as well—participants may number in the hundreds.

City Pools You can pick up a full list of city-run pools weekdays at McLaren Lodge (John F. Kennedy Dr. at Stanyan, tel. 415/753–7026 for 24-hour information) in Golden Gate Park. The three best, in our opinion, are the **Mission Pool** (19th St. at Valencia, tel. 415/695–5002), **North Beach Pool** (Lombard and Mason Sts., tel. 415/274–0200), and **Rossi Pool** (Arguello Blvd. and Anza, tel. 415/666–7014). Only the

Mission Pool is outdoors, and it's open only in the summer. There's a nominal fee to swim.

In addition, the bright, clean, and spacious **Koret Health and Recreation Center** at the University of San Francisco (Parker Ave. at Turk, tel. 415/666-6820) opens its pool Sundays from 8 to 6, but it's available only to members of the public who arrive before 2 PM. The cost is $60 for 16 swims (neighborhood residents pay $70 for 15 swims at all hours).

The **Giamona Pool** at Westmore High School (131 Edgemont Ave., Daly City, tel. 415/991–8022) is affordable *and* warm (85°). Take the Eastmore exit from I–280. It's open Sundays 1 to 4; admission is $1.

Many a lucky San Francisco kid has escaped the fog at **Marinwood Pool** (775 Miller Creek Rd., San Rafael, tel. 415/479–2335; open Apr.–Oct.). You can pay by the day or buy a season pass. Take the Lucas Valley Road exit from U.S. 101.

Tennis The San Francisco Recreation and Park Department maintains 130 free tennis courts throughout the city. For a free map of city courts, call the department's tennis information number (tel. 415/753–7100). The largest set is at **Dolores Park** (18th and Dolores Sts., tel. 415/554–9529), with six courts available on a first-come, first-served basis. The only ones you can reserve are the 21 **Golden Gate Park Courts** (tel. 415/753–7101 or 415/753–7001). Additional lighted courts can be found at **Moscone Recreation Center** (Chestnut and Buchanan Sts., tel. 415/292–2006) and **North Beach Playground** (Lombard and Mason Sts., tel. 415/274–0201).

Among the many fine private clubs are the **San Francisco Tennis Club** (645 5th St. at Brannan, tel. 415/777–2211), the **Claremont Resort and Spa** (Ashby and Domingo Aves., Oakland, tel. 510/843–3000), and the **Berkeley Tennis Club** (1 Tunnel Rd. at Domingo Ave., Berkeley, tel. 510/841–1380), where "Pop" Fuller trained Helen Wills Moody and Helen Jacobs.

Volleyball Some good places to find open games are **Marina Green** (Marina Blvd. and Scott St.), the **Big Rec Ball Field** (close to 7th Ave. and Lincoln Way in Golden Gate Park), and **Aquatic Park** (north end of Van Ness Ave.). During the summer, there's sometimes a net up in **Justin Herman Plaza** (Embarcadero and Market St.), too.

Whale Watching The annual trek of the California gray whale provides the occasion for a popular winter outing in the Bay Area. The **Oceanic Society** (tel. 415/474–3385 or 800/326–7491) runs naturalist-led full-day tours (from San Francisco) and half-day tours (from Pillar Point Harbor in Princeton, on the Peninsula), weekends December 26 through April ($32–$48 per person). From June through November, the Oceanic Society offers day-long excursions to the Farallon Islands, one of the largest seabird rookeries in the west; humpback and occasional gray whales can often be spotted throughout the season ($58 per person). The society operates a **whale hot line** (415/474–0488), an outgoing message about whale and other sea life sightings off the Bay Area coastline.

The **Point Reyes Lighthouse** (*see* Parks and Woodlands, *above*) is a popular shoreline spot to watch for whales during the winter. Bring wraps and be prepared to hike the 300 steps down. Call the Lighthouse Visitors Center (tel. 415/669–1534) for weather conditions.

Windsurfing You'll often see people windsurfing off the Golden Gate Promenade in the Marina. The bay is a great, windy place for the sport. Many of the area's sailing schools (*see above*), including Cal Adventures and Cal Sailing Club, also teach windsurfing and rent equipment.

The **Lake Merced Boat and Fish House** (1 Harding Blvd. at Skyline Blvd., tel. 415/753–1101) offers weekend morning lessons on a tamer body of water.

Spectator Sports

There are four major sporting venues in the Bay Area: **3Com Park** (formerly Candlestick Park; Candlestick Park exit off U.S. 101, tel. 415/467–1994, but for Giants and 49ers, *see below*), the **Oakland-Alameda County Coliseum** (Coliseum exit off I–880, tel. 510/639–7700), the **Cow Palace** (Cow Palace/3rd. St. exit off U.S. 101 South to Geneva Ave., then west 7 blocks; tel. 415/469–6065) in Daly City, and the **San Jose Arena** (525 W. Santa Clara St., San Jose—exit Guadalupe Pkwy. N from I–280; turn left on Santa Clara St., tel. 408/287–4275). These four arenas host everything from baseball, basketball, football, and hockey to circuses and dog shows. Tickets can be purchased by calling the box offices at the above numbers or by phoning **BASS** (tel. 510/762–2277), which means paying an extra surcharge.

The Bay Area also offers a host of major **college sports.** To find out about events and cost, phone the ticket offices at the **University of San Francisco** (tel. 415/666–2873 or 415/666–6873), **U.C. Berkeley** (tel. 510/642–5150 or 800/462–23277), **Stanford University** (tel. 415/723–1021) in Palo Alto, **Santa Clara University** (tel. 408/554–4661 or 408/554–5550) in Santa Clara, and **San Jose State University** (tel. 408/924–3267).

Auto Racing Sears Point International Raceway (junction of Hwys. 37 and 121, Sonoma, tel. 707/938–8448) offers a variety of motor events. The track is also home to the Skip Barber Racing School.

Baseball The **San Francisco Giants** (tel. 415/467–8000) play at 3Com Park. It's windy, but where else can you down espresso and sushi while watching a game? The **Oakland Athletics** (tel. 510/638–0500) play at the Oakland Coliseum. It's warmer than 3Com, but the food is no match.

Basketball The **Golden State Warriors,** the Bay Area's NBA team, play their home games at the Oakland Coliseum. Tickets can be difficult to obtain for games with top-notch teams. When they're available, you can get them at the Coliseum box office (tel. 510/639–7700) or from BASS (tel. 510/762-2277).

For a cheaper outing during the summer, consider the **Pro Am League,** which is composed of college, ex-college, European, semi-pro, and pro players. There are eight teams around the Bay Area, and they often play Sunday games at 2 PM at Kezar Stadium in Golden Gate Park. Call or stop by the Potrero Hill Recreation Center (22nd and Arkansas Sts., tel. 415/695–5009), which sponsors the games, for a schedule.

Boxing **San Francisco Golden Gloves** holds amateur matches at the Cow Palace (tel. 415/469-6065), usually in the spring.

Football The **San Francisco 49ers** (tel. 415/468–2249) play at 3Com Park. Most seats go to season-ticket holders, and even then there's a waiting list. The few tickets for scattered single games disappear almost as soon as they go on sale.

The **Oakland Raiders** returned to the Bay Area in 1995 after a 13-year sojourn in Los Angeles. Except for high-profile contests, some tickets (tel. 510/639–7700 or 510/762–2277) are usually available.

Hockey The **San Jose Sharks** of the National Hockey League play at the San Jose Arena (tel. 408/287–4275). Tickets are usually available at the box office or from BASS (tel. 510/762–2277).

The **San Francisco Spiders** of the International Hockey League play at the Cow Palace; tickets (tel. 415/469–6065 or 510/762–2277) are usually available on game day.

Horse Racing Racing dates vary from year to year, subject to state approval (tel. 916/927–7223 for information). In recent years **Golden Gate Fields** (100 Eastshore Hwy., Albany, tel. 510/559–7300) has run March through June and November through December, alternating with **Bay Meadows** (2600 S. Delaware St., San Mateo, tel. 415/574-7223), with races December through March and August through November.

Running Some 3,000 hardy spirits enter the **San Francisco Marathon,** usually held on a Sunday in July. The scenic 26-mile course ends at the Polo Field in Golden Gate Park. Fans also line the streets for the 7½-mile **San Francisco Examiner Bay to Breakers Race,** on the third Sunday in May, when more than 100,000 runners, many of them in hilarious costumes, run from the bay downtown out to the ocean.

Tennis The Bill Graham Civic Auditorium (99 Grove St. at Larkin, tel. 415/974–4000) is the site of the **Volvo Tennis/San Francisco Tournament** (tel. 415/239-4800) in early February. The **Bank of the West Classic** women's tennis tournament visits the Oakland Coliseum Arena (tel. 510/569–2121) in October.

Wrestling The Cow Palace (tel. 415/469–6065) is the site. The wrestlers are often decked out in outrageous costumes, and they love to ham it up for the audience.

Yacht Racing There are frequent races on the bay, and you can watch from the Golden Gate Bridge, among many fine vantage points. The **Yacht Racing Association of San Francisco Bay** (tel. 415/771–9500) provides details.

Best Bets for Children

The playgrounds and water parks that follow only scrape the surface of the things that kids can do on Sundays. If you look through the listings above, you'll find hordes of weekend activities that children will love.

Playgrounds

San Francisco **Cow Hollow Playground** (Baker St. between Greenwich and Filbert) is a quiet spot with a little cable car; tunnel swings; and, for adults, a shady pergola.

Golden Gate Park Children's Playground. (*See* Parks and Woodlands, *above.*)

The Jungle (555 9th St. at Brannan, tel. 415/552–4386) is ideal for a rainy day (though it can get crowded on Sundays). This indoor gym offers 15,000 square feet of crawl tubes, ball pits, track glides, slides, and assorted games. Food is served, too, and parents with older children who don't need their supervision can take refuge in the secluded "quiet room." There's also a section for young tots.

Julius Kahn Playground (W. Pacific Ave. at Spruce, in the Presidio) has three whirlwind slides and a beautiful cypress grove.

Michelangelo Park (off Greenwich St. between Jones and Leavenworth on Russian Hill) has a playground that you reach via a slide—though feet are an option, too, if you're not feeling tubular. The community garden, which adjoins the park, has a splendid view of Coit Tower.

Mountain Lake Park (Lake St. and 12th Ave.) has some of the best slides around; bring cardboard for the big one. It also has an impressive play structure, a lake with ducks, and often—not surprisingly, given its Richmond District locale—a mah-jongg game in progress.

San Francisco Zoo (Sloat Blvd. at the Great Hwy., tel. 415/753–

7080) has a wonderfully equipped playground just inside the entrance; it's second in size and equipment only to the Children's Playground in Golden Gate Park. Knowledgeable parents buy a yearly zoo pass just to bring their kids here.

South Park (between 2nd and 3rd Sts. and Bryant and Brannan), an oval patch of grass dating from the 1850s, is one of the better SoMa play areas, with nice equipment and a good climbing structure.

Stern Grove Playground (Sloat Blvd. west of 19th Ave., just to the left of the automobile entrance) nestles between a eucalyptus grove and a putting green. It's a great place to stop after you've dragged the kids to Stonestown Galleria for Sunday shopping.

East Bay **Lake Merritt Playground** (adjacent to the Oakland Museum, 1000 Oak St. at 10th St.) is a recreation oasis and a refuge for wild ducks.

Peninsula **Coyote Point Playground** (*see* Beaches *and* Zoos and Wildlife Centers, *above*) is full of chain bridges, tire swings, and great slides (bring cardboard to slide on so the kids don't wreck their pants!). You'll also find a child-friendly wildlife center, a museum, and a good beach nearby. Special holiday activities for children are another plus.

Water-Slide Parks

North Bay **Windsor Waters Works and Slides** (8225 Conde La., Windsor, tel. 707/838–7760) north of Santa Rosa—about 1¼ hours north of San Francisco—offers water slides, tunnel rides, tube rides, swimming pools, and a wading fountain.

Peninsula **Raging Waters** (2333 S. White Rd., San Jose; Tully Rd. exit off U.S. 101, tel. 408/270–8000; open May–Sept.) in San Jose has something for everyone, short to tall, tame to daredevil: waterfalls, inner-tube streams, 30-odd water slides of every stripe, and Polynesian entertainment.

7 Performing Arts

by Daniel Mangin

San Franciscans can't get enough of the arts, and Sunday is a day for indulgence. Matinee performances of "Best of Broadway" shows, prose and poetry readings, and some of the most sublime chamber music on the planet are just a few of the options. Sunday is a busy movie day, with a veritable festival of offerings from which to choose. In the summertime the Stern Grove Music Festival, concerts in Golden Gate Park, and several Shakespeare events bring culture high and low to the outdoors. And for those who appreciate the interactive arts, there are afternoon tea dances where your participation is always welcome—and comedy clubs where it may or may not be.

How to Find Out What's On

The most comprehensive guide to the performing arts in the Bay Area can be found in the "Datebook" section (a.k.a. the Pink Section) of the combined Sunday *Examiner and Chronicle.* Also useful are the Friday *Examiner*'s "Weekend" pages, which include a special column (usually on page 3) listing a dozen or so events for children.

The "alternative" *Bay Guardian* and *SF Weekly*, available at cafés and in boxes throughout the city, highlight some of the hipper and more offbeat activities for adults and kids. The *East Bay Express*, available across the bay and in selected boxes downtown, contains comprehensive listings for events in Berkeley, Oakland, and elsewhere. The *Pacific Sun*, available in boxes on the north side of town, covers the Marin County beat.

Two other good sources are the *San Francisco Arts Monthly*, available in many of the downtown art galleries and cafés, and the Convention and Visitors Bureau's **Cultural Events Calendar** (tel. 415/391–2001). The automated **MovieFone** (tel. 415/777–3456) lists dozens of films, with show times and locations.

Fort Mason Center (Laguna St. at Marina Blvd.), a former military installation now home to more than 50 arts and other organizations, has a 24-hour recorded message (tel. 415/979–3010) about its events and activities, many of which take place on Sundays.

Ticket Sources

Box Offices

Most downtown ticket services are closed on Sundays. The theater, ballet, symphony, and opera box offices, which generally open between 10 and noon on Sundays, are your best bet if you haven't purchased tickets in advance. Many of the computerized ticket agencies, such as BASS (*see below*), sell on a "best available seating" basis; if you want more control over your seating arrangements, the box offices are the places to go.

The city's charge-by-phone ticket service is **BASS** (tel. 510/762–2277), which also operates the separate **BASS Charge Performing Arts Line** (tel. 415/776–1999). The latter sells tickets to all but the smallest cultural venues in the Bay Area; its operators are able to answer more specific questions about such events than those at the other number. The regular BASS outlets at **Tower Records** and **Wherehouse** stores throughout the Bay Area are also open on Sundays.

Half-Price Tickets

Half-price tickets to Sunday stage, music, and dance performances are available from 11 to 7 on Saturdays at the **TIX Bay Area booth** (tel. 415/433–7827), on the Stockton Street side of Union Square across from Maiden Lane. If you're in town Saturday, it's worth dropping by the booth (no information about half-price events is given over the phone, nor are reservations taken) to see what's on sale for Sunday. TIX is also a full-service ticket agency for arts, culture, and sports events around the Bay Area.

Theater

The Bay Area's theater scene is highly pluralistic, with audience (and funding) support for a full range of productions, traditional and experimental. The venues are equally diverse—from state-of-the-art houses to grungy basements with coffee cans guiding the beams of hardware-store floodlights. Talent shows up on both ends of the spectrum.

The following companies (full descriptions below) have built loyal followings with quality productions: American Conservatory Theater, Berkeley Repertory Theatre, the Magic Theatre, Marin Theatre Company, and TheatreWorks. Theatre Artaud and Climate Theatre have for many seasons brought challenging experimental theater and performance works to their stages.

Sundays are matinee-only days for most of the larger houses in the city (not so with Berkeley Repertory Theatre and other out-of-town companies, which hold both matinee and evening performances), so if you are in the market for a blockbuster musical or other downtown show, be forewarned. Since many touring shows book fairly short runs, it's often difficult to get tickets for Sunday performances. Plan ahead if you can. The Sunday schedules of the medium-to-smaller companies are usually exactly the opposite of their larger counterparts: Evening performances but no matinees is the general rule.

How to Find Out What's Playing

The Pink Section, the *Bay Guardian*, *SF Weekly*, and the *East Bay Express* are all helpful. The *Chronicle* critics' opinions accompany the Pink Section listings. Even more reliable are the capsule reviews in the Friday *Examiner* "Weekend" pages and those in the *Bay Guardian*. Theater buffs may want to check out *Callboard*, published by Theater Bay Area (which also runs the TIX booth on Union Square); you can pick it up at TIX (not open Sunday) or at some local bookstores. Its "Playbill" section lists the activities of member companies and most others in town as well.

Major Houses and Companies

In the City

American Conservatory Theater (ACT). San Francisco's major theater company presents a season of approximately eight plays in rotating repertory from October through late spring. In early 1996, ACT moved back into the newly renovated **Geary Theater** (415 Geary St. at Mason , tel. 415/749–2228), which had been closed since the Loma Prieta earthquake.

Curran Theatre (445 Geary St. at Mason , tel. 415/474–3800). The Curran is home, along with the Golden Gate Theatre (*see below*), to the more intimate plays and musicals of the "Best of Broadway" series.

Golden Gate Theatre (Golden Gate Ave. at Taylor, tel. 415/474–3800). Though it's primarily a musical house, the Golden Gate hosts the larger "Best of Broadway" shows, along with the occasional Broadway-bound production.

Orpheum (1192 Market St. near the Civic Center, tel. 415/474–3800). This 2,500-seat former vaudeville house is used for the biggest touring shows.

Around the Bay

East Bay

Berkeley Repertory Theatre (2025 Addison St. at Milvia, near BART's Berkeley station, tel. 510/845–4700). The area's other major company performs classic and contemporary works at its modern, intimate theater. The Berkeley Rep season runs from fall to spring, with special events during the summer. There are Sunday matinees and evening performances of most productions.

Peninsula

San Jose Repertory Company (Center for the Performing Arts, 255 Almaden Blvd. at W. San Carlos, San Jose, tel. 408/291–2255). It's a bit of a drive from San Francisco, but the company is considered one of the area's best. It presents a full season of contemporary and classical works.

Medium-to-Small Theaters, Companies to Watch

In the City **Actors Theatre of San Francisco** (533 Sutter St. at Powell, tel. 415/296–9179). This troupe was organized in the late '80s by a group of local actors who tend to produce serious contemporary dramas.

Bay Area Playwrights Festival (Bldg. D, Fort Mason Center, Laguna St. at Marina Blvd., tel. 415/441–8822). The festival showcases local artists in workshops, readings, and a series of eight plays in late July and early August.

Bayfront Theatre (Bldg. B, Fort Mason Center, Laguna St. at Marina Blvd., tel. 415/776–8999). This venue books contemporary theater and performance art.

BRAVA! For Women in the Arts (tel. 415/641–7657). In 1995 the group purchased the York Theater (2789 24th St. at York), where it stages productions and workshops and continue its mission of developing works by women playwrights.

Center for the Arts Theater (corner of Howard and 3rd Sts., across from Moscone Center, tel. 415/978–2787). This 750-seat Yerba Buena Gardens facility hosts local and touring productions.

Cowell Theater (Fort Mason Center, Laguna St. at Marina Blvd., Pier 2, tel. 415/979–3010). A 400-seat house—with good sight lines and acoustics—the Cowell is used for performance, dance, and theater.

George Coates Performance Works (tel. 415/863–4130). One of the area's most heralded cutting-edge companies produces interdisciplinary and sometimes interactive works.

Lorraine Hansberry Theatre (620 Sutter St. at Mason, tel. 415/474–8800). The resident company here produces works by leading black playwrights and a play-reading series featuring new works.

Magic Theatre (Bldg. D, Fort Mason Center, Laguna St. at Marina Blvd., tel. 415/441–8822). An established company for new plays, the Magic is well known for its many Sam Shepard premieres in the '70s. It continues to present cutting-edge (mostly) dramatic works.

Marines Memorial Theatre (609 Sutter St. at Mason, tel. 415/771–6900). Smaller touring shows and, occasionally, locally produced ones are staged at this commercial house.

San Francisco Mime Troupe (various locations, tel. 415/285–1720 or 415/285–1717). Renowned for its wry takes on American political reality, the group fashions plays and parodies out of such unwieldy topics as labor movements and environmental warfare. **El Teatro de la Esperanza** (Box 40578, San Francisco, 94140, tel. 415/255–2320). This troupe presents bilingual work on the Chicano experience to a national audience. Local shows take place at various locations.

Theatre Rhinoceros (2926 16th St. at South Van Ness Ave., tel. 415/861–5079). The oldest active lesbian and gay theater company in the country presents shows on two stages year-round.

Theatre on the Square (450 Post St. at Mason, tel. 415/433–9500). This comfortable house on the edge of Union Square is used mostly for smaller touring dramas and musicals.

Around the Bay
East Bay

Center Repertory Theater (Regional Center for the Arts, 1601 Civic Dr. at Locust St., Walnut Creek, tel. 510/943–7469). Contemporary and Broadway-influenced fare is the focus here.

Julia Morgan Theater (2640 College Ave. at Derby St., Berkeley, tel. 510/845–8542). This intimate house was named for and built by the architect who also designed William Randolph Hearst's San Simeon. Berkeley Ballet stages its *Nutcracker* here each December.

Marin County

Marin Theatre Company (397 Miller Ave. at Evergreen St., Mill Valley, tel. 415/388–5208). Taking advantage of the North Bay's formidable talent pool, this company brings contemporary comedies, musicals, and dramas to the stage.

Peninsula **TheatreWorks** (various locations, tel. 415/903–6000). This ambitious South Bay company performs an impressive range of contemporary comedies, dramas, and musicals.

Alternative Spaces/ Performance Art

In the City **Bannam Place Theatre** (50 Bannam Pl., off Union, tel. 415/986–2701). Here a variety of smaller Bay Area companies perform classical and contemporary works.

Bernice St. Playhouse (21 Bernice St. at Division, tel. 415/863–5946). This scruffy-looking space underneath the Central Freeway hosts heavy-on-camp theater pieces and other works.

Bindlestiff Studio (185 6th St. at Folsom, tel. 415/974–1167). New plays and performance pieces take place in this small space.

Climate Theatre (252 9th St. at Folsom, tel. 415/978–2345). A breeding ground for serious local talent, the Climate produces and imports new, small theatrical works and performance art.

Encore Theater Company (various locations, tel. 415/346–7671). This innovative group presents "rarely produced drama that fosters social awareness and affirms the diversity of the human experience."

EXITheatre (366 Eddy St. at Leavenworth, tel. 415/673–3847). Tucked away in the city's intimidating Tenderloin district, this company presents plays, poetry readings, neighborhood variety shows, and staged readings.

Festival Fantochio (various locations, tel. 415/978–2345). The people at Climate Theatre (*see above*) are involved with this annual midsummer international festival of contemporary puppetry.

450 Geary Studio Theater (450 Geary St. at Mason, tel. 415/673–1172). This space presents its own productions as well as works by smaller and cutting-edge companies.

Intersection for the Arts (446 Valencia St. at 15th St., tel. 415/626–3311). Intersection often presents contemporary and classical plays, in addition to poetry readings, performance pieces, and other creative work.

The Lab (2948 16th St. at Capp, tel. 415/864–8855). Mainly a gallery, the Lab also hosts performance artists, many of them interdisciplinary.

The Marsh (1062 Valencia St. at 22nd St., tel. 415/641–0235). This Mission District venue books superb alternative/avant-garde theater, performance, comedy, and musical acts.

New Conservatory Theatre Center (25 Van Ness Ave. at Oak, tel. 415/861–8972). Two smallish rental houses make their home here; one is devoted mainly to works of interest to children and teens.

Noh Space (2840 Mariposa St. at Florida, tel. 415/621–7978). This is the headquarters of Theatre of Yugen, which bills itself as the only company in the United States to produce exclusively Noh and Kyogen works. Other troupes perform here as well.

Phoenix Theatre (301 8th St. at Folsom, tel. 415/621–4423). The Phoenix presents and produces new plays and original adaptations of works by American, British, and European playwrights. The plays the theater presents tend to be better than those it produces.

Solo Mio Festival (various locations, tel. 415/978–2345) or 415/392–4400). The Bay Area's premier celebration of performance art is held annually in late summer and early fall. Past participants have included Spalding Gray, Reno, Danny Glover, Eric Bogosian, and Annie Sprinkle.

Somar Theater (934 Brannan St. at 8th St., tel. 415/552–2131). An eclectic slate of experimental works and new and classic plays is performed here.

Theater Artaud (450 Florida St. at 17th St., tel. 415/621–7797). Performance art, avant-garde theater, and dance are among the offerings at this longstanding venue.

Summer Shakespeare Events

In the City

San Francisco Shakespeare Festival (Liberty Tree Meadow, Golden Gate Park, John F. Kennedy Dr. and Arguello Blvd., plus East Bay and South Bay locations, tel. 415/666–2221). The festival tunes up in San Jose in August, plays to overflow crowds in Golden Gate Park in September and early October, and then closes its season in Oakland in October. Arrive early for the San Francisco shows (which usually begin at 1:30 PM) and bring warm clothing, since the weather in this part of town is changeable.

Around the Bay

East Bay

California Shakespeare Festival (Bruns Memorial Amphitheatre, Gateway exit off Route 24, Orinda, tel. 510/548–9666). The most prestigious of the summer Shakespeare events presents late-afternoon Sunday matinees in a spectacular hillside setting.

San Francisco Shakespeare Festival. (*See above.*)

Marin County and Beyond

Marin Shakespeare Company (tel. 415/456–8104). The company mounts one production per season, usually a romance or a comedy, in the scenic Forest Meadows Amphitheater on Mt. Tam. Bring the kids.

Sonoma Valley Shakespeare Festival (Gundlach-Bundschu Open Air Amphitheatre, 2000 Denmark St., Sonoma, tel. 707/584–1700 or 707/575–3854). This '90s entry in the Shakespeare sweepstakes presents works by the Bard and others in a scenic winery setting. Picnicking is encouraged.

Peninsula and Beyond

San Francisco Shakespeare Festival. (*See above.*)

Shakespeare Santa Cruz (Performing Arts Complex, University of California at Santa Cruz, tel. 408/459–2121). This troupe takes a more populist approach to the Bard, tinkering with tradition in casting, costuming, and even marketing—but never the text. The repertory company usually includes one non-Shakespeare play each season.

Cabaret Theater

Club Fugazi (678 Green St. at Powell in North Beach, tel. 415/421–4222). This is the place to see the long-running (two decades-plus) *Beach Blanket Babylon*, a colorful, continually updated musical mix of cabaret, show-biz and political parodies, and tributes to local landmarks.

Eichelberger's (2742 17th St. at Florida, tel. 415/863–4177). At this restaurant, named in honor of an avant-garde theater *artiste*, you'll find offbeat (and then some) entertainment long after the kitchen closes.

Finocchio's (506 Broadway at Kearny, North Beach, tel. 415/982–9388). With its world-famous female impersonators, it's decidedly retro—which for the most part only adds to its charm. The touristy club is often closed Sundays, so call ahead.

Josie's Cabaret & Juice Joint (3583 16th St. at Market, tel. 415/861–7933). Josie's books an adventurous mix of gay and lesbian comedy, small theatrical works, and performance.

Plush Room (940 Sutter St. at Leavenworth, tel. 415/885–2800). This cabaret space at the York Hotel (a.k.a. the "Empire," one of Kim Novak's hideaways in Alfred Hitchcock's *Vertigo*) has long been a place for torch singers and jazz divas. In recent years small comedies and monologues have been performed here, too.

Music

San Francisco tends to shut down early on Saturday nights, which may explain why there's so much going on musically by Sunday afternoons. There are likely to be concerts in churches, blues at Fisherman's Wharf, the Symphony at Davies Hall, chamber music at Herbst Theatre or the Green Room, and tea dances all over on any given Sunday afternoon. In the evening the pace picks up still more. There's so much going on that only the hottest events are likely to sell out, though for best seating it's still wise to make reservations ahead.

What's Playing The Pink Section and the Friday *Examiner*'s "Weekend" listings are the best bets for classical events. Check the *Bay Guardian*, *SF Weekly*, and the *East Bay Express* for jazz and other popular music events. Or better yet, to plunge into the rock/blues/world-beat scene, scour a copy of *BAM* (*B*ay *A*rea *M*usic) *Magazine*, available at most record shops and some cafés. *BAM* has complete listings, plus reviews and the latest dirt, local and national.

Tickets Most major music halls have their own box offices, though some don't open until as late as noon. If you're worried about a sellout, phone the BASS Charge Performing Arts Line (tel. 415/776–1999), which begins taking orders at 10 AM. The regular BASS outlets at various Tower Records and Wherehouse stores open as early as 9 AM; for locations and exact hours, phone BASS at 510/762–2277.

Orchestral Music

Major Concert Venues

In the City

Davies Symphony Hall (201 Van Ness Ave. at Grove, tel. 415/431–5400). The home of the San Francisco Symphony hosts a number of Sunday matinees on its September-to-June schedule.

Herbst Theatre (Veterans Bldg., 401 Van Ness Ave. at McAllister, tel. 415/621–5344 or 415/392–4400). This is the most established venue for chamber and choral music.

Masonic Auditorium (1111 California St. at Taylor, tel. 415/776–4917). This large hall is used by San Francisco Performances and other presenters for symphonic and other musical events.

East Bay

Regional Center for the Arts (1601 Civic Dr. at Locust St., Walnut Creek, tel. 510/ 943–7469). Site of Hoffman Hall, this is acoustically one of the best medium-size venues in the Bay Area for classical music.

Zellerbach Hall (U.C. Berkeley campus, off Bancroft Way below Telegraph Ave., tel. 510/642–9988). Zellerbach is programmed exclusively by Cal Performances, which presents major classical artists from around the world.

Events and Orchestras to Watch For

In the City

Midsummer Mozart Festival (Herbst Theatre and, occasionally, Davies Symphony Hall, tel. 415/954–0850). This event is eagerly anticipated each July and August.

Philharmonia Baroque Orchestra (tel. 415/391–5252). Celebrating composers of the 17th and 18th centuries, including Handel, Vivaldi, and Mozart, the orchestra performs at halls and churches throughout the area.

San Francisco Performances (tel. 415/398–6449). Herbst Theatre is the usual venue for this major presenter of classical musical events, but the company also performs at the Green Room and other locations.

San Francisco Symphony (Davies Symphony Hall, 201 Van Ness Ave. at Grove, tel. 415/864–6000 for tickets, 415/552–8000 for information). The symphony, led by the charismatic Michael Tilson Thomas, begins its September through June concert season with an event-of-the-season gala. SFS also sponsors a Great Performers Series of guest soloists and orchestras, a concert festival on a different theme each June. The symphony's July through August Pops Concerts include weekend dates, but never Sundays.

Stern Grove Midsummer Music Festival (NW corner of 19th Ave. at Sloat Blvd., tel. 415/252–6252). Dating back to the '40s, this Sunday tradition showcases the city's symphony, opera, ballet, and other artists. It takes place in July and August in a scenic eucalyptus grove; bring something warm, since San Francisco's summer fog is apt to roll in before the performances conclude. Events always fill to capacity, so come early.

Women's Philharmonic Orchestra (tel. 415/543–2297). One of the area's best orchestras plays historical and contemporary works by women composers under the direction of JoAnn Falletta.

East Bay

Berkeley Symphony Orchestra (2322 Shattuck Ave., tel. 510/841–2800). Kent Nagano, the musical director of BSO, has been lauded for championing contemporary symphonic works.

California Symphony (Regional Center for the Arts, 1601 Civic Dr. at Locust St., Walnut Creek, tel. 510/943–7469). Musical director Barry Jekowsky oversees the presentation of a variety of music from traditional western symphonic standards to music from Asia and elsewhere.

Smaller Venues

Late Sunday afternoon is prime time for Bay Area music lovers, who are blessed with some of the most accomplished early-music ensembles in the world. There are several good chamber music and other venues in San Francisco, some as cozy as your living room, but don't overlook Berkeley, either.

In the City

Community Music Center (544 Capp St. at 20th St., tel. 415/647–6015). The center often hosts chamber music performers—along with an occasional jazz ensemble or ethnic-music group—on Sunday afternoons.

Cowell Theater (Fort Mason Center, Pier 2, Laguna St. at Marina Blvd., tel. 415/979–3010). The Cowell's acoustics make it popular with small classical and other ensembles, such as the Balinese ensemble Gamelan Sekar Jaya (*see below*).

Green Room (Veterans Bldg., 401 Van Ness Ave. at McAllister, tel. 415/621–6600 or 415/392–4400). This small room in the same building as Herbst Theatre regularly hosts chamber and vocal ensembles.

Noe Valley Ministry (1021 Sanchez St. at 23rd St., tel. 415/282–2317). With one of the city's more eccentric booking policies, this place is liable to play anything from chamber music to New Age to avant-garde.

Old First Church Concerts (1750 Sacramento St. at Van Ness , tel. 415/474–1608). For chamber music, this is one of the best venues in town. The Sunday afternoon concerts (which includes vocal soloists, new music, and jazz) often sell out; if you're in town Saturday, pick up advance tickets at the TIX booth in Union Square (*see* Ticket Sources, *above*).

San Francisco Conservatory of Music (Hellman Hall, 1201 Ortega St. at 19th Ave., tel. 415/759–3477). Concerts by faculty, graduate students, and visiting musicians, many of them quite distinguished, take place on a regular basis.

Around the Bay

East Bay

Hertz Hall (U.C. Berkeley campus, tel. 510/642–4864). The concert venue for the U.C. Berkeley Music Department is an acoustically top-notch site with a built-in pipe organ.

Julia Morgan Theater (2640 College Ave. at Derby St., Berkeley, tel. 510/845–8542). Classical, folk, and other musical events are presented here on many Sundays.

Maybeck Recital Hall (1537 Euclid Ave., Berkeley, tel. 510/848–3228). This is a beautiful, intimate room for chamber and other music.

Events and Groups to Watch

In the City **California Palace of the Legion of Honor** (100 34th Ave. in Lincoln Park, off Clement, tel. 415/863–3330). Following the restoration of the Legion's Skinner organ in late 1996, the Legion's former Sunday-afternoon concert series is expected to start up again.

Chanticleer (tel. 415/896–5866). The all-male chorus, which tours nationally and internationally, performs a dozen or so concerts locally each year.

Composers, Inc. (tel. 415/512–0641). This group presents and supports the work of living American composers.

Kronos Quartet (Herbst Theatre and other locations, tel. 415/731–3533). This quartet is rightly celebrated for its innovative interpretations of 20th-century string quartets.

Lamplighters Music Theatre (Lindland Theatre, Riordan High School, 175 Phelan Ave. at Judson, tel. 415/227–0331). Gilbert and Sullivan fans flock to Lamplighter performances; it's one of the top G & S companies in the United States.

Rova Saxophone Quartet (tel. 415/487–1701). This superb foursome performs infrequent but well-attended concerts, usually on Sundays.

San Francisco Bach Choir (tel. 415/922–1645). This 90-person choir, which has been performing for more than 60 years, specializes in the choral literature of Bach and other pre-20th-century composers. Concerts are usually held at Calvary Presbyterian Church (2515 Fillmore St. at Jackson)

San Francisco Gay Men's Chorus (various locations, tel. 415/863–4472). The chorus performs regularly, often on Sunday evenings.

San Francisco Girls Chorus (tel. 415/673–1511). This chorus, whose members range in age from 7 to 16, performs in formal concerts and at civic events.

Slavyanka Chorus (tel. 415/979–8690). A superb group of male singers, this chorus performs a cappella music of Eastern Europe.

Around the Bay
East Bay

Bay Area Pianists (First Unitarian Church, 1 Lawson Rd. at Terrace Dr., tel. 510/841–7721). A series of recitals on selected Sunday afternoons showcases award-winning classical pianists.

Gamelan Sekar Jaya (various locations, tel. 510/237–6849). This much-lauded 35-member orchestra performs music and dance of Bali around the Bay Area, sometimes in collaboration with local symphonies.

San Francisco Symphony Chamber Music Sundays (Julia Morgan Theater, 2640 College Ave. at Derby St., Berkeley, tel. 510/845–8542 or 415/584–5946). A regular series is presented by various groups comprised of symphony members.

Music in Churches

Some very fine music can be heard each Sunday in Bay Area churches as part of weekly services or concerts. Major events are listed in the Pink Section, but you may have to pop by a particular church to find out what's going on, since the telephone numbers listed below are not always answered on Sundays.

In the City **Glide Memorial Church** (330 Ellis St. at Taylor, tel. 415/ 771–6300). The gospel-rock services here, led by Reverend Cecil Williams, are uplifting musically as well as spiritually.

Love Center Church (6325 Camden St. at 65th St., tel. 510/729–0680). This is *the* spot for Sunday gospel services, with the Hawkins Family and other famous singers among the regular worshippers.

Mission Dolores Basilica (16th St. at Dolores, tel. 415/621–8203). The larger church next to this historic mission has become a popular site for a cappella and other choral recitals, hosting performances by top groups like Chanticleer.

Old First Church Concerts (1750 Sacramento St. at Van Ness, tel. 415/474–1608). This is a well-respected Sunday afternoon series (*see* Smaller Venues, *above*).
St. Mark's Episcopal Church (2300 Bancroft Way at Ellsworth St., Berkeley, tel. 510/848–5107). The church holds early evening organ concerts the second Sunday of each month.
St. Mary's Cathedral (1111 Gough St. at Geary, tel. 415/567–2020, ext. 213). A large, modern edifice ("Our Lady of Maytag," according to cynics) on the edge of the Western Addition, the cathedral often holds organ recitals or choral concerts on Sunday afternoons, usually at 3:30.
Temple Emanu-El (2 Lake St. at Arguello Blvd., tel. 415/751–2535). There's a chamber concert here on the first Sunday of every month. Pocket Opera, Klezmermania, the San Francisco Jazz Festival, and the San Francisco Chamber Orchestra also use the temple.

Around the Bay
East Bay

First Congregational Church (Dana St. at Channing Way, Berkeley, tel. 510/848–3696). The Philharmonia Baroque, the American Bach Soloists, and other groups play at this important venue for early classical music (tel. 415/392–4400 for tickets).

Opera

San Francisco's love affair with the opera predates the Gold Rush by nearly two decades. Even in the wildest days of the Wild West, Europe's most accomplished singers and conductors made it a point to pass through the city, and the tradition continues to this day at the world-famous San Francisco Opera. Smaller operatic groups perform throughout the year. The single best bet for information is the "Classical/Opera/Dance" page in the Pink Section.

Berkeley Opera (tel. 510/841–1903). The company performs classical and contemporary works at various East Bay locations.
Pocket Opera (333 Kearny St. at Bush, tel. 415/989–1855). This company has carved a niche for itself by presenting neglected chamber operas in original English translations in an annual spring series.
San Francisco Opera (War Memorial Opera House, 301 Van Ness Ave. at Grove, tel. 415/864–3330). This major international company, for the past several years under the direction of Lotfi Mansouri, presents a full season of new productions and revivals from mid-September to mid-December. Note: The opera's primary home for the 1996–97 season will be the Bill Graham Civic Auditorium while the opera house undergoes seismic retrofitting.
San Francisco Opera Center (tel. 415/565–6491). The center sponsors a "Showcase Series," usually of new operatic work or chamber operas, in a four-concert series on Sunday evenings from December to May. Its Merola Opera Program summer concerts by emerging talents are very popular.

Jazz

Several jazz joints are up and jumping by early Sunday afternoon, with some smokin' jam sessions under way by evening. Yoshi's Restaurant & Nitespot in the East Bay is highly reliable, but all the clubs below are worth checking out.

Elbo Room (647 Valencia St. at Sycamore, tel. 415/552–7788). This popular Mission District bar books an impressive slate of jazz and "new jazz" artists.
Julie Ring's Heart and Soul (1695 Polk St. at Clay, tel. 415/673–7100). A classy club with '40s-style decor, Julie Ring's hosts small but talented jazz combos and vocalists.
Kimball's East (5800 Shellmound St. off Christie Ave., Emeryville, tel. 510/658–2555). The club hosts jazz greats and popular vocalists.

Mason Street Wine Bar (342 Mason St. at Geary, tel. 415/391–3454). Torch singers swoon and croon in this mellow cocktail lounge in the heart of the theater district.

Moose's (1652 Stockton St. at Filbert, tel. 415/989–7800). Top-notch classical jazz is the regular fare Sunday evenings in the bar of this popular North Beach restaurant.

Pasand Lounge (1875 Union St. at Laguna, Pacific Heights, tel. 415/922–4498). This longtime jazz and R&B nightspot adjoins an Indian restaurant.

Around the Bay
East Bay

Johnny Love's. (*See* Dancing, *below*). **Yoshi's Restaurant & Nitespot.** The Bay Area's premier spot to hear jazz was scheduled to relocate by fall 1996 to a storefront below the Washington Street Parking Garage (at Embarcadero) in Oakland's Jack London Square. Check the *Chronicle*'s Pink Section, the *Bay Guardian*, or the *East Bay Express* for show listings.

Blues, Folk, Rock, and More

Clubs have been coming and going at a furious pace for the past few years, and the scene shows no sign of settling down. Below are some of the most reliable Sunday venues.

In the City

Bimbo's 365 Club (1025 Columbus Ave. at Taylor, tel. 415/474–0365). A speakeasylike joint, Bimbo's has some of the more brusque waiters in town and pop, jazz, blues, and rock headliners.

Blue Lamp (561 Geary St. at Taylor, tel. 415/885–1464). A great blues jam takes place every Sunday night at this downtown hole in the wall with an aura of faded opulence.

Bottom of the Hill Club (1233 17th St. at Texas, tel. 415/621–4455). This super little spot in the Potrero Hill district showcases some of the best local alternative rock and blues. Musicians hang out here—always a good sign.

Cafe du Nord (2170 Market St. at Sanchez, tel. 415/979–6545). This American-style restaurant books an audacious slate of jazz, acid jazz, blues, cabaret, and Latin music.

Coconut Grove Supper Club (1415 Van Ness at Austin Alley, tel. 415/776–1616). There's a chic, '40s ambience at this "classy joint." Tom Jones, Connie Stevens, Diahann Carroll, and other pop icons were among past headliners. The well-regarded Coconut Grove Orchestra (or a smaller trio) often backs the stars.

DNA Lounge (375 11th. St. at Harrison, tel. 415/626–1409). Alternative rock, funk, and rap are the usual fare at this hip but friendly venue. In addition, there's nightly dancing, billiards, and other diversions.

The Fillmore (1805 Geary Blvd. at Fillmore, tel. 415/346–6000). San Francisco's famous rock music hall serves up a varied plate of national and some local acts: rock, reggae, grunge, jazz, comedy, folk, acid house, and more.

Great American Music Hall (859 O'Farrell St. at Polk, tel. 415/885–0750). It's one of the most eclectic nightclubs in the country, booking blues, folk, jazz, and rock.

Last Day Saloon (406 Clement St. at 5th Ave, tel. 415/387–6343). The club presents a varied schedule of blues, Cajun, rock, and hip-hop.

Lou's Pier 47 (300 Jefferson St. at Jones, Fisherman's Wharf, tel. 415/771–0377). Blues and other sounds from this restaurant and club echo through the waterfront. Sunday sessions begin at noon.

Paragon Bar and Restaurant (3251 Scott St. at Lombard, tel. 415/922–2456). This popular hangout for the Marina's younger set presents live music—mostly bluesy rock and jazz—on Sundays.

Paradise Lounge (1501 Folsom St. at 11th St., tel. 415/861–6906). There's something offbeat for everyone here: Two stages present eclectic live music and dancing, and an upstairs cabaret showcases emerging and solo performers.

Pat O'Shea's Mad Hatter (3848 Geary Blvd. at 2nd Ave., tel. 415/752–3148). A legendary Irish hangout, the Mad Hatter is a haven for lovers of folk and other music.

The Saloon (1232 Grant St., near Columbus Ave., tel. 415/989–7666). At this atmospheric blues and R&B hangout in North Beach, the patrons are sometimes as entertaining as the tip-top performers.

Slim's (333 11th St. at Harrison, tel. 415/621–3330). One of the most popular clubs in town, Slim's specializes in what it labels "American roots music"—blues, jazz, classic rock, and the like—in addition to alternative rock and roll.

Warfield (982 Market at 6th St., tel. 415/775–7722). This erstwhile movie palace was transformed into a showcase for mainstream rock and roll. There are tables and chairs downstairs and theater seating in the balcony.

Around the Bay

East Bay

Ashkenaz (1317 San Pablo Ave. at Gilman St., Berkeley, tel. 510/525–5054). At this great, homey club in the East Bay, adults—and kids, who are always welcome—boogie to some of the best rock, blues, jazz, folk, and international music in the area.

Berkeley Square (1333 University Ave. at Bonar St., Berkeley, tel. 510/841–6555). A hangout for East Bay post-punkers, the Square schedules lo-fi, grunge, ska, heavy metal, industrial, and Gothic bands.

Blake's (a.k.a. Larry Blake's, 2367 Telegraph Ave. at Durant Ave., Berkeley, tel. 510/848–0886). There's no Sunday cover at this Berkeley club, which usually books alternative rock and blues.

Eli's Mile High Club (3629 Martin Luther King, Jr. Way, Oakland, tel. 510/655–6661). This club is considered by many aficionados to be the most authentic place to hear the blues in the Bay Area. Call ahead because it's sometimes closed on Sundays.

Freight and Salvage Coffee House (1111 Addison St. at San Pablo, Berkeley, tel. 510/548–1761). This is one of the best spots in the Bay Area for folk, blues, Cajun, and bluegrass.

Starry Plough (3101 Shattuck Ave. at Prince St., Berkeley, tel. 510/841–2082). Jazz, pop, fusion, country, and punk are among the musical styles featured at this longtime Berkeley favorite.

Marin County

Fourth Street Tavern (711 Fourth St. near Lincoln St., San Rafael, tel. 41/456–4828). A fireplace contributes to the mellow atmosphere at this "no cover, no attitude" bar that books mainly R&B and rock.

Sweetwater (153 Throckmorton Ave. off Miller Ave., Mill Valley, tel. 415/388–2820). This is a favorite hangout of many of Marin County's famous musicians, any of whom are likely to come up and jam with headliners like Clarence Clemmons and Joe Louis Walker.

Dancing

You can shake a tail feather to an international array of sounds each Sunday. Afternoon tea dances usually give way to evening events, so you can get a major workout by the time the clock strikes Monday.

In the City

Bahia Cabana Restaurant and Club (1600 Market St. at Franklin, tel. 415/626–3306). Afro-Latin music lures a citywide crowd after 10 PM on Sundays.

Cesar's Latin Palace (3140 Mission St. at Army, tel. 415/648–6611). This Mission District nightspot is home to the Latin All-Stars, who keep the Cesar's faithful up and dancing past midnight.

Club 181 (181 Eddy St. at Taylor, tel. 415/673–8181). This former speakeasy in the dicey Tenderloin district has a stylish, serpentine bar and a Sunday menu featuring DJ dancing to hip-hop, house, and funk music.

Johnny Love's (1500 Broadway at Polk, tel. 415/931–6053). Sunday at this popular restaurant and singles bar is given over to schmoozing and DJ dancing.

Metronome Ballroom (1830 17th St. at Vermont, tel. 415/252–9000). Learn how to dance from 6:30 to 7:30, then dance ballroom, Latin, and swing until 11 at this smoke- and alcohol-free space.

Oz (Westin St. Francis Hotel, 335 Powell St. at Post, tel. 415/774–0116). DJs spin Euro-house music on the hotel's top floor; the panoramic views and marble floors are reached via a glass elevator.

Pleasuredome at Club Townsend, 177 Townsend St. at 3rd St., tel. 415/985–5256. This long-running Sunday-only gay event shows no signs of slowing down; the popular DJs' trendsetting sounds keep patrons in perpetual motion.

The Stud (399 9th St. at Harrison, tel. 415/863–6623). One of the city's oldest gay bars hosts a gender-bending mix of straight, gay, and bisexual urbanites and suburbanites. The club's DJs change their tune every few months—as we headed to press, Sunday was given over to reliving the '80s.

Around the Bay
East Bay

Johnny Love's (1448 South Main St. at Newell St., Walnut Creek, tel. 510/934–4199). Johnny had so much love to share that he expanded to Walnut Creek, where he was as instantly popular (except with the club's neighbors) as he was in San Francisco. He serves up dancing to a live jazz band from late afternoon until 8 PM, then to a DJ after that.

Music in the Outdoors

In the City

Golden Gate Park Band (Bandshell at Golden Gate Park, between Music Concourse and Tea Garden Drs., tel. 415/666–7035, weekdays 8–5). The band has played free concerts on Sundays in the park for years. The usual season is April through October (concerts start promptly at 1 PM), but budget cuts have reduced the number of performances; call for details.

Around the Bay
East Bay

Concord Pavilion (2000 Kirker Pass Rd., Concord, tel. 510/671–3100). Architect Frank Gehry designed this comfortable outdoor setting for performances by nationally renowned pop, rock, jazz, blues, and country artists. The site's renovation and expansion are scheduled for completion by summer 1996.

Greek Theatre (U.C. Berkeley campus, Gayley Ave. near Hearst Ave., tel. 510/642–9988 or 510/762–2277). Booked by Bill Graham Presents, the Greek stages a disparate mix of mainstream to avant-garde (rock) acts.

Peninsula

Jazz at Filoli (Filoli Mansion, end of Cañada Rd., east from Edgewood Ave., Cañada Rd. exit off I–280, Woodside, tel. 415/366–4640). These once-a-month, June-to-October Sunday afternoon concerts are held at the beautiful Peninsula estate that was immortalized on TV's *Dynasty*. The $30 admission price includes beer, wine, and snacks; picnicking is encouraged, and box lunches (additional) are available.

Shoreline Amphitheatre (Rengstorff Ave. at Amphitheatre Pkwy., tel. 415/962–1000). It was built on a garbage dump, but there's nothing trashy about the booking policy. Only top (or top-drawing) acts (like Randy Travis, Amy Grant, and David Bowie,) take the stage.

Dance

As a center of American dance activity, the Bay Area ranks second only to New York City. Small experimental troupes, ethnic dance groups, established touring companies, and the venerable San Francisco Ballet all contribute to the vibrant scene. Bay Area dance audiences are among the most knowledgeable in the world—which makes for marvelous eavesdropping during intermission.

Although there are dozens of smallish dance troupes, many of them quite accomplished, three midsize companies are acknowledged for their longevity and innovation. The **Margaret Jenkins Dance Company** (tel. 415/863–1173) is an experimental troupe with a loyal following. Its namesake has collaborated with a number of internationally recognized talents, including Yoko Ono. **ODC/San Francisco** (tel. 415/863–6606)—ODC stands for Oberlin Dance Collective—presents the works of the collective's choreographers, foremost among them, Brenda Way. **Lines Contemporary Ballet** (tel. 415/863–3040) features a unique mixture: classical technique accented with ethnic and modern dance idioms. The company's repertoire centers on the choreography of Alonzo King.

Among the other standout troupes in the Bay Area: **Joe Goode Performance Group,** a modern company that "stretches the boundaries of dance and theater"; **Della Davidson Company,** which presents dances by emerging and established choreographers; **Theatre Flamenco of San Francisco** (tel. 415/826–1305), one of the city's oldest companies; and **Khadra International Folk Ballet,** which performs dances from a range of cultures, from Appalachian to Eastern European.

Not to be missed, either, is **Rosa Montoya Bailes Flamenco** (tel. 415/824–1960), a remarkable company presenting traditional Spanish dance and music in venues from the Herbst Theatre to Mission District bars. One final highlight of the local dance scene: the two-week **San Francisco Ethnic Dance Festival** *(see below)*.

What's Playing? The *Examiner and Chronicle*'s Sunday Pink Section lists most major dance events, as does the Friday *Examiner*'s "Weekend" section. The *San Francisco Bay Guardian, Bay Area Reporter,* and other alternative weeklies cover dance extensively.

Tickets Sunday tickets are easiest to get at the box office, although most larger events are also handled through the BASS Charge Performing Arts Line (tel. 415/776–1999).

Major Venues, Companies, and Presenters

In the City **Center for the Arts Theater** (corner of Howard and 3rd Sts., across from Moscone Center, tel. 415/978–2787). This 750-seat state-of-the-art facility programs an adventurous mix of local, national, and international dance, theater, performance, and music.

Cowell Theater (Pier 2, Fort Mason Center, Laguna St. at Marina Blvd., tel. 415/979–3010). This 400-seat space hosts some of the finest local and national artists, including Margaret Jenkins.

Footwork Studio (3221 22nd St. at Bartlett, tel. 415/824–5044). Emerging and avant-garde dance and dance-tinged performance art are presented at this Mission District loft.

San Francisco Ballet (tel. 415/865–2000). The oldest ballet company in the nation has earned an international reputation for excellence under artistic director Helgi Tomasson. From February through May, the company presents a full schedule of classical and contemporary works; its lively, entertaining version of the *Nutcracker* unfolds in December. Sunday matinees generally start at 2. Curtain time for most evening performances is 7:30. Note: The War Memorial Opera House, the ballet's usual home, will be closed at least through mid-1997 for seismic retrofitting. SFB will perform at Zellerbach Hall, the Center for the Arts Theater, and the Palace of Fine Arts until the opera-house repairs have been completed, it is hoped, by 1997.

San Francisco Ethnic Dance Festival (Palace of Fine Arts Theatre, Lyon St. off Richardson, tel. 415/474–3914). In this annual June celebration of cultural diversity, a few dozen of the Bay Area's estimated 200 ethnic dance companies and soloists perform.

San Francisco Performances (tel. 415/398–6449). This major presenter of musical events (*see above*) also produces a number of dance recitals showcasing major national and international talents, usually at Cowell Theater at Fort Mason.

Theatre Artaud (450 Florida St. at 17th St., tel. 415/621–7797). A multipurpose space for experimental, emerging, and mainstream dance, Artaud produces the popular Men Dancing series each fall.

Around the Bay
East Bay

Diablo Ballet (Regional Center for the Arts, 1601 Civic Dr. at Locust St., Walnut Creek, tel. 510/943–7469). Former San Francisco Ballet dancer Lawrence Pech is the artistic director of this young company, which performs new works and classical ballets. Its season runs from the fall to spring and mercifully does not include the *Nutcracker*.

Oakland Ballet (tel. 510/452–9288 for information, 510/465–6400 or 510/762–2277 for tickets). Under the direction of Ronn Guidi, this company has found a niche, locally and nationally, in restoring and performing pivotal works from the early 20th century. It also presents contemporary ballets during the fall and the *Nutcracker* in December. Performances are at Oakland's Paramount Theatre, Zellerbach Hall, and elsewhere in the East Bay.

Zellerbach Hall (U.C. Berkeley campus off Channing Way, tel. 510/642–9988). The hall's main programmer is Cal Performances, which presents an impressive range of local (Margaret Jenkins) and national (Alvin Ailey, Merce Cunningham, Twyla Tharp) companies.

Readings and Lectures

How to Find Out What's On

Although they've been happening for years, poetry and prose readings have undergone a boom here recently, with feature pieces in the local press contributing to the events' popularity. Up to a dozen readings and book signings are usually listed each week on page 2 of the Sunday *Chronicle*'s book review section. The paper's Pink Section lists lectures under an "Events" heading. The *Bay Guardian* and *East Bay Express* include readings in their weekly calendars. Those in need of a little oral versification will find their opportunities in the monthly *Poetry Flash*, available at Fort Mason, City Lights Bookstore, and many cafés around the city. The various **Borders Books and Music** stores in the Bay Area, including San Francisco (400 Post St. at Powell, tel. 415/399–1633), Emeryville (5800 Shellmound St. off Christie Ave., tel. 510/654–1633), and San Rafael (588 W. Francisco Blvd. off the Central San Rafael exit of U.S. 101, tel. 415/454–1400), often hold readings on Sundays. Other places to experience wisdom or whimsy are listed below.

A Different Light Bookstore (489 Castro St. at 18th St., tel. 415/431–0891). The city's leading lesbian and gay bookstore has readings most Sunday evenings at 7:30 and some afternoons as well.

Fine Arts Museums of San Francisco (tel. 415/863–3330 or 415/750–3638). Sunday afternoon lectures discussing current exhibits and other topics are often scheduled at the M.H. de Young Memorial Museum and the California Palace of the Legion of Honor (*see* Art Museums *in* Chapter 4).

Fort Mason Center (Laguna St. at Marina Blvd., events line tel. 415/979–3010). You're apt to find anything from a lecture on lace-making in Venice to an address on metaphysics in one or another of the center's buildings.

Intersection for the Arts. (*See* Theater: Alternative Spaces/Performance Art, *above*).

Modern Times Bookstore (888 Valencia St. at 20th St., tel. 415/282–9246). This left-leaning bookstore has a medium-size room for readings in the back.

Poetry Above Paradise (Paradise Lounge, 1501 Folsom St. at 11th St., tel. 415/621–1911). Each Sunday night at 8, these popular readings take place in a small room above a SoMa nightclub.

Around the Bay
East Bay

Black Oak Books (1491 Shattuck Ave. at Vine St., Berkeley, 510/486–0698). Black Oak specializes in small and alternative presses; readings take place some Sundays.

Cody's Books (2454 Telegraph Ave. at Dwight Way, Berkeley, tel. 510/845–7852). One the area's best-stocked stores holds evening readings, often on Sundays.

Marin County

Book Passage (Market Place Shopping Centre, 51 Tamal Vista Blvd. off Lucky Dr., tel. 415/927–0960 or 800/999–7909). Sunday afternoon "Mystery Teas" are frequently held here, with suspense authors reading from their works.

Comedy

In the '80s it seemed like every class clown or life-of-the-party type was cutting it up at a comedy club. The stand-up boom is but a memory, but the Sunday-night shows at the few remaining clubs in the Bay Area tend to bring out the true connoisseurs. Most shows begin at 9; admission is usually $8–$10 with a two-drink minimum.

In the City

Cobb's Comedy Club (Cannery lower courtyard, 2801 Leavenworth St. at Beach, tel. 415/928–4320). The well-established Cobb's almost always books national performers.

Josie's Cabaret and Juice Joint (3583 16th St. at Market, tel. 415/861–7933). Josie's often presents lesbian/gay comedy in the late afternoon on Sundays, sometimes as the main event.

The Punch Line/SF (444-A Battery St., 2nd floor, at Washington, tel. 415/397–7573). Home of the annual San Francisco Comedy Competition, the club hosts a Sunday night Comedy Showcase featuring up-and-coming Bay Area comics—a bargain at $5.

Around the Bay
East Bay

The Punch Line/Walnut Creek (Palm Court Center, 1661 Botelho Dr. at California, tel. 510/935–2002). This East Bay offshoot of the SF club brings in local and national comedians.

Film

Appreciation of film and its history has always run deep in the Bay Area, home to the nation's longest-running festival, as well as to the ambitious Pacific Film Archive in Berkeley. On any given weekend, any of a dozen-plus annual festivals is liable to be in full swing. Such touring events as the Festival of Animation or Tournée of Animation make regular stops in the Bay Area. On a weekend when nothing else is happening, you can still choose from any number of art, foreign, independent, or experimental films playing on more than a dozen screens (*see below*).

Or maybe you'd just like to settle into the kind of fare that put America on the cinematic map: a big, escapist Hollywood picture. Several facilities are technically superior: the **Northpoint Theatre** (2290 Powell St. at Bay, tel. 415/989–6060) shows 70mm, multitrack prints of current features (and occasional revivals like *Doctor Zhivago* or *Star Wars*); the largest of the **AMC Kabuki 8 Theatres** (1881 Post St. at Fillmore, tel. 415/931–9800) has a big screen and digital stereo THX sound (it's always the first film listed in the newspaper directory); the **United Artists Coronet** (3575 Geary Blvd. at Arguello Blvd., tel. 415/752–4400), a late-Deco first-run house, has comfortable chairs and superior sound. Art- and independent-film buffs have made an instant hit out of the five cozy **Embarcadero Center Cinemas** (1 Embarcadero Center, Clay and Battery Sts. tel. 415/352–0810). The area's few surviving movie palaces (*see below*) provide such visual pleasure that the contemporary works some of them book can't always compete.

Tickets

There are so many movie options here that Sunday afternoon shows rarely sell out—except for onetime screenings or the initial weekends of major hits. The first Sunday show at most theaters is usually a bargain matinee. Some theaters sell advance tickets by phone through **MovieFone** (tel. 415/777–3456), which also serves as an automated directory of films currently playing in the Bay Area.

Cinema Museums

East Bay **Pacific Film Archive** (2625 Durant Ave. at Bowditch St., Berkeley, tel. 510/642–1124). A repository of more than 7,000 films and videos, the PFA has an adventurous schedule, including everything from guerrilla video to acknowledged masterpieces. Sundays are often given over to screenings of classic talkies or silents from the United States and around the world.

Festivals

San Francisco International Film Festival (tel. 415/931–3456). The area's premier film event screens works from around the world, with an emphasis on Eastern European, Asian, and African films. The festival's headquarters are the AMC Kabuki 8 Theatres (*see above*), but screenings (late April–early May) are also held at the Castro Theatre and the Pacific Film Archive, among other locales.

San Francisco International Lesbian and Gay Film Festival (tel. 415/703–8650). Attended by over 50,000 enthusiastic viewers each June, this is the largest event of its kind in the world.

Mill Valley Film Festival (tel. 415/383–5346 or 415/383–0990). A cozier affair that takes place in Marin County each October, this festival is an acknowledged showcase for American independent cinema.

Other yearly festivals include **American Indian Film Festival** (San Francisco, November, tel. 415/554–0525), **Black Filmworks . . . Festival of Film and Video** (Oakland, April, tel. 510/465–0804), **Cine Latino!** (San Francisco, September, tel. 415/553–8135), **Jewish Film Festival** (San Francisco and Berkeley, July, tel. 510/548–3456), **National Educational Network** (Oakland, May, tel. 510/465–6885), and the **San Francisco Asian American International Film Festival** (San Francisco, March, tel. 415/863–0814).

Even if it isn't time for one of the yearly festivals, there's still likely to be a special onetime celebration of films, often sponsored by one of the consulates based in San Francisco. Check the "Special Film Programs" page of the Sunday Pink Section or the film listings in one of the alternative weeklies (*see above*).

Art, Foreign, Independent, Experimental Film

In the City **AMC Kabuki 8 Theatres** (1881 Post. St. at Fillmore, tel. 415/931–9800). At least one (and as many as four) of the screens at this multiplex will likely be presenting a recent high-profile art or foreign release.

Artists' Television Access (992 Valencia St. at 21st St., tel. 415/824–3890). This tattered Mission district space screens some of the rawest experimental film and video works.

Center for the Arts Theater (corner of Howard and 3rd Sts., across from Moscone Center, tel. 415/978–2787). The center's 100-seat screening room shows local and international works, from the conventional to the highly experimental.

Landmark Theatres (tel. 415/352–0810 for films and times at all theaters). The chain devotes 15 screens in six San Francisco locations to art, foreign, and independent cinema. Its flagship is the **Embarcadero Center Cinemas** (*see above*).

Roxie Cinema (3117 16th St. at Valencia, tel. 415/863–1087). The venerable Roxie books an eclectic mix of American and European art films and social and political documentaries. Its annual film noir festival includes everything from classics to totally obscure examples of the genre.

San Francisco Cinematheque (San Francisco Art Institute, 800 Chestnut St. at Jones, tel. 415/558–8129). This venue often features films and personal appearances by avant-garde artists. Sunday shows start at 7:30 or 8 PM.

Around the Bay

East Bay

Landmark Theatres has nearly two-dozen screens in the East Bay; more than half show non-Hollywood fare. Among the chain's theaters are the **Shattuck 8 Cinemas** (2230 Shattuck Ave. at Kittredge St., Berkeley, tel. 510/644–3370) and the nearby **Act 1 & 2** (2128 Center St. at Shattuck Ave., Berkeley, tel. 510/548–7200).

Marin County

There's generally an art film in one or both of the **Sequoia** theaters (listed in some newspapers as Pacific's Sequoia Twin, 25 Throckmorton Ave. at East Blithedale Ave., Mill Valley, tel. 415/388–4862) and in at least one of the many theaters at Pacific's **Northgate** multiplex (700 Northgate Dr. west of U.S. 101's Terra Linda exit, San Rafael, tel. 415/491–0608).

Peninsula

Landmark's **Belmont Art Cinemas** (100 El Camino Real, Belmont, tel. 415/591–5368) screen higher-profile art and independent works.

Movie Palaces

In the City

Alhambra Theatre (2330 Polk at Union St., tel. 415/775–2137). The Moorish-style theater got a million-dollar makeover in the late '80s. It often screens big-studio children's movies, particularly by Disney Studios. **Castro Theatre** (429 Castro St. at Market, tel. 415/621–6120). This beloved '20s movie palace programs art films, first-run independent cinema, and periodic Hollywood revivals. In between shows the organist at the Mighty Wurlitzer belts out favorite movie themes, nearly always ending with a clap-along chorus of the classic "San Francisco."

East Bay

Grand Lake Cinema (3200 Grand Ave. at MacArthur Blvd., Oakland, tel. 510/452–3556). One of the few large theaters that has been tastefully subdivided, the Grand Lake occasionally shows children's fare on Sunday afternoons.

Paramount Theatre (2025 Broadway at 21st St., Oakland, tel. 510/465–6400). Though it's mainly used for live performances, the Paramount occasionally presents classic silent and sound films. Two-hour tours ($1) are given on the first and third Saturday of the month.

Peninsula

Stanford Theatre (221 University Ave., tel. 415/324–3700). This house was the recipient of a loving makeover; it screens a regular slate of Hollywood classics and often hosts special events attended by golden-era stars and directors.

Revival Houses

Red Victorian Movie House (1727 Haight St. at Cole, tel. 415/668–3994). An ultrafunky collectively run cinema known locally as "the Red Vic," this is the the closest thing left to a bona fide repertory house in San Francisco. You're likely to find the work of everyone from Eisenstein to Ed Wood, Jr.—sometimes on the same day. Print quality may vary, but never the enthusiasm of the patrons or the worker-owners.

U.C. Theatre (2036 University Ave. at Shattuck Ave., Berkeley, tel. 510/843–6267). This theater books mainstream and art-house favorites, as well as locally produced features and documentaries. Like to get Sunday off to a campy start? Hit one of the midnight (Saturday) screenings of the cult favorite *The Rocky Horror Picture Show*, which has been running here for well over a decade.

Best Bets for Children

All the daily and weekly newspapers list events for children. Another window into family arts-and-leisure opportunities is the monthly *Parents' Press*, available at most large grocery stores and elsewhere. The **Young Audiences ArtsCard Project**'s hot line (tel. 415/863–2549) is an invaluable resource for performing arts events of interest to families. The project's ArtsCard offers substantial savings for children in grades K–12. For more information about the card, *see* Best Bets for Children *in* Chapter 4.

Arts in Parks

East Bay **Children's Fairyland.** Puppet shows and other performances take place every Sunday at this popular fairy-tale theme park for kids. *Grand and Bellevue Aves., at Lake Merritt, tel. 510/452–2259. Admission: $3 adults, $2.50 children, under 1 free.*

Arts in Museums Many of the major museums have Sunday performances for children (*see* Chapter 4 for hours and times). Below are a few additional possibilities:

In the City **De Young Museum** (Golden Gate Park, Tea Garden Dr. off John F. Kennedy Dr., tel. 415/863–3330 or 415/750–3658). The de Young (*see* Art Museums *in* Chapter 4) sponsors weekend events for children, mostly on Saturdays but occasionally on Sundays as well.

Exploratorium (3601 Lyon St. off Richardson in the Palace of Fine Arts, tel. 415/561–0360). This favorite spot (*see* Science and Technology Museums *in* Chapter 4) is primarily science oriented, but it also presents films, musical performances, and other activities.

Marin County **Bay Area Discovery Museum.** This museum, just across the Golden Gate Bridge in Marin County, presents arts and other events many Sundays. *East Fort Baker, Golden Gate National Recreation Area, tel. 415/487–4398. Admission: $7 adults, $6 children 1–18, under 1 free. Open Sun. 10–5.*

Children's Theater
In the City **New Conservatory Theatre** (25 Van Ness Ave. at Oak, tel. 415/861–8972). This smallish space regularly stages Sunday matinees of plays for children.

Young Performers Theater (Fort Mason Center, Laguna St. at Marina Blvd., tel. 415/346–5550). The theater showcases Bay Area youths in old favorites and new works.

East Bay **Regional Center for the Arts** (1601 Civic Dr. at Locust St., Walnut Creek, tel. 510/943–7469). Sunday afternoon children's theater and other cultural events often take place here.

Story Hours

In the City **Asian Art Museum** (Golden Gate Park, Tea Garden Dr. between South Dr. and John F. Kennedy Dr., tel. 415/668–7855). Storytellers relate Asian myths and tales on Sunday afternoons at 1 PM.

Book Passage (51 Tamal Vista Blvd. off Lucky Dr., Corte Madera, tel. 415/927–0960). This cheery spot hosts readings for kids every Sunday at 11 AM.

A Clean Well-Lighted Place for Books (2417 Larkspur Landing Circle and Sir Francis Drake Blvd., Larkspur, tel. 415/461–0171). Children's story hours are held here Sundays at 1 PM.

Index

NOTES

NOTES

NOTES

NOTES

NOTES

NOTES

NOTES

NOTES

Fodor's Travel Publications

Available at bookstores everywhere, or call 1–800–533–6478, 24 hours a day.

Gold Guides

U.S.

Alaska
Arizona
Boston
California
Cape Cod, Martha's Vineyard, Nantucket
The Carolinas & the Georgia Coast
Chicago
Colorado
Florida
Hawai'i
Las Vegas, Reno, Tahoe
Los Angeles
Maine, Vermont, New Hampshire
Maui & Lāna'i
Miami & the Keys
New England
New Orleans
New York City
Pacific North Coast
Philadelphia & the Pennsylvania Dutch Country
The Rockies
San Diego
San Francisco
Santa Fe, Taos, Albuquerque
Seattle & Vancouver
The South
U.S. & British Virgin Islands
USA
Virginia & Maryland
Washington, D.C.

Foreign

Australia
Austria
The Bahamas
Belize & Guatemala
Bermuda
Canada
Cancún, Cozumel, Yucatán Peninsula
Caribbean
China
Costa Rica
Cuba
The Czech Republic & Slovakia
Eastern & Central Europe
Europe
Florence, Tuscany & Umbria
France
Germany
Great Britain
Greece
Hong Kong
India
Ireland
Israel
Italy
Japan
London
Madrid & Barcelona
Mexico
Montréal & Québec City
Moscow, St. Petersburg, Kiev
The Netherlands, Belgium & Luxembourg
New Zealand
Norway
Nova Scotia, New Brunswick, Prince Edward Island
Paris
Portugal
Provence & the Riviera
Scandinavia
Scotland
Singapore
South Africa
South America
Southeast Asia
Spain
Sweden
Switzerland
Thailand
Tokyo
Toronto
Turkey
Vienna & the Danube

Fodor's Special-Interest Guides

Caribbean Ports of Call
The Complete Guide to America's National Parks
Family Adventures
Gay Guide to the USA
Halliday's New England Food Explorer
Halliday's New Orleans Food Explorer
Healthy Escapes
Kodak Guide to Shooting Great Travel Pictures
Net Travel
Nights to Imagine
Rock & Roll Traveler USA
Sunday in New York
Sunday in San Francisco
Walt Disney World, Universal Studios and Orlando
Walt Disney World for Adults
Where Should We Take the Kids? California
Where Should We Take the Kids? Northeast
Worldwide Cruises and Ports of Call

Fodor's

Special Series

Affordables

Caribbean

Europe

Florida

France

Germany

Great Britain

Italy

London

Paris

Fodor's Bed & Breakfasts and Country Inns

America

California

The Mid-Atlantic

New England

The Pacific Northwest

The South

The Southwest

The Upper Great Lakes

The Berkeley Guides

California

Central America

Eastern Europe

Europe

France

Germany & Austria

Great Britain & Ireland

Italy

London

Mexico

New York City

Pacific Northwest & Alaska

Paris

San Francisco

Compass American Guides

Arizona

Canada

Chicago

Colorado

Hawaii

Idaho

Hollywood

Las Vegas

Maine

Manhattan

Montana

New Mexico

New Orleans

Oregon

San Francisco

Santa Fe

South Carolina

South Dakota

Southwest

Texas

Utah

Virginia

Washington

Wine Country

Wisconsin

Wyoming

Fodor's Citypacks

Atlanta

Hong Kong

London

New York City

Paris

Rome

San Francisco

Washington, D.C.

Fodor's Español

California

Caribe Occidental

Caribe Oriental

Gran Bretaña

Londres

Mexico

Nueva York

Paris

Fodor's Exploring Guides

Australia

Boston & New England

Britain

California

Caribbean

China

Egypt

Florence & Tuscany

Florida

France

Germany

Ireland

Israel

Italy

Japan

London

Mexico

Moscow & St. Petersburg

New York City

Paris

Prague

Provence

Rome

San Francisco

Scotland

Singapore & Malaysia

Spain

Thailand

Turkey

Venice

Fodor's Flashmaps

Boston

New York

San Francisco

Washington, D.C.

Fodor's Pocket Guides

Acapulco

Atlanta

Barbados

Jamaica

London

New York City

Paris

Prague

Puerto Rico

Rome

San Francisco

Washington, D.C.

Mobil Travel Guides

America's Best Hotels & Restaurants

California & the West

Frequent Traveler's Guide to Major Cities

Great Lakes

Mid-Atlantic

Northeast

Northwest & Great Plains

Southeast

Southwest & South Central

Rivages Guides

Bed and Breakfasts of Character and Charm in France

Hotels and Country Inns of Character and Charm in France

Hotels and Country Inns of Character and Charm in Italy

Hotels and Country Inns of Character and Charm in Paris

Hotels and Country Inns of Character and Charm in Portugal

Hotels and Country Inns of Character and Charm in Spain

Short Escapes

Britain

France

New England

Near New York City

Fodor's Sports

Golf Digest's Best Places to Play

Skiing USA

USA Today The Complete Four Sport Stadium Guide

Fodor's Vacation Planners

Great American Learning Vacations

Great American Sports & Adventure Vacations

Great American Vacations

Great American Vacations for Travelers with Disabilities

National Parks and Seashores of the East

National Parks of the West

City Transport

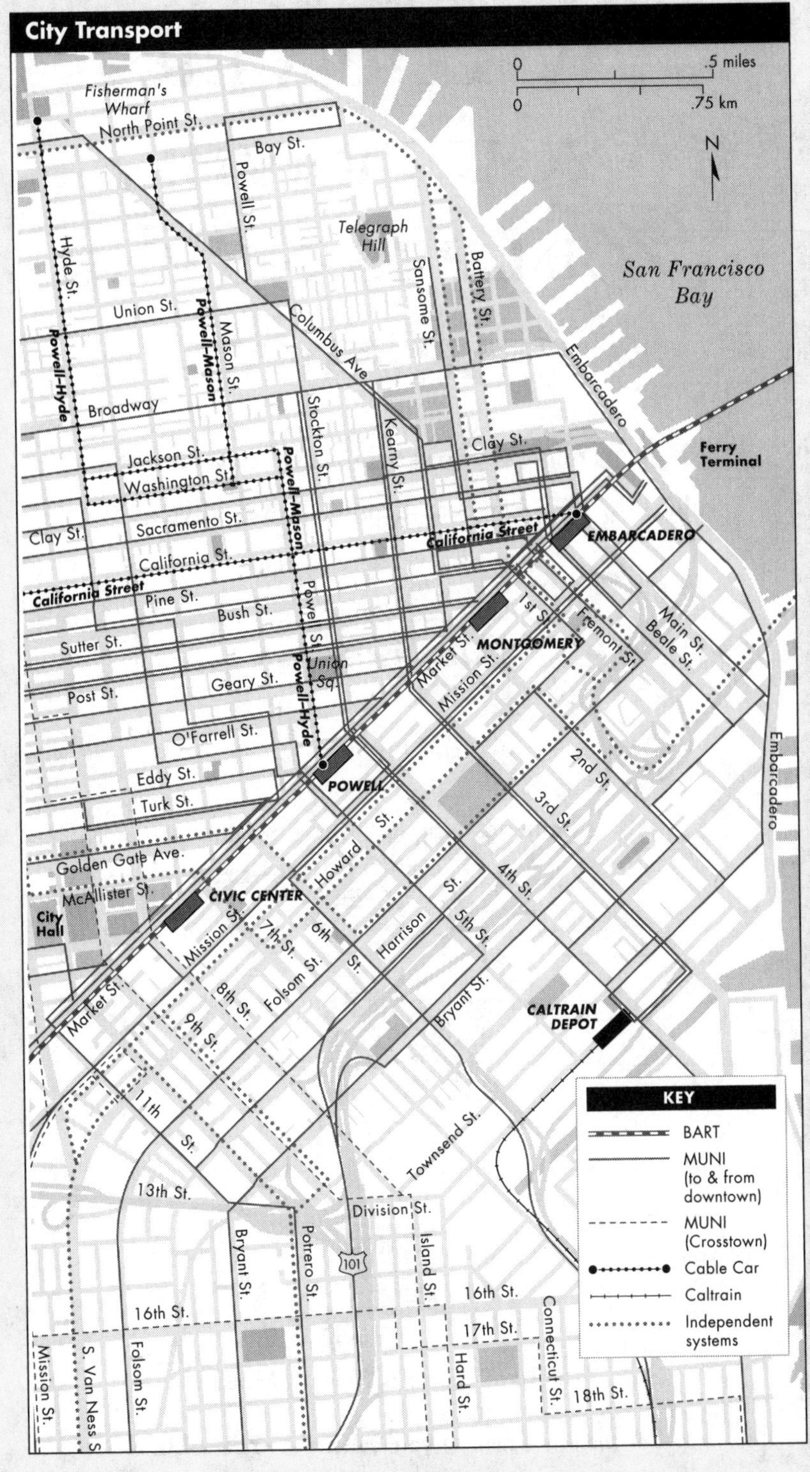

The Bay Area

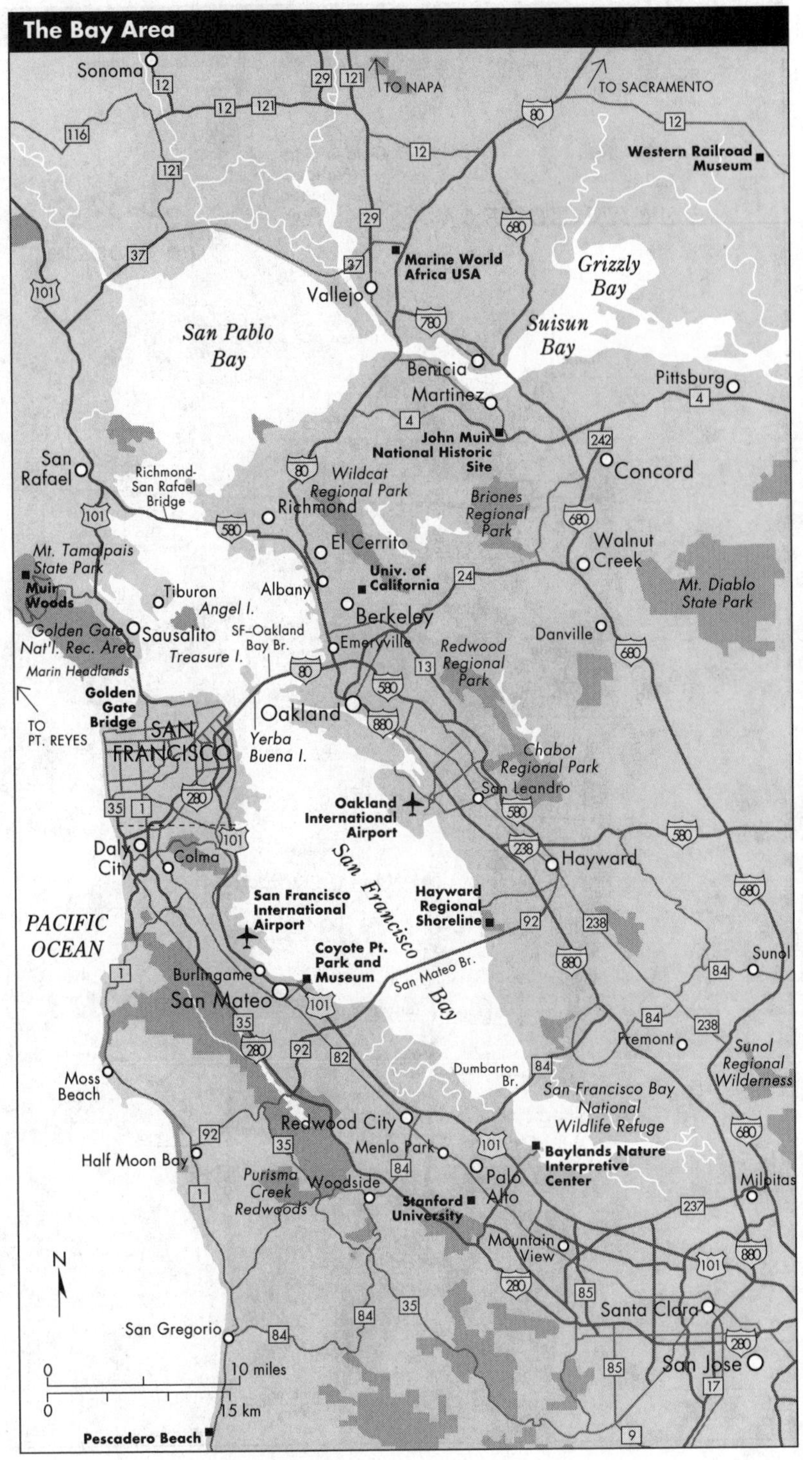

Sonoma
TO NAPA
TO SACRAMENTO
Western Railroad Museum
Marine World Africa USA
Grizzly Bay
Vallejo
San Pablo Bay
Suisun Bay
Benicia
Pittsburg
Martinez
John Muir National Historic Site
San Rafael
Richmond-San Rafael Bridge
Wildcat Regional Park
Concord
Richmond
Briones Regional Park
El Cerrito
Walnut Creek
Mt. Tamalpais State Park
Muir Woods
Tiburon
Albany
Univ. of California
Mt. Diablo State Park
Angel I.
Berkeley
Golden Gate Nat'l. Rec. Area
Sausalito
SF–Oakland Bay Br.
Danville
Emeryville
Redwood Regional Park
Marin Headlands
Treasure I.
TO PT. REYES
Golden Gate Bridge
Oakland
SAN FRANCISCO
Yerba Buena I.
Chabot Regional Park
San Leandro
Oakland International Airport
Daly City
Colma
San Francisco Bay
Hayward
San Francisco International Airport
Hayward Regional Shoreline
PACIFIC OCEAN
Coyote Pt. Park and Museum
Sunol
Burlingame
San Mateo
San Mateo Br.
Fremont
Sunol Regional Wilderness
Moss Beach
Dumbarton Br.
San Francisco Bay National Wildlife Refuge
Redwood City
Half Moon Bay
Menlo Park
Baylands Nature Interpretive Center
Purisma Creek Redwoods
Woodside
Palo Alto
Milpitas
Stanford University
Mountain View
N
Santa Clara
San Gregorio
San Jose
0
10 miles
0
15 km
Pescadero Beach

San Francisco

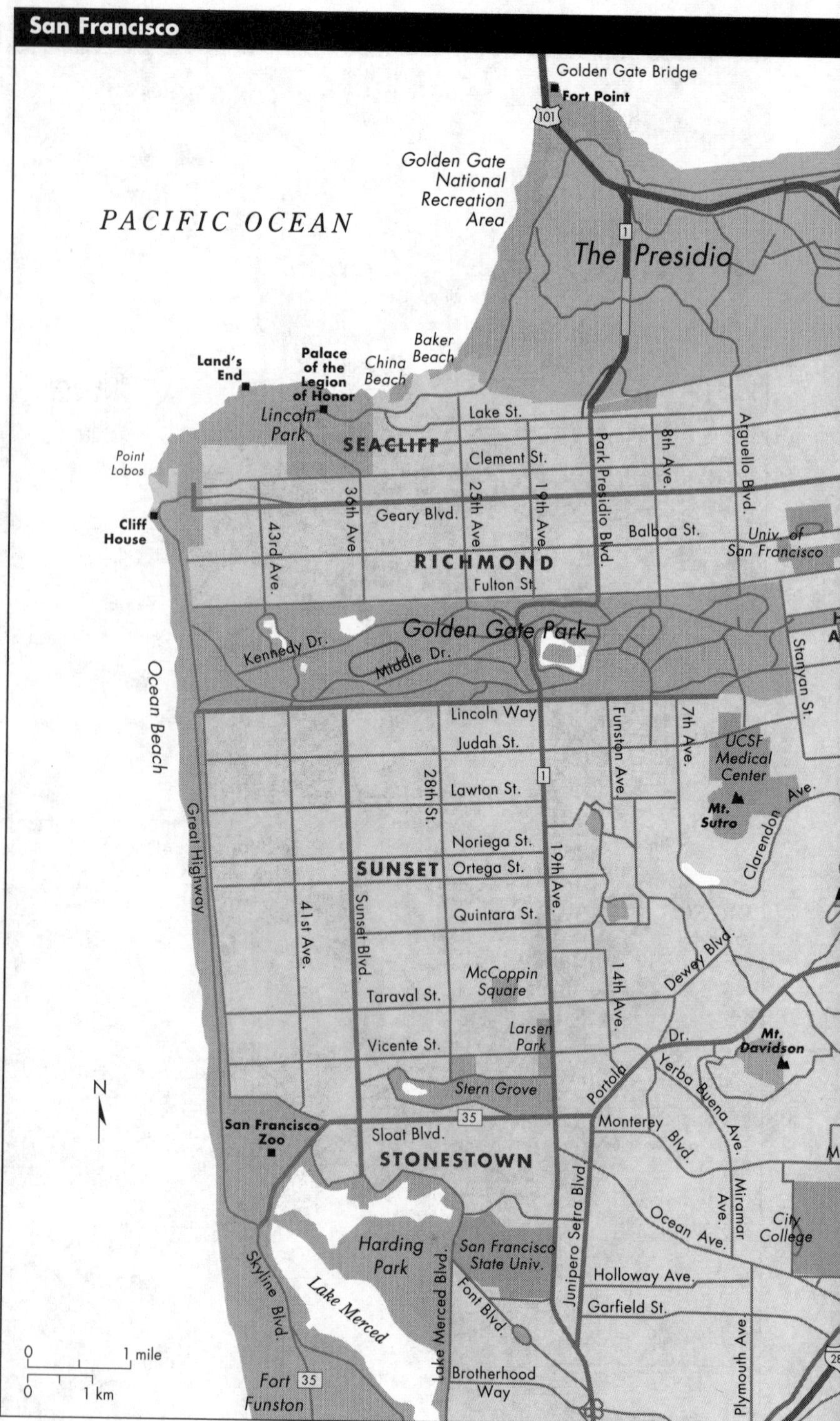
Golden Gate Bridge
Fort Point
101
Golden Gate National Recreation Area
PACIFIC OCEAN
The Presidio
Baker Beach
China Beach
Land's End
Palace of the Legion of Honor
Lincoln Park
Lake St.
SEACLIFF
Clement St.
Point Lobos
Cliff House
Geary Blvd.
43rd Ave.
36th Ave.
25th Ave.
19th Ave.
Park Presidio Blvd.
8th Ave.
Arguello Blvd.
Balboa St.
Univ. of San Francisco
RICHMOND
Fulton St.
Golden Gate Park
Kennedy Dr.
Middle Dr.
Ocean Beach
Stanyan St.
Lincoln Way
Judah St.
Funston Ave.
7th Ave.
UCSF Medical Center
Lawton St.
28th St.
Mt. Sutro
Clarendon Ave.
Noriega St.
Great Highway
SUNSET
Ortega St.
19th Ave.
Quintara St.
41st Ave.
Sunset Blvd.
McCoppin Square
14th Ave.
Dewey Blvd.
Taraval St.
Vicente St.
Larsen Park
Mt. Davidson
Stern Grove
Portola Dr.
Yerba Buena Ave.
San Francisco Zoo
35
Sloat Blvd.
Monterey Blvd.
STONESTOWN
Miramar Ave.
Ocean Ave.
City College
Harding Park
San Francisco State Univ.
Junipero Serra Blvd.
Holloway Ave.
Garfield St.
Lake Merced
Skyline Blvd.
Lake Merced Blvd.
Font Blvd.
Plymouth Ave.
Brotherhood Way
Fort Funston
0 1 mile
0 1 km
N

San Francisco Bay
Pier 39
Marina Green
Aquatic Park
FISHERMAN'S WHARF
Fort Mason
MARINA
NORTH BEACH
Coit Tower
TELEGRAPH HILL
Palace of Fine Arts
RUSSIAN HILL
(tunnel)
FILLMORE
CHINATOWN
FINANCIAL DISTRICT
Embarcadero
San Francisco–Oakland Bay Bridge
PACIFIC HEIGHTS
NOB HILL
UNION SQUARE
Yerba Buena Center
JAPAN TOWN
CIVIC CENTER
SOMA
WESTERN ADDITION
China Basin
HAIGHT-ASHBURY
Buena Vista Park
Central Freeway
Central Basin
MISSION
Mission Dolores Park
CASTRO
POTRERO HILL
San Francisco General Hospital
TWIN PEAKS
NOE VALLEY
Islais Cr. Channel
BERNAL HEIGHTS
India Basin
GLEN PARK
Hunters Point
Balboa Park
John McLaren Park
South Basin
Cow Palace
3Com Park

The Richmond, Seacliff, and Lincoln Park

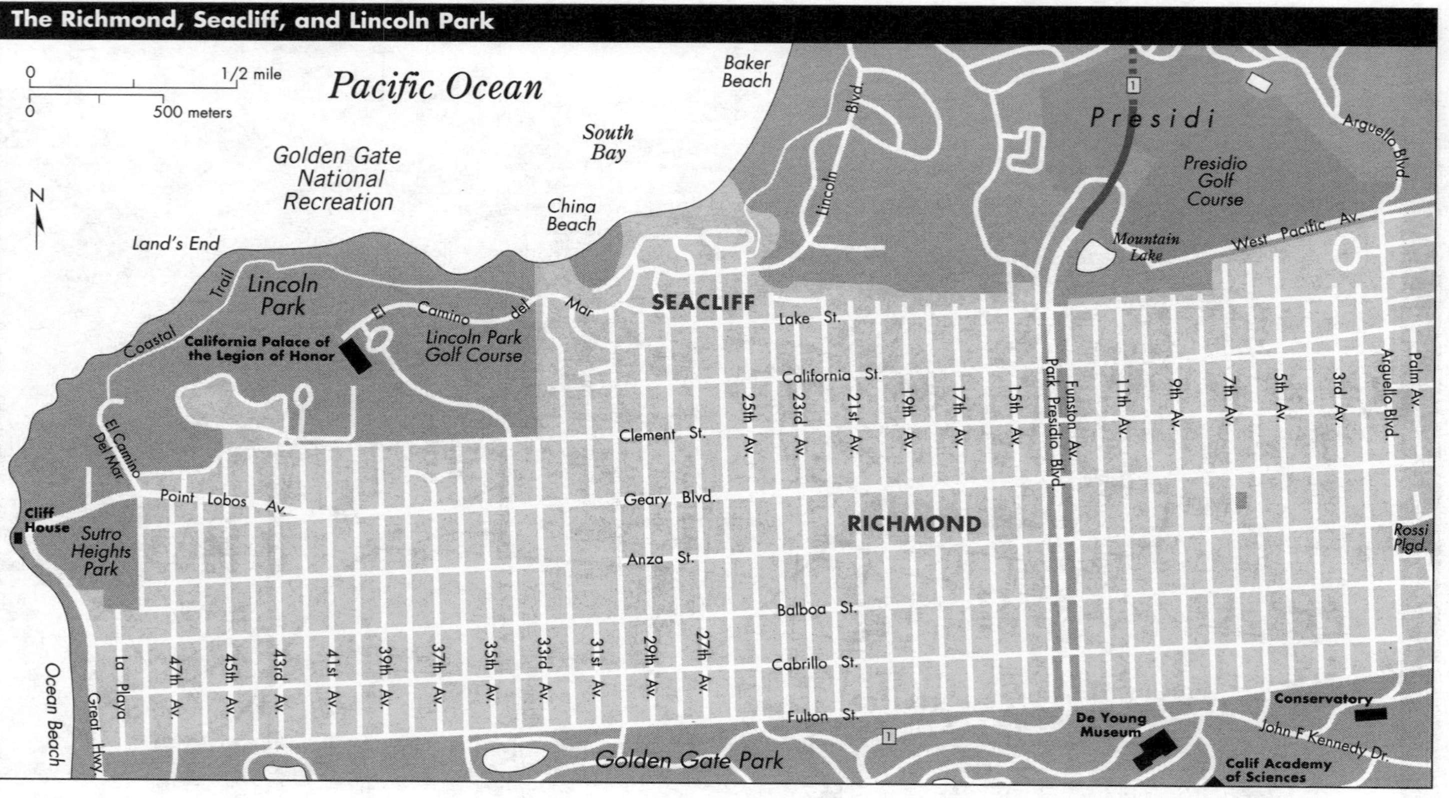
0
1/2 mile
0
500 meters
N
Pacific Ocean
Golden Gate National Recreation
Baker Beach
South Bay
China Beach
Land's End
Presidi
Presidio Golf Course
Mountain Lake
Arguello Blvd.
West Pacific Av.
Lincoln Blvd.
Palm Av.
Arguello Blvd.
3rd Av.
5th Av.
7th Av.
9th Av.
11th Av.
Funston Av.
Park Presidio Blvd.
15th Av.
17th Av.
19th Av.
21st Av.
23rd Av.
25th Av.
27th Av.
29th Av.
31st Av.
33rd Av.
35th Av.
37th Av.
39th Av.
41st Av.
43rd Av.
45th Av.
47th Av.
La Playa
Great Hwy.
Ocean Beach
Rossi Plgd.
Lake St.
California St.
Clement St.
Geary Blvd.
Anza St.
Balboa St.
Cabrillo St.
Fulton St.
RICHMOND
SEACLIFF
El Camino del Mar
Lincoln Park
Lincoln Park Golf Course
California Palace of the Legion of Honor
Coastal Trail
El Camino Del Mar
Point Lobos Av.
Cliff House
Sutro Heights Park
Golden Gate Park
Conservatory
John F Kennedy Dr.
De Young Museum
Calif Academy of Sciences
1

Golden Gate Park

Lincoln Park
Clement St.
Geary Blvd.
Sutro Heights Park
RICHMOND
Anza St.
Balboa St.
Cabrillo St.
47th Av.
43rd Av.
36th Av.
25th Av.
Park Presidio Blvd.
10th Av.
8th Av.
6th Av.
Arguello Blvd.
Queen Wilhelmina Tulip Garden
Archery Field
Dutch Windmill
Beach Chalet
Golf Course
North Lake
Buffalo Paddock
Middle Lake
J.F. Kennedy Dr.
Stables
Spreckels Lake
Lindley Meadow
Golden Gate Park Stadium (Polo Field)
Marx Meadow
Speedway Meadow
Middle Dr.
Metson Lake
Martin Luther King Jr. Dr.
Mallard Lake
Boat House
Cross Over Dr.
Stow Lake
DeYoung Museum
Asian Art Museum
Japanese Tea Garden
Music Concourse
Bandshell
Strybing Arboretum
Hall of Flowers
California Academy of Sciences
Rhododendron Dell
Conservatory
Fuschia Garden
Tennis Courts
Children's Playground
McLaren Lodge (Park HQ)
Stanyan St.
Kezar Stadium
PACIFIC OCEAN
Great Highway
Murphy Windmill
South Lake
Lincoln Way
Irving St.
Judah St.
SUNSET
Kirkham St.
Lawton St.
Moraga St.
41st Av.
Sunset Blvd.
25th Av.
19th Av.
9th Av.
7th Av.
3rd Av.
N
0
1/2 mile
0
500 meters

The Sunset

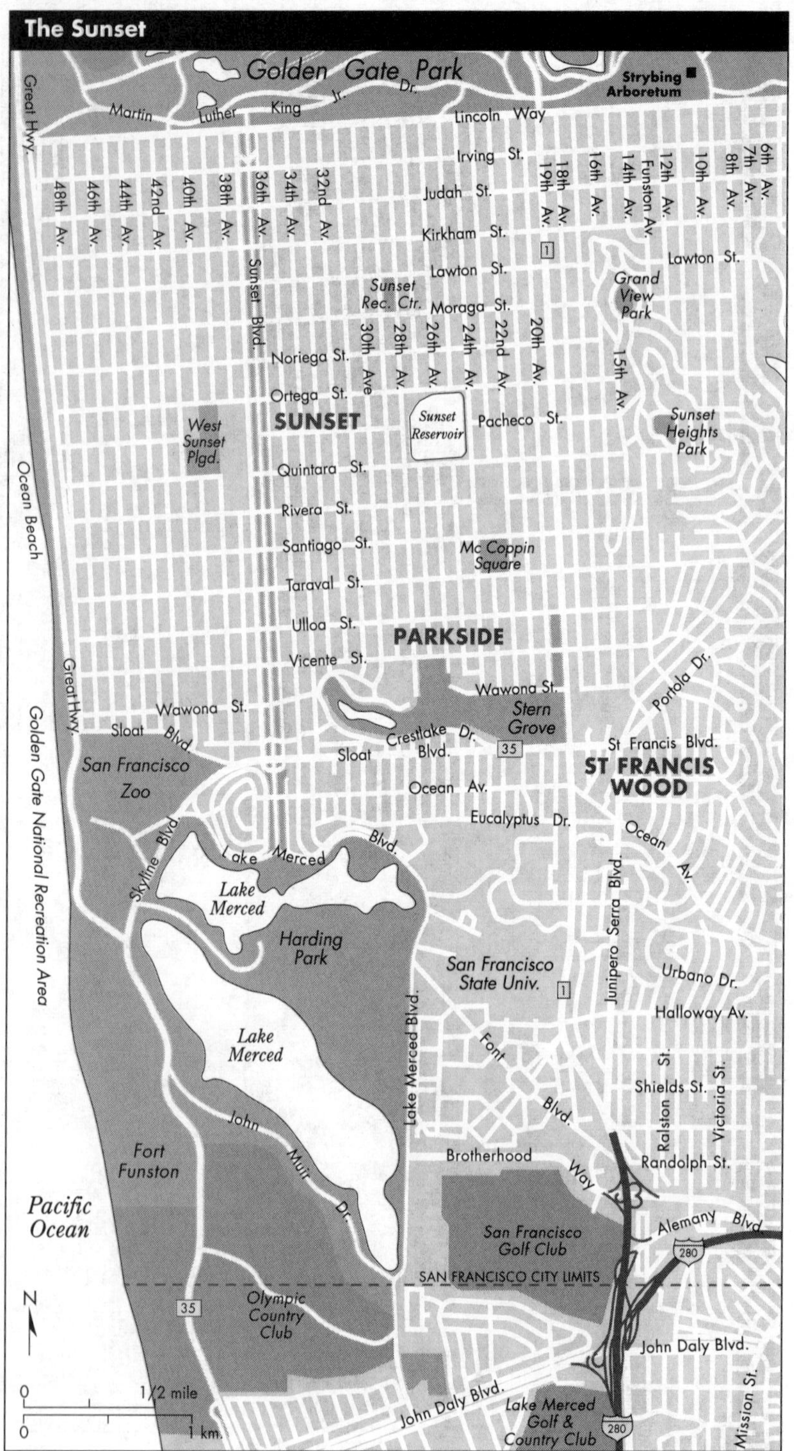
Golden Gate Park
Martin Luther King Jr. Dr.
Strybing Arboretum
Lincoln Way
Great Hwy.
Irving St.
Judah St.
Kirkham St.
Lawton St.
Moraga St.
Noriega St.
Ortega St.
Pacheco St.
Quintara St.
Rivera St.
Santiago St.
Taraval St.
Ulloa St.
Vicente St.
Wawona St.
48th Av.
46th Av.
44th Av.
42nd Av.
40th Av.
38th Av.
36th Av.
34th Av.
32nd Av.
30th Ave
28th Av.
26th Av.
24th Av.
22nd Av.
20th Av.
19th Av.
18th Av.
16th Av.
15th Av.
14th Av.
Funston Av.
12th Av.
10th Av.
8th Av.
7th Av.
6th Av.
Sunset Blvd.
Sunset Rec. Ctr.
Grand View Park
SUNSET
West Sunset Plgd.
Sunset Reservoir
Sunset Heights Park
Mc Coppin Square
PARKSIDE
Ocean Beach
Portola Dr.
Stern Grove
Sloat Blvd.
Crestlake Dr.
San Francisco Zoo
St Francis Blvd.
ST FRANCIS WOOD
Ocean Av.
Eucalyptus Dr.
Skyline Blvd.
Lake Merced Blvd.
Lake Merced
Harding Park
San Francisco State Univ.
Junipero Serra Blvd.
Urbano Dr.
Halloway Av.
Golden Gate National Recreation Area
Font Blvd.
Ralston St.
Shields St.
Victoria St.
John Muir Dr.
Fort Funston
Brotherhood Way
Randolph St.
Pacific Ocean
San Francisco Golf Club
Alemany Blvd.
280
SAN FRANCISCO CITY LIMITS
35
Olympic Country Club
John Daly Blvd.
N
0
1/2 mile
1 km.
Lake Merced Golf & Country Club
Mission St.

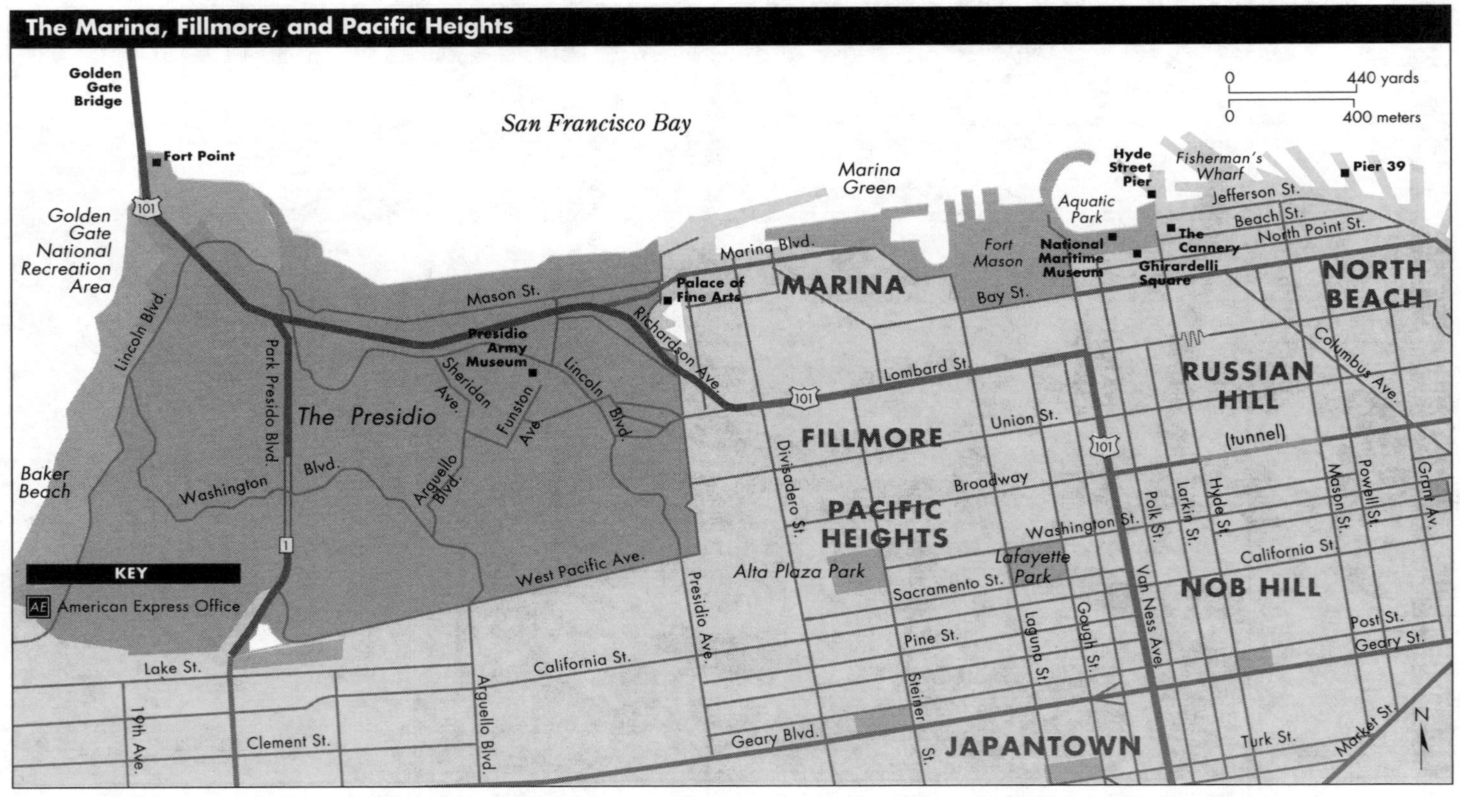
The Marina, Fillmore, and Pacific Heights
Golden Gate Bridge
San Francisco Bay
0 440 yards
0 400 meters
Fort Point
Golden Gate National Recreation Area
Lincoln Blvd.
Park Presido Blvd.
Mason St.
Presidio Army Museum
Sheridan Ave.
Funston Ave.
Lincoln Blvd.
Richardson Ave.
Palace of Fine Arts
The Presidio
Baker Beach
Washington Blvd.
Arguello Blvd.
West Pacific Ave.
KEY
AE American Express Office
Lake St.
19th Ave.
Clement St.
California St.
Arguello Blvd.
Presidio Ave.
Marina Green
Marina Blvd.
MARINA
Fort Mason
Bay St.
National Maritime Museum
Aquatic Park
Hyde Street Pier
Fisherman's Wharf
Pier 39
Jefferson St.
Beach St.
North Point St.
The Cannery
Ghirardelli Square
NORTH BEACH
Columbus Ave.
Lombard St.
RUSSIAN HILL
(tunnel)
Union St.
FILLMORE
Divisadero St.
Broadway
PACIFIC HEIGHTS
Washington St.
Alta Plaza Park
Lafayette Park
Sacramento St.
Pine St.
Laguna St.
Gough St.
Van Ness Ave.
Polk St.
Larkin St.
Hyde St.
Mason St.
Powell St.
Grant Av.
California St.
NOB HILL
Post St.
Geary St.
Steiner St.
Geary Blvd.
JAPANTOWN
Turk St.
Market St.
N

Haight, Castro, Mission, Noe Valley, and Twin Peaks

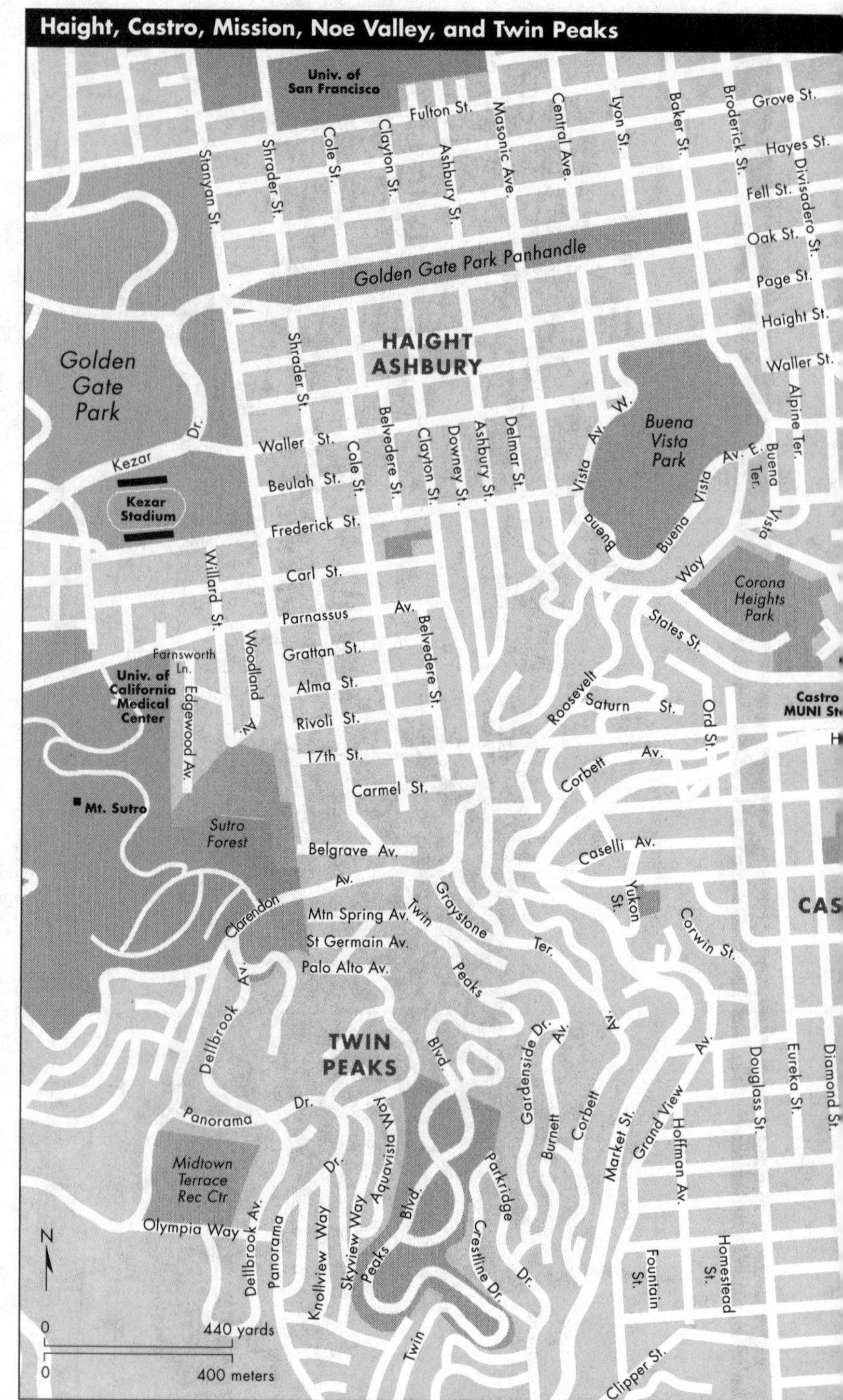

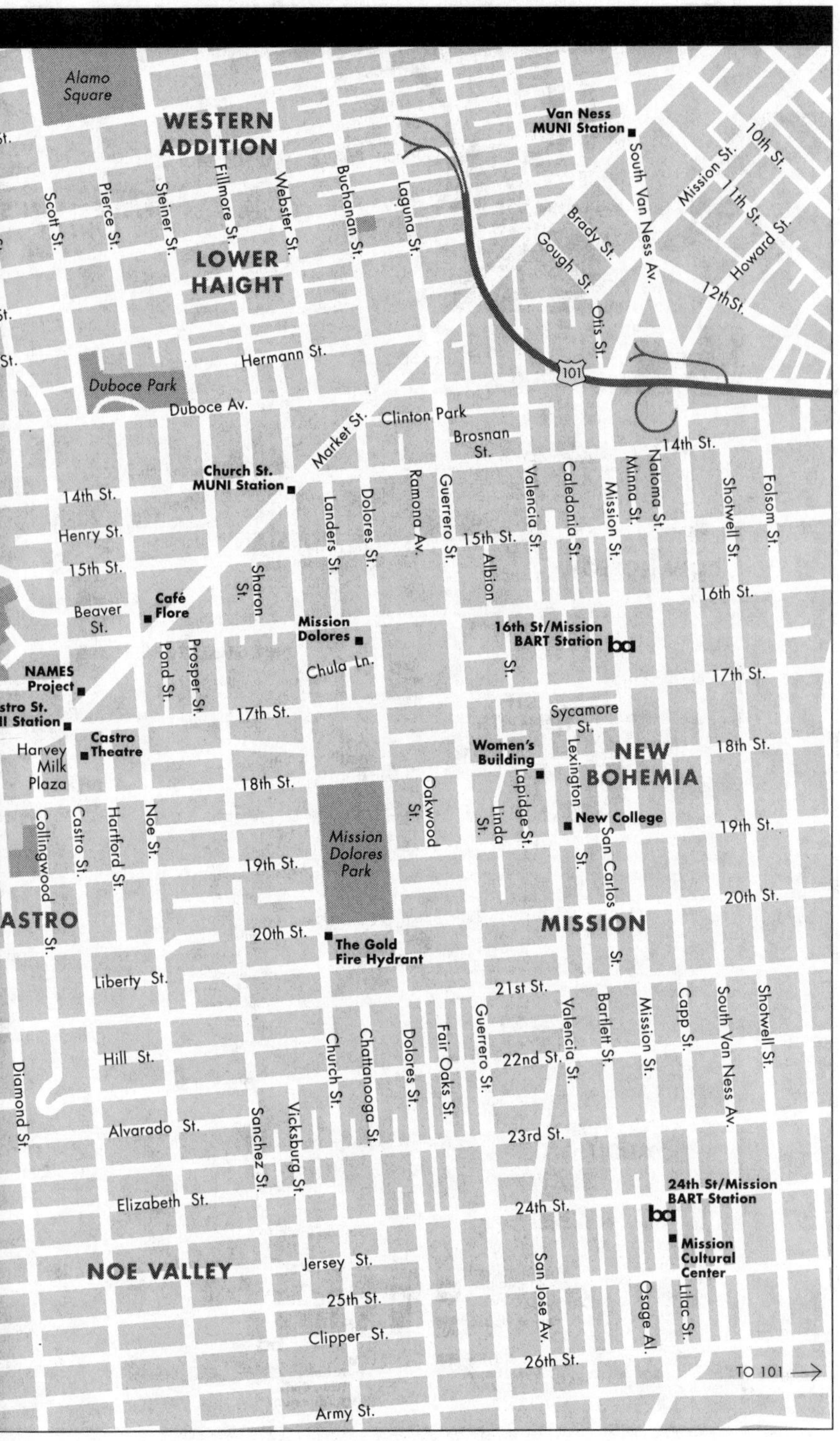
Alamo Square
WESTERN ADDITION
LOWER HAIGHT
Van Ness MUNI Station
Scott St.
Pierce St.
Steiner St.
Fillmore St.
Webster St.
Buchanan St.
Laguna St.
South Van Ness Av.
Mission St.
10th St.
11th St.
Howard St.
12th St.
Brady St.
Gough St.
Otis St.
Hermann St.
Duboce Park
Duboce Av.
Market St.
Clinton Park
Brosnan St.
101
14th St.
Church St. MUNI Station
14th St.
Henry St.
15th St.
Beaver St.
Café Flore
Sharon St.
Landers St.
Dolores St.
Ramona Av.
Guerrero St.
15th St.
Albion
Valencia St.
Caledonia St.
Mission St.
Minna St.
Natoma St.
Shotwell St.
Folsom St.
16th St.
Mission Dolores
16th St/Mission BART Station
Chula Ln.
NAMES Project
Pond St.
Prosper St.
17th St.
17th St.
Sycamore St.
Harvey Milk Plaza
Castro Theatre
Women's Building
Lexington St.
NEW BOHEMIA
18th St.
18th St.
Oakwood St.
Lapidge St.
Linda St.
New College
Collingwood St.
Castro St.
Hartford St.
Noe St.
Mission Dolores Park
19th St.
19th St.
San Carlos St.
20th St.
ASTRO
MISSION
20th St.
The Gold Fire Hydrant
Liberty St.
21st St.
Valencia St.
Bartlett St.
Mission St.
Capp St.
South Van Ness Av.
Shotwell St.
Hill St.
Church St.
Chattanooga St.
Dolores St.
Fair Oaks St.
Guerrero St.
22nd St.
Diamond St.
Alvarado St.
Sanchez St.
Vicksburg St.
23rd St.
Elizabeth St.
24th St.
24th St/Mission BART Station
Mission Cultural Center
NOE VALLEY
Jersey St.
25th St.
Clipper St.
San Jose Av.
Osage Al.
Lilac St.
26th St.
TO 101
Army St.

Embarcadero, North Beach, Chinatown, Financial District, and Civic Center

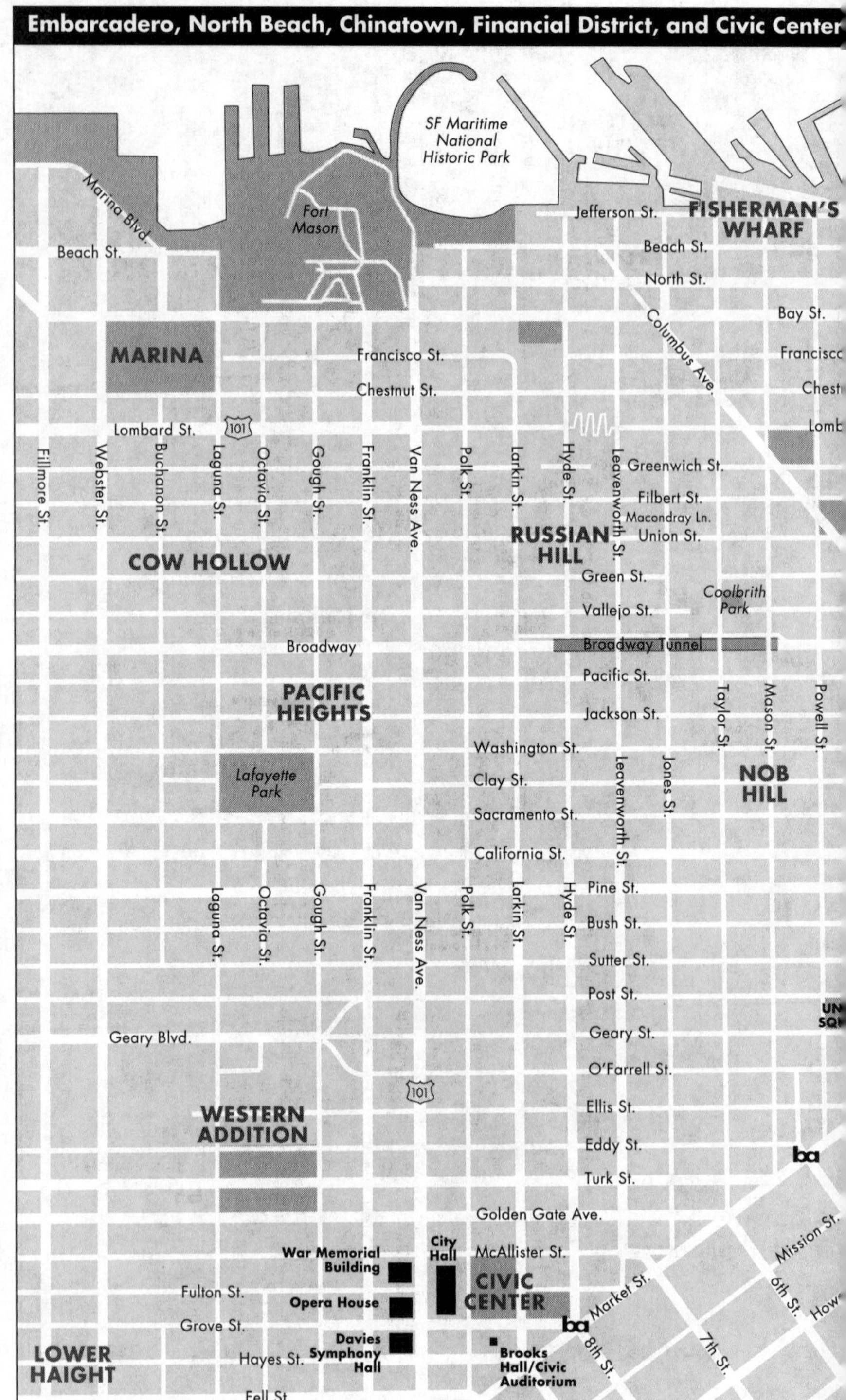

SF Maritime National Historic Park
Fort Mason
Marina Blvd.
Beach St.
Jefferson St.
FISHERMAN'S WHARF
North St.
Bay St.
Columbus Ave.
MARINA
Francisco St.
Chestnut St.
Lombard St.
101
Fillmore St.
Webster St.
Buchanan St.
Laguna St.
Octavia St.
Gough St.
Franklin St.
Van Ness Ave.
Polk St.
Larkin St.
Hyde St.
Leavenworth St.
Greenwich St.
Filbert St.
Macondray Ln.
Union St.
RUSSIAN HILL
COW HOLLOW
Green St.
Vallejo St.
Coolbrith Park
Broadway
Broadway Tunnel
Pacific St.
PACIFIC HEIGHTS
Jackson St.
Taylor St.
Mason St.
Powell St.
Washington St.
Clay St.
Lafayette Park
Jones St.
NOB HILL
Sacramento St.
California St.
Pine St.
Bush St.
Sutter St.
Post St.
Geary Blvd.
Geary St.
O'Farrell St.
WESTERN ADDITION
Ellis St.
Eddy St.
Turk St.
Golden Gate Ave.
McAllister St.
City Hall
War Memorial Building
Opera House
Davies Symphony Hall
CIVIC CENTER
Brooks Hall/Civic Auditorium
Fulton St.
Grove St.
Hayes St.
Fell St.
LOWER HAIGHT
Market St.
Mission St.
6th St.
7th St.
8th St.

0
1/2 mile
0
500 meters
N
The Embarcadero
cisco St.
hestnut St.
TELEGRAPH HILL
ombard St.
Coit Tower
Medau Pl.
Genoa Pl.
NORTH BEACH
Columbus Ave.
Romolo Pl.
Front St.
The Embarcadero
Davis St.
Walton Square
Powell St.
Stockton St.
Grant Ave.
Kearny St.
Montgomery St.
Sansome St.
Battery St.
Drumm St.
FINANCIAL DISTRICT
CHINATOWN
Ferry Building
Davis St.
Front St.
Steuart St.
Spear St.
Main St.
Beale St.
Fremont St.
1st St.
San Francisco-Oakland Bay Bridge
UNION SQUARE
Market St.
New Montgomery St.
2nd St.
3rd St.
Yerba Buena Gardens
4th St.
Hawthorne St.
SOMA
Folsom St.
5th St.
oward St.
80
Harrison St.
Brannan St.
Townsend St.
King St.

SoMa and Potrero Hill

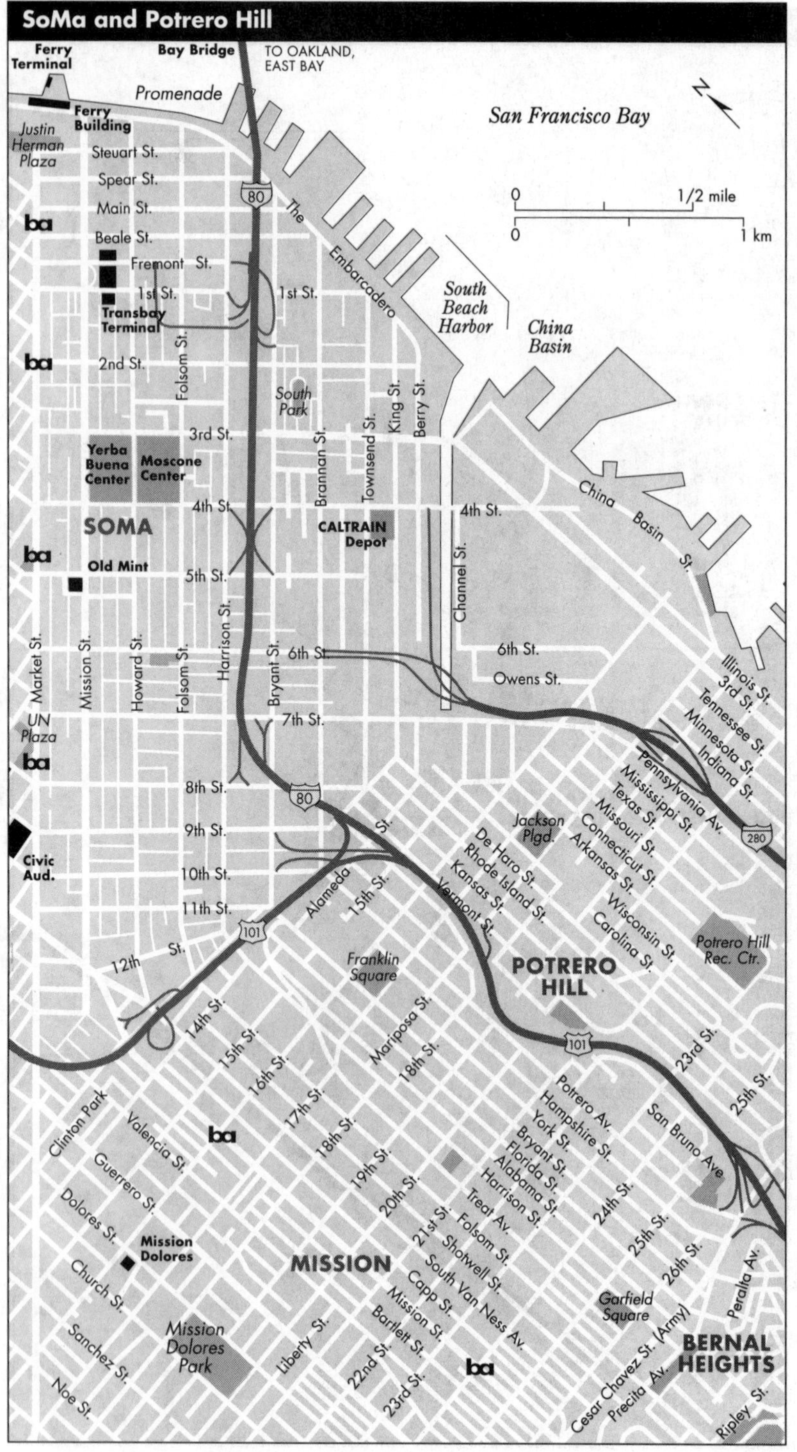
Ferry Terminal
Bay Bridge
TO OAKLAND, EAST BAY
Promenade
Ferry Building
San Francisco Bay
Justin Herman Plaza
Steuart St.
Spear St.
Main St.
Beale St.
Fremont St.
1st St.
Transbay Terminal
2nd St.
Folsom St.
The Embarcadero
South Beach Harbor
China Basin
South Park
King St.
Berry St.
3rd St.
Brannan St.
Townsend St.
Yerba Buena Center
Moscone Center
4th St.
SOMA
CALTRAIN Depot
Channel St.
China Basin St.
Old Mint
5th St.
Harrison St.
Market St.
Mission St.
Howard St.
Bryant St.
6th St.
Owens St.
7th St.
UN Plaza
Illinois St.
Tennessee St.
Minnesota St.
Indiana St.
Pennsylvania Av.
Mississippi St.
Texas St.
Missouri St.
Connecticut St.
Arkansas St.
8th St.
9th St.
10th St.
11th St.
12th St.
Civic Aud.
Jackson Plgd.
De Haro St.
Rhode Island St.
Kansas St.
Vermont St.
Alameda St.
15th St.
Wisconsin St.
Carolina St.
Potrero Hill Rec. Ctr.
Franklin Square
POTRERO HILL
14th St.
16th St.
17th St.
18th St.
Mariposa St.
23rd St.
25th St.
Potrero Av.
Hampshire St.
York St.
Florida St.
Alabama St.
San Bruno Ave
Clinton Park
Valencia St.
Guerrero St.
Dolores St.
19th St.
20th St.
Treat Av.
24th St.
21st St.
Folsom St.
Shotwell St.
26th St.
Mission Dolores
MISSION
Church St.
South Van Ness Av.
Capp St.
Peralta Av.
Garfield Square
Mission Dolores Park
Liberty St.
Bartlett St.
22nd St.
23rd St.
Sanchez St.
Noe St.
Cesar Chavez St. (Army)
Precita Av.
BERNAL HEIGHTS
Ripley St.
0
1/2 mile
1 km
80
101
280

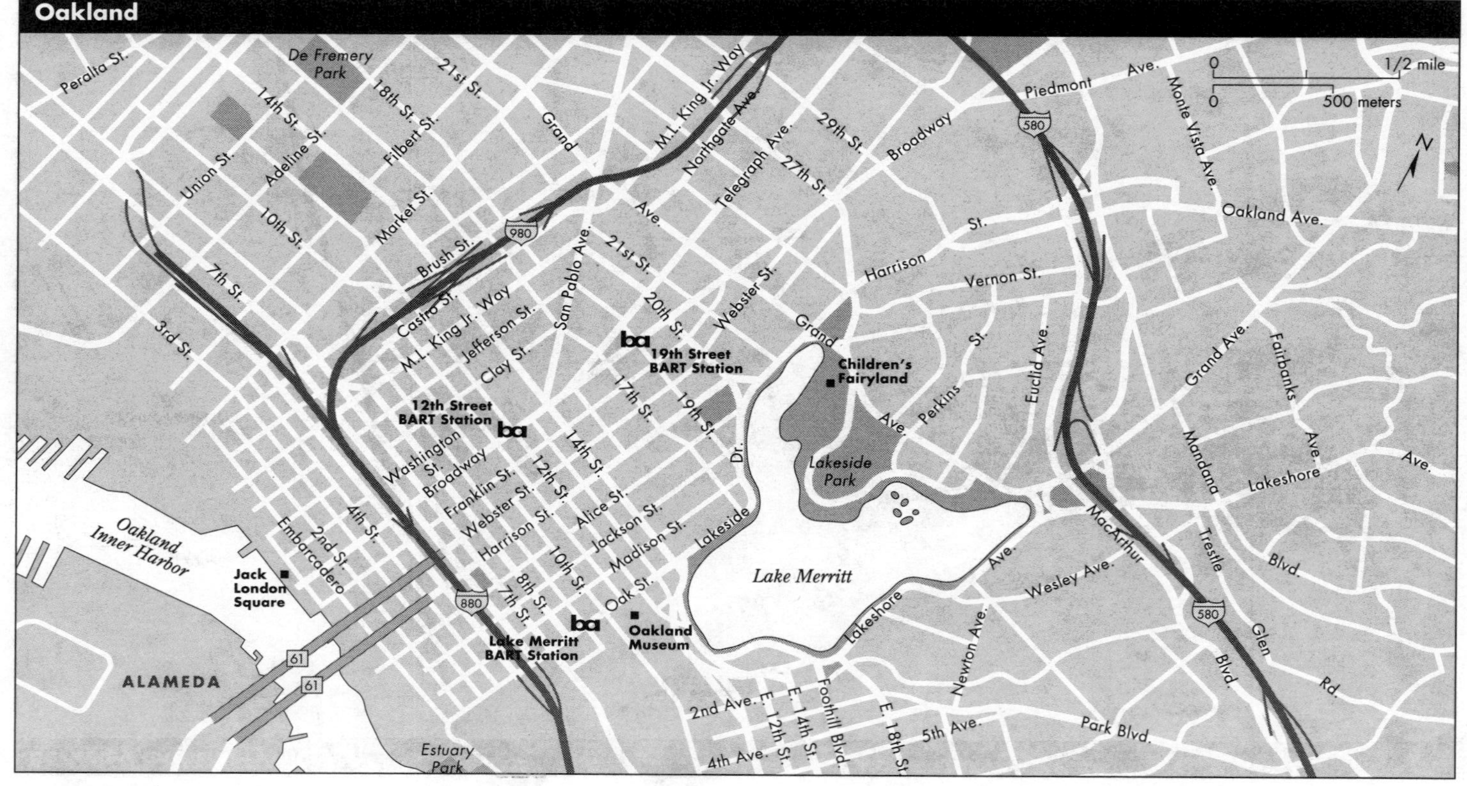
Oakland
Peralta St.
De Fremery Park
21st St.
18th St.
14th St.
Filbert St.
Adeline St.
Union St.
Market St.
10th St.
Grand
M.L. King Jr. Way
Northgate Ave.
Telegraph Ave.
29th St.
27th St.
Broadway
580
Piedmont Ave.
Monte Vista Ave.
0
0
1/2 mile
500 meters
N
Oakland Ave.
980
Brush St.
Ave.
21st St.
San Pablo Ave.
St.
Harrison
Vernon St.
7th St.
Castro St.
M.L. King Jr. Way
Jefferson St.
Clay St.
20th St.
Webster St.
Grand
19th Street BART Station
Children's Fairyland
St.
Perkins
Ave.
Euclid Ave.
Grand Ave.
Fairbanks Ave.
3rd St.
12th Street BART Station
17th St.
19th St.
Dr.
Lakeside Park
Mandana
Lakeshore
Ave.
Washington St.
Broadway
Franklin St.
Webster St.
Harrison St.
12th St.
14th St.
Alice St.
Jackson St.
Madison St.
Lakeside
Lake Merritt
MacArthur
Trestle
Blvd.
Ave.
Wesley Ave.
Oakland Inner Harbor
Jack London Square
Embarcadero
2nd St.
4th St.
880
8th St.
7th St.
10th St.
Oak St.
Oakland Museum
Lake Merritt BART Station
Lakeshore
Newton Ave.
580
Glen
Blvd.
Rd.
61
61
ALAMEDA
2nd Ave.
E. 12th St.
E. 14th St.
Foothill Blvd.
E. 18th St.
5th Ave.
Park Blvd.
4th Ave.
Estuary Park

Berkeley and Emeryville

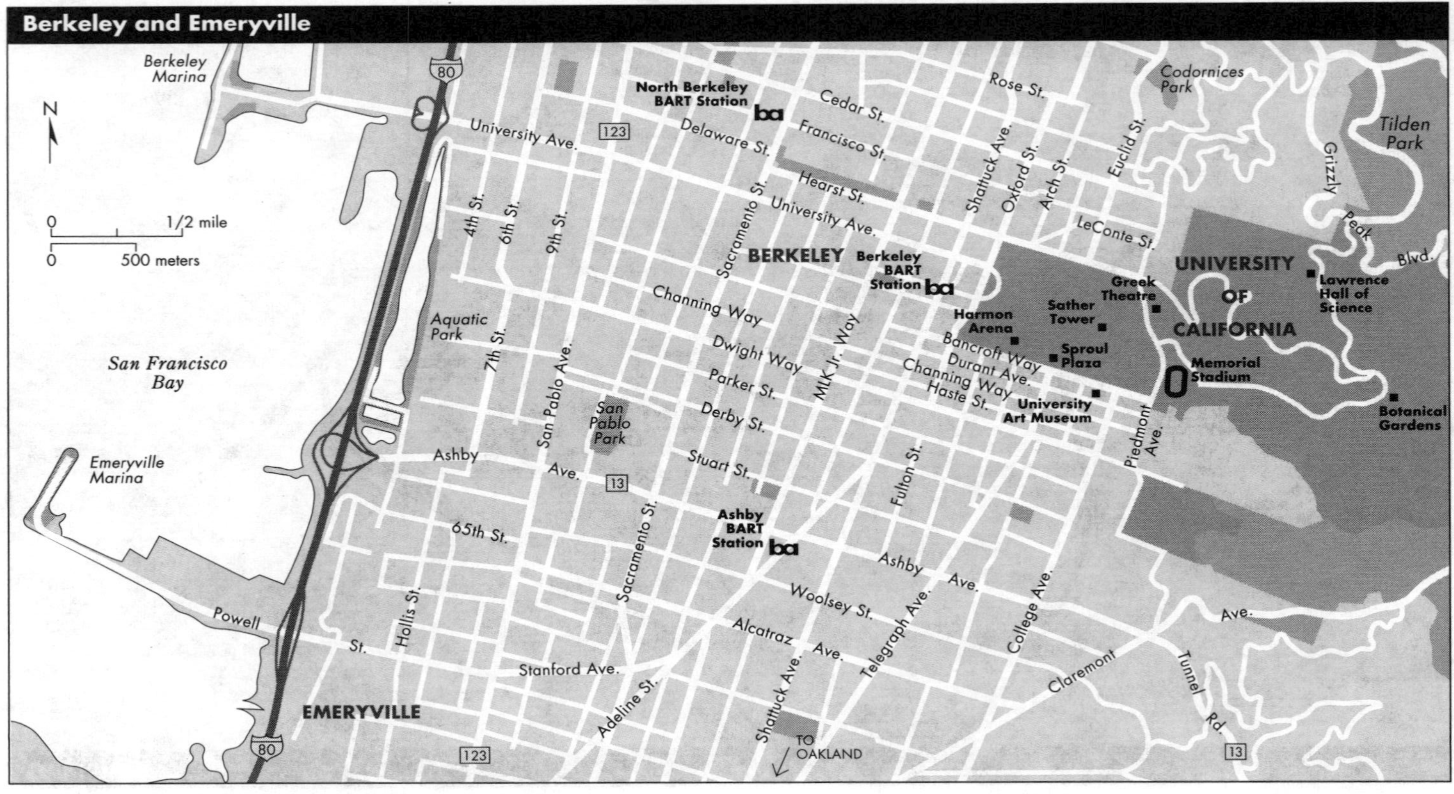

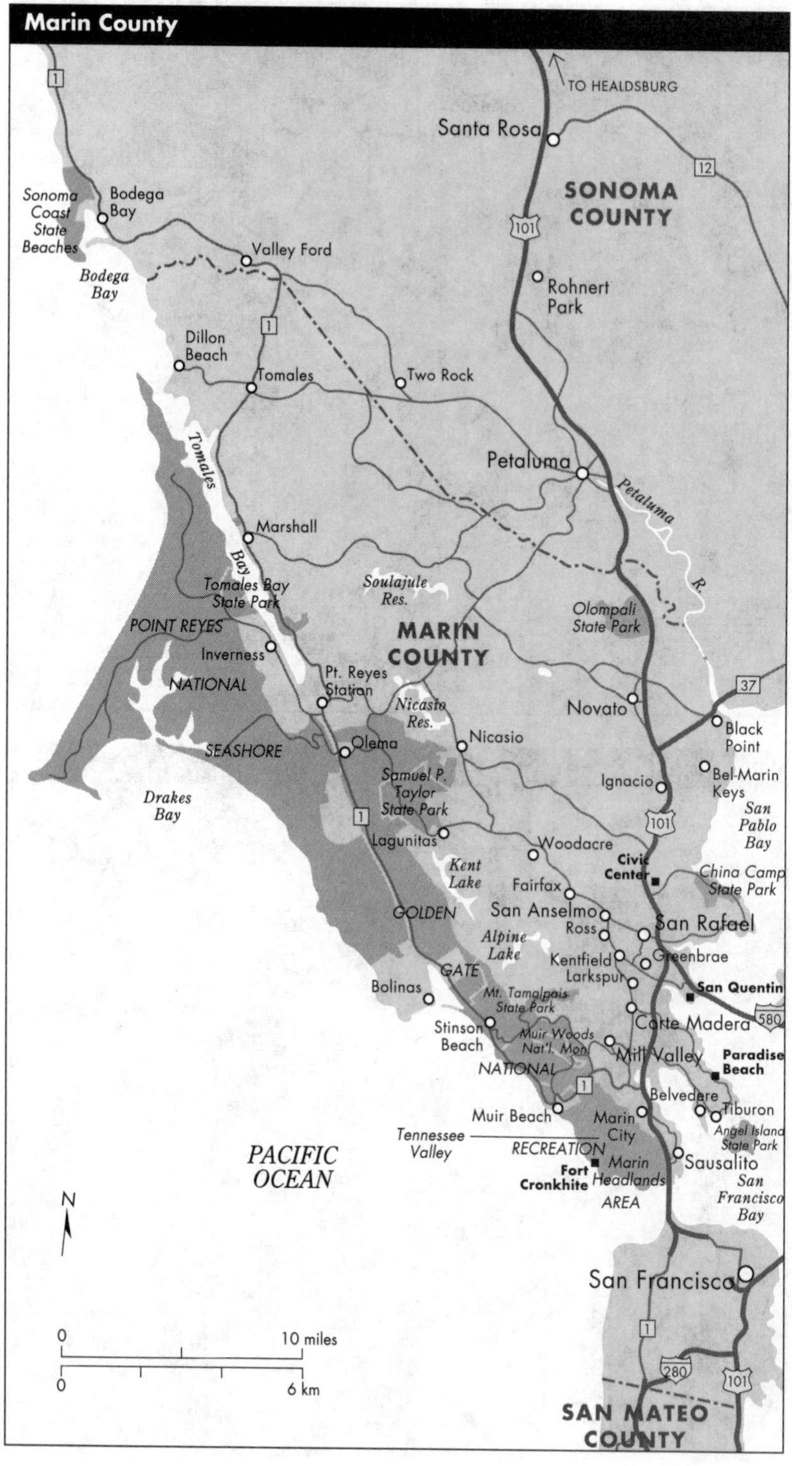
Marin County
TO HEALDSBURG
Santa Rosa
12
SONOMA COUNTY
101
Rohnert Park
1
Sonoma Coast State Beaches
Bodega Bay
Bodega Bay
Valley Ford
Dillon Beach
Tomales
Two Rock
Tomales Bay
Petaluma
Petaluma R.
Marshall
Tomales Bay State Park
Soulajule Res.
Olompali State Park
POINT REYES NATIONAL SEASHORE
MARIN COUNTY
Inverness
Pt. Reyes Station
Nicasio Res.
37
Novato
Black Point
Olema
Nicasio
Bel-Marin Keys
Ignacio
Drakes Bay
Samuel P. Taylor State Park
San Pablo Bay
Lagunitas
Woodacre
Civic Center
Kent Lake
China Camp State Park
Fairfax
San Anselmo
Ross
San Rafael
GOLDEN GATE NATIONAL RECREATION AREA
Alpine Lake
Kentfield
Greenbrae
Larkspur
San Quentin
Bolinas
Mt. Tamalpais State Park
580
Stinson Beach
Corte Madera
Muir Woods Nat'l. Mon.
Mill Valley
Paradise Beach
Belvedere
Tiburon
Muir Beach
Marin City
Angel Island State Park
Tennessee Valley
Sausalito
Fort Cronkhite
Marin Headlands
PACIFIC OCEAN
San Francisco Bay
N
San Francisco
280
0
10 miles
0
6 km
SAN MATEO COUNTY

The Wine Country

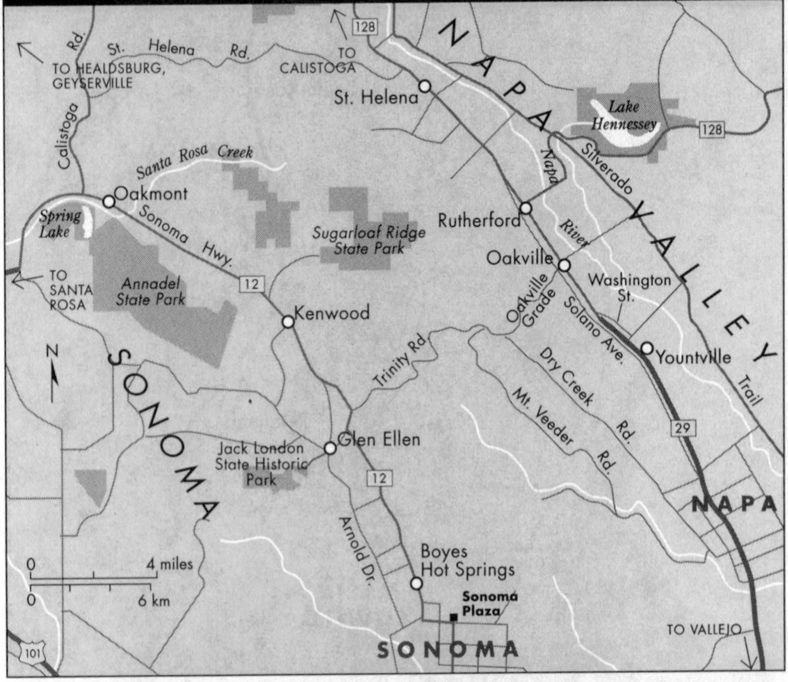

TO HEALDSBURG, GEYSERVILLE
St. Helena Rd.
Calistoga Rd.
TO CALISTOGA
128
NAPA VALLEY
St. Helena
Lake Hennessey
128
Silverado Trail
Santa Rosa Creek
Oakmont
Spring Lake
Sonoma Hwy.
Sugarloaf Ridge State Park
Napa River
Rutherford
Oakville
Washington St.
TO SANTA ROSA
Annadel State Park
12
Kenwood
Oakville Grade
Solano Ave.
Yountville
Trinity Rd.
Dry Creek Rd.
Mt. Veeder Rd.
SONOMA
N
Glen Ellen
Jack London State Historic Park
29
12
NAPA
Arnold Dr.
Boyes Hot Springs
0 4 miles
0 6 km
Sonoma Plaza
SONOMA
TO VALLEJO
101

Silicon Valley

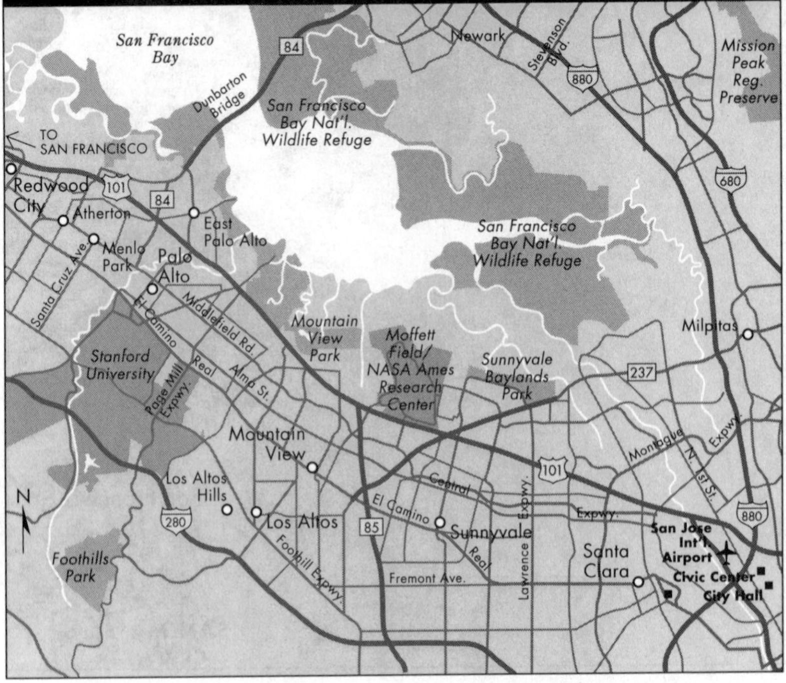

San Francisco Bay
84
Newark
Stevenson Blvd.
880
Mission Peak Reg. Preserve
Dunbarton Bridge
San Francisco Bay Nat'l. Wildlife Refuge
TO SAN FRANCISCO
Redwood City
101
84
680
Atherton
East Palo Alto
San Francisco Bay Nat'l. Wildlife Refuge
Menlo Park
Palo Alto
Santa Cruz Ave.
El Camino Real
Middlefield Rd.
Mountain View Park
Moffett Field/ NASA Ames Research Center
Milpitas
Stanford University
Alma St.
Sunnyvale Baylands Park
237
Page Mill Expwy.
Mountain View
Montague Expwy.
N. 1st St.
101
Central Expwy.
Los Altos Hills
N
El Camino Real
880
280
Los Altos
85
Sunnyvale
Lawrence Expwy.
San Jose Int'l. Airport
Foothills Park
Foothill Expwy.
Santa Clara
Civic Center
Fremont Ave.
City Hall